POLITICAL THEORY
WITHOUT BORDERS

Philosophy, Politics and Society

Edited by Robert E. Goodin
and James S. Fishkin

POLITICAL THEORY WITHOUT BORDERS
Philosophy, Politics and Society 9

WILEY Blackwell

This edition first published 2016
© 2016 John Wiley & Sons, Inc

Registered Office
John Wiley & Sons, Ltd, The Atrium, Southern Gate, Chichester, West Sussex,
PO19 8SQ, UK

Editorial Offices
350 Main Street, Malden, MA 02148-5020, USA
9600 Garsington Road, Oxford, OX4 2DQ, UK
The Atrium, Southern Gate, Chichester, West Sussex, PO19 8SQ, UK

For details of our global editorial offices, for customer services, and for information
about how to apply for permission to reuse the copyright material in this book please
see our website at www.wiley.com/wiley-blackwell.

The right of Robert E. Goodin and James S. Fishkin to be identified as the authors
of the editorial material in this work has been asserted in accordance with the UK
Copyright, Designs and Patents Act 1988.

Library of Congress Cataloging-in-Publication data applied for

Cloth: 9781119110088

A catalogue record for this book is available from the British Library.

Set in 10/12pt Sabon by SPi Global, Pondicherry, India
Printed and bound in Malaysia by Vivar Printing Sdn Bhd

1 2016

Contents

Acknowledgments

This is the ninth of the *Philosophy, Politics and Society* book series, launched by Peter Laslett in 1956. Our first debt, and the profession's, is to Peter for keeping the subject of political theory alive when (in his own famous phrase) it seemed virtually dead.

Since 2002, *Philosophy, Politics and Society* has been a joint venture, with the *Journal of Political Philosophy* publishing two special issues devoted to its theme three years apart. Every sixth year, then, the contents of those two special issues – together with a few seminal papers originally published elsewhere – are collected together and reprinted as the next volume of the *Philosophy, Politics and Society* series. The bulk of the chapters in the present volume appeared in this way in the *Journal of Political Philosophy* volume 19 number 3 (September 2011) and volume 22 number 2 (June 2014). We are grateful to those authors for agreeing to have their work reprinted here.

We are also grateful to the copyright holders for permission to reprint here the following material previously published elsewhere:

Gareth Evans, "From Humanitarian Intervention to the Responsibility to Protect," *Wisconsin International Law Journal*, 24 (3) (2006), 703–22. Reproduced by permission of the *Wisconsin International Law Journal*, the owner of the publishing rights.

Clifford Geertz, "The Judging of Nations," *Archives Européenes de Sociologie*, 18 (1977), 245–61. Reproduced by permission of the *Archives Européenes de Sociologie*, the owner of the publishing rights.

George F. Kennan, "To Prevent a World Wasteland," *Foreign Affairs*, 48 (1970), 401–13. Reproduced by permission of the Council on Foreign Relations, the owner of the publishing rights.

About the Contributors

Christian Barry is Associate Professor of Philosophy at Australian National University

Allen Buchanan is James B. Duke Distinguished Professor of Philosophy at Duke University.

Simon Caney is Professor of Political Theory and Fellow of Magdalen College at the University of Oxford.

Tony Cole is Senior Lecturer in Law at Brunel University.

Peter Dietsch is Professor of Philosophy at the Université de Montréal.

Gareth Evans is Chancellor of the Australian National University.

James S. Fishkin is Janet M. Peck Chair in International Communication at Stanford University where he is Professor of Communication and (by courtesy) Political Science.

Clifford Geertz was Professor of Social Science at the Institute for Advanced Study in Princeton.

Robert E. Goodin is Distinguished Professor of Philosophy at Australian National University.

Ran Hirschl is Professor of Political Science and Law and Canada Research Chair in Constitutionalism, Democracy and Development at the University of Toronto.

George F. Kennan was Professor in the School of Historical Studies at the Institute for Advanced Study in Princeton.

Robert O. Keohane is Professor of International Affairs in the Woodrow Wilson School of Public and International Affairs at Princeton University.

Catherine Lu is Associate Professor of Political Science at McGill University.

Claus Offe is Professor of Political Sociology at the Hertie School of Governance, Berlin.

Mathias Risse is Professor of Philosophy and Public Policy in the Kennedy School of Government at Harvard University.

Thomas Rixen is Professor of Political Science and Economics at Universität Bamberg.

Jennifer C. Rubenstein is Assistant Professor of Politics at the University of Virginia.

Ayelet Shachar is Professor of Law and Political Science and Canada Research Chair in Citizenship and Multiculturalism at the University of Toronto.

1

Political Theory Without Borders
An Introduction

Robert E. Goodin and James S. Fishkin

Political theorists of old had much to say about war and peace, and issues arising from them. Those matters apart, however, political theory's traditional focus was insistently internal – on relations among a people, and on relations between them and those ruling over them.

Those political theorists of universalist inclination have always insisted that the same principles should apply everywhere alike, of course. Virtually none of them, however, thought that literally one and the same set of institutions should rule over everyone everywhere alike.[1] Political theory's prescriptions were traditionally for the internal governance of principalities, taken one at a time.[2]

In political theory, as in political practice, proffered rules governing relations among and across principalities tended to be essentially Westphalian. They were designed to ensure that each self-contained community could get on with the business of perfecting its own institutions and practices in light of the theory's prescriptions, with minimal interference from abroad.[3] Of course there are always threats and opportunities arising from abroad – but that is the business of statesmen to manage well in the national interest. And of course there are always disasters and destitution abroad that tug at the heartstrings – but that is the business of charity and churches. Or so it had long been thought, within both political theory and political practice.

Yet the world has a way of intruding. And it did. First, with spillovers of a very literal sort – with industrial effluents threatening to poison the global biosphere upon which all life depends, including especially carbon emissions wrecking havoc with the global climate. Chapters in Part I by Kennan and Caney address those concerns, with Risse's reminding us of what it really means to treat the earth as the common property of all of humankind.

Political Theory Without Borders, First Edition. Edited by Robert E. Goodin and James S. Fishkin.

With the latest wave of globalization,[4] state borders also became increasingly porous – to the movement of people and products and financial capital. States have become sovereign over their domestic affairs largely in name only, in a great many respects. At the same time, and in consequence, the classical concerns of political theory – justice and equality, liberty and oppression – have reemerged powerfully at the global level. Global justice has grown into a veritable cottage industry, now displaying decreasing returns to scale.[5] But over and above the question of whether the same principles of distributive justice are properly applied at the global as at the national level, there are a great many other more specific matters of principle raised by those global flows of people, products and financial capital. Those issues are here explored in chapters in Part II by Dietsch and Rixen, Barry, Buchanan, Cole and Keohane, Offe, and Shachar and Hirschl.

As a result of all of that, there has been a growing reluctance to regard what happens elsewhere as of concern to people in that jurisdiction alone, as shown in the chapters in Part III. Through colonialism, earlier waves of globalization had left an awful legacy, as Lu's chapter reemphasizes; and suspending judgment for a time may have been an honorable stance in the backwash of it, as Geertz's chapter nicely recalls. But in the wake of increasing numbers (or anyway awareness) of atrocities and disasters – many connected to the phenomena described above – there has been a growing sense of global responsibility for global problems. This expanding humanitarian sensibility has led to increasing intervention abroad, by both humanitarians with guns and those without.[6] Those are the subjects of chapters by Evans and Rubenstein.

It would be wrong to claim that political theorists have fully theorized all these new developments. The critique contained in Marx's Eleventh Thesis on Feuerbach remains valid: theorists mostly just interpret the world rather than change it. Still, political theorists have not been remiss in engaging with and responding critically and creatively to the new sociopolitical and intellectual landscape that is rapidly emerging as the old Westphalian borders are increasing drained of practical relevance – as we hope this set of chapters will show.

Notes

1 Perhaps the last to argue for a world government unitary in form was Dante, in his fourteenth-century *De Monarchia*, a defence of the Holy Roman Empire. Later political cosmopolitans argued instead for a world government, federal in form, with rules of subsidiarity allowing for substantial local variation. See Robert E. Goodin, "World government is here!," *Varieties of Sovereignty and Citizenship*, ed. Sigal R. Ben-Porath and Rogers M. Smith (Philadelphia: University of Pennsylvania Press, 2013), pp. 149–65.

2 As one commentator puts it: "*A Theory of Justice* was published at a time when *globalization* was not yet a word in our everyday lexicon and few people described themselves as cosmopolitans. Virtually all political philosophers at the time assumed that the individual society was the default unit of analysis"; Samuel Scheffler, "Cosmopolitanism, justice and institutions", *Equality and Traditions* (Oxford: Oxford University Press, 2010), pp. 160–73 at p. 162.

3 That way of thinking is bracketed, roughly, by Hugh Grotius' *Law of War and Peace* (1625) and John Rawls's *Law of Peoples* (Cambridge, MA: Harvard University Press, 1999).

4 Hardly the first, as pointed out by John Quiggin, "Globalization and economic sovereignty," *Journal of Political Philosophy,* 9 (2001), 56–80.

5 The two-volume collection edited by Thomas Pogge and Darrel Mollendorf, *Global Justice: Seminal Essays* (St. Paul, MN: Paragon House, 2008) can be regarded as the capstone of this body of research.

6 Albeit in qualfied ways akin to earlier waves of humanitarian sentiment associated with the rise of capitalism; see Thomas L. Haskell, "Capitalism and the origins of humanitarian sensibility," *American Historical Review,* 90 (1985), 339–61, 547–66.

PART I
Global Spillovers

2

To Prevent a World Wasteland
A Proposal

George F. Kennan

NOT even the most casual reader of the public prints of recent months and years could be unaware of the growing chorus of warnings from qualified scientists as to what industrial man is now doing—by overpopulation, by plundering of the earth's resources, and by a precipitate mechanization of many of life's processes—to the intactness of the natural environment on which his survival depends. "For the first time in the history of mankind," U.N. Secretary-General U Thant wrote, "there is arising a crisis of world-wide proportions involving developed and developing countries alike—the crisis of human environment.... It is becoming apparent that if current trends continue, the future of life on earth could be endangered."

Study and debate of these problems, and sometimes even governmental action, have been developing with cumulative intensity. This response has naturally concentrated largely on environmental deterioration as a national problem. It is normally within national boundaries that the first painful effects of deterioration are felt. It is at the national level that the main burden of legislation and administrative effort will admittedly have to be borne, if certain kinds of pollution and destruction are to be halted.

But it is also clear that the national perspective is not the only one from which this problem needs to be approached. Polluted air does not hang forever over the country in which the pollution occurs. The contamination of coastal waters does not long remain solely the problem of the nation in whose waters it has its origin. Wildlife—fish, fowl and animal—is no respecter of national boundaries, either in its movements or in the sources from which it draws its being. Indeed, the entire ecology of the planet is not arranged in national compartments; and whoever interferes seriously with it

Political Theory Without Borders, First Edition. Edited by Robert E. Goodin and James S. Fishkin.
© 2016 John Wiley & Sons, Inc. Published 2016 by John Wiley & Sons, Inc.

anywhere is doing something that is almost invariably of serious concern to the international community at large.

II

There is today in existence a considerable body of international arrangements, including several of great value, dealing with or affecting in one way or another the environmental problem. A formidable number of international organizations, some intergovernmental, some privately organized, some connected with the United Nations, some independently based, conduct programs in this field. As a rule, these programs are of a research nature. In most instances the relevance to problems of environmental conservation is incidental rather than central. While most of them are universal in focus, there are a few that approach the problem—and in some instances very usefully—at the regional level. Underlying a portion of these activities, and providing in some instances the legal basis for it, are a number of multilateral agreements that have environmental objectives or implications.

All this is useful and encouraging. But whether these activities are all that is needed is another question. Only a body fortified by extensive scientific expertise could accurately measure their adequacy to the needs at hand; and there is today, so far as the writer of these lines is aware, no body really charged with this purpose. In any case, it is evident that present activities have not halted or reversed environmental deterioration.

There is no reason to suppose, for example, that they will stop, or even reduce significantly at any early date, the massive spillage of oil into the high seas, now estimated at a million tons per annum and presumably steadily increasing. They will not assure the placing of reasonable limitations on the size of tankers or the enforcement of proper rules for the operation of these and other great vessels on the oceans. They will not, as they now stand, give humanity in general any protection against the misuse and plundering of the seabed for selfish national purposes. They will not put a stop to the proliferation of oil rigs in coastal and international waters, with all the dangers this presents for navigation and for the purity and ecological balance of the sea. They will not, except in a degree already recognized as quite unsatisfactory, protect the fish resources of the high seas from progressive destruction or depletion. They will not seriously reduce the volume of noxious effluence emerging from the River Rhine and being carried by the North Sea currents to other regions. They will not prevent the automobile gases and the sulphuric fumes from Central European industries from continuing to affect the fish life of both fresh and salt waters in the Baltic region. They will not stop the transoceanic jets from consuming—each of them—its reputed 35 tons of oxygen as it moves between Europe and America, and replacing them with its own particular brand of poisons. They will not ensure the observance of proper standards to govern radiological contamination, including disposal of radioactive wastes, in international media. They will not assure that all uses of outer space, as well as of the polar extremities of the planet, are properly controlled in the interests of humanity as a whole.

They may halt or alleviate one or another of these processes of deterioration in the course of time; but there is nothing today to give us the assurance that such efforts will be made promptly enough, or on a sufficient scale, to prevent a further general deterioration in man's environment, a deterioration of such seriousness as to be in many respects irreparable. Even to the non-scientific layman, the conclusion seems inescapable that if this objective is to be achieved, there will have to be an international effort much more urgent in its timing, bolder and more comprehensive in its conception and more vigorous in its execution than anything created or planned to date.

The General Assembly of the United Nations has not been indifferent to the gravity of this problem. Responding to the timely initiative and offer of hospitality of the Swedish government, it has authorized the Secretary-General to proceed at once with the preparation of a "United Nations Conference on the Human Environment," to be held at Stockholm in 1972. There is no question but that this undertaking, the initiation and pursuit of which does much credit to its authors, will be of major significance. But the conference will not be of an organizational nature; nor would it be suited to such a purpose. The critical study of existing vehicles for treating environmental questions internationally, as well as the creation of new organizational devices in this field, is a task that will have to be performed elsewhere. There is no reason why it should not be vigorously pursued even in advance of the Conference—indeed, it is desirable for a number of reasons that it should. As was stated in the Secretary-General's report, "the decision to convene the Conference, and the preparations for it, should in no way be used to postpone or to cancel already initiated or planned programs of research or coöperation, be they at the national, regional or international level. On the contrary, the problems involved are so numerous and so complicated that all efforts to deal with them immediately should be continued and intensified." It will be useful to attempt to picture the functions that need to be performed if this purpose is to be achieved.

III

The first of these would be to provide adequate facilities for the collection, storage, retrieval and dissemination of information on all aspects of the problem. This would involve not just assembling the results of scientific investigation but also keeping something in the nature of a register of all conservational activities at international, national, regional and even local levels across the globe. The task here is not one of conducting original research but rather of collecting and collating the results of research done elsewhere, and disposing of that information in a manner to make it readily available to people everywhere.

A second function would be to promote the coördination of research and operational activities which now deal with environmental problems at the international level. The number of these is already formidable. To take a parallel from the American experience, it was calculated, when the President's Cabinet Committee on Environmental Quality was recently established in the White House, that there were already over 80 programs related to environmental questions being pursued just within the executive branch of the Federal Government. If a similar census were to be taken in the international field, the number would scarcely be less. A recent listing of just those bodies concerned with the peaceful uses of outer space noted 17 entities.

These activities have grown up, for the most part, without central structure or concept. There is not today even any assurance, or any means of assuring, that they cover all the necessary fields. The disadvantages of such a situation—possibilities for confusion, duplication and omission—are obvious.

A third function would be to establish international standards in environmental matters and to extend advice and help to individual governments and to regional organizations in their efforts to meet these standards. It is not a question here of giving orders, exerting authority or telling governments what to do. The function is in part an advisory one and in part, no doubt, hortatory: a matter of establishing and explaining requirements, of pressing governments to accept and enforce standards, of helping them to overcome domestic opposition. The uses of an international authority, when it comes to supporting and stiffening the efforts of governments to prevail against commercial, industrial and military interests within their respective jurisdictions, have already been demonstrated in other instances, as, for example, in the European Iron and Steel Community. They should not be underestimated here.

The fourth function that cries out for performance is from the standpoint of the possibilities in international (as opposed to national or regional) action, the most important of all. In contrast to all the others, it relates only to what might be called the great international media of human activity: the high seas, the stratosphere, outer space, perhaps also the Arctic and Antarctic—media which are subject to the sovereign authority of no national government. It consists simply of the establishment and enforcement of suitable rules for all human activities conducted in these media. It is a question not just of conservational considerations in the narrow sense but also of providing protection against the unfair exploitation of these media, above all the plundering or fouling or damaging of them, by individual governments or their nationals for selfish parochial purposes. Someone, after all, must decide at some point what is tolerable and permissible here and what is not; and since this is an area in which no sovereign government can make these determinations, some international authority must ultimately do so.

No one should be under any illusions about the far-reaching nature, and the gravity, of the problems that will have to be faced if this fourth function is to be effectively performed. There will have to be a determined attack on the problem of the "flags of convenience" for merchant shipping, and possibly their replacement by a single international régime and set of insignia for vessels plying the high seas. One will have to tackle on a hitherto unprecedented scale the thorny task of regulating industrialized fishing in international waters. There may have to be international patrol vessels charged with powers of enforcement in each of these fields. Systems of registration and licensing will have to be set up for uses made of the seabed as well as outer space; and one will have to confront, undaunted, the formidable array of interests already vested in the planting of oil rigs across the ocean floor.

For all of these purposes, the first step must be, of course, the achievement of adequate international consensus and authorization in the form of a multilateral treaty or convention. But for this there will have to be some suitable center of initiation, not to mention the instrument of enforcement which at a later point will have to come into the picture.

IV

What sort of authority holds out the greatest promise of assuring the effective performance of these functions?

It must first be noted that most of them are now being performed in some respects and to some degree by international organizations of one sort or another. The United Nations Secretariat does register (albeit ex post facto and apparently only for routine purposes) such launchings of objects into outer space as the great powers see fit to bring to its attention. The International Maritime Consultative Organization is concerned with the construction and equipping of ships carrying oil or other hazardous or noxious cargos. The United Nations Scientific Committee on the Effects of Atomic Radiation does assemble data on radiation and radioactivity in the environment and give advice to individual governments concerning standards and tolerances in this field. The Organization for Economic Development and Coöperation has recently announced its intention to work out international tolerance levels for pollutants and to tax those of its members which exceed these limits.

This list could go on for pages. Dozens of organizations collect information. Several make recommendations to governments. Some even exercise a limited coördinating role in individual fields. They cover a significant portion of needs; and they obviously cannot be ignored when it comes to the examination of the best organizational response to the problem in question. On the contrary, any approach that failed to take advantage of the work they are already accomplishing, any approach in particular that attempted to duplicate their present activity or to centralize it completely, would assuredly fail. But even in their entirety, they do not cover the whole spectrum of the functions that need to be performed, as listed above; and those that they do perform they perform, for the most part, inadequately.

The question therefore poses itself: How should these organizations be reinforced or expanded? Do they provide in themselves an adequate basis for the necessary expansion of function and activity? Or do they need to be supplemented by new organizational forms, and, if so, of what nature? Is there need for a central organization to bring all these activities under a single hat? Should there be several centers? Or none at all?

There is a view—and it is based on impressive experience and authority—which holds that there is no need for any unifying effort in these various forms of activity, at least not beyond such limited coördinating influence as United Nations bodies are able to exercise today; that any effort in this direction might only further confuse an already confused pattern; and that the most promising line of attack is for governments to intensify their support of activities already in progress, letting them develop separately according to function, letting one set of organizations continue to occupy itself with radiology, another with other forms of air pollution, another with the ecology of fresh water lakes and rivers, another with wildlife, another with oil pollution on the high seas, another with the ocean bed, etc. This is, of course, in many ways the easiest course. Existing efforts, under this procedure, are not disturbed. Existing arrangements for international control and support are not placed in question. Established competencies, sometimes conquered and defended in past years with much effort, are not jeopardized.

But there are weighty considerations that argue against such a course. A number of the existing organizations, including particularly ones connected with the United Nations, have primarily a developmental focus; yet developmental considerations are frequently in conflict with the needs of environmental conservation. Others are staffed, at least in considerable part, by persons whose professional enthusiasm runs to the exploitation of the very natural media or resources whose protection is here at stake. Others are closely connected with commercial interests engaged in just this sort of exploitation.

There is a considerable body of opinion, particularly in U. N. circles, to the effect that it is a mistake to separate the function of conservation and protection of natural resources from that of the development and exploitation of these resources for productive purposes. According to this view, there should not be separate organizations concerned with conservation. Considerations of an environmental nature should rather be built from the outset into all those activities that are concerned with the productive exploitation of natural resources, so that environmental needs would be met, so to speak, at the source.

This writer must respectfully disagree. This is an area in which exploitative motives cannot usefully be mingled with conservational ones. What is needed here is a watchdog; and the conscience and sense of duty of the watchdog must not be confused by contrary duties and undertakings. It may be boldly asserted that of the two purposes in question, conservation should come first. The principle should be that one exploits what a careful regard for the needs of conservation leaves to be exploited, not that one conserves what a liberal indulgence of the impulse to development leaves to be conserved.

V

What is lacking in the present pattern of approaches would seem to be precisely an organizational personality—part conscience, part voice—which has at heart the interests of no nation, no group of nations, no armed force, no political movement and no commercial concern, but simply those of mankind generally, together—and this is important—with man's animal and vegetable companions, who have no other advocate. If determinations are to be made of what is desirable from the standpoint of environmental conservation and protection, then they are going to have to proceed from a source which, in addition to including scientific competence and having qualified access to all necessary scientific data, sees things from a perspective which no national body—and no international one whose function is to reconcile conflicting national interests—can provide.

The process of compromise of national interests will of course have to take place at some point in every struggle against environmental deterioration at the international level. But it should not occur in the initial determination of what is and is not desirable from the conservational standpoint. This determination should at first be made, so to speak, in its pure form, or as near as one can get to it. It should serve as the point of departure for the long, wearisome, often thorny and frustrating, road of accommodation that will have to be traversed before it can be transformed into reality. But it should not itself be compromised at the outset.

Nor is this the only reason why one cannot make do with just the reinforcement of what now exists. If the present process of deterioration is to be halted, things are going to have to be done which will encounter formidable resistance from individual governments and powerful interests within individual countries. Only an entity that has great prestige, great authority and active support from centers of influence within the world's most powerful industrial and maritime nations will be able to make headway against such recalcitrance. One can conceive of a single organization's possessing such prestige and authority. It is harder to conceive of the purpose being served by some fifty to a hundred organizations, each active in a different field, all of them together presenting a pattern too complicated even to be understood or borne in mind by the world public.

All of this would seem to speak for the establishment of a single entity which, while not duplicating the work of existing organizations, could review this work from the standpoint of man's environmental needs as a whole, could make it its task to spot the inadequacies and identify the unfilled needs, could help to keep governments and leaders of opinion informed as to what ought to be done to meet minimum needs, could endeavor to assure that proper rules and standards are established wherever they are needed, and could, where desired, take a hand, vigorously and impartially, in the work of enforcement of rules and standards. It would not have to perform all these various functions itself—except perhaps where there was no one else to do so. Its responsibility should be rather to define their desirable dimensions and to exert itself, and use its influence with governments, to the end that all of them were performed by *someone*, and in an adequate way.

This entity, while naturally requiring the initiative of governments for its inception and their continued interest for its support, would have to be one in which the substantive decisions would be taken not on the basis of compromise among governmental representatives but on the basis of collaboration among scholars, scientists, experts, and perhaps also something in the nature of environmental statesmen and diplomats—but true international servants, bound by no national or political mandate, by nothing, in fact, other than dedication to the work at hand.

VI

It is impossible to picture an entity of this nature without considering, in the first instance, the possible source of its initiation and sponsorship in the international community. Who would take the lead in establishing it? From whom would it draw its financial resources? Who would constitute the ultimate sanction for its existence and its authority?

Obviously no single government could stand as the patron for such an agency. To seek, on the other hand, the sanction of the entire international community for its inception and activity would scarcely be a promising undertaking. Aside from the fact that this would then necessitate procedures practically indistinguishable from those of the United Nations itself, it would mean involving in the control and operation of the entity to be established a host of smaller and less developed countries which could contribute very little to the solution of the problems at hand. It would also involve formidable delays and heavy problems of decision-taking. Were this to be the course selected, one would do better to content one's self, throughout, with the existing facilities of the United Nations, which represent just about the limit of what can be accomplished on the basis of a universal, or near-universal, governmental consensus.

One is driven to the conclusion that if anything very constructive is going to be accomplished along this line, the interest and initiative will have to proceed from a relatively small group of governments; and logic suggests that these should be those of the leading industrial and maritime nations. It is they whose economies produce, in the main, the problem of pollution. It is they, again, who have the means to correct it. It is they, finally, who have the scientific and other resources to analyze the problem and to identify the most promising lines of solution. The devastation of the environment is primarily, though not exclusively, a function of advanced industrial and urban society. The correction of it is primarily a problem for the advanced nations.

One can conceive, then, by an act of the imagination, of a small group of advanced nations, consisting of roughly the ten leading industrial nations of the world, including communist and non-communist ones alike, together (mainly for reasons of their maritime interests) with the Scandinavians and perhaps with the Benelux countries as a bloc, constituting themselves something in the nature of a club for the preservation of natural environment, and resolving, then, in that capacity, to bring into being an entity—let us call it initially an International Environmental Agency—charged with the performance, at least on their behalf, of the functions outlined above. It would not, however, be advisable that this agency should be staffed at the operating level with governmental representatives or that it should take its decisions on the basis of intergovernmental compromise. Its operating personnel should rather have to consist primarily of people of scientific or technical competence, and the less these were bound by disciplinary relationships to individual governments, the better. One can imagine, therefore, that instead of staffing and controlling this agency themselves, the governments in question might well insert an intermediate layer of control by designating in each case a major scientific institution from within their jurisdiction—an Academy of Science or its equivalent—to act as a participating organization. These scientific bodies would then take over the responsibility for staffing the agency and supervising its operations.

It may be argued that under such an arrangement the participating institutions from communist countries would not be free agents, would enjoy no real independence, and would act only as stooges for their governments. As one who has had occasion both to see something of Russia and to disagree in public on a number of occasions with Soviet policies, the writer of this article is perhaps in a particularly favorable position to express his conviction that the Soviet Academy of Sciences, if called upon by its government to play a part in such an undertaking, would do so with an integrity and a seriousness of purpose worthy of its great scientific tradition, and would prove a rock of strength for the accomplishment of the objectives in question.

The agency would require, of course, financial support from the sponsoring governments. There would be no point in its establishment if one were not willing to support it generously and regularly; and one should not underestimate the amount of money that would be required. It might even run eventually to as much as the one-hundredth part of the military budgets of the respective governments for the same period of time, which would of course be a very substantial sum. Considering that the threat the agency would be designed to confront would be one by no means less menacing or less urgent than those to which the military appropriations are ostensibly devoted, this could hardly be called exorbitant.

The first task of such an agency should be to establish the outstanding needs of environmental conservation in the several fields, to review critically the work and the prospects of organizations now in existence, in relation to those needs, to identify the main lacunae, and to make recommendations as to how they should be filled. Such recommendations might envisage the concentration of one or another sort of activity in a single organization. They might envisage the strengthening of certain organizations, the merging of others. They might suggest the substance of new multilateral treaty provisions necessary to supply the foundation for this or that function of regulation and control. They might involve the re-allotment of existing responsibility for the development of standards, or the creation of new responsibilities of this nature. In short, a primary function of the Agency would be to advise governments, regional organizations and public opinion generally on what is needed to meet the environmental problem internationally, and to make recommendations as to how these needs can best be met. It would then of course be up to governments, the sponsoring ones and others as well, to implement these recommendations in whatever ways they might decide or agree on.

This, as will be seen, would be initially a process of study and advice. It would never be entirely completed; for situations would be constantly changing, new needs would be arising as old ones were met, the millennium would never be attained. But one could hope that eventually, as powers were accumulated and authority delegated under multilateral treaty arrangements, the Agency could gradually take over many of the functions of enforcement for such international arrangements as might require enforcement in the international media, and in this way expand its function and designation from that of an advisory agency to that of the single commanding

International Environmental Authority which the international community is bound, at some point, to require.

All this, however, belongs to a later phase of development which it is idle to attempt to envisage in an enquiry so preliminary as this. In problems of international organizations, as in war, one does well to follow the Napoleonic principle: *"On s'engage et puis on voit."* To engage oneself means, in this instance, to bring into being the personality. The rest will follow.

VII

The above is intended only as a suggestion of certain lines along which international action in this field might usefully and hopefully proceed. In the mind of the writer, these considerations would have validity even if founded only on the strictest and narrowest view of the environmental factors alone. They need no extraneous arguments for their justification.

It would be wrong, however, to close this discussion without noting that no such undertaking could be without its political and psychological by-products. The energies and resources men have to devote to international activities are not unlimited. To the extent that a place can be found in their hopes and enthusiasms for constructive and hopeful efforts, these must proceed at least to some extent at the expense of the sterile, morbid and immensely dangerous preoccupations that are now pursued under the heading of national defense.

Not only the international scientific community but the world public at large has great need, at this dark hour, of a new and more promising focus of attention. The great communist and Western powers, particularly, have need to replace the waning fixations of the cold war with interests which they can pursue in common and to everyone's benefit. For young people the world over, some new opening of hope and creativity is becoming an urgent spiritual necessity. Could there, one wonders, be any undertaking better designed to meet these needs, to relieve the great convulsions of anxiety and ingrained hostility that now rack international society, than a major international effort to restore the hope, the beauty and the salubriousness of the natural environment in which man has his being?

3

Two Kinds of Climate Justice
Avoiding Harm and Sharing Burdens *

Simon Caney

> There exists a solidarity among men as human beings that makes each co-responsible for every wrong and every injustice in the world, especially for crimes committed in his presence or with his knowledge. If I fail to do whatever I can to prevent them, I too am guilty.
>
> —Karl Jaspers[1]

I. Two Kinds of Climate Justice

The overwhelming majority of climate scientists hold that humanity is facing the prospect of severe climate change and the Assessment Reports of the Intergovernmental Panel on Climate Change (IPCC) contain some stark warnings. In the IPCC's Fourth Assessment Report, the 'best estimate' of the increase in global mean temperatures in the period between 1980–1999 and 2080–2099 ranged from 1.8°C (B1 scenario) and 4.0°C (A1F1 scenario). If we consider the 'likely range' of temperature increases in this period, we see that the figures range from between a 1.1°C increase (B1) and 6.4°C increase (A1F1).[2] These changes—and the sea level rises and severe weather events associated with climate change—will have disastrous effects on human and non-human life.

One can distinguish between two ways of thinking about climate justice. One starts by focusing on how the burden of combating the problem should be shared fairly among the duty-bearers. An agent's responsibility, then, is to do her fair share. Its concern is with what I shall term *Burden-Sharing Justice*. A number of principles of burden-sharing justice have been proposed

Political Theory Without Borders, First Edition. Edited by Robert E. Goodin and James S. Fishkin.
© 2016 John Wiley & Sons, Inc. Published 2016 by John Wiley & Sons, Inc.

and assessed. Three, in particular, have been suggested—the principle that those who have caused the problem should bear the burden; the principle that those who have the ability to pay should bear the burden; and the principle that those who have benefited from the activities that cause climate change should bear the burden.[3]

One might, however, look at the issue from a second point of view. This second perspective takes as its starting point the imperative to prevent climate change, and it works back from this to deduce who should do what. Its focus is primarily on ensuring that the catastrophe is averted (or at least minimised within reason). This perspective is concerned with the potential victims—those whose entitlements are threatened—and it ascribes responsibilities to others to uphold these entitlements.[4] This approach focuses on what I shall term *Harm Avoidance Justice*.

Ideally, both perspectives would coincide. However, in many areas of human life it is clear that these two kinds of perspective can clash. To see this consider, what is by comparison with climate change, a fairly trivial example. Consider a familiar academic context where certain important administrative tasks need to be allocated. If we make fair burden-sharing our priority, then we may allocate it to an individual *A*, who has not yet done her fair share. On the other hand, if we make getting the job done properly our priority, we may baulk at giving it to *A* if, say, *A* is unreliable and will not do the job properly. So although, ideally, both kinds of justice would coincide, there is no guarantee that this will occur. We, therefore, need an account which includes both kinds of responsibility, and which determines which should take priority when the two conflict.

We can think of other—less trivial—examples where both perspectives apply and where they may not happily coincide. This tension will arise whenever four conditions apply:

1 there is an important goal the realization of which involves a burden;
2 the equitable sharing of the burden requires a certain distribution of burdens *Di* (Burden-Sharing Justice);
3 to make sure that the goal is achieved requires a distribution of burdens *Dii* (Harm Avoidance Justice); and
4 *Di* and *Dii* do not coincide.

Conditions (1)–(4) occur in a number of different contexts. Consider, for example, the ethics of waging war. One goal obviously is to prosecute a just war successfully. At the same time, pursuing this imposes severe harms on some, and we need to comply with principles of just conduct (*jus in bello*). Although it is unusual to frame *jus in bello* as being concerned with the fair distribution of harms, that is essentially what is at stake.[5] However, there might be cases where the importance of (2) clashes with (3) and we are forced to consider whether it can be justified to violate the principles of just conduct. We may face what Michael Walzer terms a 'supreme emergency', where we have to choose between acting in such a way that we secure the specified goal (*jus ad bellum*) or by acting in ways that distribute the harms equitably (*jus in bello*).[6] Another case where we face a similar dilemma might include dealing with the financial crisis. On the one hand, we might say 'it's crucial that we have a stable economy and therefore there is a case for bailing out the banks'. On the other hand, we might say that some bankers brought this about, and so they should bear responsibility for that, and that precludes bailing them out.

So the distinction between the two kinds of justice is hopefully a familiar one. Before proceeding further, it is worth noting that the distinction between *Harm Avoidance Justice* and *Burden-Sharing Justice* is <u>not</u> identical to that between a backward-looking approach and a more forward-looking one. One might think so on the grounds that an approach focusing on avoiding harm is concerned with a certain outcome—one in which people can enjoy certain kinds of entitlements. However, while a harm-avoidance-oriented approach is forward-looking (and thus the elision seems plausible), a burden-sharing approach is not necessarily backward-looking. Those who focus on how burdens should be shared do often appeal to non-backward-looking considerations such as 'who has the ability to pay?'[7]

Let us return now to the case of climate change. As I have noted above, much of the ethical discussion of climate change has focused on what I have termed *Burden-Sharing Justice*. I think that such discussions are crucial. Nothing that follows challenges the need for such analyses. However, they are, I maintain, incomplete: we also need to analyse matters from the point of *Harm Avoidance Justice*. Climate change poses serious existential threats to many people's lives and to the very existence of some communities. Its effects will be extremely harmful, possibly catastrophic, for millions of people. Given this, I think we have reason to focus on what would most effectively prevent the onset of dangerous climate change, and then consider what responsibilities would follow from that.[8] My aim in this paper, then, is to develop a normative account of climate change that takes as its starting point the assumption that it is of paramount importance that humanity avoids dangerous climate change.[9] I shall begin by considering two approaches which, like mine, are animated by a concern to prevent dangerous climate change from occurring (Sections II–III), before then setting out and seeking to defend my own account (Sections IV–VI).

II. Prioritising Prevention 1—International Paretianism

The first prevention-oriented approach I wish to consider is that set out by Eric Posner and David Weisbach in their book *Climate Change Justice* (2010). Posner and Weisbach start from a commitment to preventing dangerous climate change and argue that to realize this commitment we must adopt what they term 'International Paretianism'.[10] Their claim is nicely encapsulated in the following passage:

> Any treaty must satisfy what we shall call the principle of International Paretianism: all states must believe themselves better off by their lights as a result of the climate treaty. International Paretianism is not an ethical principle but a pragmatic constraint: in the state system, treaties are not possible unless they have the consent of all states, and states only enter treaties that serve their interests.[11]

Broken down into its constituent parts, Posner and Weisbach's argument is as follows:

(P1)   It is necessary to have a climate treaty with which major emitters comply.

(P2)   To be <u>feasible</u> an effective climate treaty must serve the interests of high emitting states (from 'Feasibility' to 'Pareto Superiority').

Therefore,

(C)   A climate treaty must serve the interests of high emitting states.

This argument is unclear in a number of respects. In particular, (P2) is ambiguous in two ways. First, although Posner and Weisbach refer to 'feasibility'[12] it is not clear what they mean by this. To say that 'X is feasible' might mean, inter alia, that X is (i) 'possible' or (ii) 'likely to happen', or (iii) 'will happen'.[13] Posner and Weisbach do not consider the different ways in which this concept can be interpreted. In what follows I shall assume, in the first instance, that when they say that a treaty is feasible they mean that it is *possible* for agents (in this case, governments) to comply with it (interpretation (i)). Later on, I consider interpretations (ii) and (iii). Whichever interpretation we use, I argue, their argument is unsuccessful.

Second, Posner and Weisbach do not say what baseline they are using. However, to say that a treaty must be Pareto-superior one must specify what it is Pareto-superior to, and then explain why this is an appropriate baseline. To see why this matters, consider three possible baselines. The claim might be that for the members of any given state, S, a treaty at t_2 (and thereafter) should be Pareto-superior to:

(a)   the situation members of S face at t_1 (the status quo ex ante);
(b)   the situation members of S would face at t_2 (and thereafter) if no treaty were signed; or
(c)   the situation members of S would face at t_2 (and thereafter) if a treaty were signed and other states credibly threatened punitive sanctions if S did not agree to and comply with the treaty.

In one passage Posner and Weisbach explicitly endorse (a), writing that 'a treaty … satisfies International Paretianism' if it 'advances the interests of all states relative to the status quo'.[14] If, though, this is their considered view, then it is highly implausible, for (a) may not be a live option after t_1 has elapsed. Consider, for example, the following situation.

Suppose that a coalition of states implements a climate treaty and suppose that this coalition credibly threatens to punish a state, S, if it does not sign up to and comply with this treaty. In these circumstances, S may have a good self-interested reason to comply—even if what S agrees to is worse than the status quo at t_1 (option a), and even if it is worse for the members of S than a world without a climate treaty would be at t_2 (option b). Options (a) and (b) are not relevant baselines because they are not available to S at t_2. (c), though, is relevant. Suppose, finally, that the sanctions that the coalition will impose on S are worse for S than the burdens involved in compliance. In this kind of case, states may then rationally agree to something that worsens their condition at t_2 when compared with t_1. This is highly relevant for international environmental diplomacy because some states, coalitions of states, and international organizations can threaten to impose sanctions on non-complying states. Climate treaties, thus, need not be Pareto-superior to the status quo.

Suppose that Posner and Weisbach address these concerns and provide a plausible conception of feasibility and the baseline. Their argument is still unsuccessful. To see why, it is worth distinguishing between two different kinds of perspective when thinking about the feasibility of a climate treaty. In particular, one can distinguish between, on the one hand, the perspective of a state that is a major emitter (call this the *internal point of view*), and, on the other hand, the perspective of others (perhaps the representatives of other states) who are trying to persuade major emitters to reduce their emissions (call this *the external point of view*). It is vital to make this distinction because the argument from International Paretianism has force only from the external point of view, but lacks it from the internal point of view.

To explain: while it might be true that if someone wishes to design a treaty that an emitter will sign up to and comply with then the first agent (assuming she cannot compel the emitter, or that she can but has good reason not to do so) should take this consideration into account. She has reason to try to design a treaty which caters to the interests of the emitting state. However, this gives the emitter no reason at all not to sign up without the inducement. The emitter cannot say (to borrow Posner and Weisbach's words) that '[f]easibility rules out' signing this treaty.[15] He cannot because it is not true: it is quite possible for him to do this. He, therefore, cannot appeal to the infeasibility of committing himself to Pareto-inferior policies because it is *not* infeasible for him to reduce his emissions. Infeasibility here is not a bar. It should be called what is it, namely 'unwillingness'.

The argument I am making here is structurally analogous to that which G. A. Cohen levels against Rawls's treatment of the talented in his defence of the Difference Principle. As Cohen points out, whereas people other than the most talented may say that it is necessary to reward the talented to ensure that they work to the benefit of the least advantaged, this is not an argument that the talented themselves can make (barring cases of akrasia).[16]

Posner and Weisbach's argument gains whatever credibility it might possess because they present their claim in the passive mood. They write, for example, that 'only a treaty that satisfies International Paretianism—that is, that advances the interests of all states relative to the status quo—is feasible'.[17] But this *passive* way of putting it is misleading.[18] Treaties are agreed to by *agents* and we need to examine it from their point of view. From the point of view of the members of a high emitting political community, it is just not true that it is not possible for them to sign up to a treaty that leaves them worse off. They can.

Posner and Weisbach might make two replies. First, they might protest that they are not using 'feasible' to mean 'is possible'. Rather, they might argue, they are using 'feasible' to mean 'is likely to happen' or, perhaps, 'will happen'. This, however, does not help their case for the same argument applies against this. From the external point of view, it is defensible to argue that 'concessions need to be made to high emitters because without that they are not *likely to* comply (or *will not* comply)'. But if a high emitting country like the USA simply says 'this treaty needs to reward us because unless it does so then we are not likely to comply' (or, just, 'we will not comply'), then it is hard to see why this counts as a justification at all. It is a prediction of expected behaviour and perhaps a threat. Pointing out that a proposed obligation is not possible is relevant. But saying that, though it is possible for one to do X, one *is not likely to comply* with it (or, more baldly, one *will not comply with it*) has no argumentative power. To posit that 'ought' implies 'can' is reasonable (if not uncontroversial), but to claim that 'ought' implies either 'is likely to' or 'will' is obviously implausible.

At this point, Posner and Weisbach might adopt a second tack. They might argue that it is not *possible* for elected representatives to reduce emissions in such a way that their citizens were worse off, because if they did so they would be voted out of office, and, if their successors pledged to adopt a climate policy that would leave their citizens worse off they too would suffer the same outcome. Elected representatives are beholden to their electorate and the latter would punish them. It is therefore not possible for a government to enact and put into practice a radical mitigation policy.

In reply: this has some plausibility, but it does not save Posner and Weisbach's argument for it just entails that members of the political community *as a whole* have a duty to reduce emissions. So governments have a responsibility to cut emissions; and electors too have a pro tanto duty not to punish them for such action. Indeed, they have a (pro tanto) duty to punish them for any deviation from this course of action. Also the politicians in this scenario have a responsibility to persuade the electorate of the need for mitigation and adaptation. So both elected and electors have responsibilities. The key point is that it is possible for the members of the political unit <u>as a whole</u> to act in ways that reduce emissions, and this is all that my argument above needs.

The objection thus, remains intact. Posner and Weisbach's claim that the only feasible climate treaty is one that improves the lot of all signatories is mistaken.

III. Prioritising Prevention 2—Acting Without Sacrifice

Having considered one approach that puts preventing climate change at the forefront of its concerns, let us now consider a second approach—one inspired by recent work by Duncan Foley and John Broome. Foley and Broome have both argued that mitigating climate change does not actually involve any sacrifice.[19] I will focus on Broome's discussion of it, in his recent book *Climate Matters* (2012), because he stresses there that this conclusion has considerable political significance for it enables humanity to overcome the current impasse in climate negotiations and implement an effective climate treaty.

Broome reasons as follows. Those who emit greenhouse gases are not internalizing the costs of their activity. Climate change is, thus, what economists term an 'externality'. Externalities are inefficient. Therefore, it follows from this that we can move from where we are to a more efficient outcome.[20] Specifically, we could move to a situation where emitters stop their harmful activity and thus do not inflict harm on others (whom Broome calls 'receivers'), and, crucially, the emitters are also no worse off.[21] What does this mean in practice? How could we leave those who would emit no worse off? Broome's proposal is that we borrow from the future—for example, using up some natural resources we would otherwise leave for future generations—and compensate people for refraining from emitting dangerous amounts of greenhouse gases.[22] We can thus achieve what Broome terms 'efficiency without sacrifice'.[23]

It is important to be clear that Broome does not think that this is the best outcome. He prefers what he terms 'efficiency with sacrifice'. This requires current emitters to stop their harmful behaviour and not be compensated by taking benefits from the future. Broome holds that 'efficiency with sacrifice' is better for two reasons. His first is essentially utilitarian. His second is that justice requires that the cost of emitting be picked up by the actual polluters (and not by their more affluent descendants). Justice, in his view, requires that the polluter should pay. For these two reasons, 'efficiency with sacrifice' is better than 'efficiency without sacrifice'.[24]

However, Broome is keen to emphasize that, for pragmatic reasons, we might aim for 'efficiency without sacrifice'. It is for this reason that his argument is very relevant here. For, in line with my emphasis on preventing climate change, Broome canvasses 'efficiency without sacrifice' as a way of breaking the political deadlock. As he puts it, 'it has the moral purpose of moving the political process forward'.[25]

Broome (and Foley's) argument has considerable appeal. However, I think it fails to show that a 'no sacrifice' option is available. Before presenting my central concern, it is worth noting a limitation in Broome and Foley's argument. Their argument critically depends on the empirical assumption that climate change is an inefficiency: that is, both assume that there are other outcomes which contain more welfare. This may be true, but it is not obviously true, and depends on empirical assumptions about the aggregate impacts of climate change and the costs and benefits of mitigating (and adapting to) climate change. Broome emphasizes that emitters are imposing external costs on others. This is true. But it does not, in itself, entail that this is a case of an 'externality', *if that is understood to entail that there is a more efficient distribution available*. For it is, of course, possible to have cases where A imposes an external cost on B, where the benefit to A gained by this activity is greater than the harm to B. In this kind of case, preventing the external cost will result in a net loss to society, and so would be termed inefficient. Of course, it might still be the right thing to do.

We can thus distinguish between two kinds of cases where A imposes external costs on others—those where the benefits to A are less than the harm to B (harm with inefficiency) and those where the benefits to A are more than the harm to B (harm without inefficiency). For Broome and Foley's argument to go through the first possibility must be correct. Broome does not say much in defence of this assumption.[26] I should make clear that I am not challenging this empirical claim. My point is the more modest one of making clear that the Foley-Broome argument depends on a key empirical premise. If this is mistaken—if, for example, mitigating climate change prevents harm but nonetheless results in a net loss of welfare—then their argument fails.

Suppose that we grant this. The central weakness in Broome's argument lies in its assumption that it is possible to act now and to pass on all of the costs to future people. I do not deny that it is possible to pass on some costs to future generations. Current generations can, for example, use certain natural resources that they would have otherwise passed on to future generations. Is it, however, possible to pass on all the costs? I think we have good reason to be sceptical of this, and to believe that mitigation may impose costs on some for which they cannot be compensated. Consider those who work in professions that depend for their existence on fossil fuels. A radical programme of mitigation of the kind required to avert dangerous climate change would require laying off many who work in heavy industry, manufacturing, coalmining, and construction. However, for very many people having a job is a crucial and non-substitutable source of well-being. Their job provides not only money (which can, of course, be provided in other ways) but also certain other goods which may be essential to having a fulfilling life. It gives them a sense of purpose and meaning in life; it defines their identity, and is often tied up with their sense of self-respect. For such people, to live a fulfilling life requires, as a necessary condition, earning a living (rather than just getting money), making their own way in the world, and using skills they have developed over the years. Being made redundant robs them of all of these goods and thereby removes a source of well-being that cannot be made up by providing other goods.[27] To this we should then add that, in very many cases, those laid off will be unable to reskill and learn new professions. In such cases, mitigation will necessarily incur a sacrifice— one that cannot be passed on to others. More generally, the point is this: the fact that a policy removes a source of well-being from A but makes B much better off does not entail that B can transfer some of that benefit to A so that A is no worse off. The enforced unemployment of those in fossil fuel-dependent jobs is a case in point. Lest my argument be misunderstood: my claim is not that this entails that mitigation should not be pursued (after all the abolition of slavery probably also led to loss of jobs). It is just that if we engage in it, it is likely to impose a considerable sacrifice on some.

IV. Prioritising Prevention 3—Taking the Institutional Context and the Political Challenges Seriously

Having criticised two approaches that might both appear to help us make progress in preventing dangerous change, I shall now outline and then defend my own prevention-oriented approach. The two preceding accounts have both sought to minimize the sacrifices that need to be made—either by acceding to the self-interest of high emitting states and not requiring them to make any sacrifices (International Paretianism), or by not requiring anyone to make any sacrifices (Efficiency Without Sacrifice).

My account starts from the recognition that, even if some costs can be passed on, some sacrifices have to be made. Given this, we cannot just assume that agents will comply with their duties to mitigate and enable adaptation to climate change. Unless one thinks that agents will spontaneously comply with such burdensome responsibilities—and our experience of human nature and the inconclusive nature of the negotiations on climate change for the last two decades have surely taught us that such a belief would be naïve in the extreme—anyone serious about preventing climate change (and thus avoiding harm) needs to reflect on how to respond to current and future non-compliance.

There are two distinct kinds of response to this challenge. To elaborate on these it is, however, necessary to distinguish here between two kinds of responsibility—what can be termed *first-order* and *second-order responsibilities*. First-order responsibilities, as I employ that term, are responsibilities that certain agents have to perform (or omit) certain actions. In the context of addressing climate change these *first-order* responsibilities include responsibilities to mitigate climate change (through reducing emissions and maintaining greenhouse gas sinks), to enable adaption, and to compensate people for harm done. *Second-order responsibilities*, by contrast, refer to responsibilities that some have to ensure that agents comply with their *first-order responsibilities*.[28] (This is a rough formulation of the distinction, and I will refine it later.)

Now with this distinction on hand, we can outline the two kinds of response to current and future non-compliance. The first operates at the *first-order* level and says that when there is non-compliance, others should cover some, if not all, of the *first-order responsibilities* of those who do not comply.[29] I have defended this kind of response elsewhere.[30]

Whilst undoubtedly important, this kind of response is insufficient. To adopt this approach, and only this approach, wrongly treats levels of non-compliance as a given, and then responds to it in a reactive way, seeking merely to cope with it. Since, however, agents operate in social, economic, and political contexts, it is possible to structure these contexts in ways which induce agents to comply with their *first-order* responsibilities. Given this, and given the paramount importance of preventing dangerous climate change, we therefore have good reason to design these contexts to enable greater compliance and thereby avoid harm. It would be irresponsible to ignore these opportunities for reducing non-compliance, and then hope that those who comply with their responsibilities will cover for the failings of others.[31] Put more succinctly: the first response needs to be supplemented with an account of *second-order responsibilities*.[32]

Given this, my aim in the remainder of this article is to outline and motivate support for an account of *second-order responsibilities*. The most logical way to derive such an account is to start by identifying what needs to be done to minimize the prospects of dangerous climate change (the 'tasks'). Then, with an account of the tasks in hand, we can use this to ascertain who is best placed to perform these tasks (the 'second-order agents'), and the qualities they must possess (the 'traits'). Having outlined what needs to be done and by whom, I turn then (in Section V) to provide a normative justification which can establish why these agents are under an obligation to perform these tasks (the 'normative rationale').

This account of *second-order responsibilities*, I will argue, yields four important normative conclusions: it (i) draws attention to different kinds of action than are commonly mentioned; (ii) identifies a wider range of agents than is normally proposed; (iii) results in a different apportionment of responsibilities; and (iv) rests on a distinct normative basis for ascribing responsibilities.

I shall begin, then, by describing the approach to be adopted in the remainder of this section, before turning in the next section to justify it.[33]

A. Task delineation

As noted above, if our aim is to avert dangerous climate change, then it makes sense to commence our analysis with an account of what needs to be done to achieve this goal. In order to do this, we need to specify the content of the *second-order responsibilities* required to avert dangerous climate change. Without claiming to be exhaustive, one might identify at least six kinds of action that agents can perform.[34]

The first, is <u>enforcement</u>: those who have (or could have) the political power to set up enforcement mechanisms may have a responsibility to do so. To give one example, Joseph Stiglitz has proposed that the WTO should employ trade sanctions against states that do not make an appropriate reduction in greenhouse gas emissions.[35] In addition to enforcing compliance (or, perhaps, as an alternative to doing this), one might also compel an agent to disclose its level of greenhouse gas emissions. Such enforced transparency does not, in itself, compel an agent to comply, but it may often, nonetheless, lead to greater compliance because agents do not wish to look bad in the eyes of others. Such transparency initiatives can operate through what Geoffrey Brennan and Philip Pettit call the 'economy of esteem'.[36]

A second type of second-order course of action is <u>incentivization</u>. Whereas enforcement imposes a burden on non-compliers, incentivization offers benefits to them in exchange for compliance. Organizations like the WTO and

EU can, and do, insist that those belonging to them, and those seeking to join, must satisfy certain criteria. Such organizations can thus withhold membership (and, therefore, the benefits of such membership) from states that do not comply with their mitigation and adaptation responsibilities.

A third type of second-order action is what we might term <u>enablement</u>. By this I mean the capacity to enable others to engage in mitigation or adaptation. For example, some agents' willingness to comply with their first-order responsibilities to reduce their greenhouse gas emissions may be undermined because low-carbon alternatives may be difficult to find (or, in a variation on this, because the low-carbon alternatives are quite expensive). Given this, one way that some can affect whether agents comply with *first-order responsibilities* to mitigate is by: (a) facilitating scientific research (into clean technologies, new energy sources, and ways of increasing energy efficiency); and (b) transferring these scientific innovations widely so that people may reduce emissions more easily. For example, one way to enable agents to comply is by designing urban spaces so that people can move around (between their homes, workplaces, schools, and leisure activities) in ways which do not involve emitting high levels of greenhouse gases.[37]

At this point it is worth noting that 'enablement' can take us beyond *second-order* action as I defined it above. For as well as assisting people to do what they have a *first-order* responsibility to do, enablement can also have the consequence that agents who previously lacked a particular *first-order* responsibility (either because they could not engage in the necessary action or because they could do so but only at unreasonable cost) can now— because of enablement—be expected to bear that responsibility. The generation and transfer of clean technology can, for example, enable the world's least advantaged to develop, and in doing so gives them an opportunity, but also a responsibility, to do so in ways that do not exacerbate climate change. We should thus reconceive *second-order* responsibilities so that they are not simply (i) responsibilities to ensure that agents comply with their *first-order* responsibilities, but also (ii) include responsibilities to create possibilities for some to be allocated some new *first-order* responsibilities that they previously lacked. (This is the reformulation promised above when I first introduced the distinction.)

Consider now a fourth kind of second-order policy. Some agents can influence the behaviour of others by <u>creating norms</u> that discourage high emissions lifestyles (or, alternatively, that foster a commitment to adaptation). To employ a term coined by Cass Sunstein, some can act as 'norm entrepreneurs'.[38] Norms can be tremendously influential for they define what options count as appropriate and what not. To take two recent examples, attitudes towards smoking in confined spaces and attitudes to drink-driving have changed dramatically in the UK in the last thirty to forty years. If we consider now international politics, the importance of norms and taboos in explaining state behaviour has also been attested to by a number of justly influential 'constructivist' works in international relations. Representative examples include Neta Crawford's work on the role of norms in decolonization and the abolition of slavery, Martha Finnemore's work on UNESCO, the Red Cross, and the World Bank, and Nina Tannenwald's compelling analysis of the 'nuclear taboo'.[39]

In addition to norm-creation, some can affect the way in which activities that cause greenhouse gas emissions are framed. To illustrate: the coverage of the cost of petrol is frequently framed by national media solely in terms of increasing the cost of living of drivers (and those whose livelihood is affected by transportation), and not at all in terms of its impact on greenhouse gas emissions. Those who are able to frame the issue so that the link with environmental degradation is brought out can thus affect norms of 'appropriateness'.[40]

Consider now a fifth kind of second-order policy—namely underlining resistance to effective climate policies. As Naomi Oreskes and Erik Conway have convincingly argued in *Merchants of Doubt*, oil companies have sought to spread misinformation about the nature, extent, and causes of global warming.[41] In addition to this, it has been persuasively argued that media representations of climate change are often misleading, and hence that the public understanding of climate science is often poor and out of line with the scientific consensus.[42] One service that some (in the media) can provide is to give an accurate portrayal of the state of climate science, reporting the levels of agreement on the existence of anthropogenic climate change, as well as including the areas of considerable uncertainty. In addition to this, others (notably climate scientists and national science academies) can, and often do, rebut factual and other errors propounded by those who deny climate science.[43]

To this list we can also add civil disobedience. Citizens can discourage, impede, and even prevent their governments from engaging in activities which increase emissions above an acceptable level by engaging in civil disobedience. They can—and often do—seek to block the construction of new motorways and new airports (or new runways at existing airports). By doing so they prevent, or at least obstruct, the ability of governments to default on their *first-order responsibilities*.[44]

Demographic policy. The six kinds of second-order policy listed above will affect the norms, opportunities, and constraints that agents face. A seventh way of affecting the extent to which society mitigates climate change (and can adapt to climatic changes) is to affect demographic change.[45] This may include affecting both the total number of people who are born, as well as the composition of the world's population (that is, how many are born in countries with high emissions-lifestyles). Those who can affect demographic change—for example, through education, providing affordable contraception, protecting the civil and political rights of women, and by increasing the opportunities available to women—can thus affect the volume of future emissions (and people's capacity to adapt).[46]

B. Kinds of actors

Given this an account of what needs to be done, the next logical step is to consider who has the capacity to perform these tasks. To do so we might refer to each of the tasks presented above and then infer from this who can do what. Doing this will confirm that some actors that one might expect would have *second-order responsibilities* (such as governments and international institutions) can indeed play a pivotal role. However, it will also draw attention to the contribution that other less obvious actors can make.

If we begin, for example, with enforcement then the relevant agents of justice clearly include political actors such as states and international institutions like the WTO, the IMF and the World Bank. Furthermore, and in line with my response to Posner and Weisbach, it also implies that citizens can play a kind of enforcement role for they can punish governments that fail to put in place environmental policies.[47] In addition to this, powerful agents can create new institutions with enforcement powers.

A similarly conventional picture emerges if we consider incentivization. Again, we can see that governments and international institutions can play a significant role. As noted above, membership of the organizations like the European Community and the World Trade Organization is often extremely beneficial, and given this, such organizations can use this to induce compliance by stipulating that those joining their organizations must honour certain environmental standards.

If we examine other tasks, however, we arrive at less conventional answers. Consider enablement for example. As I noted above, one important kind of enablement is technological innovation and diffusion. Given this, research councils, university science departments (who often have large research budgets), and corporations all have a capacity to make a significant contribution by orienting their research capacities to promoting these goals. As I also noted above, the layout of cities and towns can make a significant difference to the emissions that result from transportation. Given this, it follows that urban planners have a significant role to play—not a conclusion that has been stressed by the existing literature on climate ethics.

Reflecting on other tasks also reveals the role that can be played by other actors that one might not immediately consider to be potential agents of justice. For example, if we turn now to norm-creation, we can see that a significant role can be played by figures as diverse as church leaders, poets, novelists, charismatic individuals, and gifted communicators. To see the potential role played by communicators think, for example, of the influential science writer Rachel Carson, whose work, *Silent Spring* ([1962] 1965), chronicled the impacts of pesticides and had an enormous galvanising impact on environmentalism.

If we turn now to consider undermining resistance, we can also see that those who can communicate the findings of climate science effectively—such as climate scientists and science journalists—have an important role to play. We might think here, for example, of the role played by scientists like James Hansen. Also, those who are highly trusted—especially those who are regarded as reliable by communities which tend to resist climate change initiatives—can perform a vital function.[48]

Reflection on who can discharge *second-order responsibilities* thus reveals the role that a wide variety of very different actors can play—including not just government departments, but also journalists, scientists, writers, research councils, churches, urban planners, officials responsible for demographic policy, and charismatic individuals.

C. Traits

We might also note that the criteria for who should have some *second-order responsibilities* are not the same as the criteria for who should be subject to *first-order responsibilities*. Someone may be under a duty to mitigate climate change (a *first-order responsibility*) simply in virtue of their unjustly high emissions in the past. By contrast, to be under a duty to perform some *second-order responsibilities* (most notably those that require performing a leadership role) may require certain virtues or character traits.[49] For example, if they are to act as 'norm entrepreneurs', and to be effective at accurately conveying information and persuading people to act, then agents must enjoy a certain moral authority and enjoy good standing among others. They must be regarded as trustworthy by others and command respect. Some bearers of *first-order responsibilities* should, thus, not be bearers of *second-order responsibilities*.[50]

V. The Power/Responsibility Principle

Section IV sought to introduce the idea of *second-order responsibilities* and to flesh out the kinds of *tasks* that need to be performed and the *agents* who can best perform them. It did not, however, give any argument as to why the agents designated in Section IV have this kind of responsibility. It was primarily descriptive.

My aim in this section is to address this lacuna and provide a justification of why the kinds of agents specified in Section IV have a duty to undertake *second-order responsibilities*. To begin our analysis, it is worth noting that one unifying feature of the account outlined in Section IV is that it attributes responsibilities to those who can make a valuable difference. Put more succinctly, it operates on the principle that 'with power comes responsibility' (hereafter the *Power/Responsibility Principle*). It posits that those with the power to compel or induce or enable others to act in climate-friendly ways have a responsibility to do so. Since I am using the concept of power, I need to make clear how I am defining it. For the purposes of this article, I follow Robert Dahl who writes that 'A has power over B to the extent that he can get B to do something that B would not otherwise do'.[51]

The dictum that 'with power comes responsibility' is often voiced, especially in times of crisis. For example, Franklin Roosevelt wrote in his 'Jefferson Day Address' that '[t]oday we have learned in the agony of war that great power involves great responsibility'.[52] Similar sentiments were echoed by Winston Churchill who famously said that '[t]he price of greatness is responsibility'.[53] The phrase has entered into popular consciousness.[54]

For all this, the precise principle I am invoking has rarely received philosophical analysis. In *The Idea of Justice*, Amartya Sen affirms what looks like a similar principle. He refers to what he terms the 'obligation of effective power'.[55] However, when he explicates this it becomes clear that he simply means the capacity to aid people, which is not quite the principle I am analysing. A related point can be made with reference to David Miller's analysis of responsibilities. Miller refers to what he terms 'the principle of *capacity*' which he defines as stating 'that remedial responsibilities ought to be assigned according to the capacity of each agent to discharge them'.[56] Again this is an important principle, but it does not distinguish between different ways of having a capacity to help others. Consider, for example, the oft-invoked principle that burdens of mitigating climate change and enabling adaptation should be borne by those with the greatest ability to pay (the 'Ability to Pay' Principle). This is a kind of capacity principle. However, it is quite distinct from the Power/Responsibility Principle for two reasons. First the Power/Responsibility Principle—unlike the Ability to Pay Principle—is focused on *second-order responsibilities*. Furthermore, and even more importantly, many of those who have the power to make a difference do not have that power because of their access to financial resources and thus their ability to pay. The sources of their power may lie in their role in the political process (e.g., politicians or urban planners), or their knowledge and expertise (e.g., those capable of scientific innovations), or their powers of persuasion (e.g., norm entrepreneurs). The Power/Responsibility Principle is, thus, a distinct kind of capacity principle. Furthermore, as we shall see soon, it rests on a distinct kind of justification.

Why should we accept it? I shall not seek to provide a general account of when this principle applies and why. I shall, however, try to show why it applies in this context and thus why, given the prospect of dangerous climate change, those who can take up *second-order responsibilities* and thereby promote the ideal of *Harm Avoidance* have, modulo certain conditions, a duty to do so. My claim appeals to the following highly plausible assumptions.[57]

1   Emergency. First, humanity faces a prospect of disastrous harms. To refer again to the IPCC, its Fourth Assessment Report chronicles severe threats to life (from heat stress, extreme precipitation, and storm surges), health (with increased exposure to several infectious diseases), access to water and to food (resulting in malnutrition and hunger).[58]

In addition to this, the time left to prevent the onset of dangerous climate change is quickly running out. According to one influential account, humanity must emit less than a trillion tonnes of carbon if it is to have a 50% chance of avoiding bringing about an increase in global mean temperatures of 2°C from pre-industrial temperatures. At the moment, we have emitted over half a trillion tonnes, and, at the time of writing and using current projections, the trillionth tonne will be emitted in approximately 2040. There is thus an urgent need for decisive action.[59]

2   Effectiveness. Second, certain agents can reduce, or severely limit, the chances of these dire outcomes. Though their capacities vary, the second-order agents listed in the preceding section can all make a marked difference to whether people comply with their *first-order responsibilities*. In many cases, they have considerable leverage.
3   A Crucial and Privileged Causal Role. In addition to this, the agents identified in the previous section do not simply have the capacity to effect change. It is also the case that they have a capacity that many others lack. Their action is, thus, crucial in the sense that if disaster is to be averted, these kinds of agents must act.

Though it may be too strong to say that the intervention of *all* these agents is necessary, it is plausible to suggest that the action of many of them in concert is necessary (and sufficient) to provide the right kind of choice-architecture to avert dangerous climate change. Unlike others, they can make a major difference.[60] For example, energy experts can play a critical role by cooperating to produce low-carbon technologies and thereby help, among other things, developing countries develop in a clean way. This is a role that almost all other actors cannot perform. And, organizations like the WTO and EU can exert a leverage that other actors simply cannot. In other words, second-order agents have a capacity that others lack. Whether dangerous climate change is averted thus depends on whether a sufficient number of second-order agents take up these roles.

4 <u>No Sufficiently Weighty Countervailing Considerations</u>. The final step maintains that the second-order agents listed in the preceding section do not, in general, have countervailing responsibilities that take priority. I suspect that this is the most contentious step in my argument.

Before considering two challenges to it, we should note that—as mentioned above—the reasoning for the Power/Responsibility Principle as a *second-order* principle, is quite distinct from the reasoning normally mooted in support of the standard accounts of *first-order* responsibilities, including, for example, the Ability to Pay Principle. Consider the various reasons that have been given in support of the idea that burdens should be borne in accordance with people's ability to pay. Some defend it on the grounds that making those with the greatest wealth bear the lion's share of the burden would result in the 'least aggregate sacrifice'.[61] Second, some defend the same conclusion but appeal instead to 'the principle of equal sacrifice'.[62] Third, some might defend it by reference to a more general commitment to equality. What is relevant in this context is that, as we have just seen, the argument for the Power/Responsibility Principle is distinct from all of these. Whereas these arguments for the Ability to Pay Principle focus on the fairest or most efficient way of sharing the burden, the argument for the Power/ Responsibility Principle adduced above is, by contrast, that acting on it is necessary to protect those whose interests are threatened. It puts harm prevention first.[63]

Let us turn now to consider ways that someone might resist the above argument, especially step [4]. First, someone might say that some of those designated second-order agents might have countervailing obligations. For example, it is commonly asserted that governments have a special responsibility to their own citizens to promote their interests.

In reply: This is plausible, but such responsibilities are clearly not absolute. We recognize that when a great deal is at stake such special responsibilities can be overridden. For example, I may have a special responsibility to keep a promise to meet someone, but if on my way there I encounter someone in great need and, if it is the case not only that I can play an effective role but my contribution is critical, then we recognize that this should take priority. Second, many second-order agents will not have countervailing responsibilities. For example, research scientists, church leaders, and charismatic individuals will not generally have fiduciary responsibilities that require them to abstain from the actions I described. In addition to this, governments with vulnerable populations will have a fiduciary responsibility to induce compliance with mitigation responsibilities. Finally, governments may have responsibilities that converge with mitigation policies—for example, a responsibility to improve air quality may call for a reduction in emissions and thus converge with mitigation policies.

A critic might then press a second objection. They might say that undertaking *second-order responsibilities* may impose excessive costs on the duty-bearers. Three points can be made in reply. First, it is worth noting that for many of the second-order agents I specified above, complying with their second-order responsibilities (as listed in IV.A) imposes little or no cost on the actor. Consider, for example, political organizations that can insist that new members meet certain environmental standards if they are to join. In many cases this imposes no burden on the organization: rather what they are doing is making a decision that might impose a cost on the would-be member. Or consider spokespersons for influential social organizations (like churches): their affirmation of environmental goals need not generate any extra cost on them. Or consider urban planners: they can ensure that built up areas be designed in such a way as to facilitate the use of cycling, to minimize sprawl, and to ensure that housing, schools, recreation, and shops are close to each other. This might conceivably impose costs on some, but the key point is that it does not impose costs on the urban planners. They therefore cannot object that the posited duty is too onerous on them. Consider, too, government officials who implement 'transparency' initiatives: this too may impose burdens on others but, as Brennan and Pettit note, it is not costly for the officials.[64] Finally, it is worth observing that some measures can actually reduce the burdens born by many taxpayers. For example, eliminating subsidies to fossil fuels (which in 2011 came to 523 billion dollars) would result in a net gain for taxpayers, or no let loss if the funds were diverted elsewhere (such as investing in clean technology).[65]

A second point can also be made to the 'excessive cost' concern, namely that, in some of the cases under consideration, those being asked to perform *second-order responsibilities* may be being asked to perform tasks that they are already obligated to perform. For example, it is arguable that journalists have a duty to report the existing degree of consensus concerning climate change.

This leaves a third point. Some costs will no doubt remain. Clearly, however, we cannot reject a view simply because it imposes costs on some: after all, inaction by all second-order agents would also result in the imposition of costs on others (the victims of climate change). In determining how much sacrifice the putative bearers of *second-order responsibilities* should bear, it is worth noting three further considerations. First, the costs on second-order agents are likely to be small when compared to the costs of inaction. Second, it is instructive to make a comparison with other cases where there is a call for sacrifices. Consider, for example, humanitarian intervention. Very few reject humanitarian intervention out of hand in all cases, and where some do, it is often because of practical concerns about whether such interventions succeed. But humanitarian intervention frequently results in deaths of troops on the intervening side. This prompts the following thought: If we are willing to send some to their death to defend others, then can we reasonably object to imposing non-lethal sacrifices on people to defend similarly important interests (in life, physical integrity, health, and subsistence)? Third, it is worth noting that those who take up *second-order responsibilities* might be able to seek compensation for their efforts at a later date.[66] Their position can be contrasted with the victims of climate change because if action is not undertaken, then they may have very meagre (sometimes non-existent) capacities to seek compensation.

Thus neither way of arguing that there are overwhelming countervailing considerations seems promising.[67] Given this then: *since* there is a prospect of disastrous effects on people's lives and *since* some agents not only can play an effective role, but their action is critical to avoiding these disastrous impacts; and, finally, *since* these agents lack compelling countervailing reasons for action we are, I think, driven to the conclusion that those agents with the power to discharge *second-order responsibilities* have a duty to do so.[68]

One final point: If the argument given above is correct, then some agents may have two distinct kinds of responsibilities—some *first-order* and some *second-order*. I have emphasized that the second order responsibilities are governed by a different principle (the Power/Responsibility Principle) to the first-order responsibilities (such as the Ability to Pay or Polluter Pays Principles). However, that agents' responsibilities in the two domains are governed by different principles does not necessarily entail that the distributions in one domain (the first-order) should not take into account those in another (the second-order). For example, it is consistent with my argument that those who undertake burdensome *second-order* responsibilities can be compensated by allocating to them reduced *first-order* responsibilities. (To give an analogy: someone who takes on the burdensome (*second-order*) task of being a head of department might be given reduced (*first-order*) teaching responsibilities.)

VI. Concluding Remarks

It is time now to conclude. I have argued that we should examine the ethical challenges posed by climate change from two different perspectives—what I have termed *Burden-Sharing Justice* and *Harm Avoidance Justice*. Much of the normative analysis of the responsibilities relating to climate change has focused solely on *Burden-Sharing Justice*. My aim in this article has been to examine what an approach that prioritizes avoiding harm would look like. In doing so, I have examined two approaches which attempt to do this, but found both wanting because neither recognizes that averting dangerous climate change requires that some make sacrifices. Acknowledging the need for some sacrifices entails that we take seriously the need to create and sustain an institutional context which induces people to comply with their duties to mitigate and to enable adaptation. It calls, that is, for an account of second-order responsibilities.

Such responsibilities, so I have argued, should be guided by what I term the Power/Responsibility Principle where this asserts that, under certain circumstances, those with the power to ensure that agents comply with their first-order responsibilities have a responsibility to use their power to protect people from the existential threats posed by climate change. This principle differs in its *application*, *nature*, and *justification* from those principles commonly invoked in discussions of climatic responsibilities. It differs in its *application* for it is directed towards second-order responsibilities, not first-order ones; it differs in its *nature* because, as I argued above, it cannot be assimilated to common principles such as the Ability to Pay Principle or the Polluter Pays Principle; and, it differs in its *justification* because it can be grounded (as I have done here) on a commitment to avoiding catastrophe, rather than appeals to equitable burden-sharing.[69]

The Power/Responsibility Principle takes us out of a realm where the focus is just on responsibilities to reduce emissions and to engage in adaptation, for it also provides an account of the more explicitly political responsibilities that are needed if we are to avoid severe climatic changes.

Notes

* I presented this paper at the CSSJ workshop on 'Justice and the Global Commons' at the University of Oxford (December 2012) and the Department of Government, University of Gothenburg (April 2013) and am grateful to the audiences at both, and in particular to Sverker Jagers (my respondent in Gothenburg), Bengt Brülde and Göran Duus-Otterström for their comments. I am also grateful to the three referees of the journal (one of whom revealed himself to be Stephen Gardiner) for their illuminating comments, and to Patrick Briône, Pablo Gilabert, Aaron Maltais, and Sridhar Venkatapuram for helpful suggestions.
1 Jaspers 2001, p. 26.
2 Solomon et al. 2007, p. 70.
3 I have discussed these in Caney (2005; 2010a). There is now a considerable literature on these issues. For some important contributions, see the papers by Gardiner, Shue, Jamieson, and Baer among others in Gardiner et al. (2010).
4 Elsewhere I have referred to these two perspectives as 'entitlement-bearer' and 'duty-bearer' justice (Caney 2010b, p. 199: cf. p. 219 where the possibility that the conceptions of justice may clash is noted). The same distinction is made, but without reference to climate change, in Shue (1996, pp. 164–6).
5 Cf. McMahan 2010.
6 See Walzer 1977, ch. 16.

7 The distinction I have in mind is thus distinct from the distinction between 'deontological models of blame-responsibility' and 'consequentialistic utilitarian models of task-responsibility' that Robert Goodin invokes (1995, p. 88: cf. pt. III, chs. 5, 6, 7).

8 I am indebted here to a presentation by Robert Goodin at the conference on 'Political Thought and the Environment' (University of Cambridge, 25 May 2012), which similarly emphasized the importance of adopting this perspective.

9 A complete analysis of *Harm Avoidance Justice* would need to specify what constitutes 'dangerous' climatic changes (UNFCCC Art. 2). Furthermore, should *all* harms be prevented? Or only up to a certain level? If so, what level? These are important questions which merit answers, but which raise complex normative and empirical issues. Given the complexity of this issue, and given limitations of space, I will not attempt to give a precise definition of dangerous climate change in this paper. I will simply take it to refer to changes in the climate system which pose severe threats to the core interests of many people.

10 Posner and Weisbach 2010, p. 6.

11 Ibid., footnote omitted.

12 E.g., ibid.

13 For an instructive discussion of political feasibility, see Gilabert and Lawford-Smith (2012).

14 Posner and Weisbach 2010, p. 143.

15 Ibid., p. 6.

16 See Cohen 1991, esp. secs. 3 and 4; see also Cohen 2008, ch. 1.

17 Posner and Weisbach 2010, p. 143: see also p. 6.

18 See also Cohen's comment on how the 'incentives argument' sounds plausible only when expressed in an 'impersonal form' (1991, pp. 272–3; 2008, p. 35).

19 See Foley (2008) and Broome (2012, ch. 3).

20 Broome 2012, pp. 37–8.

21 Ibid., p. 44.

22 Ibid., p. 44; see also Rendall 2011.

23 Broome 2012, pp. 45ff.

24 For these two arguments, see Broome (2012, pp. 45–6).

25 Ibid., p. 48; see also pp. 15, 38.

26 In a footnote, Broome (2012, p. 194 fn. 3) notes that both William Nordhaus (2008, p. 180) and Nicholas Stern (2009, p. 85) maintain that not mitigating climate change would be inefficient. He also cites Foley (2008).

27 For a survey of some relevant empirical data, see Price, Friedland, and Vinokur (1998, pp. 303–16).

28 For this distinction, see Onora O'Neill (2005, pp. 428, 433–6). See also O'Neill's highly illuminating discussion of agents of justice, and in particular her treatment of what she terms 'primary' and 'secondary' 'agents of justice' in O'Neill (2001, pp. 181ff.). Note that O'Neill changes her terminology between these two essays in a way that might cause confusion: she refers to those who enact what she calls (in 2005) 'second-order responsibilities' as 'primary agents of justice' (2001, p. 181). In addition, in her 2001 (p. 181) paper, she refers to those who enact

what she calls (in 2005) 'first-order responsibilities' as 'secondary agents of justice'. This change in terminology obviously does not affect her analysis.

29 See Shue's (1996, pp. 171–3) discussion of 'default duties'.

30 See Caney (2005, pp. 766–7, 769–72), which argues that agents have a duty—within certain limits—to make up for the failings of others. For an alternative view that denies this, see Miller (2008, pp. 152–5); (2011; cf. 2008, p. 153). For a compelling critique of Miller's (2011) views, see Stemplowska (2011).

31 It would also be unfair on the compliers too. See here Elizabeth Cripps's (2013, pp. 141–50) illuminating discussion of what she terms 'promotional duties' and the three reasons she gives in support of them. Cripps offers a different way of thinking about climatic responsibilities, and would reject the emphasis that my account places on first-order responsibilities. For an evaluation of her framework see Caney (forthcoming).

32 For an earlier brief affirmation of the two distinct kinds of response to non-compliance, see my discussion of principles D3 and D4 in Caney (2005, p. 769). Sections IV and V of this paper are an attempt to develop an account of what I there referred to as D4.

33 The need for agents to perform what I am terming *second-order responsibilities* has not received much discussion in the literature on climate ethics. For two valuable exceptions, see Cripps (2013, ch. 6) and Maltais (forthcoming). (See also Henry Shue's [2011] important discussion of leadership, though I think his focus is more on the *first-order* level.) Maltais' paper distinguishes between the responsibility to mitigate climate change and the responsibility to create effective international cooperative frameworks. He maintains, however, that states should create 'conditions for achieving effective international action' by 'implement[ing] domestic reforms that rapidly accelerate our ability to make the transition to economies with very low GHG emissions' (p. 2). They should, that is, facilitate cooperation by leading by example and by 'demonstrating the compatibility of economic welfare and emissions reduction' (p. 2, see also pp. 6–7). In what follows, I defend a broader conception of both the *second-order* agents and also the types of actions they should adopt.

34 The agents in question might include, but are not restricted to, individuals, firms, trade unions, churches, states, and international institutions.

35 Stiglitz 2006, pp. 176–8.

36 See Brennan and Pettit 2004.

37 For a discussion of the environmental costs of 'sprawl', see Williamson (2010, ch. 8).

38 See Sunstein 1996, p. 909.

39 See Crawford 2002, Finnemore 1996, and Tannenwald 2007. See also Finnemore and Sikkink 1998, pp. 887–917.

40 See James March and Johan Olsen's (1989, pp. 23–4, 160–2) seminal work on the 'logic of appropriateness'.

41 See Oreskes and Conway 2010, ch. 6.

42 See Boykoff 2011.

43 We should though be aware of the many pitfalls that climate scientists face when they seek to communicate scientific findings and climate projections to the wider public.

44 For an argument for civil disobedience in order to protect future generations from environmental harm, see Carter (1998).

45 For a discussion, see Cafaro (2012).

46 See Bongaarts and Sinding 2011, pp. 574–6.

47 See also the perceptive remarks by Steve Vanderheiden on the role that 'followers', as well as 'leaders', can play (2012, pp. 465–6, 468).

48 Here we might think, for example, of the distinguished climate scientists Kerry Emmanuel (MIT) and Richard Alley (Penn State), both of whom made considerable efforts to inform the general public about climate change, and both of whom have made it very clear that they generally self-identify as Republicans (Gillis 2013).

49 Note: my claim is about some *second-order responsibilities* (such as those that involve playing a leadership role and persuading others to comply), but not necessarily all of them.

50 For a related point, see also O'Neill (2005, p. 435).

51 Dahl 1957, pp. 202–3.

52 See <http://georgiainfo.galileo.usg.edu/FDRspeeches/FDRspeech45-1.htm>. Roosevelt did not deliver this speech because he died before he was scheduled to give it.

53 Kennedy 1999, p. 255.

54 It is, for example, associated with a character (Uncle Ben) in the Spider-Man comic series.

55 Sen 2009, p. 205: cf. pp. 205–7, 271.

56 Miller 2001, p. 460.

57 To be clear, my claim here is that these four conditions are collectively *sufficient* to impose (second-order) responsibilities on the powerful.

58 For a comprehensive overview of climatic impacts, see Parry, Canziani, Palutikof, van der Linden, and Hanson (2007). For a summary of the effects of climate change on core human rights, see Caney (2009).

59 I am here relying on Allen et al. (2009), Meinshausen et al. (2009), and <www.trillionthtonne.org>.

60 For an excellent discussion of this point (that where some are dependent on some others who are the only ones who can ensure protection, then those others are under an obligation to protect) see Goodin (1985, esp. p. 34, see also ch. 5). My account is structurally similar to Goodin's 'vulnerability model', but unlike Goodin I am applying it only to *second-order responsibilities*, whereas he is applying it to those (see the discussion of collective responsibilities, 1985, pp. 136–41), but also to what I am terming *first-order responsibilities*.

61 Pigou 1929, pt. II, ch. 1.

62 See Miller 2008, p. 125: cf. pp. 146–51. J. S. Mill also invokes the idea of 'equality of sacrifice' (Mill 1965, bk. V, ch. II, esp. p. 807).

63 To be sure, one could distinguish between two approaches to ascribing *second-order responsibilities*. One would be to focus on fairness to all *second-order* duty-bearers. The second would be to focus on harm prevention and put that first. I am exploring the second option here.

64 Brennan and Pettit 2004, p. 258.

65 This figure comes from the International Energy Authority, <http://www.worldenergyoutlook.org/resources/energysubsidies/>.
66 For a related consideration, see Miller (2011, p. 237).
67 A third way that someone might resist [4] is by arguing that the measures needed to avoid dangerous climate change have disadvantages so great that it would be better to allow dangerous climate change than to adopt these measures. I assume here that this is not the case.
68 Though it focuses on the realization of first-order duties of justice rather than promoting welfare, the underlying line of reasoning has a structural similarity to that advanced by Peter Singer (1972, pp. 231ff). I am grateful to Ingmar Persson for drawing this to my attention.
69 Note, I am not claiming either that it cannot be grounded on a commitment to fairness among second-order duty bearers or that it is incompatible with that commitment.

References

Allen, Myles R. et al. 2009. Warming caused by cumulative carbon emissions towards the trillionth tonne. *Nature*, 458, 1163–6.
Bongaarts, John and Steven Sinding. 2011. Population policy in transition in the developing world. *Science*, 333, 574–6.
Boykoff, Maxwell T. 2011. *Who Speaks for the Climate?* New York: Cambridge University Press.
Brennan, Geoffrey and Philip Pettit. 2004. *The Economy of Esteem*. New York: Oxford University Press.
Broome, John. 2012. *Climate Matters: Ethics in a Warming World*. New York: Norton.
Cafaro, Philip. 2012. Climate ethics and population policy. *Wiley Interdisciplinary Reviews: Climate Change*, 3, 45–61.
Caney, Simon. 2005. Cosmopolitan justice, responsibility, and global climate change. *Leiden Journal of International Law*, 18, 747–75.
Caney, Simon. 2009. Human rights, responsibilities, and climate change. Pp. 227–47 in Charles Beitz and Robert Goodin (eds), *Global Basic Rights*. Oxford: Oxford University Press.
Caney, Simon. 2010a. Climate change and the duties of the advantaged. *Critical Review of International Social and Political Philosophy*, 13, 203–28.
Caney, Simon. 2010b. Markets, morality and climate change: what, if anything, is wrong with emissions trading? *New Political Economy*, 15, 197–224.
Caney, Simon. Forthcoming. The collective duty to create just institutions. In Peter French (ed.), *Forward-Looking Collective Moral Responsibility. Midwest Studies in Philosophy*, 38.
Carson, Rachel. [1962] 1965. *Silent Spring*. London: Penguin.
Carter, Alan. 1998. In defence of radical disobedience. *Journal of Applied Philosophy*, 15, 29–47.
Cohen, G. A. 1991. Incentives, inequality, and community. *Tanner Lectures on Human Values*. Available at: <http://tannerlectures.utah.edu/_documents/a-to-z/c/cohen92.pdf>.

Cohen, G. A. 2008. *Rescuing Justice and Equality*. Cambridge MA: Harvard University Press.

Crawford, Neta C. 2002. *Argument and Change in World Politics: Ethics, Decolonization, and Humanitarian Intervention*. Cambridge: Cambridge University Press.

Cripps, Elizabeth. 2013. *Climate Change and the Moral Agent*. Oxford: Oxford University Press.

Dahl, Robert A. 1957. The concept of power. *Behavioral Science*, 2, 201–5.

Finnemore, Martha. 1996. *National Interests in International Society*. Ithaca, NY: Cornell University Press.

Finnemore, Martha and Kathryn Sikkink. 1998. International norm dynamics and political change. *International Organization*, 52, 887–917.

Foley, Duncan K. 2008. The economic fundamentals of global warming. Pp. 115–26 in Jonathan M. Harris and Neva R. Goodwin (eds), *Twenty-First Century Macroeconomics: Responding to the Climate Challenge*. Cheltenham: Edward Elgar.

Gardiner, Stephen; Simon Caney; Dale Jamieson; and Henry Shue, eds. 2010. *Climate Ethics: Essential Readings*. New York: Oxford University Press.

Gilabert, Pablo and Holly Lawford-Smith. 2012. Political feasibility: a conceptual exploration. *Political Studies*, 60, 809–25.

Gillis, Justin. 2013. An antidote for climate contrarianism. *New York Times*, 4 January. Available at: <http://green.blogs.nytimes.com/2013/01/04/an-antidote-for-climate-contrarianism/>.

Goodin, Robert E. 1985. *Protecting the Vulnerable*. Chicago: University of Chicago Press.

Goodin, Robert E. 1995. *Utilitarianism as a Public Philosophy*. Cambridge: Cambridge University Press.

Jaspers, Karl. [1947] 2001. *The Question of German Guilt*, trans. E. B. Ashton. New York: Fordham University Press.

Kennedy, David M. 1999. *The American People in World War II*. Volume II: *Freedom from Fear*. New York: Oxford University Press.

Maltais, Aaron. Forthcoming. Failing international climate politics and the fairness of going first. *Political Studies*.

March, James G. and Johan P. Olsen. 1989. *Rediscovering Institution*. New York: Free Press.

McMahan, Jeff. 2010. The just distribution of harm between combatants and non-combatants. *Philosophy & Public Affairs*, 38, 342–79.

Meinshausen, Malte et al. 2009. Greenhouse-gas emission targets for limiting global warming to 2°C. *Nature*, 458, 1158–62.

Mill, J. S. [1848] 1965. Principles of Political Economy. Vol. III in J. M. Robson (ed.), *Collected Works of John Stuart Mill*. Toronto: University of Toronto Press.

Miller, David. 2001. Distributing responsibilities. *Journal of Political Philosophy*, 9, 453–71.

Miller, David. 2008. Global justice and climate change: how should responsibilities be distributed? *Tanner Lectures on Human Values*, 24–25 March. Available at: <http://tannerlectures.utah.edu/_documents/a-to-z/m/Miller_08.pdf>.

Miller, David. 2011. Taking up the slack? Responsibility and justice in situations of partial compliance. Pp. 230–45 in Carl Knight and Zosia Stemplowska (eds), *Responsibility and Distributive Justice*. Oxford: Oxford University Press.

Nordhaus, William. 2008. *A Question of Balance: Weighing the Options on Global Warming Policies*. New Haven, CT: Yale University Press.

O'Neill, Onora. 2001. Agents of justice. *Metaphilosophy*, 32, 180–95.

O'Neill, Onora. 2005. The dark side of human rights. *International Affairs*, 81, 427–39.

Oreskes, Naomi and Erik M Conway. 2010. *Merchants of Doubt: How a Handful of Scientists Obscured the Truth on Issues from Tobacco Smoke to Global Warming*. New York: Bloomsbury Press.

Parry, Martin; Osvaldo Canziani; Jean Palutikof; Paul van der Linden; and Clair Hanson, eds. 2007. *Climate Change 2007: Impacts, Adaptation and Vulnerability—Contribution of Working Group II to the Fourth Assessment Report of the Intergovernmental Panel on Climate Change*. Cambridge: Cambridge University Press.

Pigou, A. C. 1929. *A Study in Public Finance*. 2nd edn. London: Macmillan.

Posner, Eric A. and David Weisbach. 2010. *Climate Change Justice*. Princeton, NJ: Princeton University Press.

Price, Richard H.; Daniel S. Friedland; and Anuram D. Vinokur. 1998. Job loss: hard times and eroded identity. Pp. 303–16 in J.H. Harvey (ed.), *Perspectives on Loss: A Sourcebook*. Philadelphia. PA: Taylor & Francis.

Rendall, Matthew. 2011. Climate change and the threat of disaster: the moral case for taking out insurance at our grandchildren's expense. *Political Studies*, 59, 884–99.

Sen, Amartya. 2009. *The Idea of Justice*. London: Penguin.

Shue, Henry. 1996. *Basic Rights: Subsistence, Affluence, and US Foreign Policy*. 2nd edn. Princeton, NJ: Princeton University Press.

Shue, Henry. 2011. Face reality? After you!—A call for leadership on climate change. *Ethics & International Affairs*, 25, 17–26.

Singer, Peter. 1972. Famine, affluence, and morality. *Philosophy & Public Affairs*, 1, 229–43.

Solomon, Susan; Dahe Qin; and Martin Manning. 2007. Technical summary. Pp. 19–91 in Susan Solomon et al. (eds.) *Climate Change 2007: The Physical Science Basis. Contribution of Working Group I to the Fourth Assessment Report of the Intergovernmental Panel on Climate Change*. Cambridge: Cambridge University Press.

Stemplowska, Zosia. 2011. *Doing more than one's fair share (version 2—December)*. Unpublished.

Stern, Nicholas. 2009. *A Blueprint for a Safer Planet: How to Manage Climate Change and Create a New Era of Progress and Prosperity*. London: Bodley Head.

Stiglitz, Joseph E. 2006. *Making Globalization Work*. London: Allen Lane.

Sunstein, Cass R. 1996. Social norms and social roles. *Columbia Law Review*, 96, 903–68.

Tannenwald, Nina. 2007. *The Nuclear Taboo: The United States and the Non-Use of Nuclear Weapons Since 1945*. Cambridge: Cambridge University Press.

Vanderheiden, Steve. 2012. Coaxing climate policy leadership. *Ethics & International Affairs*, 26, 463–79.

Walzer, Michael. 1977. *Just and Unjust Wars*. Harmondsworth, Middlesex: Penguin.

Williamson, Thad. 2010. *Sprawl, Justice, and Citizenship: The Civic Costs of the American Way of Life*. New York: Oxford University Press.

4

The Human Right to Water and Common Ownership of the Earth*

Mathias Risse

"Thousands have lived without love, not one without water," so W. H. Auden finished his poem "First Things First." And right he was. Only oxygen is needed more urgently than water at most times. But a key difference that makes water a more immediate subject for theorists of justice is that, for now, oxygen is normally amply available where humans live. Historically, the same was true of water since humans would not settle in places without clean water. Nowadays, however, water treatment plants and delivery infrastructure have vastly extended the regions where humans can live permanently. Population increases have prompted people to settle in locations where access to clean water is precarious.

While we need other nutrients as well, we can survive without any one of them for quite some time. Without water we die within days. Water is life-giving and non-substitutable. A second crucial point about water is that it is part of nature. Its existence is not owed to human accomplishments. My goal here is to argue in support of a human right to water and a global water compact to regulate its distribution. I do so in a way that develops the aforementioned two points about water within a theory of global justice I recently presented, which is especially suitable to capture the significance of water for human life and to show that there is a genuinely *global* responsibility for the distribution of water.[1] A human right to water is discussed in two forms: a right to safe drinking water and a right to sanitation. I support both. I talk of a "human right to water" to refer to both rights, and distinguish between them where appropriate.

Political Theory Without Borders, First Edition. Edited by Robert E. Goodin and James S. Fishkin.

According to the World Health Organization (WHO), each human being requires at least 20 liters of clean water for daily consumption and basic hygiene.[2] However, many countries in Latin America, Africa, Asia and the Middle East lack sufficient water resources or have so far failed to develop these resources or the necessary infrastructure. According to a 2006 UN Development Programme report, "one part of the world sustains a designer bottled water market that generates no tangible health benefits, another part suffers acute public health risks because people have to drink water from drains or from lakes and rivers."[3] The world has met the Millennium Development Goal of halving the proportion of people without sustainable access to safe drinking water, well in advance of the 2015 deadline. Nonetheless, insufficient access to clean water remains a ubiquitous problem, posing an impediment to development and may even be a security risk.[4]

The human rights framework is the leading proposal for a globally acceptable normative approach to regulating human affairs. It matters therefore greatly whether there is a human right to water. There has been an intense debate about this topic in recent years. Lawyers and social scientists have discussed whether international law generates such a right, what precisely it would mean, and what difference it could make (perhaps for the better, by promoting development or by preventing excessive privatization, or perhaps for the worse, by wrestling control over water from indigenous peoples or by preventing appropriate privatization). Philosophy comes late to this debate. But if we are to accept a human right to water, it must have solid normative foundations. Before turning to that subject, let me say a bit about the legal and political situation that provides the background to our inquiry.

The Universal Declaration of Human Rights does not mention water, nor does the International Covenant on Economic, Social and Cultural Rights (ICESC). Both the Convention on the Elimination of Discrimination against Women and the Convention on the Rights of the Child do mention water, but only in contexts concerned with the eponymous women and children. In 2002, then, the Committee on Social, Economic, and Cultural Rights, charged with assessing the implementation of ICESC, recognized a human right to water as being implied by the provisions of that covenant. In its General Comment 15, the committee asserts:

> The human right to water entitles everyone to sufficient, safe, acceptable, physically accessible and affordable water for personal and domestic uses. An adequate amount of safe water is necessary to prevent death from dehydration, to reduce the risk of water-related disease and to provide for consumption, cooking, personal and domestic hygienic requirements.

The Comment discusses extensively what a human right to water amounts to, and what its corresponding duties are. In 2010, the UN General Assembly recognized rights to water and sanitation. Also in 2010, the Human Rights Council adopted a resolution acknowledging that both rights are implied by the right to an adequate standard of living. Both resolutions have advanced the political acceptance of these rights. Nonetheless, neither the experts on the Committee on Social, Economic, and Cultural Rights nor the UN General Assembly or its Human Rights Council can readily create binding international law.[5]

Sanitation might appear less worthy a subject for a human right than drinking water. However, water for drinking and water for sanitation come from the same water system around us. We are highly vulnerable to water: there are water-borne diseases humans catch from dirty water, water-scarce diseases stemming from insufficient access, water-based diseases originating from organisms that live in water, and water-related diseases spread by animals that live near water. Poor sanitation is causally related to all these hazards. Moreover, the drinking of water and the disposal of urine and feces belong to the same metabolic cycles for which water is so essential. Two thirds of our bodies consist of water. A right to safe drinking water makes sure we receive enough safe water for resupply. A right to sanitation guarantees that conditions allow for the safe disposal of human waste, which to some extent is just contaminated water, but also involves water as a medium.

I

Let us turn to the philosophical debate. This section offers an overview. Economic and social rights enable individuals to participate actively in community life and to be competitive in commercial life by providing them with some substantive (often material) prerequisites to those ends (education, food, housing, social security, private property, etc.). A human right to water would be among these rights. Two questions arise: whether there are such rights at all, and if so, whether a right to water is among them. There is hardly any philosophical discussion about a human right to water itself.[6] But there has been much discussion about whether economic and social rights count as human rights. Some philosophers insist it is in light of general features of rights that such (alleged) rights are of the wrong sort to be human rights. Despite the significance of water for life, there could then be no human right to water. Section II rebuts these reservations.[7]

To be sure, this rebuttal only shows that there *could* be such rights, not that there *are*. And if there are, one still needs to argue that a human right to water is among them. One may wonder, for instance, how such a right bears on practical choice, say, how it can be consistent with markets for water and sanitation. Or perhaps such a right would be unduly specific. Why proclaim it when we have a right to an adequate standard of living? Does this presuppose a judgment about priorities among the components of well-being that we may want to avoid? There is also an inflation worry: do we devalue the currency by declaring too many rights? Finally, one may think there is something about water that should detach it from the international responsibilities associated with human rights (especially on the account we will use in the present study). To argue that there are economic and social rights, in general, and a human right to water, specifically, we need an actual account of human rights that delivers such rights.

There are economic and social rights, *and* there are human rights to safe drinking water and to sanitation, according to the conception of human rights as membership rights in the global order I have recently presented.[8] My conception integrates an idea that initially would seem to have little to do with human rights: that humanity collectively owns the earth, the resources and spaces that exist without human accomplishments. The idea that the earth is collectively owned by humanity was pivotal to the political philosophy of the seventeenth century. At that time European expansionism had come into its own. Questions about how to divide up the planet arose forcefully among the conquering nations. The Old Testament (where the divine gift of the Earth was recorded) was as secure a starting point for such debates as these religiously troubled times permitted. Philosophers such as Hugo Grotius, Thomas Hobbes, Samuel Pufendorf and John Locke disagreed about how to capture this ownership status and the conditions under which parts of the earth can be appropriated. Section III looks at Locke's take on collective ownership with a focus on what he says about water.[9]

Revitalizing the standpoint of collective ownership is sensible in light of the problems of global reach that now preoccupy us and that concern our use of the earth, such as questions about immigration and our responsibility for future generations. What is at stake is the sheer space in which our existence takes place. There turns out to be a conceptual link between collective ownership and human rights. In virtue of the fact that humanity collectively owns the earth, persons possess a set of natural rights that capture their status as co-owners. The existence of states puts these rights in jeopardy. A set of associative rights must ensure that states preserve these natural rights. ("Associative" rights are rights individuals have in virtue of being subject to certain political or economic structures.) These associative rights are among the membership rights in the global order, and, as such, are human rights. Within that conception the human right to water emerges vindicated. Sections IV through VI develop these matters.

As we see in Section VII, my account of collective ownership also allows us to formulate ideas about the proportionate distribution of human beings across the earth. If countries fail to occupy resources and spaces in a proportionate manner, they can be expected to admit more people or to relinquish resources or spaces. What matters is the overall value of a region for human purposes. Water is increasingly important for determining a region's value. Water-rich countries have a duty to make good on that human right if other countries are unable to do so for their citizens. I conclude by arguing in support of a global compact on water, including a monitoring body that keeps track of global distribution of water. As we notice in passing, Thales of Miletus and the Old Testament gave water pride of place. Contemporary theories of global justice should do the same.

II

In its 1993 Vienna Declaration and Program of Action, the UN famously states that "all human rights are universal, indivisible and interdependent and interrelated."[10] However, there have been philosophical doubts about economic and social rights as human rights. Prominent among them are arguments to the effect that it is because of certain features of rights that economic and social rights could not be human rights. Since this is familiar territory I only briefly discuss the two most influential objections.[11]

The *Nature-of-Rights objection* insists that regardless of how we think of the moral urgency of the issues behind economic and social rights, we should not think of them in terms of *rights*. Talking about a (moral) right to something involves identifiable addressees with an ability to make good on the realization of the right and with relevant connections to the holder. But for economic and social human rights this could not be done.

The response is that human rights can sensibly be *aspirational*. Aspirational rights are rights one can only progressively realize, but that do not, thereby, forfeit their status as rights. (Strict rights are those that can be realized right now.) A human right to X is a moral demand that X be realized, if it is possible to do so, and that appropriate steps towards the creation of conditions be taken under which X can be realized, if that is not possible right away. The obvious worry is that this response renders rights indistinguishable from mere goals (which do not impose duties on particular agents). But it does not. Even rights one cannot realize immediately have *duty* bearers with the ability to *contribute* to the realization of the right and with relevant connections to the holder. Duty bearers should help create circumstances under which the right can later be implemented. There is much potential for disagreement about who needs to do how much towards the realization of certain rights. But this does not undermine the conceptual possibility of aspirational rights. Moreover, human rights are a source of moral progress partly *because* they render unavoidable the question of who needs to do what.[12]

Strictly speaking (in my view of human rights, see below), the duty holder is always the global order as such. We must then determine which entities in the global order must do what towards the realization of the rights in question. A person's state must protect her rights, strict and aspirational ones, as appropriate. The international community has a duty to defend strict rights by intervening as appropriate if the government fails. The global order must aid governments that need assistance, intervening as appropriate if countries refuse to make efforts toward realizing aspirational rights.

One may worry that within states it would be unsatisfactory to claim that, say, some constitutional rights are for future realization, and if so, the same applies to human rights. But this objection assumes that the context in which a right to X is held does not matter for what is involved in there being such a right and in being a duty holder. We are primarily used to (legal and moral) rights that hold within *states*. Those rights are plausibly linked to rather immediate realization. But it is not true that such rights are rights to begin with (among other reasons) because they are readily realizable. It is the other way round: they are readily realizable because state power has a certain nature, and so rights that hold within states can be conceptualized in this way. Human rights, in my view, hold within and against the global order. It is because of the differences between states and the global order that it might be problematic for rights guaranteed by constitutions to be aspirational, but not for human rights. There is always a link between rights and duties, but what precisely it is depends on the context in which the rights are held.

A second objection to counting economic and social rights as human rights is the *Inferior-Urgency objection*. If X is a human right, then it is no less urgent than any other human right. Economic and social rights are less urgent than some other rights that everyone accepts are human rights. Therefore, economic and social rights are not human rights.

One way of understanding what is at stake is that civil and political rights are said to be more essential to survival than economic and social rights. But that point is misguided. Civil and political rights provide security, while economic and social rights protect one's ability to make a living. That ability is as essential to survival as security. Therefore, some economic and social rights must be of as paramount an importance as some civil and political rights. A second understanding of what is at stake is that there is greater urgency in the provision of civil and political rights than in the provision of social and political rights, in the sense that satisfying the former can be more readily *expected of duty holders* than satisfying the latter. The rationale is that civil and political rights are negative rights: they merely require that duty holders refrain from inflicting harm. Economic and social rights are positive: they require measures to supply rights-holders with something. Not harming is more significant than doing good.

But first of all, just about every right involves positive and negative elements. Abstaining from abuse is always one aspect of what it is for such a right to be realized. But in addition, the state must take measures to make sure officials are trained and supervised in such a way that they do not abuse their powers. Economic and social rights often require the provision of material benefits to people, or the creation of opportunities that allow them to secure these benefits. But there is also a requirement that others refrain from interfering with individuals as they go about doing so. The division of rights into negative and positive ones is misleading.

A second reply is that even if there were a difference in urgency between civil and political rights on the one hand, and economic and social rights on the other, this difference would not preclude any kind of rights from being human rights. Any conception of human rights would have to explain why a certain list of rights is being proposed as a list of human rights. If all things considered a conception is plausible, the present objection would have little bite.

III

So there is nothing about the nature of rights that excludes the possibility of economic and social rights, which would ipso facto exclude a right to water. But this does not show that such rights *are* human rights. To show they are, we need a conception of human rights that delivers them. Below we discuss my proposed conception, and it is only once we have that conception that we can ask about a right to water. That conception integrates the idea of collective ownership of the earth. In preparation, let us look at one of the classic explorations of collective ownership in Locke's *Second Treatise of Government*. The discussion of property in his chapter V is stage-setting for philosophical reflection on the foundations of property. We are interested in what he says about water.[13]

Water is a venerable topic of philosophical and religious writing. In the Western canon water enters early. Thales of Miletus believed water was the origin of everything. The Presocratics started philosophy by seeing the world as orderly and comprehensible. The original version of that thought made water essential. In the biblical Book of Genesis we read that before giving shape to this creation, "the Spirit of God was hovering over the waters" (Genesis 1:2). Water became God's point of departure for further deeds. The Old Testament also mentions God as a giver of water. In Exodus 15, the Israelites are saved when God reveals a tree whose contact with available bitter water makes it sweet. However, when collective ownership of the earth was discussed in the 17th century, it was not this idea of God as a giver of water, and thus the significance of water for life, that set the tone. Instead, the idea that water was abundant and worthless became prevalent.

Water appears three times in chapter V of Locke's *Second Treatise*. He begins by stating that, by revelation and natural reason, the earth can be considered common property of all of humanity. The revelation is recorded in Genesis.[14] Locke explores how there can be private property of resources that were originally given to humanity in common. Each person owns her body, and thus her labor. When she "mixes" her labor with something that is commonly owned, this object is thereby appropriated. An apple becomes mine when I pick it. Everybody has a license to appropriate in this way, without anybody else's consent. One illustration for how things are removed from the common pool involves water:

> Though the water running in the fountain be every one's, yet who can doubt, but that in the pitcher is his only who drew it out? His labor hath taken it out of the hands of nature, where it was common, and belonged equally to all her children, and hath thereby appropriated it to himself.[15]

Next Locke introduces constraints on acceptable property acquisition. Nobody is supposed to acquire more than she can enjoy: nothing must be spoiled or destroyed. When land appropriation occurs initially, such acquisition would leave "enough and as good" for others. Again he illustrates the matter in terms of water:

> No body could think himself injured by the drinking of another man, though he took a good draught, who had a whole river of the same water left him to quench his thirst: and the case of land and water, where there is enough of both, is perfectly the same.[16]

The remainder of chapter V explores how the development of money affects what property holdings people may have. The final mention of water occurs when Locke explains the decisive contribution of labor to the value of things:

> Bread, wine and cloth, are things of daily use, and great plenty; yet notwithstanding, acorns, water and leaves, or skins, must be our bread, drink and cloathing, did not labour furnish us with these more useful commodities: for whatever bread is more worth than acorns, wine than water, and cloth or silk, than leaves, skins or moss, that is wholly owing to labour and industry; the one of these being the food and raiment which unassisted nature furnishes us with; the other, provisions which our industry and pains prepare for us, which how much they exceed the other in value, when any one hath computed, he will then see how much labour makes the far greatest part of the value of things we enjoy in this world …[17]

It is indeed not the theme of the precious water from Exodus that animates Locke, but an idea we can trace to another revered source, Cicero's *On Duties*. In Book I, 52, Cicero lists fresh water alongside fire and council as something one should give freely because it is useful to the receiver and of no trouble to the giver. This classic passage makes water a subject for an account of *beneficence*, rather than *justice*.[18] For Locke, water exists in abundance and has little commercial value, not only at the early stages of acquisition, but also in his time. Still, appropriation can occur although it adds no value to the water. But, then, appropriation mustalso be possible once there no longer is abundance. However, since the earth was given to humanity in common, "for the support and comfort of their being," at that later stage everybody must still have access to enough water to survive.[19] It requires detailed investigations of Locke to assess just what this may mean. But rather than pursuing this matter, let us see what we can make of ideas of collective ownership in the present, and explore how water fares on that approach.

IV

While Locke took the biblical standpoint of the earth as a divine gift, he also thought this view should be acceptable even if humankind had never received that revelation. Indeed, that the earth originally belongs to humankind collectively remains plausible without religious input. But the approach must be developed with some care. Philosophically, much can be gained by developing, in secular ways, the idea that humanity collectively owns the earth, since this original ownership status has strong implications for what individuals and groups can do with portions of three-dimensional space. Once we develop this secular version we find an important connection to human rights. Sections IV and V develop this approach. Sections VI and VII explain what this theory says about water.

Three points are straightforward enough: first, the resources and spaces of the earth are valuable and necessary for any human activities to unfold; second, those resources have come into existence without human interference; and third, the satisfaction of basic human needs matters morally. These points must be considered when individual accomplishments are used to justify property rights strong enough to determine use across generations.[20] *Egalitarian Ownership* is the view that the earth originally belongs to humankind collectively, in the sense that all humans, no matter when and where they are born, must have *some* sort of symmetrical claim to it. ("Original" ownership now does not connote with time, but is a moral status, one that pertains to the "original" resources and spaces, the resources and spaces of the earth as they exist without human interference.) This is the most plausible view of the ownership of natural resources in light of the three points just mentioned. Egalitarian Ownership is detached from the complex set of rights and duties the civil law delineates under the heading of property law.[21] At this level of abstraction from conventions and codes—that themselves have to be assessed in relation to views on original ownership—all Egalitarian Ownership states is that all humans have a symmetrical claim to original resources. The considerations motivating Egalitarian Ownership speak to raw materials only, not to what human beings have *made* of them. The distinction between what "is just there" and what humans have shaped is blurred. But by and large, we understand well enough the idea of what exists without human interference.[22]

One may object that the idea of humanity's collectively *owning* the earth is misguided in light of the environmental problems that now are (or should be) so high on our agenda. But Egalitarian Ownership does not presuppose the arrogance associated with an interpretation of the biblical account that subjects the rest of creation to the human will, an attitude that shows, say, in Calvin's view, that God took six days to create the world to demonstrate to human beings that everything had been prepared for them. In that way my approach differs from its seventeenth century predecessors, many of whose defenders took no issue with this implication.[23] Egalitarian Ownership captures a relationship among human beings and can accommodate concerns, say, about the value of nature or the value of non-human animals: *to the extent* that nature is at our disposal, no human being has a privileged claim. Valuing nature intrinsically, as sublime or awesome, as providing a context where life obtains meaning to begin with, or even as in some sense sacred, is consistent with my view.

Conceptions of Egalitarian Ownership differ in terms of how they understand the symmetry of claims to original resources. There are, roughly, four types of ownership-status entities may have: *no* ownership; *joint* ownership—ownership directed by collective preferences; *common* ownership—in which the entity belongs to several individuals, each equally entitled to using it within constraints; and *private* ownership. Common ownership is a right to use something that does not come with the right to exclude other co-owners from also using it. If the Boston Common were held as *common* ownership when it was used for cattle, a constraint on each person's use could be to bring no more than a certain number of cattle, a condition driven by respect for other co-owners and the concern to avoid the infamous Tragedy of the Commons. Yet, if they held the Common in *joint* ownership, each use would be subject to a decision process to be concluded to the satisfaction of each co-owner. Joint ownership ascribes to each co-owner property rights as extensive as rights of private ownership, except that others hold the same rights: each co-owner must be satisfied on each form of use.

So, there are various interpretations of Egalitarian Ownership: resources could be jointly owned, or commonly owned, or each person could have private ownership of an equal share of resources, or its value equivalent. These conceptions all carve out a pre-institutional space of natural rights that constrain property conventions, which in turn regulate what these natural rights leave unregulated. I submit that Common Ownership is the most plausible conception.[24] While I cannot offer a complete argument for this proposal here, I can elaborate on what common ownership means, what it entails, and why it should be considered the preferred interpretation of Egalitarian Ownership.[25] The core idea of common ownership is that all co-owners ought to have an equal opportunity to satisfy basic needs to the extent that this turns on obtaining collectively owned resources. This formulation, first, emphasizes an equality of status; second, it points out that this equality of status concerns opportunities to satisfy needs (whereas there is no sense in which each co-owner would be entitled to an equal share of what is collectively owned, let alone to the support of others in getting such a share, any more than co-owners of the Boston Common had a claim to such a share or to the support of others to obtain it); and third, it does so insofar as these needs can be satisfied with resources that are collectively owned.

To put this in standard Hohfeldian rights terminology, common ownership rights must include liberty rights accompanied by what Hart (1982) calls a "protective perimeter" of claim rights.[26] To have a liberty right is to be free of any duty to the contrary, and obviously, common ownership rights must include at least rights of that sort; that is, co-owners are under no duty to refrain from using any of the resources of the earth. But the symmetry of claims postulated by Egalitarian Ownership demands more than liberty rights. In light of the intuitions supporting Egalitarian Ownership, to count as an interpretation of it, Common Ownership must guarantee some minimal access to resources, that is, impose duties to refrain from interference with certain forms of use of resources. So, we must add that protective perimeter of claim rights to the liberty rights. We can obtain enough mileage from the original intuitions to require that common ownership rights (for Common Ownership to serve as an interpretation of Egalitarian Ownership) be conceived of in sufficientarian terms, in the sense that no co-owner should interfere with the actions of another to the extent that they serve to satisfy basic needs. I do not think these intuitions can be pressed beyond that. Equal Division and Joint Ownership press these intuitions too far. But we must add one more right to Common Ownership as we have understood it thus far. We must also make sure individuals can maintain their co-ownership status under more complex arrangements. A necessary condition for the acceptability of such arrangements is that the core purpose of the original rights can still be met. That core purpose is to make sure co-owners have the opportunity to meet their basic needs. In Hohfeldian terminology, co-owners have *immunity* from living under political and economic arrangements that interfere with their having such opportunities.

Let me address a typical *reductio* through which right-libertarians often ridicule collective ownership. Can somebody seriously claim, asks Murray Rothbard, that a newborn Pakistani baby has a claim to a plot in Iowa that Smith just transformed into a field?[27] As soon as one considers such implications of collective ownership, says he, one realizes its implausibility. Smith has claims on the strength of his plight, but the baby has none. Yet, collective ownership of the sort I defend (Common Ownership) does not grant each and every individual claims to each and every object. Not any nugget of gold found on the ocean floor has to be shared among all human beings. That our baby has claims to resources on a par with Smith's is consistent with him/her not having claims on Smith to vacate *that* land. Collective ownership is not so easily shown to be absurd. However, the discussion of this attempted *reductio* also serves to highlight that certain complaints, one might have thought humanity's collective ownership helps us articulate, cannot be made from this standpoint (assuming Common Ownership is the right conception of it). People in Slovenia or Chile do not have a claim specifically to the oil and gas riches of other countries merely because they do not find such resources where they live themselves.

V

I continue to say that humanity "collectively" owns the earth if the precise form of ownership does not matter. Otherwise I will talk about Common Ownership. In any event, one way of putting our result from Section IV is that these terms are interchangeable. The existence of a system of states dividing up the world's resources must be reconciled with Common Ownership. Each state, in virtue of its immediate access to individuals' body and assets, might deprive them of such opportunities, but so might other states by refusing them entry if they cannot satisfy basic needs. When individuals cannot satisfy basic needs where they live, other states that have this ability but refuse entry would not merely fail to aid them; they would deny them the opportunity to satisfy these needs. Under these conditions we must ask what to make of the immunity individuals have from living under political and economic arrangements that interfere with those subject to them having opportunities to satisfy their basic needs.

Common ownership rights are natural, pre-institutional rights. Once institutions are founded, guarantees must be given to co-owners that institutional power will not be used to violate their status. Since such a violation is threatened by the system of states per se, such guarantees take on the form of moral demands against that system of states. Responsibilities that arise in the manner I have sketched must be allocated at the level of the state system as such, as collective responsibilities, rather than resting exclusively with individual states and, then, only with regard to their members.

These considerations take us to a conception of *human rights*. Cohen (2006) sensibly proposes that human rights have three features: they are universal and owed by every political society to everybody; they are requirements of political morality whose force does not depend on their expression in enforceable law; and they are especially urgent requirements.[28] Any more specific account of human rights, says Cohen, has to meet these constraints, as well as two methodological assumptions: fidelity to major human rights documents, so that a substantial range of these rights is accounted for; and open-endedness (we can argue in support of additional rights). Yet, these criteria do not entail commitments with regard to a range of questions about such rights. It is the function of a *conception* of human rights to provide fuller answers to such questions. For instance, accepting these criteria does not imply human rights must be understood as protecting essential features of personhood, as for instance Griffin argues.[29] A different way of adding detail to these criteria is to think of "human" rights as rights individuals hold qua members of the global and political order that ipso facto, but contingently, includes *everybody*. What I have argued above is work towards such a conception. That is, humanity's collective ownership generates a set of rights, namely membership rights in the global order.

In what sense are human rights held in virtue of membership in the global order? This order is the system of states that covers most of the land of the earth, as well as the network of organizations that provides for "global governance." At the political level, the state system is governed by a set of rules, the most significant of which are codified by the UN Charter. At the economic level, the Bretton Woods institutions (International Monetary Fund, World Bank, later the General Agreement on Tariffs and Trade/World Trade Organization) provide a cooperative network intended to prevent wars and foster worldwide economic improvement. These institutions, jointly with the more powerful states acting alone or in concert, shape the economic order. Importantly, for there to be enough structure to the global order to render that term ("global order") applicable, and an accompanying capacity for coordinated action, is a minimal condition for the existence of rights held within that order. And, indeed, there is enough structure of that sort. Being a member of that order merely means to live on the territory covered by it, which by now all human beings do, if for no other reason than because they all live on the territory of some state. So it makes sense to speak of rights that are held in virtue of membership in the global order.

Once we see how collective ownership of the earth generates membership rights in the global order, it is natural to turn around the direction of inquiry and explore whether there are other bases on which such rights could be held. There are indeed, such as the idea of common humanity (which to most readers will be more naturally tied to human rights than collective ownership). I have explored this elsewhere.[30] What matters now is this: using collective ownership for a derivation of membership rights generates two *fundamental guarantees* states and other powerful organizations must give, and whose realization is a global responsibility. First, they must make sure their power does not render individuals incapable of meeting basic needs; second, they must provide opportunities for individuals to lead a life at least at subsistence level. A good deal of work still needs to be done to get from these guarantees to a sizeable list of human rights. But if such guarantees exist, the dangers imposed on individuals through the existence of the global order are neutralized vis-à-vis the status of which individuals are ensured in virtue of their common ownership rights.

VI

We can now harvest some important results about water. To begin with, my approach does deliver economic and social rights. In addition to ensuring that the power of states and other organizations is not used to render individuals incapable of meeting basic needs, such organizations must provide opportunities for individuals at least to meet basic needs. Everybody must have the opportunity to enjoy a minimally adequate standard of living, as far as food, clothing, and housing are concerned. But this reasoning merely delivers a small set of rights, since we can derive only a requirement to protect everybody's ability to satisfy basic needs.

However, we can adopt a broader understanding of what rights are entailed by our starting points. According to that reading, rights provide more *robust* protection. We are assessing what set of associative rights should protect a bundle of natural rights of vital importance, rights needed to ensure individuals can meet basic needs. But in the pre-institutional scenario where these rights hold, no agent is as powerful as the state. It is in light of the power of states, and of the importance of the rights that are at stake that control mechanisms must be imposed especially on states to ensure the individuals' status as co-owners prevails. The permanence and reliability of that protection matter critically. So, we should adopt the broader view of what rights are entailed by our starting points that generates more robust protection.

Recall the first fundamental guarantee, that states must make sure their power does not render individuals incapable of meeting their basic needs. On a narrow reading, this standpoint does not deliver much beyond basic rights to life and physical integrity. On the broader reading, co-ownership status is not preserved merely if it so happens that states do not render individuals incapable of meeting basic needs. States must be *bound* to refrain from doing so. Their power must be limited so that they cannot simply elect to become abusive. Adding ideas of robustness responds to the nature of the state as an entity that (generically, ignoring phenomena such as failed states) is overwhelmingly more powerful than individuals, and organized in complex ways that permit abuse in many forms. Ensuring that individuals are robustly protected in light of the dangers posed by the state system requires such constraints, although we cannot achieve perfect protection. To rights to life and bodily integrity we must add individual liberties (e.g., freedom from forced labor, of conscience, of expression and association, of movement, and freedom to emigrate), as well as political rights (e.g., to accountable representation), and due process rights (e.g., a fair trial).

The second fundamental guarantee is that states must provide opportunities for individuals to lead a life at least at subsistence level. On a narrow reading we merely obtain a set of rights that protect people's ability to live at subsistence level, such as rights to food, clothing and housing. But here too, a broader understanding is available that generates a more robust set of rights. At least in societies with sophisticated economies that make it difficult to satisfy needs without actively participating in society, an elementary right to education and a right to work, understood as a right not to be excluded from labor markets, can be supported within such societies. Such rights constitute robust protection of the rights to food, clothing and housing that the narrower understanding already delivered.

Without water humans cannot survive. Therefore, this right "to food" must include a right to safe drinking water. According to the more robust understanding, such a right includes a claim to enough safe drinking water to be an active member of society. Given the present understanding of human rights, it is then up to the global order to distribute the global water resources accordingly, and to assume a shared responsibility to develop local infrastructures to assist with accessing and distributing water. If people find themselves without water, and their state cannot help, other agents in the global order must either make sure they have water or else allow them to move elsewhere. States can exclude people, and thus restrict their liberty right, only if they jointly give guarantees to people wherever they live. Since even minor deficiencies in our supply with safe water can seriously debilitate human beings, this guarantee must include safe drinking water.

Section 2 recorded some concerns about a right to water: that we would have to assess how such a right bears on practical choice, that is, how it may be compatible with markets for water; that it may be too specific and presuppose a problematic judgment about priorities among components of well-being; that we may devalue the currency by proclaiming too many rights; and that there may be good reasons not to tie water to international duties. As far as the first point is concerned, a right to water has often been enlisted to resist privatization of water resources. For instance, in the late 1990s, the Bolivian government sought to improve the provision of municipal services by, among other things, privatizing water services. To cover their investments the companies involved raised the price of water substantially. In the city of Cochabamba these measures encountered such heavy resistance that the government ultimately undid the changes. During these protests several grassroots organizations issued the Cochabamba Declaration according to which "water is a fundamental human right and a public trust to be guarded by all levels of government, therefore, it should not be commodified, privatized or traded for commercial purposes."[31]

But nothing in the account of human rights that we discussed licenses such a move. What the theory delivers is that a human right must constrain private markets to make sure everybody has access to enough safe water. This in turn implies that water has to be available at reasonable prices (prices that to do not interfere with other purchases required to maintain a decent life, and on which the original ownership status of the water exerts downward pressure). But, although water occurs naturally, one might say, pipes do not. Nonetheless, fees must be kept at rates that do not interfere with the requirement that everybody have access to water at reasonable prices.

The concern about over-specificity is toothless on account of the special status water has among nutrients. We *must* prioritize access to water as a component of well-being. The worry about rights inflation fails for the same reason. Finally, that there is something about water that makes it unsuitable for international duties is false. Precisely the opposite is true, and making that clear is one of the distinctive implications of resorting to my account of human rights in this context: there is a genuinely global responsibility for making sure everybody can enjoy access to water to which co-owners of the earth are entitled. The state system is acceptable only if it meets that responsibility.

A human right to sanitation also emerges, in any event, on the more robust understanding of human rights that I just introduced. The basic thought behind the derivation of rights from collective ownership is that co-ownership generates entitlements to access to natural resources that must be either preserved or adjusted appropriately when individuals live in states. A right to water is an example of a right that preserves access to something to which individuals qua co-owners must have access. A human right to basic education, for instance, adjusts for lack of access. Such a right applies at least in any slightly sophisticated society, since the existence of states means that co-owners will often not have the possibility to make a living by accessing natural resources. As a substitute for this lack of access we need empowerment to participate in society. A right to sanitation involves both aspects (preservation of access to something to which co-owners must have access, and appropriate adjustment to life in states). It involves a guarantee to use the local water system, in this case for purposes of hygiene, and thus for the maintenance of health. But such a right also captures an adjustment to life in societies where particular health hazards are generated, or exacerbated through our organized ways of living together. Hygiene is an example of such a health concern. In a nutshell, there is human right to sanitation because co-owners are allowed to help themselves to naturally existing water systems to protect themselves against health hazards that, to a large extent, arise because of human living arrangements.

To put this point in perspective, let me add that a general human right to basic health care cannot be derived from collective ownership. Such a right is not necessary to neutralize the state system's ability to interfere with co-ownership. After all, access to such care does not turn on access to original resources as much as, say, sanitation does, but instead turns on human services and ingenuity. As opposed to the human services and ingenuity that are at stake in a right to basic health care, human rights to safe drinking water and sanitation capture different aspects of a general right to use the world's water systems for survival.

Let us review what my approach implies about water. Collective ownership (especially Egalitarian Ownership) is plausible because the resources and spaces of the earth are nobody's accomplishment, but are required for human needs to be satisfied. Common Ownership, the conception I find most plausible, implies that each individual must have the opportunity to satisfy basic needs, to the extent that this turns on natural resources and spaces of the earth. In light of the significance of water for all forms of life, this includes a right to make use of the earth's water. This reasoning integrates the two crucial points about water with which we started: water is essential to all forms of life, and its existence is not owed to any human accomplishments. The state system interferes with the co-owners' ability to satisfy basic needs by exericising their liberty right to water.

Crucially, guaranteeing access to safe drinking water and basic sanitation becomes a *genuinely global responsibility*, a condition of the very acceptability of the state system, which on my account is characteristic of human rights. It is highly laudable that there are regional agreements that regulate the use of water resources that are shared among various countries. For instance, there are agreements between US states and Canadian provinces to strengthen protection against what some consider abusive water withdrawal practices within the Great Lakes basin. But, in the future, we do need to go beyond such regional arrangements. The particular theoretical set-up of my account is especially useful for showing that there is the aforementioned genuinely global responsibility for guaranteeing access to safe drinking water and basic sanitation.

VII

There is more to say about water on my approach. For one thing, we can explore who has to make good on a human right to water. But, we can also extend our horizon beyond the issues addressed by human rights. The vast majority of water is used for agriculture (upwards of 70%), followed by industry (say 15–20%) and then personal consumption (10–15%), of which drinking water is only a fraction. Many "water justice" issues involve disputes over water for agriculture that are not covered by the (legal or moral) definition of human rights to safe drinking water and sanitation. Often these are questions of transboundary water allocation on which human rights provide little guidance, but which collective ownership also illuminates.

I focus mostly on obligations pertaining to the actual provision of water, rather than support that may be necessary to create infrastructure. However, we should notice that often physical water shortage is not the issue when people lack water for drinking and sanitation. There is often enough water, but it is used for other purposes. Agriculture is frequently the only way for people (say, in rural Africa) to make a living, but water used for irrigation is unavailable for drinking needs. In such situations, a human right to water entails a duty to help with the provision of infrastructure to optimize use of water for agriculture or other essential purposes, while also making sure there is enough water for drinking and sanitation.

To approach the topics I mentioned in the first paragraph of this section, let me develop the ownership standpoint a little further. Note, first, how my argument on collective ownership bears on *immigration*.[32] We must ask under what conditions would-be immigrants can reasonably be expected to accept borders. Countries are justified in excluding others *only if* sufficiently many people populate their spaces. "Sufficiently many" means the number of these people is proportionate to the value for human purposes of the resources and spaces thereby removed from general use. We arrive at an idea of relative over- and under-use, and thus of *proportionate use*, of portions of the earth, an idea that is helpful for water distribution problems. A population under-uses its share of three-dimensional space if the per-capita value of what they occupy is higher than the world average across states. The average person in such a state can access more resources and spaces than people around the world can on a per-country average. They over-use if the per-capita value of what they occupy is lower than the world average among states. Under-users can be reasonably expected to permit immigration. Alternatively, they should relinquish some territory or resources. Over-users may decline further requests for immigration. They are doing enough in permitting a proportionate share of humanity to make a living.

Assessing how many people are proportionate to the value for human purposes of certain resources is not a matter of population density that proceeds in terms of sheer territorial extension. Territories of the same size might differ vastly in terms of soil quality, resource endowment, climatic conditions and other variables. A host of biophysical factors shape the value of a territory for human purposes, as do technological constraints. Much of the empirical work needed to make the relevant valuing operation precise is currently unavailable. Another complication is that one needs to wonder exactly what counts as "use" in the relevant sense (not merely what is in circulation, but also, say, what is accessible in the ground, but not yet in circulation), a point that matters greatly for the case of water (see below).

It is in any event the *overall* value for human purposes of whole regions that determines whether a country proportionately uses a portion of the earth. If countries have large amounts of certain resources, people who live elsewhere do not, therefore, have a claim on a share of those particular resources. It is not the case that each country should have its share of oil, gas, copper or coal. But things are different *for water*. Water is special among the raw materials humans have integrated into their lives as resources. Unlike any other resource (except oxygen, which, however, is amply present where people normally live) water must either be made available to human beings everywhere, or alternatively, people who live in countries where there is not enough water to allow for the realization of the human right to water must be permitted to move to countries where water is available.

This situation calls for a *global compact on water*, which must include a monitoring body. This body would take inventories of global water resources and assess how they contribute to the overall value for human purposes of regions of the earth. It must identify which countries (a) under-use their regions and (b) are water-rich (on a per-capita basis). As far as the human right to water is concerned, it is in the first instance those countries satisfying conditions (a) and (b) that are responsible for making good on the global responsibility of ensuring all human beings can access water. They could do so either by plainly transferring water (and thus relinquishing full ownership over water on their territory) if other countries cannot realize the right to water for their citizens, or else by allowing for more immigration, primarily from countries that (a) over-use resources, and specifically (b) suffer from water shortages. Donor countries could, thereby, make a contribution to global distributive justice for which they would get credit when it comes to assessing what they must contribute overall.[33]

But the global compact idea (and Common Ownership) has broader applications than what we can say about the *human right* to water. With populations growing, living standards rising in many places, and climate change disrupting patterns of water supply, availablity of clean water is increasingly important for the value for human purposes of three-dimensional spaces. Thereby, water also becomes increasingly important for assessing whether countries over- or under-use their portion of the world. Recall also that many "water justice" issues involve disputes over transboundary water allocation for agriculture, or for industrial use, which are not generally addressed by human rights. Here too, ideas of over- and under-use allow us to make progress.

For instance, suppose a river runs through several countries and affects people's lives in different ways (e.g., the Mekong). In some parts the river is used for fishing, but elsewhere mostly for transportation or generation of energy. Suppose country A wants to build a dam to generate hydroelectric power. The dam might affect the water flow and, let us suppose, would negatively affect fishing downstream. If "downstream" is still in A, my approach does not offer any advice since it is formulated at the level of countries. One could perhaps apply the same ideas to different regions of a country (a case in point being the 1922 Colorado River Compact, an agreement among seven US states in the basin of the Colorado river governing the allocation of rights to the river's water), but that is not what the theory is, in the first instance, designed to do. But, if "downstream" is in country B, and B complains, the monitoring body should assess the impact of the construction on relative over- and under-use in A and B.

What should *not* matter for the resolution—once there is enough water to meet subsistence needs—is how much water overall A or B possess, or their absolute wealth. What matters at that stage is how the overall value of resources and spaces is affected for whose assessment availability of water is but one (albeit increasingly important) factor. That is, what matters is the per-capita value of what A and B occupy (before and after the construction), and the relative change in their situations. One might say that water matters twice: it must itself be sufficient, and its availability is one factor in the aggregrate value of resources.

If A is an under-user both before and after, but B's over-use is exacerbated, B has a rightful complaint. If A and B are over-users before and after, but afterwards A's situation has been somewhat ameliorated at the expense of an exacerbation of B's over-use situation to about the same extent, B has a rightful complaint. I have picked easy cases, and others are more complex. For instance, what if both A and B are over-users before and after, but A's over-use improves by quite a margin at the cost of a minor exacerbation in B's situation? Or how should we think about a case where A is an under-user before, but an over-user after the construction, whereas B is an under-user before, and an over-user afterwards? Difficult questions arise, but they are questions about fair division that are independent of water issues and that, therefore, I set aside. My point is only that this is the kind of use to which a global water compact and its monitoring body should put the idea of proportionate use of regions of the earth.[34]

Let me end by describing why such a monitoring body would indeed face a difficult task. It is vexing to determine which countries are "water-rich" in the sense that they—if they also generally under-use resources—can be expected to be the first to share water. More generally, it is vexing to determine how water contributes to the overall value of a region for human purposes. First of all, we must note the difference between water *volume* and yearly *renewable supply.* Countries might have a topography that creates lakes and a climate that prevents evaporation. For instance, Canada harbors 20% of the global water that is contained in lakes.[35] Based on that, one might wish to conclude that Canada should be among the first to be summoned when water is scarce elsewhere. Perhaps so, but one way of illustrating the intended impact of the remainder of this discussion is that it renders that kind of inference more problematic than it may seem. The renewable supply is the amount of fresh water that is fully replaced annually through precipitation. (Canada's share of world supply is 6.5%, to continue that example.) If the supply is gone, it will be replaced next year. If the volume is diminished, it may not be replenished. An assessment of the overall value for human purposes of regions of the earth must distinguish between these two manners of access to water.

A second complication is that humans are not the only water users. Collective ownership is a relationship among humans that is meant to capture that all of us have the same claim to resources and spaces. That relationship does not imply that other creatures should not also have an opportunity to consume resources, or that the preservation of ecosystems (of which hydrological systems are an essential component) does not, by itself, at least have aesthetic value that demands preservation. A third complication stems from the instrumental value of ecosystems. Wetlands and forests, for instance, play a critical role in purifying water. This kind of instrumental value of nature accrues mostly to the immediate environment. But ecosystems might also contribute to the cycle of transforming CO_2 into oxygen, a contribution to life everywhere on earth and not just where that ecosystem happens to be located.[36]

More work is needed to develop these ideas of a global water compact and its guiding idea of proportionate use of resources, and spaces of the earth. Much of it is work in disciplines other than philosophy. Nonetheless, despite these complications, a global water compact that includes a monitoring body is required to make sure human beings have the kind of access to which they are entitled as co-owners. This relatively concrete result also mirrors our more general finding. Unlike Cicero and, following his example, Locke and others, we can no longer think of fresh water as abundant, and thus a suitable illustration of what *beneficence* requires. Water is an essential subject for a global theory of *justice.* Thales and the Old Testament rightly gave water pride of place. Contemporary theories of global justice should do the same.

Notes

* Many thanks to Robert Goodin, Mika LaVaque-Manty, Sharmila Murthy and Henry Shue for very helpful comments, as well as to the participants of a Radcliffe Exploratory Seminar on the Human Rights to Water and Sanitation at Harvard University and a colloquium at the University of Graz for their insights. I am also grateful to Charles Beitz for helpful conversations.

1 Risse 2012.

2 <http://hdr.undp.org/external/hdr2006/water/10.htm.> The UNDP 2006 Human Development Report provides much information on the global water crisis. See also the biennial report *The World's Water* by the Pacific Institute (e.g., Gleick 2011). On the overall water situation, see World Water Assessment Programme (2003; 2009). For the range of conceptual (legal) and practical issues connected to a human right to water, see Dubreuil (2006). Water is vital as a solvent and an essential part of a multitude of metabolic processes within the body. As the Quran states, "by means of water, we give life to everything" (21:30), first of all, we may add, to our own bodies. For historical approaches to water regulation across cultures, see Salzman (2006). For historical and contemporary water conflicts, see also Shiva (2002).

3 <http://hdr.undp.org/en/media/HDR06-complete.pdf>, p 35.

4 Most water is used for agriculture (upwards of 70%) followed by industry (15–20%) and personal consumption (10–15%), of which drinking water is a fraction. Arguably, for now, the biggest security threat is when agricultural water is tapped. About a decade ago, there was much concern about "water wars." The more recent thinking seems to be that countries find ways to cooperate over water but that water could exacerbate conflicts. See the 2012 Global Water Security report produced by US intelligence agencies, available at <http://www.dni.gov/index.php/newsroom/press-releases/96-press-releases-2012/529-odni-releases-global-water-security-ica>.

5 For the legal discussion, see: Dubreuil (2006); Staddon et al. (2012); Winkler (2012); Riedel and Rothen (2006); and Murthy (forthcoming); see also Gleick (1999) and Albuquerque (2012). On global waters politics and governance, see Dobner (2010). On General Comment 15, see Riedel (2006), Tully (2005) and Langford (2006). Perhaps we should take it at face value that major human rights treaties ignore water: water was not supposed to become part of the international responsibilities associated with human rights. This stance was taken, for instance, by the Canadian government (Craven 2006). Another possibility is that the framers of those documents took the availability of water for granted. Water conflicts are more prevalent now than when those documents were crafted. According to a morsel of wisdom attributed to Benjamin Franklin, "only when the well is dry, we know the worth of water." On account of population increases and climate change, water conflicts have come to stay. Here we will not be further concerned with exploring why water appears so rarely in human rights documents and with other issues of legal interpretation that arise in this context.

6 Exceptions are Bleisch (2006) and Ladwig (2007). But see also Ingram et al. (2006) and Veigha da Cunha (2009). Sultana and Loftus (2012) also discuss philosophical issues.

7 Most philosophers of human rights, like most practitioners, now accept that such rights are human rights although the precise list of such rights is debatable. Main voices of resistance have included Maurice Cranston (1973) and Carl Wellman (1995; 1999). The most outspoken opponent among practitioners is Aryeh Neier ((2012), chapter 3). Shue (1980, p. 23) offers a classic argument to the effect that the enjoyment of any rights presupposes both basic civil and political rights (a basic right to physical security) and basic economic and social rights (to subsistence). What is remarkable in light of the general negligence of the topic of water is that Shue explicitly included within subsistence "unpolluted water."

8 Risse 2012.

9 See Buckle (1991) and Tuck (1999) for these discussions.

10 <http://www.unhchr.ch/huridocda/huridoca.nsf/(symbol)/a.conf.157.23.en.>

11 For nuanced discussion, see Beitz (2009, pp. 161–74); see also Sen (2009, pp. 379–85) and Pogge (2002, pp. 67–9) and Griffin (2000).

12 Often writers on human rights flee the suggestions that social and economic rights are aspirational. For instance, by way of constrast to the position taken here, Pogge (2000; 2002) argues that all human rights are strict because the lack of fulfillment of basic economic and social rights is a function of how the global order operates, a failing that *should* and *could* be remedied immediately.

13 Except for the recent revival of left-libertarianism, inquiries about collective ownership have been almost invisible since the Rawlsian renaissance of political philosophy. But this approach is present in international law, where for forty years the term "common heritage of mankind" has been applied to the high seas, the ocean floor, Antarctica and outer space. For "common heritage of humankind," see Attfield (2003, pp. 169–72) and Malanczuk (1997, 207–8); see also Buck (1998). For left-libertarianism, see Vallentyne and Steiner (2000a; 2000b).

14 1:26, and 9:2–3. See also *Psalm* 115:16.

15 Locke, *Second Treatise*, sec. 29.

16 Ibid., sec. 33.

17 Ibid., sec. 42.

18 This Cicero passage is quoted by Grotius in *On the Laws of War and Peace,* bk 2.2.11 and discussed more in 2.2.12. See Grotius 2005. Like Locke, Grotius thought fresh water was abundant and should be left to everybody's use. Pufendorf, in his *Two Books on the Duty of Man and Citizen*, also lists water, fire and advice as things nobody should be refused (bk I.8.4). See Pufendorf 1991. In the middle of the eighteenth century, Emer de Vattel would again list water as an example of something that is so abundant it should not be refused anyone, see *Law of Nations*, Chapter IX, sec. 126 (a section called "Things, the Use of which is Inexhaustible"). See Vattel 2008. Seneca's *On Benefits,* another inspiration for the seventeenth century, also treats water as an example of something that is abundantly available (see 4.29). See Seneca 2010. It is a long way from there to an attitude expressed by John F. Kennedy on several occasions, that "the first country that is able to [transform sea water into fresh water at a reasonable price] will earn far more prestige than we lost by being second in outer space," <http://www.presidency.ucsb.edu/ws/index.php?pid=60400&st=salt+water&st1=>. Linton (2010) explores the many ways in which societies have integrated water into their practices, including its transformation into a resource.

19 Locke, *Second Treatise*, sec. 26.
20 There is an enormous literature on the foundations of property; see Becker (1977), Reeve (1986), or Ryan (1987) for overviews.
21 Honoré 1961.
22 A more difficult question is under what conditions man-made products, including improvements of original resources, should no longer be accompanied by special entitlements of those who made them or their offspring. See Risse (2012, ch. 8) for discussion. Egalitarian Ownership formulates a standing demand on all groups that occupy parts of the earth to inhabit the earth in a manner that respects this symmetrical status of individuals with regard to resources. That Egalitarian Ownership operates in this way should be intelligible and acceptable even within cultures where individuals are not seen as property owners. Nothing about Egalitarian Ownership precludes such cultures from being acceptable to their members even if they do not treat individuals themselves as property holders. At the same time, even cultures that do not see individuals themselves as property holders must indeed be acceptable to those who live in them especially because all individuals have symmetrical claims to original resources, no matter how precisely we understand such acceptability.
23 The biblical story can be read in different ways, see White (1967) and Passmore (1974, chs. 1, 2). Passmore (1974) contains a wealth of information about the diversity of attitudes towards nature that have been held across cultural traditions. For the reference to Calvin, see Passmore (1974, p 13).
24 In capital letters, "Joint Ownership" and "Common Ownership" are names of interpretations of Egalitarian Ownership and, hence, views about ownership of the earth, whereas in small letters "joint ownership" and "common ownership" are general forms of ownership of anything.
25 For detailed discussion, see Risse (2012, ch. 6).
26 Hart 1982, p. 171. For the Hohfeld terminology, see Edmundson (2004, ch. 5).
27 Rothbard 1996, p. 35. Hospers (1971, p. 65) makes a similar point.
28 Cohen 2006.
29 Griffin 2008.
30 Risse 2012a, ch. 11.
31 The Cochabamba Declaration contrasts with an international statement, the Dublin Statement, published in 1992. Issuing the first major recognition of water as a commodity, the governments represented at the 1992 International Conference on Water and the Environment declared that "water has an economic value in all its competing uses and should be recognized as an economic good." For both declarations, see Salzman (2006). See Bakker (2012), for the relationship between a human right to water and privatization. See also: Murthy (forthcoming); Dobner (2010, ch. 3); Bakker (2010, ch. 5); and Barlow and Clarke (2002). Related is also the issue of bottling water, private suppliers profiting from packaging natural resources; see Gleick (2010).
32 Risse 2012.
33 Petrella (2001), for one, argues for a global water compact. He considers water a common heritage. Such a compact would in some ways be parallel to the efforts embodied in the United Nations Framework Convention on Climate Change to produce what amounts to a global compact on carbon sinks. Some have argued

there for a distinction between "subsistence emissions" and "luxury emissions" analogous to a distinction that becomes available in the present context between "subsistence water" (needed for sufficiency) and "luxury water." But, note also that as climate change produces drought and flooding, it undermines to some degree my underlying claim that the existence of water is not owed to human accomplishments. For example, climate change that disrupts the Indian monsoon will be a human "accomplishment" of sorts that deprives people of now naturally occurring water. The same is true for the anthropogenic melting of the glaciers that feed the great South Asian rivers. So, reliable availability of water may not in the past have depended on human action, but it will in the future.

34 It is worth noting here that in 1997, the United Nations adopted the Convention on the Law of Non-Navigational Uses of International Watercourses (or Watercourse Convention). This Convention pertains to the uses and conservation of all waters that cross international boundaries (both surface and ground water). The Convention has three primary principles. First, states should use an international watercourse in a way that is "equitable and reasonable" vis-à-vis other states sharing that watercourse. Second, states should take "all appropriate measures" to prevent "significant harm" to co-riparian states. Third, states should "consult" with co-riparian states and provide "timely notification" of any changes in use that could have significant, adverse effects on those co-riparian states. The Convention also outlines seven factors designed to ensure that an international watercourse is utilized in an "equitable and reasonable manner." Notably, in the absence of agreement or custom to the contrary, no use of an international watercourse enjoys priority over other uses, but disputes about use must be resolved with "special regard being given to the requirement of vital human needs." For this Convention, as well as for its legal context and possible implications for the case of Iraq, see Murthy (2010). As of 2012, the Convention has not yet been ratified by enough countries to enter into force.

35 Sprague 2007.

36 For discussion of these points, see also Bakker (2010, ch. 5). See Bakker (2007) for insightful assessments of Canada's water situation.

References

Albuquerque, Catarina de. 2012. *On the Right Track: Good Practices in Realizing the Rights to Water and Sanitation*. Private printing. Available at <http://www.ohchr.org/Documents/Issues/Water/BookonGoodPractices_en.pdf>

Attfield, Robin. 2003. *Environmental Ethics: An Overview for the Twenty-First Century*. Oxford: Polity.

Bakker, Karen, ed. 2007. *Eau Canada: The Future of Canada's Water*. Vancouver: UBC Press.

Bakker, Karen. 2010. *Privatizing Water: Governance Failure and the World's Urban Water Crisis*. Ithaca, NY: Cornell University Press.

Bakker, Karen. 2012. Commons vs. commodities: debating the human right to water. Pp. 19–45 in Sultana, Farhana, and Alex Loftus, eds. 2012. *The Right to Water: Politics, Governance, and Social Struggles*. London: Earthscan.

Barlow, Maude, and Tony Clarke. 2002. *Blue Gold: The Fight to Stop the Corporate Theft of the World's Water*. New York: New Press.

Becker, Lawrence. 1977. *Property Rights: Philosophical Foundations*. Boston: Routledge and Kegan Paul.

Beitz, Charles. 2009. *The Idea of Human Rights*. Oxford: Oxford University Press.

Bleisch, Barbara. 2006. The human right to water—normative foundations and ethical implications. *Ethics and Economics*, 4, 1–23.

Buck, Susan. 1998. *The Global Commons: An Introduction*. Washington, DC: Island Press.

Buckle, Stephen. 1991. *Natural Law and the Theory of Property: Grotius to Hume*. Oxford: Clarendon Press.

Cicero, Marcus Tullius. 1993. *On Duties*, ed. E. M. Atkins. Cambridge: Cambridge University Press.

Cohen, Joshua. 2006. Is there a human right to democracy? Pp. 226–49 in Christine Sypnowich (ed.), *The Egalitarian Conscience: Essays in Honor of G. A. Cohen*. Oxford: Oxford University Press.

Cranston, Maurice. 1973. *What Are Human Rights?* New York: Taplinger.

Craven, Matthew. 2006. Some thoughts on the emergent right to water. Pp. 37–47 in Riedel, Eibe, and Peter Rothen, eds. 2006. *The Human Right to Water*. Berlin: Berliner Wissenschaftsverlag.

Dobner, Petra. 2010. *Wasserpolitik. Zur politischen Theorie, Praxis und Kritik globaler Governance*. Frankfurt: Suhrkamp.

Dubreuil, Céline. 2006. *The Right to Water: From Concept to Implementation*. World Water Council.

Edmundson, William. 2004. *An Introduction to Rights*. Cambridge: Cambridge University Press.

Gleick, Peter. 1999. The human right to water. *Water Policy*, 1, 487–503.

Gleick, Peter. 2010. *Bottled and Sold: The Story Behind Our Obsession with Bottled Water*. London: Island Press.

Gleick, Peter, ed. 2011. *The World's Water: The Biennial Report on Freshwater Resources*. Washington, DC: Pacific Institute.

Griffin, James. 2000. Welfare rights. *Journal of Ethics*, 4, 27–43.

Griffin, James. 2008. *On Human Rights*. Oxford: Oxford University Press.

Grotius, Hugo. 2005. *The Rights of War and Peace*, ed. Richard Tuck. Indianapolis, IN: Liberty Fund.

Hart, H. L. A. 1982. *Essay on Bentham*. Oxford: Oxford University Press.

Honoré, A. M. 1961. Ownership. *Making Law Bind: Essays Legal and Philosophical*. Oxford: Clarendon Press.

Hospers, John. 1971. *Libertarianism*. Los Angeles: Nash Publishing.

Ingram, Helen, John Whitely and Richard Perry. 2006. Introduction: the importance of equity and the limits of efficiency in water resources. *Water, Place, and Equity*. Cambridge: MIT Press.

Ladwig, Bernd. 2007. Kann es ein Menschenrecht auf Wasser geben? Pp. 45–59 in Beate Rudolf (ed.), *Menschenrecht Wasser?* Frankfurt: Peter Lang.

Langford, Malcolm. 2006. Ambition that Overleaps Itself? A response to Stephen Tully's critique of the General Comment on the right to water. *Netherlands Quarterly of Human Rights*, 24, 433–59.

Linton, Jamie. 2010. *What is Water? The History of a Modern Abstraction*. Vancouver: UBC Press.

Locke, John. 1960. *Two Treatises of Government*, ed. Peter Laslett. Cambridge: Cambridge University Press.

Malanczuk, Peter. 1997. *Akehurst's Modern Introduction to International Law*, 7th edn. London: Routledge.

Murthy, Sharmila. Forthcoming. The human right(s) to water and sanitation: history, meaning and the controversy over privatization. *Berkeley Journal of International Law*.

Murthy, Sharmila. 2010. Iraq's constitutional mandate to justly distribute water: the implications of federalism, Islam, international law and human rights. *George Washington International Law Review*, 42, 749–85.

Neier, Aryeh. 2012. *The International Human Rights Movement: A History*. Princeton, NJ: Princeton University Press.

Passmore, John. 1974. *Man's Responsibility for Nature*. London: Duckworth.

Petrella, Riccardo. 2001. *The Water Manifesto: Argument for a World Water Contract*. London: Zed Books.

Pogge, Thomas. 2000. The international significance of human rights. *Journal of Ethics*, 4, 45–69.

Pogge, Thomas. 2002. *World Poverty and Human Rights: Cosmopolitan Responsibilities and Reforms*. Cambridge: Polity.

Pufendorf, Samuel. 1991. *On the Duty of Man and Citizen according to Natural Law*, ed. James Tully. Cambridge: Cambridge University Press.

Reeve, Andrew. 1986. *Property*. Atlantic Highlands: Humanities Press.

Riedel, Eibe. 2006. The human right to water and General Comment No. 15 of the Committee on Economic, Social and Cultural Rights. Pp. 19–36 in Riedel, Eibe, and Peter Rothen, eds. 2006. *The Human Right to Water*. Berlin: Berliner Wissenschaftsverlag.

Riedel, Eibe, and Peter Rothen, eds. 2006. *The Human Right to Water*. Berlin: Berliner Wissenschaftsverlag.

Risse, Mathias. 2012. *On Global Justice*. Princeton, NJ: Princeton University Press.

Rothbard, Murray. 1996. *For a New Liberty: The Libertarian Manifesto*. San Francisco: Fox and Wilkes.

Ryan, Alan. 1987. *Property*. Milton Keynes: Open University Press.

Salzman, James. 2006. Thirst: a short history of drinking water. *Yale Journal of Law and the Humanities*, 18, 94–121.

Sen, Amartya. 2009. *The Idea of Justice*. Cambridge, MA: Harvard University Press.

Seneca, Lucius Annaeus. 2010. *On Benefits*, trans. Brad Inwood and Miriam Griffin. Chicago: University of Chicago Press.

Shiva, Vandana. 2002. *Water Wars: Privatization, Pollution, and Profit*. Cambridge: South End Press.

Shue, Henry. 1980. *Basic Rights: Subsistence, Affluence and U.S. Foreign Policy*. Princeton, NJ: Princeton University Press.

Sprague, John. 2007. Great wet worth? Canada's myth of water abundance. Pp. 23–36 in Bakker, Karen, ed. 2007. *Eau Canada: The Future of Canada's Water*. Vancouver: UBC Press.

Staddon, Chad, Thomas Appleby and Evadne Grant. 2012. A right to water? Geographico-legal perspectives. Pp. 61–78 in Sultana, Farhana, and Alex Loftus, eds. 2012. *The Right to Water: Politics, Governance, and Social Struggles*. London: Earthscan.

Sultana, Farhana, and Alex Loftus, eds. 2012. *The Right to Water: Politics, Governance, and Social Struggles*. London: Earthscan.

Tuck, Richard. 1999. *The Rights of War and Peace*. Oxford: Oxford University Press.

Tully, Stephen. 2005. A human right to access water? A critique of General Comment No. 15. *Netherlands Quarterly of Human Rights*, 23, 35–63.

UNDP. 2006. *Human Development Report 2006: Beyond Scarcity: Power, Poverty and the Global Water Crisis*. New York: United Nations Development Program.

Vallentyne, Peter, and Hillel Steiner, eds. 2000a. *The Origins of Left-Libertarianism: An Anthology of Historical Writings*. New York: Palgrave.

Vallentyne, Peter, and Hillel Steiner, eds. 2000b. *Left-Libertarianism and Its Critics: The Contemporary Debate*. New York: Palgrave.

Vattel, Emer de. 2008. *The Law of Nations*. Indianapolis, IN: Liberty Fund.

Veigha da Cunha, Luis. 2009. Water: a human right or an economic resource? Pp. 97–114 in M. Ramon Llamas, Luis Martinez-Cortina, and Aditi Mukherji (eds.), *Water Ethics: Marcelino Botin Water Forum 2007*. London: CRC Press.

Wellman, Carl. 1999. *The Proliferation of Rights: Moral Progress or Empty Rhetoric?* Boulder, CO: Westview Press.

Wellman, Carl. 1995. *Real Rights*. New York: Oxford University Press.

White, Lynn. 1967. The historical roots of our ecological crisis. *Science*, 55, 1203–7.

Winkler, Inga. 2012. *The Human Right to Water: Significance, Legal Status, and Implications for Water Allocation*. Portland: Hart Publishing.

World Water Assessment Programme. 2009. *Water in a Changing World*. Paris: UNCESCO Publishing.

World Water Assessment Programme. 2003. *Water for People, Water for Life*. Paris: UNESCO Publishing.

PART II
Global Flows

5

Tax Competition and Global Background Justice*

Peter Dietsch and Thomas Rixen

A globalized economy raises intricate questions of distributive justice.
Some of these have come under scrutiny in the literature. Under what
conditions can international trade be regarded as respecting norms of
fairness? Are wages at the subsistence level a necessary step on the path
to growth or a form of exploitation? Who does and who should benefit
from the profits generated by the exploitation of natural resources? Yet,
one important determinant of global justice, namely questions of international taxation, has received little attention in the philosophical debate.[1]
While the importance of taxation as a means of implementing *domestic*
public policy and conceptions of justice is widely acknowledged—and
indeed often taken for granted—issues of *international* tax justice are
mostly neglected. Tax competition between states puts pressure on
domestic fiscal regimes. Mobile factors of production have the opportunity to "shop around" to minimize their tax burden. This interdependence
of national tax regimes generates external effects that undermine the
de facto sovereignty of states. As a consequence, tax competition tends to
exacerbate inequalities of income and wealth both within countries and
across borders.

One way to address these issues is to condemn the distributive outcomes and to propose redistributive policies to correct what are perceived to be unjust inequalities. This approach is largely remedial. A
second possibility is to examine the rules of the game of international
taxation themselves, and to make sure they do not contain any unjust
bias. This approach, which is geared towards the prevention of injustice
in the first place, is the approach favored here. To what extent does

Political Theory Without Borders, First Edition. Edited by Robert E. Goodin
and James S. Fishkin.
© 2016 John Wiley & Sons, Inc. Published 2016 by John Wiley & Sons, Inc.

the fiscal interdependence between countries call for a normative inter-dependence in the form of obligations towards other countries that governments have to respect in designing their fiscal policy? How can we delineate legitimate fiscal interdependence from illegitimate tax competition? These are the questions addressed in this article. They target the conditions of *global background justice* that need to be met to guarantee rules of international taxation that are free from unjust bias.[2] The reference point for a just international order is one where states have *effective* sovereignty over their fiscal affairs. Self-determination of this kind serves as the normative premise of our argument. It provides the foundation for advocating functionally differentiated supranational institutions but, importantly, delineates our approach from calls for a wholesale transfer of fiscal sovereignty to a supranational or even world government.

The article is structured as follows. In a first step, we sketch the impact of three different kinds of tax competition—for portfolio capital, so-called paper profits, and foreign direct investment (FDI)—on the *de facto* sovereignty of states. We show how tax competition exacerbates social inequalities in order to explain why it is a case of background injustice and should thus be on the radar of theories of justice (Section I).

The central part of the article then lays out two principles of international taxation designed to both protect and circumscribe the fiscal prerogatives of the state. First, a membership principle which holds that deriving the benefits of membership in any given country grounds an obligation to pay one's taxes there. This principle substantially curtails competition for portfolio investment and paper profits. Second, a constraint on fiscal policy that rules out fiscal arrangements which can be shown *both* to be based on strategic intent—luring in foreign capital—*and* to have a collectively negative outcome—reducing the aggregate extent of fiscal self-determination. This constraint serves as a tool to assess the legitimacy of fiscal measures to attract FDI. Taken together, the membership principle and the fiscal policy constraint allow us, we argue, to delineate legitimate fiscal interdependence from illegitimate tax competition (Section II).

In Section III, we address the question of how these principles could be implemented. We propose the establishment of an International Tax Organization (ITO) after the model of the World Trade Organization (WTO) and endorse unitary taxation with formulary apportionment (UT+FA) as a reform of corporate taxation. We also evaluate the political feasibility of our proposal.

In Section IV, we discuss the objection that our principles are incompatible with defending a cosmopolitan theory of global justice. Furthermore, we elaborate on the normative status of our account as one of global background justice. Section V concludes.

I. How Tax Competition Undermines Fiscal Self-Determination

In this section we show that tax competition leads to policy changes that are not legitimately chosen by the states involved, but forced upon them by competitive pressures.[3] In other words, tax competition undermines the self-determination of states. We first explain what fiscal self-determination entails and then how tax competition undermines it.

A. The content of fiscal self-determination

In order to establish the fiscal prerogatives of the state, it is useful to step back and consider what the purpose of taxation is. At the most basic level, it is needed in order to finance public goods.[4] Due to collective action problems their provision generally requires a central enforcement institution, the state. Therefore the prior public good paid for by taxes is the state itself. The state can be viewed as a complex exchange between individuals, performed in order to supply themselves with the public goods necessary to pursue their individual life plans. Under a pluralism of conceptions of the good life, the legitimacy of the state is generally grounded in a democratic form of government, where those subject to the coercively enforced rules of the state are also the authors of these rules.

Importantly, for the purposes of the present section, we take it for granted that polities should be granted considerable autonomy in designing their state institutions. In the fiscal context, a stylized definition of collective self-determination entails two basic choices. These choices respectively concern the size of the public budget (level of revenues and expenditures) and the question of relative benefits and burdens (extent of redistribution). Importantly, these choices of policy objectives extend to the means selected to realize them, like for instance the calibration of the tax mix between direct and indirect taxes. While there are certainly many different views on how these two evidently interdependent choices ought to be made, there is widespread agreement that they constitute the fiscal prerogatives of the state.[5] This is the substantive content of fiscal self-determination or tax sovereignty.[6]

Three points are worth mentioning. First, we make the simplifying assumption that governments perfectly track their citizens' preferences.[7] We acknowledge that this is an unrealistic assumption, since government actions often are the result of rather messy and contentious political processes, in which different groups of citizens pursue different interests. It is, in reality, not necessarily true that differences in political preferences *within* the polity of a state are less important than differences *between* polities. Second, a distinction needs to be made between *de jure* and *de facto* tax sovereignty. As will become clear in the next subsection, effective self-determination in fiscal matters requires the latter. Third, self-determination is not to be understood in absolute terms. Instead, effective protection from illegitimate interference by other states requires limits on self-determination. Spelling out these limits lies at the heart of this article.

B. The consequences of tax competition

Tax competition is defined as interactive tax setting by independent governments in a non-cooperative, strategic way. For tax competition to exist there must be *fiscal interdependence*. This condition is met if tax bases are sensitive to international tax differentials. Tax base mobility must be legally possible and it must actually occur.[8] Favorable tax conditions to attract foreign capital can be brought about in various ways, such as a reduction in tax burdens (be it by reducing tax rates or defining tax bases in favorable ways), fashioning preferential tax regimes for foreigners, or creating (or not closing) tax loopholes, for example through implementing bank secrecy rules or a lax enforcement of existing rules.

Tax competition primarily targets capital, which is mobile internationally.[9] Governments use different strategies and tax instruments depending on the kind of capital targeted. Three kinds of capital can be distinguished. First, in the area of portfolio capital of individuals and firms, so-called "tax havens" often have low or zero tax rates. More importantly, they offer strict bank secrecy rules as well as certain legal constructs such as trusts that enable individuals to hide their ownership vis-à-vis tax administrations in their state of residence. The taxpayer's behavior in these cases constitutes illegal tax evasion. Due to its illegality it is hard to come up with reliable figures, yet the available evidence suggests that these policies have a real impact. Estimates of the worldwide yearly revenue losses to government coffers range from USD155–255 billion.[10]

Second, governments compete for so-called paper profits. Through various techniques, such as manipulating transfer prices (especially of intangible assets) and thin capitalization, multinational enterprises (MNEs) can assign profits made in high-tax countries to their subsidiaries in low-tax countries without relocating real business activity. Such "tax planning" activity of MNEs is not necessarily illegal; it constitutes (legal) tax avoidance.[11] Despite different approaches, all empirical investigations into this issue come to the same conclusion: the transfer of taxable profits is very sensitive to taxation, and companies make ample use of these possibilities. The decisive factor in attracting mobile profits is the nominal tax rate, because companies shift only those profits that cannot be offset against depreciation and other tax benefits.[12] Again, governments may also decide to compete via specially designed regimes to attract paper profits. For example, the regime of Special Financial Institutions (SFI) in the Netherlands allows foreign companies to channel capital through them in order to realize tax benefits.

Third, there is competition for FDI in the form of real business activity, for example the location decisions of MNEs. These business decisions depend on various factors such as countries' respective levels of education, costs of labor, and quality of infrastructure. But the effective tax burden also plays a role. Empirical studies come to the conclusion that raising taxes decreases the inflow of FDI. However, the direction and strength of the correlation is strongly affected by the method of measurement and the kinds of tax rates investigated.[13] In their quest to attract FDI, governments may either lower the general business tax rate or engage in designing so-called preferential tax regimes, which grant tax advantages to foreigners only (ring fencing).

Standard economic theory predicts a "race to the bottom" in capital taxation and the under-provision of public goods in all jurisdictions.[14] While this extreme outcome cannot be observed empirically, it can be shown that tax competition undermines the fiscal self-determination of states, that is, their ability to effectively set the size of the budget and the extent of redistribution. In OECD countries, nominal corporate tax rates have fallen from an average of 50% in 1975 to an average of 25.7% in 2010. Over the same period, nominal top personal income tax rates have fallen from 70% to 41.4%. These rate cuts were refinanced by broadening the bases on which taxes are applied ("tax cut cum base broadening"). As a result, corporate tax revenue as a percentage of GDP remained stable at an average of about 2.5%, whereas income tax revenue even rose from 11.2% to 12.8% of GDP.[15] The trend towards low nominal tax rates and broad tax bases is an attempt to defend against the outflow of mobile profits and at the same time prevent an adverse revenue effect.[16]

While revenue losses did not occur, the "tax cut cum base broadening" policy affects the distribution of the tax burden among different kinds of taxpayers. For one, there is an effect within the business sector: highly profitable MNEs benefit, while nationally organized small and medium-sized enterprises are more heavily burdened. Second, the tax burden is shifted from capital to labor. This is also visible in the general trend to increase indirect taxes, such as consumption taxes. Last but not least, competitive downward pressure on corporate tax rates affects the distributional characteristics of the personal income tax. If the nominal corporation tax rate is lowered, then it is worthwhile for private individuals to re-label their income by incorporating. In order to prevent such arbitrage, policy makers often align the corporate tax rate and the top rate on personal income, thus flattening the personal income tax schedule.[17]

For developing countries, the dynamics of a race-to-the-bottom have a more visible impact. The pressure from tax competition on public finances is comparable to OECD countries, but developing countries usually do not have the administrative resources to stabilize their revenues by broadening tax bases. On the contrary, in many countries the base has been narrowed.[18] A significant part of the revenue loss is directly due to the shifting of paper profits. One study estimates the annual revenue loss of developing countries from transfer pricing to be USD 160 billion.[19]

Overall, the empirical evidence shows that tax competition undermines fiscal self-determination.[20] While states still possess the formal right to set tax policies (*de jure* sovereignty), they cannot effectively pursue their desired policy goals (*de facto* sovereignty). Developed countries are able to maintain the size of the budget (the first component of self-determination), but this can only be achieved by compromising the desired extent of redistribution (the second component of self-determination). By contrast, developing countries are not able to prevent revenue losses and thus lose out on both components of fiscal self-determination. In this respect, tax competition increases existing inequalities between countries of the global North and South. For these reasons, we consider international tax competition in its present form to be a case of background injustice. In the absence of an institutional framework to regulate it, it introduces multiple kinds of bias into the international fiscal regime that lack justification.

II. Two Principles of Global Background Tax Justice: Membership and Fiscal Policy Constraint

The last section specified the content of fiscal self-determination and demonstrated how it is endangered by tax competition. Just like in the case of individual liberty, to be effective the liberty to make these collective choices is restricted by the same liberty for the citizens of other countries. The two principles we will advance in this section spell out these restrictions and are meant to ensure that countries have an effective right to tax that reflects their polities' choices about the size of the state budget and the desired extent of redistribution. The membership principle is based on the intuition that capital mobility renders this liberty fragile and that it therefore needs to be protected. The fiscal policy constraint argues that this liberty can be abused and therefore calls for it to be circumscribed.

A. The first principle: Membership

Imagine you live on a street with two health clubs. One high-end club with expensive equipment and all kinds of freebies like club towels and shaving equipment, and one less fancy club that lacks the rowing machines, has only three step masters instead of ten and no freebies. Unsurprisingly, the membership fee of the high-end club is almost three times that of its no-frills competitor. You are a member of the no-frills club. One day, you discover that your membership card actually lets you pass the turnstile at the high-end club, too. You keep quiet and start working out there. As it turns out, quite a few members of the no-frills club frequent the fancy club. A month later, you bump into a friend in the washrooms of the high-end club. "What are you doing here?" he asks. With a sheepish look on your face, you tell him about your discovery. He is enraged. "You guys are free-riding on our membership fees." He informs the manager and, the next day, the high-end club starts issuing new membership cards. This reaction appears justified.

For the purposes of our argument, the analogy between countries and health clubs is a useful one. There are places, such as the Scandinavian countries, that provide more services like state-financed daycare, more generous unemployment insurance, and so on, but in turn also "charge" more in terms of taxes.[21] There are others, like England, where citizens prefer to have a leaner set of services and hence pay less. Certain forms of tax planning that involve shifting one's tax base to a low-tax jurisdiction without moving the underlying activity itself are parallel to using the high-end health club on your no-frills card. When a company uses the services of a country—that is, its infrastructure, human capital, and so on—to produce a certain commodity, but then shifts the paper profit made with this economic activity to low-tax jurisdictions through practices like transfer pricing or thin capitalization, the citizens who finance these services have a legitimate complaint. Tax evasion on portfolio capital, as suggested by its illegality, represents an even blunter form of abuse and can be likened to jumping the turnstile at the high-end health club when no one is watching.

We are now in a position to formulate our first principle of international taxation, the membership principle:

> *Natural and legal persons should be liable to pay tax in the state of which they are a member.*

In order to apply the principle, it is necessary to define membership. Our definition is the following: individuals and companies should be viewed as members in those countries where they benefit from the public services and infrastructure.[22] This conception of membership is related to, but distinct from, what is called the "benefit principle" or the principle of "fiscal equivalence" in the public finance literature.[23] The *benefit principle* is usually contrasted with the *ability to pay principle*.[24] Whereas the latter justifies redistribution, the former does not and makes taxes strictly proportional to the individual benefits taxpayers receive in return. Our conception of membership is more general and comprises both of these principles. It is compatible with what has been called "group fiscal equivalence,"[25] which demands that the *collective* benefits of the group of citizens should be proportional to the amount of taxes paid. It thus allows for redistribution among individuals and corporations. As implicit in our notion of fiscal self-determination, the citizens of a state may (or may not) decide that it is appropriate to tax higher incomes at higher rates.[26] On this issue, the above analogy between the health clubs and countries breaks down. True to its objective to re-establish the *de facto* sovereignty of states, the membership principle is silent on the actual tax system chosen by polities. It merely stipulates that polities should have an *effective* right to tax individuals and companies as they see fit.

The remainder of this section is dedicated to two sets of comments on the membership principle. The first concerns its relation to existing principles, rules, and practices of international taxation. The second set of comments gauges the potential impact of respecting the membership principle on international taxation.

Our definition of membership is broad enough to encompass the major intuitions of diverse theories of international taxation. In the international tax literature, there is agreement that a nexus of some sort between taxpayer and country is required to justify taxation. Yet, there is disagreement about the proper nature of this nexus—should it be economic, social, political, or territorial allegiance, or a combination of these? The disagreement has never been fully resolved at the level of principles.[27] This is unsurprising, given that each pure solution has distributive consequences that favor the material revenue interests of certain groups of countries over others.[28]

Nevertheless, a working compromise has been found. According to the so-called "international tax principles," *individuals* are assessed on a residence basis, because residence determines where they benefit from public services and where they should therefore be counted as a member. *Companies* benefit from public services and infrastructure in the country where their substantive activities take place. Beyond a certain threshold of economic activity, they are therefore liable to tax in source countries, that is, those countries where the income was generated. For MNEs whose activities spread across borders, membership comes in degrees and should correspond to the distribution of its economic activities among countries. This justification for a combination of the residence and source principles of international taxation is commonly accepted. While the detailed definition of membership for particular cases remains a thorny and often controversial issue that keeps many tax experts busy, the distribution of taxing rights broadly follows this pattern, which is in line with our membership principle.

However, there are two practical problems. First, even though their underlying rationale is in line with our membership principle, the actual international tax rules, which are made up of domestic tax laws, bilateral double tax agreements (DTAs), and non-binding model conventions of international organizations, create certain overlaps (so-called double taxation) and gaps (double non-taxation) in countries' taxing rights.[29] As described in Section I, these grey zones can be exploited by sophisticated taxpayers to minimize their tax bill, thus violating the membership principle. Second, tax arbitrage aside, the current rules are badly enforced. There is no international authority overseeing state compliance, and administrative assistance and information exchange between countries is underdeveloped. Hence, it becomes possible to pass under the radar of tax authorities, thus violating the membership principle.

This brings us to our second set of comments. How would respecting the membership principle change the international tax landscape? While the detailed answer depends on the way it is institutionalized, a general observation can be made. The membership principle ensures that tax competition is brought closer to Tiebout's idealized notion of "voting with your feet."[30] Tiebout's model is generally presented as a *justification for* tax competition. It is argued that competition among jurisdictions leads to an efficient allocation of public funds as individuals self-select into different jurisdictions according to the match between the various tax-expenditure packages on offer and their fiscal preferences.[31] A crucial assumption of the model is that there are neither positive nor negative externalities for other countries stemming from the provision of "local" public goods. Yet, this assumption will generally not hold. When public goods are modeled more realistically as generating externalities, they will be underprovided if left to the market. Under these conditions, H. W. Sinn has shown that tax competition is nothing other than the introduction of the market mechanism "through the backdoor" and fails to produce an efficient allocation of public funds.[32]

While the costs and benefits of government action will never align perfectly in an economically interdependent world, the membership principle works to minimize the gap between them. It prohibits the hiding or shifting of part of the tax base from one's residence state in the case of individuals and from the source state in the case of MNEs. If it were implemented, two of the three kinds of tax competition, namely targeting portfolio capital and paper profits, would be curtailed and free-riding would no longer be possible. Any relocation of residence in the case of individuals and of real investment in the case of companies, however, would be unproblematic, since in those cases taxes are paid where the benefits from public services and infrastructure are obtained. A shift from the *status quo* to a world where the membership principle is respected would be a shift from a world of (merely) *virtual* tax competition for portfolio capital and paper profits to a world of *real* tax competition for FDI.

Note, however, that the membership principle not only sanctions the relocation of real investment but, by making virtual tax competition impossible, it is likely to make the competition for 'real' FDI more intense. If taxpayers cannot realize tax advantages by shifting portfolio capital or paper profits anymore, the incentive for actual relocation increases.[33] If this is so, it becomes all the more important to determine whether real tax competition is in line with fiscal self-determination and, if so, to what extent.

B. The second principle: A constraint on the design of fiscal policy

There is a basic difference between the three kinds of tax competition laid out in Section I. Whereas in the case of competition for portfolio capital and paper profits, countries aim to attract the tax base of people who remain members of another jurisdiction, competition for FDI implies a change of membership for the individuals or corporations who follow their capital to the new jurisdiction. The former phenomenon has been called "poaching" by the OECD,[34] reflecting intrusion or free-riding on someone else's fiscal territory; the latter phenomenon could be labeled "luring." In this section, we argue that some, though not all, cases of luring are problematic from a normative perspective and that, hence, fiscal self-determination needs to be curtailed in certain ways.

A limitation of sorts to fiscal self-determination should not come as a surprise. After all, it is a constitutive feature of any right that, in order to be effective across its various holders, it will have to be limited. Against this background, while the membership principle is designed to *protect* fiscal self-determination, the constraint on fiscal policy to be developed in the present section *circumscribes* it.

To motivate the normative relevance of cases of luring, consider the case of Ireland. For decades, Ireland had a tax rate between 10% and 12.5% on corporate profits, which drew in up to 25% of the FDI American corporations made in Europe.[35] This arrangement was a major factor behind the—by European standards—phenomenal growth of the Irish economy in the decades immediately preceding the 2008 financial crisis, and is therefore regarded by many economic commentators as a useful and effective tool of public policy. Any argument that claims luring to be problematic from a normative perspective will have to engage with this classic case for tax competition invoked by those countries that successfully employ it to promote economic growth.

So, what is wrong with luring from a normative perspective? We will discuss two tentative replies to this question and argue that while both are unsatisfactory when considered on their own, taken together they can both delineate the problematic aspects of luring and help formulate an adequate regulatory response. In a nutshell, one might object to luring either because it produces bad outcomes or because the intentions behind it are objectionable. We will start with the former.

a) An outcome-based constraint. As has been demonstrated in Section I, tax competition undermines the fiscal prerogatives of the state. It puts pressure on a government's capacity to realize their citizens' preferences concerning the size of the state as well as the level of redistribution. This is so even if the membership principle were fully implemented, because as argued above tax competition will generally not function as perfect Tiebout competition since it does generate fiscal externalities across jurisdictions.

These considerations prepare the ground for an outcome-based principle as one candidate for a constraint on fiscal policy: *A tax policy is legitimate if it does not produce a collectively suboptimal outcome. A collectively suboptimal outcome is here defined as one where the aggregate extent of fiscal self-determination of states is reduced.*

Such a principle would not only rule out all effective tax competition, that is, tax competition that actually succeeds in luring FDI, but it would impose far more drastic limits on fiscal policy. Suppose that, in a two-country world, the English have a preference for a leaner state and lower level of redistribution than Swedes. Suppose also that, to realize these preferences, the English lower their corporate tax rate. This leads to an inflow of Swedish FDI to England. In that scenario, the English continue to live out their fiscal preferences to the same extent as before, whereas the Swedish face a new constraint on their fiscal sovereignty. In the aggregate, the extent of fiscal self-determination of all countries is reduced. Even though England is not purposefully luring in Swedish capital, this is the outcome of its policy, and the above principle would therefore have to consider it illegitimate. The candidate principle would undermine precisely the kind of fiscal sovereignty that the membership principle is designed to protect and, in this sense, overshoot its target. It would fail to delineate mere fiscal interdependence from illegitimate tax competition.

b) An intention-based constraint. Rather than trying to delineate legitimate fiscal interdependence from illegitimate tax competition by appeal to outcomes, an alternative strategy is to focus on the intention that motivates the tax policy in question. Is it not the fact that Ireland *deliberately* tries to lure in foreign corporations and their capital that raises hackles and poses problems from a normative viewpoint? Could an argument be made that this is objectionable?

Such an argument can appeal to the intuition that fiscal prerogative trumps strategic intent. Consider the following two cases. First, the England-Sweden case discussed above. The tension between the fiscal prerogatives of the two countries here is constitutive of a fiscally interdependent world without tax harmonization. Privileging the fiscal prerogatives of Sweden over those of England seems unwarranted and overshoots the target. Second, think again of the Irish case. Here, the tension does not occur between two sets of fiscal prerogatives, but between the strategic intent of Ireland and the fiscal prerogatives of other countries. After all, the practice of luring in more members does not form one of the fiscal prerogatives of the state.

The fiscal prerogatives of other countries trump the strategic intent of the Irish in this case.

It is worth highlighting that, at least in one respect, an intention-based constraint is an improvement on the outcome-based constraint discussed above. While the latter was not able to drive a wedge between mere fiscal interdependence and tax competition, the criterion of strategic intentions does exactly that. This is a considerable advantage.

However, an appeal to intentions suffers from an important drawback of its own. If one condemns instances of strategic luring of foreign capital, does this condemnation not have to extend beyond tax competition narrowly defined? If strategic intent is the normative hitch, what should one make of investments in infrastructure or in human capital? Ruling out strategic intent across the board would not only deprive governments of substantive policy tools, but it might also have negative consequences in some contexts. Take the example of strategic infrastructure investments. Suppose Belgium invests in high-quality and specialized infrastructure in order to attract entrepreneurs from various countries, who profit from the fact that many people and firms from the same sector are geographically close. Over time a highly interdependent cluster develops. These agglomeration effects will positively impact growth in the country.[36] As a reaction, other countries may follow suit in promoting infrastructure or technology clusters. The result is a race to the top. While it is true that the initial move by Belgium tempo-rarily violates the fiscal prerogatives of other countries, the resulting economic growth and tax revenues will allow the other countries to realize their preferences in terms of fiscal prerogatives in the long run.[37] In these cases, there is no need to rule out strategic considerations.

Like an outcome-based constraint, an intention-based constraint over-shoots the target, albeit in a different way. It cannot distinguish regulatory competition with good *versus* bad collective outcomes. We submit that the difficulties of these approaches taken in isolation can be overcome by combining them into a mixed constraint.

c) A mixed constraint. An adequate constraint on the design of national fiscal policies is one that weighs the necessary protection of fiscal sover-eignty against the costs it imposes on other countries.[38] We believe that such a constraint should be sensitive both to the intention behind the fiscal policy in question and to the consequences on aggregate *de facto* fiscal sovereignty. What would such a mixed constraint look like?

Consider the intentions component first. While the basic practical question of how to assign intentions to a state in the first place will be discussed in Section III, we are here concerned with the criterion that decides whether an intention is strategic or not. We propose the following test. *Suppose the ben-efits of a tax policy change in terms of attracting tax base from abroad did not exist. Would the country still pursue the policy under this hypothetical scenario? If yes, the policy is evidently not motivated by strategic considerations and therefore is legitimate. If not, it is strategically motivated, but the verdict depends on the impact of the policy on the aggregate fiscal self-determination of all countries.*

"Strategic" here implies that a policy is justified by the prospect of luring in mobile capital from abroad rather than by appeal to the fiscal prerogatives of the state defined in Section I. The counterfactual nature of the criterion allows us, on a conceptual level, to elicit the motivation of a country in pursuing any given fiscal policy.[39] Note that it also captures cases of mixed motives, where a country lowers a certain tax rate *in part* because this reflects the conception of justice of its citizens, *but also* because of the strategic value of doing so for attracting foreign tax base.

Second, the causal impact of a specific fiscal policy on the fiscal prerogatives of all affected states will have to be evaluated. The criterion for assessing this impact is the one already discussed above: *a tax policy is legitimate if it does not produce a collectively suboptimal outcome, that is, a negative impact on the aggregate extent of fiscal self-determination.* While unsatisfactory on its own, it combines with the test for strategic intention to provide a good yardstick to evaluate fiscal policies. If this assessment were to be tackled entirely as a projection into the future, it would be too speculative in nature to be reliable. Yet, as we set out in detail in Section III, we propose an arbitration procedure under which countries bring forward cases that their fiscal prerogatives *have been* violated by the fiscal policy of others. The at least in part backward-looking character of this procedure renders the task of evaluating outcomes feasible.

Even though we acknowledge that both assessing intentions and evaluating outcomes remain daunting prospects, we believe they are feasible. As Section III will argue, there are precedents in the practice of international law that justify this optimism.

To sum up the conceptual implications of our proposed mixed constraint as well as its advantages over the two candidate constraints discussed before, consider Table 5.1.

Table 5.1 A mixed constraint on fiscal policy

		Outcome	
		Good	Bad
Intent	Independent	1	2
		✓	✓
	Strategic	3	4
		✓	☒

Fiscal policies that are formulated independently of their impact on international capital flows *and* have a positive outcome (quadrant 1 of the matrix) are clearly unproblematic. A domestically motivated decision to invest in infrastructure which then has positive knock-on effects on the infrastructure abroad ("race-to-the-top") could be an example.

Fiscal policies that are formulated independently *but* have a negative outcome (quadrant 2) are problematic, but ruling them out would impose too powerful a constraint on the design of fiscal policy (as demonstrated by the England—Sweden case).[40] Doing so is the weakness of a purely outcome-based constraint as discussed above.

Fiscal policies that are formulated strategically *but* have a positive outcome (quadrant 3) may at first appear to violate fiscal sovereignty, but a closer look reveals they do not because they lead to a race to the top (as demonstrated by the Belgium example). A drawback of a purely intention-based constraint is that it would rule out strategically motivated policies irrespective of their effects.

Finally, policies that are formulated strategically *and* have a negative outcome (quadrant 4) are problematic on both counts and should therefore be prohibited. This is what our mixed constraint is designed to do. The Irish case falls into this category.

Before moving on to questions of implementation, we need to discuss one potential objection to our partial appeal to intentions in evaluating fiscal policy. Suppose the citizens of a developing country are motivated by social justice reasons to build more hospitals and, in order to do so, decide to lower their country's taxes to attract the necessary capital from abroad. Is this part of their fiscal self-determination or should it count as a strategic consideration? Would we not deprive poor countries of an important source of redistribution if it turned out that such a strategic policy contributes to a race-to-the-bottom? We believe that our principle can answer these questions. First, we submit that this policy should indeed count as motivated by strategic considerations. Capital that is attracted to the developing country to build a hospital is not available to build a hospital elsewhere. Second, this does not mean that building the hospital in the developing country is not important and does not preclude the possibility that richer countries have an obligation of assistance towards this project. But this obligation should not be discharged in the form of a bias in the way the jurisdictional structure of international taxation is set up. It should rather be dealt with via explicit redistribution.[41] This illustrates that a complete account of tax justice has two components—the fair rules of the game that lie at the heart of this article and redistributive obligations, which we bracket here. Attempting to assess redistributive obligations before the fair rules of the game have been determined amounts to a Sisyphean task. Redistribution to correct for an institutional bias and injustice is analogous to swimming against the current—it takes a lot more energy while getting you less far.

In fact, this issue is not simply hypothetical. There is a debate about the legitimacy of developing country tax havens. When OECD countries began to pressure tax havens to abandon their harmful tax policies (see below), some of them argued that they had chosen to become tax havens because they saw no other possibility to initiate economic development.[42] Rich countries may well have an obligation to compensate these states.

III. Institutionalizing the Two Principles

It is notoriously difficult to derive concrete institutions from abstract principles, because there will generally be more than one way to institutionalize a principle. In the face of this institutional indeterminacy, we limit ourselves here to demonstrating that there is an institutional solution that satisfies the conditions embodied in our principles. As a further caveat, we stress that the following sketch cannot, due to space constraints, do full justice to the complex issues of international tax law. But it should suffice to outline some possible institutional implications of our proposal.

Any institutional solution must: (1) provide a forum for governments to negotiate agreements on the rules of international taxation; and (2) make sure that the rules are enforced. In the following we propose the establishment of an International Tax Organization (ITO) and discuss the basic institutional design features required to ensure it is up to the two tasks.[43] The ITO should become the forum for negotiating and defining the rules in line with the membership principle and the fiscal policy constraint. To ensure a level playing field, all states should be members and adequately represented in the ITO's decision-making procedures, which, in a world of power politics, does of course represent a challenge in its own right.[44]

A. Institutionalizing the membership principle

On the basis of our two principles several reforms become imperative. First, governments have to abolish all rules that make it impossible for other countries to enforce the membership principle. Thus, strict bank secrecy regulations, the supply of other deliberately nontransparent legal constructs, and the refusal to exchange information with other tax administrations will be ruled out. The requirement to exchange tax-relevant information with other countries could be implemented through a system of multilateral automatic exchanges of information.

Second, an ITO with inclusive membership would provide an ideal forum to reconsider the membership rule in the case of MNEs. How should the rights to tax shares of the profit of an MNE be allocated among jurisdictions? This issue is a very thorny one in international tax practice that has so far been resolved through so-called separate entity accounting and arm's length standard (ALS) transfer pricing.[45] As set out in Section I, both the indeterminacy of applying this standard and the difficulties in its enforcement can be exploited by MNEs to lower their tax bills. One possible solution would be to switch to a system of unitary taxation with formula apportionment (UT+FA).[46] This would require governments to agree on a common and consolidated corporate tax base. MNEs would have to determine their worldwide profit in one single report, and they would be allowed to consolidate profits and losses of entities in different countries. The worldwide profit would then be apportioned to the respective countries in which the MNE operates on the basis of a predetermined formula. The formula should reflect the real economic activity in each country by referring to factors such as property, sales, and payroll. This would make it impossible for companies to engage in the shifting of paper profits and would thus be a major step forward in the implementation of the membership principle.

B. Institutionalizing the fiscal policy constraint

As we have already acknowledged, defining rules that respect the constraints on fiscal policy will be difficult. First, the outcome on which we focus, namely constraints on aggregate fiscal self-determination of countries as a result of national tax policies, may not be easily observed, especially across alternative regulatory regimes. However, in principle it should be possible for a government to make the case, and support it with empirical evidence, that it has lost tax base to another country that has recently changed its tax policies. Second, and more importantly, the fact that intentions are unobservable invites hypocrisy. It will be possible for governments to misrepresent their intentions, that is, to attribute any tax reforms to the preferences citizens have about the size of the budget and the extent of redistribution, even if in reality they pursue the strategic aim of attracting foreign tax base. In order to avoid hypocritical political discourses and long but futile attempts to distinguish honest from dishonest representations of intentions, the institutionalization of the principle should as much as possible rely on objectively observable proxies for the defendant's intentions. To get off the hook, the defendant would need to show that the tax policy change in question has actually had beneficial effects collectively.

While a detailed and legally applicable definition of the objective factors that indicate a bad outcome and a strategic intention of the defendant is a task for tax lawyers, and thus beyond the scope of this article, it is clear that data on capital flows, economic growth rates, or distributive results are readily available and could be used by the parties to a tax dispute. Reference to these indicators is routinely made in all kinds of debates on policy design; international fiscal policy is no exception in this respect. Nevertheless, given the many factors that affect economic outcomes and the complex relationships among them, controversies over the right interpretation of these data are likely. In case of controversy, what is needed is an accepted independent third party that can settle the dispute through an authoritative interpretation of the facts. As described in the following section, what we envisage is a judicial or quasi-judicial system in which disputes among governments over tax policy can be settled. Here, it is worth noting that courts assess intentions on a regular basis in the international arena. For example, the International Court of Justice (ICJ) has to assess the intentions of the alleged offender in applying the genocide convention.[47] The WTO is another case in point. Under the rules on non-tariff trade barriers, policies with protectionist effect are generally prohibited. However, in case a country pursues a policy with the intention of protecting consumers' health and safety and can prove its good intentions, an exception to the rule of non-protectionism is granted. As in our proposal, the WTO institutionalized this rule by focusing on the observable implications of countries' intentions. A government has to provide valid scientific evidence of the claimed adverse effects on consumers' health and safety.[48]

In addition to these considerations, it is possible to derive one necessary, but not sufficient, condition for satisfying the fiscal policy constraint: all forms of preferential tax regimes for foreigners (ring fencing) must be abolished. The only plausible explanation for such discriminatory arrangements is strategic intent to lure in foreign capital. As to its consequences, discrimination of this kind will generally not have positive effects in the sense of a race to the top.

C. Enforcement

What would it take to effectively enforce our two principles? Monitoring compliance should be relatively straightforward since governments can be expected to launch a complaint if other governments violate either or both of the two principles. Yet, what is needed is an independent authority that will process the complaints and eventually enforce the rules. Effective enforcement is needed to ensure compliance with the two principles, because the structure of tax competition is such that every individual country has an incentive to deviate from the collectively desirable rules. The ITO could install a dispute settlement procedure after the WTO model to satisfy this requirement.[49] In case a member state complains that the tax practices of another member violate the rules, they can, as a first step, try to resolve the conflict in consultations. If they are unsuccessful, the case will be transferred to the dispute settlement body (DSB), which effectively functions like an independent judiciary, because a panel report (judgment) can only be blocked if all member states unanimously agree on blocking it. Since parties know that there will be effective enforcement of decisions in the DSB, it can be expected that they will resolve many cases in consultation. This procedure has the advantage of avoiding excessive litigation and leaves room for political negotiations and decisions.

One potential objection to the ITO is that it is another non-majoritarian institution which is provided with substantial enforcement powers but lacks democratic accountability and legitimacy.[50] This is an important concern. Yet, we believe that the *status quo*, with its hollowing out of effective fiscal sovereignty through tax competition as described in Section I, is even more problematic in this respect. Although it *formally* guarantees democratic accountability, *de facto* this is not the case. Conversely, while an ITO may reduce the scope of fiscal policy issues for which there is direct democratic accountability, it would make sure that the latter can actually work effectively in this restricted realm.

D. The contrast with the status quo and feasibility issues

How does our proposal for the future rules of international taxation compare with the institutional status quo? Is it feasible in the sense that it relies on solutions that have successfully been put to work in other contexts or policy fields?

As described in Section I, the current situation is characterized by harmful tax competition. This fact has not gone unnoticed by governments and international organizations. Accordingly, they have launched policy initiatives to address this situation. We now very briefly summarize the results of the two most important instances—the efforts of the OECD and the EU. The ongoing OECD initiative against harmful tax competition[51] has so far hardly brought any tangible progress. It focuses on information exchange on request, which is provided for in bilateral tax treaties. Under the on-request system, the requesting state has to present initial evidence of international tax evasion in order to receive the required information about foreign funds of its residents. Yet, precisely the kind of information required to mount an initial case is often secret and thus on-request information exchange is ineffective. Routine, electronic (that is, automatic) and multilateral exchange of information on the funds of non-residents to their respective home countries, as foreseen in our proposal, can address this problem.[52] Moreover, the OECD can only issue non-binding recommendations and countries are not obliged to implement them.[53]

The EU has been somewhat more successful in its initiatives against harmful tax competition. With respect to business tax competition, the Council agreed on a soft law Code of Conduct in 1997. Member states entered into a non-binding commitment to remove so-called preferential tax regimes. Despite being non-binding, the code developed some bite because compliance with it was made a condition of accession for the Central and Eastern European countries. Also, the Commission applied the principles contained in the code to its state aid rules, which thus increased compliance among the EU-15 states.[54] Currently, the EU is considering adopting a system of unitary taxation with formula apportionment.[55]

In the area of portfolio tax competition the EU has passed the Savings Tax Directive, which took effect in July 2005. This directive targets tax evasion on interest income by requiring automatic information exchange among countries on the savings of foreign residents. While the directive has significant loopholes, it is important in that it shows that automatic international information exchange can be implemented in practice.[56]

Our proposal significantly improves upon these initiatives. In line with the demands of our two principles we propose an international framework that is much stronger than the current global tax institutions, which cannot make universally binding rules and lack international levers of enforcement. Moreover, the OECD, as today's most important international tax forum, is made up only of industrialized countries, a fact that has invited the criticism of imperialism. The proposed ITO with its encompassing membership would remedy this shortcoming.

The experience at the regional level of the EU shows that creating an institutional framework with more effective powers of enforcement is indeed feasible. The EU uses one of the specific policies we recommend, namely automatic information exchange, and is seriously debating another one, UT+FA. At the same time, note that our proposal, while it does involve a redefinition of fiscal sovereignty, does not require the transfer of core fiscal prerogatives to the international level. No supra-national power to tax is established. Instead, the basic idea is that the international community protects national fiscal self-determination by imposing certain limits on the fiscal choices of nation states. The existence of the WTO is testament to the fact that creating an international organization to define and enforce these constraints is achievable.[57]

An additional argument for the feasibility of our proposal is that it does not envisage harmonization of national tax policies. While harmonization is portrayed as the relevant alternative to tax competition in large parts of the literature,[58] it is also clear that there are strong political objections against it. We submit that our principles can address the undesirable aspects of tax competition without implying full harmonization. First, respect of the membership principle and the fiscal policy constraint does not entail harmonization. Suppose the English really do have a preference for a smaller state and less redistribution than the Swedish. Neither of our principles will stop them from designing a tax structure that reflects these preferences. In turn, nothing we have said will prevent the Swedes from making a democratic choice that the best way to finance a relatively generous welfare state is to shift a considerable portion of the tax burden onto labor and consumption and to tax capital lightly, as they in fact do. However, the proposed constraint on fiscal policy prohibits the very same policies if they are based on strategic considerations and have negative consequences.

Second, even in a world where different polities have divergent preferences about the size of the state and the extent of redistribution, our two principles will create *some* pressure towards convergence. This is so because countries with preferences for a relatively large state and/or a high extent of redistribution will now have to bear the real costs of these preferences in terms of part of their tax base voting with its feet. At the other end of the spectrum, however, the danger of a race to the bottom would be eliminated by our two principles for the very same reason. Countries with smaller state budgets and a lower level of redistribution would also be forced to bear the full costs of their tax structure, rather than being able to finance part of their public services by strategically attracting foreign tax base. The fiscal externalities generated in both directions under our two principles are those minimally present under conditions of fiscal interdependence between states.[59] They ensure a maximum—though less than perfect—correspondence between the convictions of members of the respective polities and the fiscal structure of those polities.

IV. Toward What Kind of Global Justice?

We have pointed out that the membership principle and fiscal policy constraint serve to protect the *de facto* sovereignty of states and their capacity to implement the conception of justice of their citizens domestically through their fiscal policy. Yet, what about global justice? Arguably, the most disturbing inequalities in today's world are ones between individuals across borders rather than between citizens of the same state.

Our account owes two explanations in this context. First, we need to justify granting states fiscal self-determination in the first place—a question that we bracketed in Section I. Without such a justification, which requires a theory about the fundamental relationship between social justice, democracy, and global justice, our principles could be accused of being constructed on theoretical quicksand. We do not aim here to provide a full-fledged justification of the state. Instead, our objective is to survey a number of potential justifications of the state and to argue that the theories of global justice that underpin them—notably cosmopolitan ones—are not at odds with our principles and the fiscal self-determination the latter imply. Second, a clarification concerning the normative status of the two principles is in order.

In the second part of this section, we will elaborate on what we have in mind when presenting them as principles of *global background justice*.

A. The normative grounds of self-determination

Consider the following formulation of the basic tenet of cosmopolitanism: "moral cosmopolitanism holds that all persons stand in certain moral relations to one another: we are required to respect one another's status as ultimate units of moral concern—a requirement that imposes limits upon our conduct and, in particular, upon our efforts to construct institutional schemes."[60] Moral cosmopolitanism is to be distinguished from legal cosmopolitanism, which calls for a global order in which people have "equivalent rights and duties."[61] While the latter, more radical version of cosmopolitanism is indeed incompatible with state autonomy, most cosmopolitan theorists endorse the more moderate variant of the cosmopolitan ideal.[62]

It is not our goal here to endorse cosmopolitanism or any other theory of global justice. We merely aim to anticipate and counter the objection that the principles of international taxation developed in Section II and the self-determination of states they advocate conflict with moral cosmopolitanism as defined above. To this end, we will now sketch three ways in which a moral cosmopolitan can accept, or even endorse, the self-determination of states.

First, a cosmopolitan may hold that "to respect one another's status as ultimate units of moral concern" actually *requires* a certain level of state autonomy.[63] How so? Consider a purely justice-based cosmopolitan theory, that is, one that proposes one theory of global justice to apply to all human beings across the globe. Such a position runs into the objection of pluralism concerning conceptions of justice. Given pluralism, so the objection against this position runs, imposing *one* conception of justice on everyone in fact fails to respect as ultimate units of moral concern those who do not share it. This objection can be defused by introducing a democracy-based component into cosmopolitanism. This component requires that people have a say in the decisions that affect their interests. Note that this does not provide us with a justification for the self-determination of states as such, but for a multi-level governance structure that states plausibly form a part of. Under this structure, political issues are dealt with at the governance level that best corresponds to the scope of the policy in question—for example, environmental issues will be dealt with at a higher level of governance than questions of educational policy. The upshot of this position is what Simon Caney calls a mixed cosmopolitan view that is sensitive both to a minimal—that is, pluralism-defying—notion of global justice and to the importance of political participation. A position of this type accepts a certain level of state self-determination on *normative* grounds. While some constraints based on considerations of global justice may apply to the level of self-determination in question, there is no incompatibility with the membership principle and fiscal policy constraint as such.

Second, a cosmopolitan may defend state self-determination as the most effective means to promote the interests of individuals worldwide. In particular, he may believe it to offer a more effective way of serving these interests than concentrating collective decision-making at the highest level, that is, in the hands of a world government. As Robert Goodin puts it, the special duties that states have towards their citizens are the best way of discharging "the general duties that everyone has towards everyone else worldwide."[64] Besides, granting autonomy to states offers protection from domination as well as immunity from the larger unit. This allows states to be more responsive to local interests and to reduce the burdens of decision-making.[65] A position of this type accepts a certain level of state self-determination on *instrumental and conditional* grounds. If it turns out that there is an institutional alternative that serves the interests of individuals worldwide in a better way, the justification of self-determination will be undermined. The same qualification would apply to an endorsement of the membership principle and the fiscal policy constraint on these grounds.

Finally, for those cosmopolitans who remain unconvinced by the two previous arguments, there is another, pragmatic reason to grant states some autonomy nonetheless. A theory of justice with practical ambitions is well-advised to take some features of the world as given, rather than attempting to reform everything at once. Arguably, the division of world politics into states is a good candidate for such a feature, given that a world without states has to be viewed as utopian from today's perspective.

Note that adopting a pragmatic stance of this kind does not imply accepting the *current* state system as just. One might argue that those states benefiting from the international structure in unjust ways incur a series of redistributive obligations towards those who get short-changed under the *status quo*. We agree that such redistributive duties exist today. However, this article relegates them to the background. Our focus here has been to design fair rules of the game to govern fiscal interdependence between states. It is to a series of comments on the normative status of these rules that we turn in the next subsection.

In sum, a cosmopolitan theorist has at least three potential reasons to accept the kind of state self-determination inherent in our principles. Given that our position promotes the *effective* sovereignty of states, statists among the global justice theorists should equally find it an attractive view to hold. It seems fair to conclude that accepting our two principles does not impose an undue constraint on the theory of global justice one may want to defend.

B. An Account of Background Justice in International Taxation

The literature on global justice has been dominated by questions concerning the relation between principles of domestic justice versus principles of global justice. While cosmopolitan theorists generally defend continuity between the two, their critics hold that the global sphere is significantly distinct from the domestic level.[66] One of these alleged differences will occupy us here, namely the question of whether a global basic structure exists that gives rise to concerns of global distributive justice.[67]

On the one hand, a number of so-called "practice-dependent" views argue, first, that the content of our conceptions of justice is dependent on the practices they regulate and, second, that no clear structures and rules of the required kind exist at the global level to give rise to concerns of distributive justice.[68] On the other hand, this position has recently been contested in two ways. First, Andreas Follesdal has argued that several of the practices of international relations are in fact *constitutive* of a global basic structure and, hence, that issues of global justice do indeed arise.[69] Second, and more importantly in our context, Miriam Ronzoni has suggested that "the most pressing issue is not whether we *have* a global basic structure, but whether we *need* one."[70] Ronzoni makes the case that the absence of a global basic structure in the face of inequalities should not lead us to conclude that these inequalities somehow fall outside the purview of justice, but instead calls for the *creation* of such a basic structure. Internationally as well as domestically, certain rules may be required to guarantee the fairness of interactions between individuals. Ronzoni submits that "under circumstances of intense international interaction and interdependence the conditions of effective sovereignty, and hence of *international background justice*, may be eroded."[71] Consequently, she advocates the creation of functionally differentiated supranational institutions that have the (legitimate) authority to set certain rules for appropriate conduct.

This is precisely the kind of claim we have attempted to substantiate with respect to international tax competition in Section I. The current institutional setting undermines effective sovereignty. The two principles put forward in Section II are designed to restore this sovereignty and to guarantee international background justice. In fact, Ronzoni explicitly cites tax competition as one policy area where she considers international background justice to be violated and calls for interdisciplinary research on this issue. Delivering on this research program is a principal objective of this article.

Let us add two comments on this categorization of our account as one of international background justice. First, the idea of background justice emphasizes institutional reform over redistributive obligations. It favors preventative institutional reform to remedial redistribution of income. That said, note that implementing our two principles will, as a by-product, lead to a significant reduction in global inequalities.

Second, this short section cannot claim to present a comprehensive treatment of the rich literature on global justice. Our limited objective here has been to elucidate the nature of our contribution to the literature. The membership principle and fiscal policy constraint represent principles of global background justice.

V. Conclusion

This article was motivated by the intuition that some effects of tax competition on fiscal self-determination can be qualified as unjust. The two principles defended above serve as a normative toolkit to specify to what extent the interdependence of states in fiscal matters calls for normative interdependence. The membership principle rules out any *poaching* of foreign capital, that is, the practice of attracting capital of non-members of a state. The fiscal policy constraint prohibits certain instances of *luring*, that is, the practice of inviting foreign individuals and corporations to follow their capital. Luring is problematic if it is *both* motivated by strategic intent *and* leads to a negative outcome collectively in terms of the aggregate extent of fiscal self-determination. To put these principles into practice, we propose the creation of an International Tax Organization (ITO), whose job description would include the settling of disputes between states about compliance issues.

To be sure, a world in which the two principles are respected is not yet a just world. It is merely a world that guarantees international background justice in one important way: national polities would regain the capacity to make collective fiscal choices about the size of the budget and the level of *domestic* redistribution. In other words, the principles ensure that the costs of fiscal choices fall on those who make them, at least to the extent that this can be achieved under conditions of fiscal interdependence. However, the two principles will have to be complemented by substantive principles of *global* tax justice. While these necessarily build on the work done in this article, they also ask the question of whether states have normative obligations to make transfer payments to other states and, if so, what they are. We hope to address this issue in future work.

Notes

* Versions of this article have been presented at the Canadian Political Science Association (Montréal, 2010), the ECPR General Conference (Reykjavik, 2011), the Social Science Research Center Berlin (WZB) as well as at the Centre de Recherche en Éthique de l'Université de Montréal (CREUM). For comments on previous drafts of this article we thank participants at these events and, in particular, Kim Brooks, Ryoa Chung, Matthias Ecker-Ehrhardt, Tim Gemkow, Anja Görnitz, Monika Heupel, Dominic Martin, Mihaela Mihai, Jean-Pierre Vidal, Lora Viola, Daniel Weinstock, David Wiens, Jurgen de Wispelaere, and Michael Zürn. Special thanks are due to Barbara Buckinx, Miriam Ronzoni, and Christian Schemmel for detailed written comments and to Georg Simmerl for his research assistance. We acknowledge financial support from the Humboldt Foundation, the German Academic Exchange Service (DAAD), and the Social Sciences and Humanities Research Council of Canada (SSHRC).

1 Notable exceptions are Gillian Brock, "Taxation and global justice: closing the gap between theory and practice," *Journal of Social Philosophy*, 39 (2008), 161–84; Alexander W. Cappelen, "The moral rationale for international fiscal law," *Ethics & International Affairs*, 15 (2001), 97–110 and Miriam Ronzoni, "The global order: a case of background injustice? A practice-dependent account," *Philosophy & Public Affairs*, 37 (2009), 229–56. Brock discusses challenges of international taxation similar to the ones at the heart of this article, yet her account of potential solutions differs from ours in that she focuses on various kinds of global taxation rather than principles to make national taxation more effective. Cappelen analyses the current distribution of international rights to tax through the lens of theories of distributive justice. Ronzoni, whose work we shall discuss in more detail later, identifies tax competition as an instance of background injustice.

More common are contributions from lawyers and economists discussing normative principles of international taxation. See e.g. Richard A. Musgrave and Peggy B. Musgrave, "Inter-nation equity," *Modern Fiscal Issues*, ed. R. M. Bird and J. G. Head (Toronto: University of Toronto Press, 1972), pp. 63–85; Reuven S. Avi-Yonah, *International Tax as International Law* (New York: Cambridge University Press, 2006).

2 See Ronzoni, "The global order." The idea of background justice is discussed in detail in Section IV.

3 As is generally the case with competition, the pressure it exerts is not external to competitors' individual acts, but is in fact constituted by them. Nevertheless, competition presents a structural constraint on each individual actor, as it could only be eliminated or mitigated collectively. In that sense policy reactions by individual states are 'forced upon' them by competition.

4 The category of public goods is broadly construed here. It includes not only public infrastructure but also less tangible goods like the maintenance of a legal order or the redistribution of income and wealth.

5 Reuven S. Avi-Yonah, "Globalization, tax competition, and the fiscal crisis of the welfare state," *Harvard Law Review*, 113 (2000), 1573–676; James M. Buchanan and Richard A. Musgrave, *Public Finance and Public Choice* (Cambridge: MIT Press, 1999), pp. 29–103.

6 We discuss the normative foundations of the (fiscal) self-determination of states in Section IV.

7 For a discussion of the problems associated with this assumption see Alexander Cappelen, "Responsibility and international distributive justice," *Real World Justice*, ed. A. Follesdal and T. Pogge (Dordrecht: Springer, 2005), pp. 215–28 at pp. 220–22.

8 John D. Wilson and David E. Wildasin, "Capital tax competition: bane or boon," *Journal of Public Economics*, 88 (2004), 1065–91 at pp. 1065–6.

9 States may, in theory, also compete to attract mobile individuals via taxes on labor income. Empirically, while there is some competition for individuals in very high income brackets, labor tax competition is insignificant. Cf. Peter Schwarz, "Does capital mobility reduce the corporate-labor tax ratio?" *Public Choice*, 130 (2007), 363–80. We bracket labor tax competition in this article.

10 Jeffrey Owens, "Written testimony of Jeffrey Owens, Director, OECD Center for Tax Policy and Administration before Senate Finance Committee on Offshore Tax Evasion, 3 May 2007" <http://finance.senate.gov/imo/media/doc/050307testjo1.pdf>; Tax Justice Network (TJN), "Tax us if you can: the true story of a global failure," *Tax Justice Network Briefing Paper* (London: Tax Justice Network International Secretariat, 2005).

11 Former British chancellor Denis Healey famously said that the difference between avoidance and evasion is the "thickness of a prison wall." For a description of these and other techniques of shifting paper profits, see e.g. Brian J. Arnold and Michael J. McIntyre, *International Tax Primer* (Den Haag: Kluwer Law International, 1995), pp. 8–17. The fact that 60% of world trade is intra-firm indicates that the tax base at stake is significant.

12 Ruud A. de Mooij and Sjef Ederveen, "Corporate tax elasticities: a reader's guide to empirical findings," *Oxford Review of Economic Policy*, 24 (2008), 680–697; Michael P. Devereux, "The impact of taxation on the location of capital, firms and profit: a survey of empirical evidence (with Data Appendix by Giorgia Maffini)," *Working Paper* (Warwick: University of Warwick, 2006). The fact that profit shifting is possible may explain the weaker effect of tax policies on FDI. As long as MNEs can realize tax savings without business relocations, the competition for FDI and paper profits is in a substitutive relationship. We return to this issue in Section II.

13 De Mooij and Ederveen, "Corporate tax elasticities."

14 See e.g. Wilson and Wildasin, "Capital tax competition," pp. 1069–70.

15 OECD Centre for Tax Policy and Administration, "OECD tax data base" <www.oecd.org/ctp/taxdatabase>; Steffen Ganghof, *The Politics of Income Taxation* (Colchester: ECPR Press, 2006), p. 1.

16 See e.g. Andreas Haufler and Guttorm Schjelderup, "Corporate tax systems and cross country profit shifting," *Oxford Economic Papers*, 52 (2000), 306–25.

17 Simon Loretz, "Corporate taxation in the OECD in a wider context," *Oxford Review of Economic Policy*, 24 (2008), 639–660; Steffen Ganghof and Philipp Genschel, "Taxation and democracy in the EU," *Journal of European Public Policy*, 15 (2008), 58–77.

18 Michael Keen and Alejandro Simone, "Is tax competition harming developing countries more than developed?" *Tax Notes International*, 34 (2004), 1317–25.

19 Christian Aid, "Death and taxes: The true toll of tax dodging" (London: Christian Aid, 2008).

20 Some observers argue that the policy choices described above—tax cuts cum base broadening, increasing reliance on indirect taxes, and low tax burdens on capital—are not caused by tax competition. They argue that these policies reflect a general shift towards market-conforming taxation that governments have

implemented irrespective of competitive pressures. Cf. e.g. Sven Steinmo, "The evolution of policy ideas: tax policy in the 20th century," *British Journal of Politics and International Relations*, 5 (2003), 206–36. While it is true that there are also domestic efficiency reasons for implementing these policies, our foregoing sketch of the mechanisms shows—in line with most of the public finance literature—that these changes are to a significant extent driven by the pressures of tax competition. For more on this debate, see Thomas Rixen, "Taxation and cooperation: international action against harmful tax competition," *Globalization. State of the Art and Perspectives*, ed. S. A. Schirm (London: Routledge, 2007), pp. 61–80. However, as we will discuss in Section II, if such policies were indeed chosen for domestic reasons only, they would not indicate a violation of self-determination but an instance of it.

21 We put "charge" in inverted commas here, because we do not mean to imply adherence to the benefit principle. See also discussion below.

22 While, as we will briefly discuss below, this definition of membership is not detailed enough to resolve all cases of ambiguous membership assignments, it does nonetheless exclude certain conceptual possibilities. It should be emphasized, for example, that our definition of membership is distinct from citizenship. Permanently non-resident citizens should not be liable to tax in their country of citizenship. Conversely, temporary resident aliens, even though they generally do not have a democratic voice in state decisions, should be. We bracket these debates here.

23 Mancur Olson, "The principle of 'fiscal equivalence': the division of responsibilities among different levels of government," *American Economic Review*, 59 (1969), 479–87.

24 See e.g. Joel Slemrod and Jon Bakija, *Taxing Ourselves* (Cambridge: MIT Press, 2004), pp. 61–6.

25 Thielemann, Ulrich, "Grundsätze fairen Steuerwettbewerbs—Ein wirtschafts-ethisches Plädoyer für einen Steuerleistungswettbewerb," *Regulierung oder Deregulierung der Finanzmärkte*, ed. B. Britzelmaier, S. Geberl, H.-R. Kaufmann and M. Menichetti (Heidelberg: Physica-Verlag, 2002), pp. 113–32.

26 It has been proposed to replace the corporate income tax with user fees, which are unrelated to the profit made by the enterprise. The idea behind this is that redistributive taxation should only occur among individuals, and the distributed profit of companies would be taxable on the individual level as dividend income. Under our notion of fiscal self-determination governments would be free to choose such a system. But they may also be of the opinion that corporations can be viewed as (legal) persons that should be incorporated in a redistributive scheme. See e.g. Reuven S. Avi-Yonah, "Corporations, society, and the state: a defense of the corporate tax," *Virginia Law Review*, 90 (2004), 1193–1254.

27 See e.g. Peggy B. Musgrave, "Fiscal coordination and competition in an international setting," *Retrospectives on Public Finance*, ed. L. Eden (Durham: Duke University Press, 1991), pp. 276–305; Cappelen, "The moral rationale."

28 See e.g. Musgrave and Musgrave, "Inter-nation equity"; Thomas Rixen, *The Political Economy of International Tax Governance* (Basingstoke: Palgrave Macmillan, 2008), pp. 57–116.

29　For a discussion of the gaps and overlaps in the international tax regime with references to the vast legal and economic literature on the topic, see Rixen, *The Political Economy of International Tax Governance*, pp. 66–85.

30　Charles M. Tiebout, "A pure theory of local expenditures," *Journal of Political Economy*, 64 (1956), 416–24.

31　See e.g. Dennis C. Mueller, "Redistribution and allocative efficiency in a mobile world economy," *Jahrbuch für Neue Politische Ökonomie*, 17 (1998), 172–90.

32　Hans-Werner Sinn, "The selection principle and market failure in systems competition," *Journal of Public Economics*, 66 (1997), 247–74. While Sinn and other contributors to the economic literature on tax competition frame this result in terms of welfare losses, we focus on the negative impact on fiscal self-determination (see Section I). Potential trade-offs between these two perspectives are set aside in this article.

33　Michael Keen, "Preferential regimes can make tax competition less harmful," *National Tax Journal*, 54 (2001), 757–62; Dhammika Dharmapala, "What problems and opportunities are created by tax havens?" *Oxford Review of Economic Policy*, 24 (2008), 661–79 at pp. 671–6.

34　OECD, *Harmful Tax Competition* (Paris: OECD, 1998), p. 16.

35　See "A survey of Ireland," *The Economist*, 16 October 2004.

36　As the literature on economic geography points out, these agglomeration economies also open up room for taxing capital without automatically leading to capital flight. See for instance Richard E. Baldwin and Paul Krugman, "Agglomeration, integration and tax harmonisation," *European Economic Review*, 48 (2004), 1–23.

37　That said, it remains of course an empirical question whether a race to the top actually materializes.

38　See also Peter Dietsch, "Rethinking sovereignty in international fiscal policy," *Review of International Studies*, 37 (2011), 2107–20.

39　The counterfactual nature of the criterion is in part inspired by Calvin Normore, "Consent and the principle of fairness," *Essays on Philosophy, Politics & Economics*, ed. C. Favor, G. Gaus and J. Lamont (Stanford: Stanford University Press, 2010), pp. 225–45.

40　An anonymous referee pointed out another interesting case that falls into this category. Suppose a country stratifies its tax structure in a way that frees up "armies of lawyers and accountants" to work "in more productive ways," thereby creating a more attractive business environment and attracting FDI. Provided this policy is formulated independently, our constraint deems it legitimate even if it leads to a reduction in the aggregate level of self-determination.

41　As Christian Schemmel pointed out to us, whether the developing country should be allowed to engage in tax competition if the transfers from richer countries are not forthcoming is a different, and interesting, issue.

42　See Jason C. Sharman, *Havens in a Storm: The Struggle for Global Tax Regulation* (Ithaca, NY: Cornell University Press, 2006).

43　Calls for an International Tax Organization can be found in the literature, see e.g. Vito Tanzi, "Is there a need for a World Tax Organization? *The Economics of Globalization*, ed. A. Razin and E. Sadka (Cambridge: Cambridge University Press, 1999), pp. 173–186; Frances M. Horner, "Do we need an International

Tax Organization?" *Tax Notes International*, 24 (2001), 179–87. However, so far no attempt has been made to derive the institutional design from the functional requirements of the issue to be dealt with.

44 The decision-making procedures of the World Bank and the International Monetary Fund, which are heavily biased in favor of developed countries, provide a cautionary tale in this context.

45 According to the ALS, foreign branches or subsidiaries of an MNE are to be taxed as if they were independent market participants, exchanging goods and services at arm's length (i.e. market) prices, see e.g. Lorraine Eden, *Taxing Multinationals* (Toronto: University of Toronto Press, 1998), pp. 32–52.

46 There is an extensive literature in law and public finance on UT+FA and how it compares to separate entity accounting. For an overview, see e.g. Michael J. Graetz, *Foundations of International Income Taxation* (New York: Foundation Press, 2003), pp. 400–35.

47 See Convention on the Prevention and Punishment of the Crime of Genocide, art. 2 (December 9, 1948, UN General Assembly Resolution 260).

48 Bernhard Zangl, "Judicialization matters! A comparison of dispute settlement under GATT and the WTO," *International Studies Quarterly*, 52 (2008), 825–54 at pp. 840–1.

49 For a description of the WTO dispute settlement process, see e.g. ibid.

50 We thank an anonymous referee for pushing us to address this issue.

51 See e.g. OECD, *Harmful Tax Competition*; OECD, "The Global Forum on Transparency and Exchange of Information for Tax Purposes," *Information Brief* (Paris: OECD, 2011).

52 For more on automatic and multilateral exchange of tax information, see David Spencer, "Tax information exchange and bank secrecy," *Journal of International Taxation*, 16 (2005), 22–30; Ronen Palan, Richard Murphy and Christian Chavagneux, *Tax Havens* (Ithaca, NY: Cornell University Press, 2010), pp. 244–5.

53 For a fuller consideration of these issues and a more detailed account of the OECD project, see e.g. Rixen, *The Political Economy of International Tax Governance*, pp. 130–42; Sharman, *Havens in a Storm*; Rixen, "From double tax."

54 Philipp Genschel, Achim Kemmerling and Eric Seils, "Accelerating downhill: how the EU shapes corporate tax competition in the single market," *Journal of Common Market Studies*, 49 (2011), 1–22 at pp. 12–3.

55 European Commission, "Council directive on a common consolidated corporate tax base (CCCTB)," COM(2011) 121/4.

56 Thomas Rixen and Peter Schwarz, "How effective is the European Union's Savings Tax Directive? Evidence from four EU member states," *Journal of Common Market Studies*, 50 (2012), 151–68.

57 As an anonymous referee rightly emphasized, the general analysis of feasibility should also be sensitive to issues of trajectory, that is, questions regarding the (dis)incentives different countries have to accept or promote a multilateral regulatory framework of international taxation. We bracket this issue here.

58 Bruno S. Frey and Reiner Eichenberger, "To harmonize or to compete? That's not the question," *Journal of Public Economics*, 60 (1996), 335–49.

59 Note that these fiscal externalities suffice to impose some of the discipline in government spending that some theorists see as one of the important advantages of tax competition. See for instance Geoffrey Brennan and James M. Buchanan, *The Power to Tax* (Cambridge: Cambridge University Press 1980).

60 Thomas W. Pogge, "Cosmopolitanism and sovereignty," *Ethics*, 103 (1992), 48–75 at p. 49.

61 Ibid.

62 They include: Charles Beitz, *Political Theory and International Relations* (Princeton, NJ: Princeton University Press, 1999); Simon Caney, *Justice Beyond Borders: A Global Political Theory* (Oxford: Oxford University Press, 2006); Thomas Pogge, *World Poverty and Human Rights* (Cambridge: Polity Press, 2008).

63 Simon Caney, "Cosmopolitan justice and institutional design: an egalitarian liberal conception of global governance," *Social Theory and Practice*, 32 (2006), 725–56 defends an argument of this sort.

64 Robert E. Goodin, "What is so special about our fellow countrymen?" *Ethics*, 98 (1988), 663–86 at p. 681.

65 These are some of the classic reasons given for a federal structure. See e.g. Andreas Follesdal, "Federal inequality among equals: a contractualist defense," *Global Justice*, ed. T. Pogge (Oxford: Blackwell, 2001), pp. 242–61 at pp. 251–53; Wallace E. Oates, "An essay on fiscal federalism," *Journal of Economic Literature*, 37 (1999), 1120–49. In addition, the existence of several smaller units allows for different experiments of life.

66 See for instance the following two review articles: Simon Caney, "International distributive justice," *Political Studies*, 49 (2001), 974–97 and Philippe van Parijs, "International distributive justice," *A Companion to Contemporary Political Philosophy*, ed. R. E. Goodin, P. Pettit, and T. Pogge (Oxford: Blackwell, 2007), pp. 638–52.

67 John Rawls defines the basic structure of society as "the way in which the major social institutions distribute fundamental rights and duties and determine the division of advantages from social cooperation"; *A Theory of Justice* (Oxford, Oxford University Press, 1999), p. 6. Here, we are interested in the *global* basic structure.

68 See for example, Andrea Sangiovanni, "Global justice, reciprocity, and the state," *Philosophy & Public Affairs*, 35 (2007), 1–39; Saladin Meckled-Garcia, "On the very idea of cosmopolitan justice: constructivism and international agency," *Journal of Political Philosophy*, 16 (2008), 245–71. While we distance ourselves from one aspect of their position here, a lot more would have to be said to do their contributions justice.

69 Cf. Andreas Follesdal, "The distributive justice of a global basic structure: A category mistake?" *Politics, Philosophy & Economics*, 10 (2011), 46–65.

70 Ronzoni, "The global order," p. 243.

71 Ibid, pp. 248–49.

6

Sovereign Debt, Human Rights, and Policy Conditionality*

Christian Barry

International policies often make the conferral of aid, debt relief, or additional trading opportunities to a country depend upon its having successfully implemented specific policies, achieved certain social or economic outcomes, or demonstrated a commitment to conducting itself in specified ways. Such policies are *conditionality arrangements*.[1] My aim in this article is to explore whether conditionality arrangements that would make the conferral of debt relief depend on whether the debtor country achieves a certain status with respect to the human rights fulfilment of its population can be justified. I argue that many objections that are typically advanced against conditionality arrangements are unconvincing, and that the possible benefits of human rights conditionality are sufficient to warrant serious intellectual and practical exploration. Whether or not particular arrangements are justified cannot be determined in advance of such exploration.

I. Human Rights Concerns About Sovereign Debt

A. Human rights

Let us say that a person's human rights are *fulfilled* when she has access to the natural and social resources that are ordinarily required for persons to achieve a level of civic status and standard of living that are *minimally* adequate, and when her access to these resources is secure. A person's human rights *claims* are claims that social affairs be arranged so that they have

Political Theory Without Borders, First Edition. Edited by Robert E. Goodin and James S. Fishkin.
© 2016 John Wiley & Sons, Inc. Published 2016 by John Wiley & Sons, Inc.

access to these resources, and that this access be secure. I will refer to cases in which people fail to command the resources ordinarily required to achieve a minimally adequate level of civic status and standard of living, or where their command over such resources is insecure, as human rights *underfulfilment.*

For a person to achieve a minimally adequate level of civic status and standard of living is generally thought to involve her being protected from various forms of mistreatment, such as slavery, torture, arbitrary arrest, and egregious forms of discrimination; afforded some meaningful role in shaping the policies and social institutions of the society in which she lives; having protection of freedoms (such as freedom of speech and association) that would ordinarily be required for her to play such a role; being subject to a political process that takes some account of her interests; and being able to command the basic necessities (food, drink, shelter, and so on) necessary to meet the elementary needs that all human beings have.[2]

Like any understanding of human rights, this one is hardly uncontroversial. It does not include (though it also does not rule out) the significantly more demanding standards that have been articulated in various legal human rights instruments, such as the right to vote in periodic and genuine elections, or the right to the highest attainable standard of physical and mental health.[3] It also includes more in the category of human rights than some philosophical accounts of human rights would allow. Finally, I have left open the nature of the duties correlative to human rights claims of particular persons, as well as what more precisely a minimally adequate level of civic status and standard of living consist in. Since nearly all of the issues I will discuss in the remainder of this article arise regardless of the more specific conception of human rights that is adopted, however, this understanding of human rights will suffice for my purposes.

B. Sovereign debt

Sovereign debt obtains when agents have lent resources to the national governments of sovereign states, and these agents have claims to repayment that have at least *prima facie* legal validity.[4] The claim to repayment, in turn, depends on the existence of a debt contract involving the national government and the lender.

On the borrower side, sovereign debt contracts are entered into by national governments ('sovereign debtors'). On the lender side, they are entered into by national governments ('official/bilateral creditors'), international financial institutions such as the IMF, World Bank, or regional development banks ('multilateral creditors'), or commercial banks and bondholders ('private creditors'). Until the early 1980s, private lending constituted credit extended by commercial bank syndicates, but virtually all of their claims have been passed on in the bond market. The ability of national governments to enter into debt contracts can serve an important role in the sound management of their affairs, and thus also their ability to fulfil the human rights of their populations. Governments can smooth out their spending over revenue cycles through short-term borrowing during months of revenue shortfall, and repay the debt in surplus months. By taking out short-term loans in foreign currency, they can smooth international transactions over time and thus help to limit short-term volatility in the exchange rate. Similarly, governments can maintain spending without having to raise taxes during periods of economic recession by taking out medium-term loans, which they repay in the next boom period. Governments can also borrow for investment in longer-term projects, such as improvements in infrastructure, education, and health care, without imposing the burden of financing them solely on present taxpayers. Since improvements in a country's highways or ports, schools, and hospital care, for example, benefit future taxpayers, long-term borrowing allows the government to share the present costs of such projects with future taxpayers through interest and principal repayments.

C. How debt can undermine human rights

It is hard to imagine, in the modern world at least, how most countries, whether poor or rich, could govern themselves well or reliably fulfil the human rights of their people without their national government enjoying *some* rights (though not necessarily rights of unlimited scope) to borrow in the name of their present and future citizens. Sovereign debt raises serious human rights concerns, however, when very high levels of debt significantly limit the ability of countries to manage their affairs effectively. High debt levels can limit the capacities of governments to provide the social services necessary to ensure even a minimally adequate standard of living for their people, and divert resources and energy from the pursuit of short- and long-term strategies that further their peoples' well-being. These effects are particularly acute in the poorest countries. For example, in 2000 Tanzania spent *nine times* more on debt service than on health, even though 1.6 million of its citizens lived with AIDS; in 2005, Malawi spent twice on debt servicing what it spend on public health;[5] and in 1994, payment of debt service by Mozambique surpassed its spending on health, education, police, and its judicial system *combined*.[6] But so-called middle-income countries (Turkey, Argentina, and Greece in recent years) can also be very significantly affected by their external debts. In Argentina, for example, where life expectancy at birth is 75 years and approximately 97 per cent of the population is literate, nearly half the population was pushed below the national poverty line by the severe economic crisis in 2002, the year following the debt default and

the collapse of its fixed exchange rate system.[7] Moreover, even the populations of poor and middle-income countries that are deemed not to be in
'crisis' often suffer very significant social costs as a result of the extent to
which their governments' budgets are devoted to servicing their debts.
Brazil, for example, has typically committed above 20 per cent of its fiscal
revenue to debt interest payments alone.[8] This significantly understates the
burdens imposed by these debts, since Brazil's high external debts have
helped engender even larger internal debts that have had significant negative
consequences for a great many of its people.

Economists typically caution against 'debt overhang'—the acquisition of
large debts, which creates a climate of permanent financial fragility in a
country, leaving that country in a financial and economic slump without
domestic revenue to pay for current expenditures. Because of its financial
instability, the country is deemed to be high-risk from an investment perspective. Creditors demand a higher interest rate on investment finance—if
they are willing to lend at all—since many of them may have substantial
outstanding debt claims on the country.[9] Financial crises and the debts that
often engender them can also lead the crisis countries to increased dependence
on international institutions, which arguably limits the capabilities of
their citizens to exercise any sort of meaningful control over their policies
and institutions.

II. The Claims of Creditors

Suppose that some country becomes heavily indebted, and that its
government can service its debt obligations (as contractually defined) only
by severely cutting back expenditure on education, health, and security.
Suppose further that these cutbacks will predictably lead to human rights
underfulfilment among people in its population. We would then be faced
with the question of whether the government (and ultimately, the population)
of this country ought to bear the costs of the country's earlier decision to
borrow—or whether these costs ought to be pushed onto others, such as
creditors or other agents. The answer to this question has seemed plainly
obvious to some advocates of human rights. How, they ask, can we reasonably demand that a country repay its debts when this will predictably lead
to human rights underfulfilment in its population, especially since others
(such as wealthy countries or financial institutions) could arguably bear the
financial costs of non-repayment of these debts in a way that would not lead
to comparably regrettable outcomes? Kunibert Raffer has argued, for
example, that 'one must not be forced to fulfil contracts if that leads to inhumane distress, endangers one's life or health, or violates human dignity.
Civilized laws give unconditional preference to human rights and human

dignity.'[10] This view is also endorsed by the many advocates of the Fair and Transparent Arbitration Process (FTAP), inspired by Raffer's work and modelled on Chapter 9 of the US Bankruptcy Code, which governs the bankruptcy of municipalities. The FTAP would ensure that the basic human rights (somehow understood) of citizens of debtor countries are given higher priority than creditors' rights in the management of debt crises.[11] Of course, even if it is decided that the costs of debts should not be borne entirely by the population of the indebted country, this does not mean that creditors alone should be left to absorb these losses. One could imagine a general compensation scheme, into which all countries pay according to some formula, which provides resources to heavily indebted countries to meet their debt obligations without sacrificing the provision of goods and services to their people, while also protecting to some degree the claims of the creditors.[12] It might plausibly be argued, however, that the degree to which assistance ought to be provided to heavily indebted counties should depend not only on how heavily burdened the population of the debtor country would be in absolute and relative terms were the country to pay its debts, and how costly it would be for others to offset the costs that it would otherwise face, but also upon *how the country became* heavily indebted in the first place. David Miller, for example, has recently argued that if the plight of poorer populations can be attributed in large measure to decisions for which they are responsible, this can considerably lessen the responsibilities of others to take on costs to assist them.[13]

If a country has acted negligently, either through severe imprudence or recklessness, it might therefore be argued that the costs resulting from this cannot fairly be pushed onto others, even if the country can *now* shoulder these costs with great difficulty and at significant sacrifice.[14] In short, in such cases it may be that creditors or other agents lack responsibilities to take on costs to alleviate the burdens of such debts and can permissibly demand full repayment of the loans in question. However, it seems extremely unlikely that considerations concerning national responsibility would provide grounds for concluding that the burdens resulting from sovereign indebtedness should be borne solely by the populations of the indebted countries. This is so for several reasons. First, there is a great deal of sovereign debt that cannot plausibly be characterised as resulting from the imprudence or recklessness of borrowing countries. The unstable global environment in which sovereign debtors and creditors operate produces many changes to the circumstances of debtor countries. These changes are not only impossible for debtors to control, but also quite difficult or impossible to foresee. Natural disasters or regional and global financial crises provide vivid examples of such instability.

In response to this, it may be argued that these simply are the risks of borrowing money. That is, while specific circumstances are impossible to foresee, any borrower is aware (or at least should be aware) that there are general risks that accompany borrowing money, which include the risks of financial crises and natural disasters. It is of course a common feature of contracts that those who engage in them are usually supposed to assume the risk that fulfilling the conduct that is required of them by the contract will turn out to be more difficult, and perhaps much more difficult, than anticipated.[15] However, it is also acknowledged—in morality and in law—that there are contexts in which this supposition no longer holds. For example, if an unanticipated tsunami of unprecedented ferocity, or a contagious global or regional financial crisis that no reasonable observers could have either predicted or anticipated, wreak havoc on some country's economy, these events can plausibly be viewed as falling outside the 'normal' background risks that agents ought to have considered when entering into contracts or making other financial decisions. Indeed, contract law and the law of torts have made legally relevant the distinction between ordinary and extraordinary events that lead to the non-performance of contracts or the non-payment of damages. When extraordinary events (including so-called 'acts of god') lead to non-performance of contracts, the duty to perform them is excused in many legal systems, and the contract is viewed as 'impracticable'.[16] When the performance of a contract becomes impossible for reasons other than the negligence of the contracting parties, it can sometimes be treated as void under the so-called doctrine of frustration.[17] In practice, debtor countries are often in so vulnerable a condition that refraining from entering into debt contracts with creditors (even particular creditors) is not a reasonable option for them. In domestic legal contexts, contracts of this kind are often viewed as non-binding, either because they were entered into under severe duress, or because enforcing them would be 'unconscionable'.[18]

Second, while it may seem appropriate to attribute debt crises entirely or mainly to the negligent conduct of a *country*, it may be implausible to hold the vast majority of the country's present and future people solely, mainly, or in some cases even partially liable to shoulder the costs that such crises engender. One reason for this relates to the fact that those agents who take out a loan and those who are obliged to repay it are different. It is the finance ministers and other public officials of a country's government who make the decision to borrow money in the name of the country, but it is largely present and future citizens and other subjects taxable by the government who are asked to repay it. This does not mean that the populations of countries are not ordinarily liable to repay debts accrued by their governments. Indeed, when a creditor's claims on individual agents result from decisions or policies that have been adopted by the agent's political community, and where she either played some role in choosing the policy *or* at least had her interests given adequate weight by those making the decision, there is (as David Miller and others have argued) at least a *prima facie* case for taking her to be obliged to honour them.[19] The present or past governments of many excessively indebted countries, however, are not even *minimally* representative of the interests of those they rule. They fail to give due consideration to the interests of their people, in both the making of decisions and in the decisions themselves.[20] An often-cited example is Zaire, which accumulated $12 billion in foreign debt under the dictator Mobutu Sese Seko, but there are many more.[21]

To see why debts are problematic if they arise as a result of governments failing to be minimally representative of the interests of those they rule, consider that when a state borrows, it is effectively selling a resource to the creditor, namely, the future revenues necessary to cover interest and repayment of principal. The government will in turn raise the revenues, in large measure from those subject to its taxation.[22] It is thus selling a right to part of the future taxable income of those subject to its tax authority. As with any other resource, owners retain the right to decide whether or not to sell it unless they have transferred this right to some other agent. That an agent other than the owner of some resource can have the right to sell it, or undertake binding financial decisions in the name of the owner, is commonplace. But it is normally required that agents who have such rights, such as stockbrokers or trustees, must either have been granted that right voluntarily by the owner and/or are bound by a fiduciary duty to act in the best interest of the owner. Insofar as the owner has not voluntarily granted a right to sell its resources or undertake other financial transactions in her name, under normal circumstances *no other agent* is deemed to have acquired such rights. And if agents who have been granted such a right fail to exercise it responsibly (act in breach of duty), they can be held liable (personally and/or through their employers) for damages to the owner. It is hard to see how governments that are not minimally representative of the interests of the people they rule could have acquired a right to sell part of the future incomes or other revenue sources of all persons subject to its tax authority. First, the vast majority of these persons cannot plausibly be viewed as having voluntarily conferred this right to them.[23] Second, the government has ordinarily acted in negligence of its fiduciary duties to its people. It seems quite implausible that oppressive elites should be entitled to incur debts in the names of those whom they impoverish (or worse) and bind present and future citizens of their country (along with others subject to their tax authority) to repay it.[24] And it seems equally problematic that a creditor should be permitted to provide a government with resources that there are strong reasons to believe will be used to impose significant social costs on the present and future people of that government's country. Indeed, it seems quite wrong that such creditors could *escape* responsibility for compensating for the harms (such as significant human rights underfulfilment) that they have thus enabled and in many cases benefited significantly from.

These considerations not only provide reason not to hold the populations of many debtor countries fully (and in some cases even partly) liable to shoulder the severe social costs of their excessive indebtedness, especially when these involve human rights underfulfilment, but also a reason in many instances to hold the creditors and beneficiaries of these loans responsible for shouldering the cost of some or all of them. It also provides reason to hold creditors and beneficiaries of these loans liable to compensate for whatever further costs may have been initially imposed on the citizens of the country as a result of such loans.

III. Debt Relief and Conditionality

A. Debt relief

Let us assume that some creditors and other agents have reason to take action to promote the human rights of the populations of severely indebted countries, and that others (for example, private creditors) are at the very least obliged not to enable or become complicit in their underfulfilment. How might these agents best discharge their responsibilities? One obvious suggestion is that they should offer direct and immediate debt relief to the debtor countries, thereby freeing up resources that the governments of these countries could devote towards fulfilling the human rights of their populations.

Debts are *relieved* when creditors reduce the amount of debt that they own without receiving debt service (direct payment on the debt) in return. Debt relief can occur either when the creditor simply reduces the contractual value of the debt, or when it reduces the value of the contracted debt in exchange for something other than direct payment on that debt, such as equity (in the form of rights to future resource extraction, or a stake in a government owned company or other property). The granting of debt relief, however, may not only fail to promote the fulfilment of human rights within the debtor country, but be counterproductive to this aim. The reasons for this are straightforward: it does not follow from the fact that, if some government did not pay X-amount in debt service, it *could* use the money saved to better fulfil the human rights of its population; that if this government did not pay X-amount in debt service, it *would* use the money saved to better fulfil the human rights of its population. Governments of indebted countries might not use the additional resources made available to them through debt relief to reduce these social costs, and might indeed use them instead in a way that raises these costs. This may be because the government is corrupt or otherwise inefficient in managing the provision of public resources. There is certainly reason to believe that many governments of severely indebted countries suffer from problems of these kinds, and that resources made available through relief have sometimes been wasted (or worse) for these reasons.[25] Reducing the debt burden of a country will do little to promote the fulfilment of the human rights of its population if its government uses the revenues freed up by debt relief on military equipment that does not enhance the security of its people, or to buy the latest-edition Mercedes to transport its ministers, or if its expenditures benefit only a few relatively well-off segments of the population. As a director of the Uganda Debt Network, Patrick Tumwebaze, expressed this concern, "[i]f there are no strings attached I'm afraid the money will not be useful for Uganda … It could benefit a few, those at the political helm, but not the poorest of the poor."[26]

Countries that receive debt relief may lack the infrastructure to use the resources with much effectiveness.[27] Indeed, in some cases reducing a country's debt may lead to an increase in the burdens on its population and contribute significantly in other ways to their deprivations. This would be likely to occur if the additional resources made available to a government through debt relief are used to more effectively repress minority groups, or to strengthen politically a government that might otherwise be replaced by one which would adopt much sounder economic policies.[28]

Conversely, if governments use additional resources made available through debt relief to restore public services and infrastructure, for example in health and transportation and the provision of vaccinations or school supplies, then debt relief may contribute significantly to human rights fulfillment of the population of the country.

In sum, there is no necessary connection between reduction in the contractual value of debt and reductions of the burdens borne by the populations of the indebted countries. And it seems quite wrong to relieve debt service obligations when doing so will aggravate human rights problems. If one does this knowingly, one would become complicit in enabling human rights underfulfilment, a quite serious form of wrongdoing. An important consideration in determining whether or not debt relief programs are justified at all, then, is whether and to what extent such programs reduce the human rights underfulfilment and other significant social costs that would otherwise be imposed wrongfully on the populations of highly indebted countries.

B. The prima facie case for human rights conditionality

A conditionality arrangement is an arrangement by which some agent (or set of agents) makes the conferral of some benefit to another agent (or set of agents) contingent on the latter's satisfaction of some set of conditions. A conditionality arrangement in debt relief involving two agents (creditor and debtor) obtains when the debt relief conferred to the debtor is made to depend on whether the debtor satisfies some set of condition(s). Any condition could conceivably figure in a debt relief conditionality arrangement. Typically, however, conditions in such arrangements concern different aspects of the debtor's conduct. In some cases, they refer to specific actions that debtor may undertake. In other cases, they refer to some outcome that debtor might hope to achieve through their conduct, such as reducing unemployment to some specified level, or increasing the enrolment ratio of young girls in primary education by a certain increment.

Human rights conditionality in debt relief would make the conferral of debt relief depend upon the debtor having some specified human rights *status*. This status can be understood as some function of the debtor's human rights *achievements* (for example, the extent to which the human rights of those living within its territory are fulfilled) and what might be called its human rights *efforts* (for example, the extent to which it implements, or shows evidence that it will implement in the future, a plan oriented towards fulfilling the human rights of those living in its territory).[29] In some cases, the arrangement may require that the benefits provided be used specifically ('earmarked') for policies oriented towards human rights fulfilment. The status demanded by any particular conditionality arrangement may be an admixture of achievement and effort, or may involve only one of these elements.

Prima facie, it seems plausible that human rights conditionality arrangements could contribute to debt relief that promotes the fulfilment of human rights. As noted above, there is no guarantee that reducing the contractual value of debt will lead to the reduction of human rights underfulfilment, and it may instead aggravate it. By making the provision of additional resources through debt relief available to the governments of countries *only if* these governments commit to conducting themselves in a way that is likely to promote the fulfilment of human rights, such arrangements can create incentives for these governments to respond to the urgent needs of their people. Under the rules of such arrangements, resources that would otherwise have been provided through debt relief could be withdrawn if debtor governments fail to follow through on their commitments to reducing (or at least taking steps to reduce) these underfulfilments.

IV. Objections to Conditionality in Debt Relief

We may nevertheless have compelling reasons not to institute conditionality arrangements for debt relief. This may be because such arrangements are, all things considered, relatively ineffective in achieving (or are counterproductive to) ethically valuable debt relief, or inferior to a strategy of collecting the debt service payments and then spending them oneself to fulfil the human rights of the debtor population or other people throughout the world.[30] Determining whether or not this is the case is impossible without detailed empirical investigation, and doing this is beyond the scope of this article. Instead, I will focus here on several types of argument that might be used to criticise conditionality arrangements. If any of these arguments apply to the case of human rights conditionality in debt relief, then even if such arrangements were effective in bringing about debt relief that promoted the fulfilment of human rights, we will have good reason to reject them. Conversely, if there are forms of human rights conditionality that can withstand these objections, then these initiatives warrant serious consideration. Considering these objections also helps to indentify the features that conditionality arrangements ought to have if they are to deliver on the promise of promoting human rights fulfilment.

A. Obligations to provide debt relief unconditionally

One reason why a conditionality arrangement may be deemed inappropriate is that creditors may allegedly have very weighty ethical reasons to provide debtors with the benefit of the proposed arrangement *unconditionally*. This idea can be illustrated through a simple example from another domain. Suppose that one agent, A, has acquired resources from another agent, B, to which B has a rightful claim, either by forcefully taking them from her or acquiring them from others who lacked the power to confer valid title to them. It would in this case seem quite inappropriate indeed for A to condition the transfer of these resources to B on B's having satisfied some criteria. A lacks any claim to these resources whatsoever, while B has a valid claim to them; thus A should arguably simply transfer the resources to B. It seems plausible to say that if I have stolen your watch or bought it from someone who has stolen it, then I must simply return it to you. And I must do this almost regardless of what you plan to do with your watch once you get it back. Many activists have claimed that *any* conditionality in debt relief is inappropriate for precisely this reason. They argue that, because of the considerations described earlier in this article, the resources that would be transferred to creditors in connection with many debts properly belong to the debtor countries, even if they lack a legal claim to them. Once these facts are recognised, it seems an easy route to the conclusion that the appropriate policy response is immediate and unconditional cancellation of such debts. In its Sofia Moria Declaration, for example, the government of Norway urged that, 'The UN must establish criteria for what can be characterised as illegitimate debt, and such debt must simply be cancelled.'[31]

With respect to debts to which creditors seem obviously to lack moral, if not legal, claims; it is certainly true that the creditors lack a moral right to the resources represented by payments on the debt. For this reason, it is surely not just *up to them* which conditions may be attached to the conferral of these benefits. It does not follow from this, however, that such debts should be cancelled immediately and unconditionally. There are several reasons for this. Consider first the simple case described very schematically above, in which A and B are both individual persons. If B has a rightful claim to something in A's possession, this will make many conditions that might otherwise be legitimately placed on its return seem inappropriate. It would be inappropriate, for example, if in such a case A were to require that B provide some special favours, or to offer her equity in some enterprise, before she returned her property. Nevertheless, there are still some conditions that would not seem inappropriate in this case. If A has strong evidence that B will use a returned resource to purchase a gun to hold up a storeowner, a returned cudgel to harm his children, or a returned shotgun to shoot A (or perhaps to commit suicide); he may (and indeed *must*) withhold the good until there are assurances that these harmful outcomes will not occur. The conditions might be justified in such a case if they provided the only or most reliable means of protecting A, B, or third parties from seriously harmful behaviour.

A second reason why debts should not necessarily be cancelled unconditionally relates to the fact, stressed above, that debt relief (like most aid) is typically granted to a country's government, and not directly to its people. For reasons noted earlier, making additional resources available to a country's government may not lead to its people acquiring access to these resources in any meaningful sense. Government officials and others may use these resources for their own purposes, including purposes that are contrary to the interests of vast majority of its people. Now, if it were the government rather than the people of a country that had a rightful claim to these resources, this might not seem quite so problematic. It is generally maintained, however, that insofar as 'countries' have claims to the additional resources represented by aid or debt relief, these resources properly belong to its people, and not to its government. Indeed, one of the main bases for the appeal of the claim that some sovereign debts do not give rise to morally valid claims by creditors is that these debts represent resources that the government of a country has taken unfairly from its people. And it is very often because of this that it is argued that these resources be returned to them through debt relief. If it is the people of a country that have a claim to the resources made available through debt relief, then placing conditions on when a country's government can receive these resources cannot so easily be rejected. And when the conditions—such as the human rights conditions under examination here—are oriented towards effectively ensuring that the rightful owners of these resources (that is, the people of the country) acquire access to them, it may on the contrary seem seriously objectionable if they are not instituted.

Human rights conditions are of course oriented towards ensuring that resources made available to governments will indeed be used to the benefit of their people, and in particular the poor and vulnerable. For this reason, it might seem hard to reject such conditions for the reasons examined above, even in those cases where a creditor lacks an ethical claim to the resources conferred as debt relief.

There are some human rights conditions, however, that might indeed seem inappropriate with respect to the relief of debts of this kind. Suppose, for example, that debt relief is offered to some poor democratic country only on the condition that it uses the conferred relief to improve the living standards of its very poorest people. It would seem that the debtor could plausibly argue that since the resources represented by the debt relief belong properly to its people as a whole, it would be inappropriate that such distributional constraints be imposed upon it. This argument would not necessarily be decisive, of course; particularly if it could be shown that the costs resulting from the debt have fallen particularly heavily on the less advantaged persons within the country. Still, it does seem that there should be a strong presumption against attaching conditions to the cancellation of illegitimate debts of countries that attain a human rights status that can be considered minimally adequate.

There may also be benefits which we feel ought to be provided to some agent, A, independent of any conditions, even if A does not have a claim to them. If A is dying of thirst and the only source of water available belongs to me, he may not have a legal claim to my water, but arguably I ought to give him some of it independent of his meeting any (or very nearly any) conditions. And it might similarly be argued that if the debtor country has or is at risk of a public health crisis as a result of high prevalence of HIV but is unable to purchase antiretroviral drugs because it spends resources on debt repayment, its creditors ought to relieve some of these burdens by reducing the contractual value of its debt. Here again, however, the fact that debt relief is granted to a country's government, and not directly to its people seems quite important, since the creditors would in this case seem only to have a reason to confer benefits unconditionally to the people who are put at risk by the current situation, and not to their government. And because of this, it may be quite problematic not to attach conditions to the country's government receiving debt relief when this seems the most effective way of ensuring that the benefits reach these people. If a country is granted debt relief because the resources freed up through such relief are needed to address pressing public health concerns, but its government fails to use the resources conferred to it in this way, it may in the future be wrong for creditors to fail to make future relief conditional on some demonstration of the government's commitment to using the relief to achieve this or other important ends.

B. Ethically dubious benefits

A conditionality arrangement involving the transfer of some benefit might be deemed inappropriate because there are very weighty ethical reasons against providing the benefit *whether or not* those receiving it fulfil the conditions stipulated in it. In some cases this may be because there are always very weighty ethical reasons against providing the benefit in question to another agent. This type of reason for deeming a conditionality arrangement to be problematic seems not to apply to debt relief, since surely we do not generally have weighty ethical reasons against granting to persons who presently have a legal duty to provide us with some resource the privilege of not doing so.

With respect to other benefits—for example ivory acquired through the killing of elephants—the benefits provided may involve conduct that there are weighty moral reasons against only in specific circumstances, such as when elephants are an endangered species, or can be killed only in a cruel manner.

In still other instances, the provision of the benefit may be ethically dubious not because of intrinsic features of the benefit, but because of the specific characteristics of those providing or receiving it: there may be nothing wrong in itself about transferring firearms, but there may always be very weighty moral reasons against transferring them to young children. This may also be true in cases involving collective agents. There may always be very weighty moral reasons not to provide small arms or high-tech surveillance equipment to murderous dictatorial governments or even to decent governments that lack the capacity to control the illicit acquisition and transfer of such equipment within the territory they govern.

There may be potential recipients of debt relief to whom it would be inappropriate to grant such relief because their increased command over resources could reasonably be expected to lead to significant and unjustified harm. Insofar as there are governments of this type, however, this would suggest not that human rights conditionality arrangements involving them would be objectionable, but that there are weighty reasons against granting any debt relief whatsoever to regimes of some types on human rights grounds.

It is of course true that human rights conditionality arrangements for debt relief could be problematic either because the human rights status that is demanded as a condition of debt relief is unduly minimalist, or because it is poorly conceived and thus unlikely to make any real positive difference to a country's people. For example, such arrangements might allow debt relief to a government that was making very small and half-hearted steps towards implementing protections against various forms of mistreatment and enacting social policies that would alleviate malnutrition and other severe deprivations, while at the same time also acting in ways that substantially undermined these reforms.

These considerations show not that human rights conditionality in debt relief is necessarily inappropriate, but that such arrangements must ensure that the human rights status demanded of potential debtors be such that it does not have these characteristics.

At the very minimum, human rights conditionality in debt relief ought to incorporate conditions that are sufficiently demanding (and rigorous enough in holding the debtor accountable for meeting them) that the likely effect of granting the debt relief to such debtors will not be such that human rights underfulfilment within its population is greater than it would have been without the relief. It may of course turn out that no feasible conditionality arrangement could have these features, but there is no reason to assume that this is the case.

C. Demanding ethically dubious conduct by debtor

Conditionality arrangements can also be inappropriate because the conditions that they stipulate demand that debtors do things that they ought not to do. It may be that the conduct required would be such that there are *always* very weighty moral reasons against it. It is not difficult to imagine conditionality arrangements for debt relief that could be inappropriate for this reason. An arrangement in which the creditor confers debt relief to the debtor on the condition that the debtor invades or takes steps to undermine the legitimate governments of peaceful neighbouring countries, or that it implement social and economic policies that would impose significant additional hardships on its people or the people of other countries, for example, seems to be inappropriate for this reason.

But could human rights conditionality arrangements in debt relief be deemed inappropriate on these grounds? This seems very unlikely, at least if the human rights standards incorporated into the arrangement are understood in the way described earlier in this article. After all, such arrangements would demand only that governments secure (or take sufficient steps towards securing) for their people the social and natural resources that are ordinarily required for them to achieve a civic status and standard of living that is minimally adequate. Few plausible conceptions of ethics would maintain that there are weighty moral reasons *against* a government's conducting itself in this way. In another type of case, the conduct demanded of the debtor may not be ethically objectionable in itself, but might be so under the circumstances that obtain when the arrangement is in operation. There may be nothing wrong *as such* with, for example, making cuts in governmental spending on education and health, or adopting contractionary economic policies. Indeed, such policies may be important means for some countries to balance their budgets and ensure their long-term economic stability. But there may be weighty moral reasons against undertaking such policies in some circumstances, such as when these policies seem very likely to lead avoidably to public health crises or aggravate seriously the hardships of the poor for the foreseeable future.

Could human rights conditionality arrangements be inappropriate for this reason? Some have claimed that they can, on the ground that the urgency of improving the living standards of people in poor countries requires that priority be given to rapid economic development, even though this may lead to the nonfulfilment of human rights, particularly those relating to what are sometimes called 'basic' or 'core' labour standards—specified levels of wages and working conditions that are deemed minimally adequate—or civil and political rights. The reason that is typically offered for prioritising development over fulfilment of such human rights is that promoting their fulfilment can act as an obstacle to the development process. It is sometimes even argued that development can only take place *through* the underfulfilment of such human rights.

If this charge were true, then it might plausibly be argued that policies requiring greater fulfilment of some human rights of a country as a condition for providing benefits to it might require that its government act against weighty moral reasons that apply to it. This is of course an empirical claim and, as such, it may be questioned on empirical grounds. It is far from obvious that development requires (or even permits) that any (let alone all) human rights go unfulfilled. First, the fulfilment of some human rights can plausibly be understood as constitutive of development; promoting the fulfilment of these rights is a form of promoting development itself.[32] In addition, fulfilling human rights may be instrumentally valuable because they facilitate other aspects of development. For example, the elimination of child labour may help to bring about universal basic education which may in turn help to foster economic growth, or higher wages may foster increased productivity.[33] Indeed, countries often improve their human rights fulfilment, including rights to political participation and rights to certain wages and working conditions, without any apparent impediment to their development.[34]

There is a valid concern implicit in this type of charge, however, which is that the human rights conditions incorporated in a conditionality arrangement must explicitly recognise the economic and social constraints facing potential debtors of debt relief or other benefits. The human rights standards incorporated into such arrangements ought, therefore, to be defined in way that makes it very unlikely that efforts towards their fulfilment would be likely to significantly thwart other valuable objectives. In addition, such arrangements should give explicit allowance to countries that demonstrate good faith efforts to fulfil human rights to an extent and in a manner appropriate to their level of development, even when this falls short of fulfilling them completely. Unless human rights conditionality arrangements operate in a context-sensitive manner, they are likely to be unjustified.

D. Imposing impermissible conditions

A conditionality arrangement may be inappropriate because it contains conditions that are ethically problematic even though there is nothing intrinsically wrong with the conduct that they require. There are a number of reasons why this might be so. It might be argued that requiring countries to adopt certain policies would be objectionable since they would involve 'undue meddling' in that country's affairs. There may be nothing wrong with the policies demanded in the conditions themselves, and it may indeed even be very good for the prospective beneficiary of debt relief to implement them. It may nevertheless be inappropriate for others to strongly encourage them to do so by providing them with incentives through conditionality arrangements. Such incentives might be alleged to undermine self-determination and local autonomy. This concern might seem particularly important when the prospective recipient of debt relief needs it very badly, and has few (or no) viable alternatives to entering into the agreement to obtain it. Vivien Collingwood has argued that in such contexts some conditions (such as those comprising the World Bank's conception of 'good governance') may plausibly be viewed as constituting a "form of cultural hegemony, an attempt to impose contested values on states that have not previously embraced them."[35] If Collingwood is correct, then such conditionality arrangements could plausibly be viewed as objectionable because they involve morally problematic forms of coercion.

Surely some conditionality arrangements for debt relief (including many existing conditions placed on debt relief) could plausibly be rejected for this reason. Suppose, for example, that the debtor is a poor country that is in desperate need of development finance. Assume further that the debtor's government is at least minimally representative of the interests of its people. Is it appropriate for the creditor to offer to make additional finances available to the debtor only on the condition that the debtor adopts a series of policies that would offer significant benefits to the creditor, but which would not be very likely to benefit, and may even involve some risk of harm to, the debtor's population? Is it permissible even for them to demand unwanted policy changes that are highly controversial among economists and social scientists, as often occurs at present? In such a case, the creditor may be ethically free not to offer debt relief or some other benefit to the debtor at all, and it may be perfectly reasonable for the debtor to adopt the policies specified in the conditions given the situation in which it finds itself. It may nevertheless be inappropriate for the creditor to make the adoption of such policies a condition for the provision of debt relief.

Human rights conditionality arrangements for debt relief could be regarded as objectionable in this way insofar as they employ human rights conditions that depend on highly controversial interpretations of human rights that seem closely tied to some particular cultural or political tradition. This does not show, however, that all such human rights conditionality in debt relief would be inappropriate. To avoid being objectionable for this reason, the human rights conditions incorporated in arrangements for the conferral of debt relief would need to be specified abstractly enough that they permit appropriate context-specific variation in their interpretation and application.

It is hard to see how insisting that countries must possess a certain status with respect to human rights (when human rights are understood in the way stipulated earlier in this article) could be plausibly viewed as a form of cultural hegemony. Indeed, some of these protections seem to be necessary for ensuring national self-determination and local autonomy. A society in which many persons are not afforded a meaningful role in shaping the policies and social institutions of the society in which they live is arguably not self-determining or autonomous, or at least not so in ways that are worth protecting at the expense of permitting widespread human rights underfulfilment and other significant social costs to its population. Prohibitions against various forms of mistreatment, demands that people be granted a meaningful role in shaping the affairs of their society, and that they have access to resources normally sufficient to avoid severe ill health or other deprivations, are not unique to any political tradition. Even if the explicit conditions themselves do not depend on controversial interpretations of human rights, however, they may be applied in a manner that reflects a commitment to such interpretations. To avoid being potentially objectionable for this reason, the procedures that would determine whether the conditions are met ought to be rule-based and impartial. In addition, it would be highly desirable that any agency charged with determining whether or not human rights conditions are met be widely viewed as distinct from creditor countries or countries whose governments are influenced substantially by creditors.

Any human rights conditionality in which creditors, or countries in which creditors are influential, determine whether there has been compliance with these standards and decide whether it is justified to withhold relief, would clearly lend itself to opportunistic misuse. Such opportunistic misuse would not be as readily possible in conditionality arrangements that prevented individual countries from making unilateral determinations of this kind. A transparently constituted and functioning representative body could be charged with interpreting the human rights conditions stipulated in the arrangements, as well as determining how they apply in particular cases. The findings and reasoning of the body could also be presented for public scrutiny. Approaches to fact-finding and adjudication of this kind are familiar, even if sometimes difficult to implement fully in practice. They may be found in both domestic and international settings.[36]

Another possible reason for deeming conditionality in debt relief to be inappropriate has recently been interestingly explored in different contexts by Robert Goodin.[37] If conditionality arrangements are justified, it must be justifiable to confer upon agents the power to enact such arrangements. Now, as Goodin suggests, powers are typically conferred for specific purposes that have an ethical justification—and it may be inappropriate (and indeed impermissible) for agents to whom such powers are conferred to use them for other purposes.[38] If this test of the permissible application of powers is satisfied when these powers are applied to a specific purpose, then the application of these powers to the purpose in question can be referred to as *germane*. In general, it is suggested that an agent's power should be deemed germane to some policy issue area only if one of the reasons why the agent should be granted the power would be to promote desired effects within that very policy issue area.

Goodin illustrates this idea with the example of the US ban on Cuban exports.[39] Whatever one thinks of the potential efficacy of the US ban on trade with Cuba in promoting ethically valuable outcomes, one might question whether it is legitimate to use the extension or withdrawal of rights to trade as a means of bringing about regime change (a stated aim of the trade embargo at least since the passage of the Helms-Burton act in 1996). Altering the form of government of one's trading partners simply does not, it might plausibly be argued, further the purposes that are served by granting governments the power to permit or prohibit trade. Since regime change is an objective that is arguably not germane to the purpose of granting governments powers over trade policies, rights to trade may not in his view be restricted in order to achieve this objective.

It might similarly be argued (though Goodin himself does not) that the reasons for which powers are conferred on governments to place conditions on the provision of benefits to other countries do not include the altering of the domestic policy decisions of the countries to whom such benefits might be conferred. It might be concluded that debt relief is therefore not a germane instrument to apply in attempting to influence domestic policies, and this makes conditionality agreements inappropriate. I shall call this the 'nongermaneness' ground for deeming certain conditionality arrangements in debt relief to be objectionable.

It is not difficult to think of conditionality arrangements in debt relief that might indeed be regarded as inappropriate because they are nongermane. Imagine, for example, some country offering debt relief to another only on the condition that the Prime Minister of the debtor country (herself guilty of no great misdeeds) is removed from power.

Could human rights conditionality be deemed objectionable for this reason? To answer this question requires reflection on the reasons why two distinct powers should be conferred on governments. The first is the power to confer debt relief in the first place. The second is the power to place conditions on the debt relief that one grants. One reason why the power to grant debt relief should arguably be conferred to governments and other agents is that those powers enable such actors to promote improved living standards. They may improve living standards in various ways. First, by granting debt relief, they may help restore an indebted country's economy, and to create the conditions for it to undertake needed reforms and to improve the living standards of its people, including the alleviation of human rights underfulfilment and other harms suffered by its people. Second, by granting debt relief they may increase the debt service that the indebted country can be expected to pay in the medium and long term (for all the reasons mentioned above), thus also leading to improved living standards of those (including themselves) who stand to gain from the payment of the debt. Our reason to confer to agents the power to grant privileges of nonrepayment to indebted countries is also a reason to confer upon them the power to make such relief contingent on the prospective debtors of this relief satisfying certain conditions.

As discussed above, there is no guarantee that debt relief will lead to improved living standards, and it may instead decrease them. Allowing agents to place conditions on such relief can enable them to better serve the purpose that justifies the conferral of the power to grant such relief in the first place, so long as the conditions are oriented towards improving living standards or other purposes relevant for the justification of this power, and are realised in institutional arrangements that protect against their opportunistic misuse. Second, these powers are arguably granted to governments and other agents to help ensure that the people on whose behalf they act observe ethical obligations that apply to them. Insofar as some firm, country, or other collective agent is in a position to cancel the legal obligations to repay debts to which they have no rightful claim, they have fairly compelling reasons to do so since acting otherwise could implicate their members or those they represent in unfairly harming those who are servicing these debts.

People who know (or should have known) that they are receiving resources as a result of a debtor country's having serviced such a debt can plausibly be viewed as having violated their moral duties by enabling or by becoming complicit in practices that unfairly harm others. Since governments and other collective agents can, to some extent at least, help ensure that their members do not engage in such conduct by adopting appropriate policies with respect to debt contracts, this provides a good reason to confer to them the power to set such policies.

There are similar reasons to grant some power to place conditions on the terms under which debt relief might be offered. Due to the considerations discussed earlier in this article, simply transferring benefits to the government of a country that is paying such debts unconditionally may aggravate, instead of alleviate, the human rights underfulfilment and other significant social costs borne by the country's population. If governments and other collective agents are conferred the power to place conditions on debt relief that are oriented towards making it the case that the populations of indebted countries are not harmed unduly by servicing these debts, then these agents are able to ensure that their members do not contribute to or be complicit in practices that unfairly harm others, while at the same time prevent them from contributing to significant harms of other kinds.

E. Unfair procedures

A conditionality arrangement may also be deemed inappropriate because its procedures are objectionable in various respects. There are a number of reasons why this might be so. The procedures of a conditionality arrangement may be poorly designed in a way that makes them prone to opportunistic misuse. For example, the procedures may enable creditors to delay relief that ought to be provided to debtors by arbitrarily making it harder for them to show that the conditions incorporated in the arrangement have been met. The procedures may also enable debtors to cheat creditors easily by withholding information that is relevant to determining whether the conditions have been met. This latter possibility may be of particular concern when the conditions are relevant to ensuring that the benefits provided to the debtor benefit its people and that they do not instead aggravate their hardships.

It is easy to see how conditionality arrangements in debt relief, including those involving human rights conditions, could be inappropriate for this reason. It does not follow, however, that they need be. To avoid the risk of being objectionable for this reason, the procedures that determine whether the conditions are met would need to be not only rule-based and impartial, but also have the effectively resourced capacity to ensure that abuses of these rules do not occur.

In all conditionality arrangements, some agent or set of agents will be allocated authority to determine whether or not the conditions have been met. A conditionality arrangement may involve unfair procedures if such authority is improperly allocated. Imagine, for example, a case in which a creditor lacks an ethically valid claim to repayment of some part of a country's debt. It may of course be questioned whether conditionality can be justified at all in such a case. But let us suppose (for reasons canvassed above) that at least conditions oriented towards ensuring that the population of the debtor country received the benefits of such relief were justified.

It could nevertheless be problematic that the creditor be granted authority to determine whether the conditions for debt relief were met, at least insofar as there are other reasonably reliable agents in whom such authority could be entrusted. There are several reasons for this. First, in the case imagined, the resources do not belong to the creditor, and indeed it may seem problematic that the creditor continues formally to claim title to them. Entrusting the resources, and the responsibility for setting and tracking the conditions for their conferral to the debtor country, to an independent agent or institution would not only eliminate incentives for opportunistic misuse of the arrangement by creditors or other agents, but would also make clear the nature of the entitlements to these resources. What is more, others (notably including debtor countries themselves) will have much more confidence in a conditionality arrangement if authority for implementing it lies with an independent agent rather than with creditors, particularly if the claims these creditors have to the resources are generally thought to be ethically questionable.

Under existing programs for debt cancellation for the poorest countries, such as the HIPC (Highly-Indebted Poor Countries) Initiative and Multilateral Debt Relief Initiative (which resulted from the G-8's June 2005 decision on multilateral debt cancellation), qualifying countries must have complied with IMF-designed and monitored conditionalities in order to benefit from them. While IMF conditionalities may be motivated by legitimate reasons to ensure that the cancelled resources are used for defensible purposes, they are seen as highly controversial by developing countries.[40] Instead, peer-run trust accounts that provide a check on the policies of the countries receiving the benefits—but are *not* controlled by creditors—might provide a desirable alternative.[41] As part of the condition for allowing a cancellation or reduction to go forward, a country might be required to deposit an amount equal to its monthly debt payments into this trust account, from which the money will be transparently allocated to social expenditures on poverty alleviation, health care, and education or other means of addressing human rights underfulfilment in the population of the debtor country. Since payments into the fund could be made in regular instalments, potential abuses could be halted in time with in-progress audits. A further check on the fund's spending could be provided by an independent international arbitral body. Approaches to fact-finding and adjudication of this kind are familiar, even if sometimes difficult to implement fully in practice.

V. Conclusion

To show that some particular human rights conditionality arrangement for debt relief is desirable would clearly require developing in much greater detail the characterisation of the human rights standards, the composition of the arbitral body making determinations about whether such conditions are met, and the rules according to which such a body would make its assessments, that I have provided here. It would also involve detailed empirical assessment of the likely effects of such a scheme, and of whether it would be feasible to bring about and maintain. Even if some such arrangement could be shown to be desirable, it would not follow from this that it should be made a priority for action. Still, given the severity of human rights concerns engendered by debt crises, and the real risk that granting debt relief may aggravate rather than mitigate such problems, exploring further such arrangements would be a very worthwhile practical task.

Notes

* I am indebted to Lina Eriksson, Pablo Gilabert, Matt Peterson, Thomas Pogge, Matt Ravvin, Sanjay Reddy, Jennifer Rubenstein, Lydia Tomitova, Scott Wisor, and the Editor and anonymous reviewers of this journal for critical feedback on earlier versions of this article.

1 Policy analysts sometimes distinguish between 'conditionality', which they understand as a policy in which benefits of some kind are provided to prospective recipients only on condition that they meet certain conditions, and 'selectivity', which they understand as a policy whereby prospective recipients of some benefit can expect to receive a larger amount than others depending on their satisfaction of certain conditions. In this article, I will understand conditionality as encompassing both such types of policies.

2 For further discussion of these elements, see Charles Beitz, 'Human rights as a common concern', *American Political Science Review*, 95 (2001), 269–82.

3 For a discussion of the plausibility of minimalist accounts of human rights, See Joshua Cohen, 'Minimalism about human rights: the best we can hope for?' *Journal of Political Philosophy*, 12 (2004), 190–213.

4 I assume that it makes sense to distinguish between legally valid and morally valid claims, even though determinations of legal validity may arguably partly depend on some moral considerations, and the fact that one having a legally valid claim may be seen as an important consideration in determining whether one has a morally valid claim. Conflicts between legally valid and morally valid claims and obligations will be most pronounced when legal systems are unjust or when they contain many 'gaps', but it is unlikely that such conflicts can ever be completely removed.

5 Jubilee Debt Campaign, 'Malawi', *The Debt Crisis*, <www.jubileedebtcampaign. org.uk/Malawi+3481.twl>.

6 World Health Organization, 'Debt', *Trade, Foreign Policy, Diplomacy and Health*, <www.who.int/trade/glossary/story014/en/index.html>.

7 Economic Commission on Latin America and the Caribbean, *Statistical Yearbook for Latin America and the Caribbean: 2005*, (Santiago: United Nations, 2006) table 1.6.1. More precisely, 45.4% of the urban population fell below the poverty

line—that is, had an annual income of less than twice the cost of a basic food basket—in 2002, roughly double what it had been in 1990.

8 As the Economist Intelligence Unit notes: 'The share of fiscal revenue absorbed by debt interest payments in Brazil is particularly striking considering that the country's tax burden, at more than 35% of GDP, is one of the highest among emerging markets and close to the levels typical of more developed countries.' Economist Intelligence Unit, 'Brazil finance: is it investment grade?' *Views Wire*, 23 May, 2007, <www.viewswire.com/index.asp?layout=VWArticleVW3&article_id=1542214339&rf=0>.

9 As discussed in Thomas Palley, 'Sovereign debt restructuring proposals: a comparative look', *Ethics & International Affairs*, 17 (2003), 26–33.

10 Kunibert Raffer, 'Risks of lending and liability of lenders', *Ethics & International Affairs*, 21 (2007), 85–106.

11 See, for example, Erlassjahr, 'A fair and transparent arbitration process for indebted southern countries', *Updated Submission to Financing for Development*, September 2001, <www.erlassjahr. de/content/languages/englisch/dokumente/ftap_englisch_rz.pdf>.

12 Needless to say, such a scheme could also create undesirable incentives, since it would reduce the risk to creditors of extending loans.

13 See David Miller, 'Justice and global inequality', *Inequality, Globalization and World Politics*, ed. A. Hurrell and N. Woods (Oxford: Oxford University Press, 1999), pp. 187–210; *National Responsibility and Global Justice* (Oxford: Oxford University Press, 2007).

14 The intuition here factors prominently in John Rawls, *The Law of Peoples* (Cambridge, MA: Harvard University Press, 2001), esp. pp. 117–18.

15 See, for discussion, Peter S. Atiyah, *Introduction to the Law of Contract*, 5th ed. (Oxford: Oxford University Press, 1995), esp. pp. 212–15.

16 For discussion of such measures, see Alan O. Sykes, 'The doctrine of commercial impracticability in a second-best world', *Journal of Legal Studies*, 19 (1990), 43–94; Richard A. Posner and Andrew M. Rosenfield, 'Impossibility and related doctrines in contract law: an economic analysis', *Journal of Legal Studies*, 6 (1977), 83–118.

17 For discussion, see Atiyah, *Introduction to the Law of Contract*, pp. 229–44.

18 It is worth noting that the domestic law of many countries has traditionally regarded with great suspicion loans to poor persons in distress, such as by payday lenders or check cashers. See, for discussion, John Cartwright, *Unequal Bargaining: A Study of Vitiating Factors in the Formation of Contracts* (Oxford: Clarendon Press, 1991).

19 See David Miller, 'Justice and global inequality' and *National Responsibility and Global Justice*.

20 Cohen, 'Minimalism about human rights: the best we can hope for?'

21 Cf. Michael Kremer and Seema Jayachandran, 'Odious debt', *Policy Brief 103*, (Brookings Institution: Washington, D.C., 2002), <www.brookings.edu/comm/policybriefs/pb103.htm>. A good case can be made that many of the 40-odd countries in the Highly Indebted Poor Countries (HIPC) Initiative fall into this category.

22 Alternatively, governments may repay debts from other revenue streams that might otherwise be allocated toward public spending.

23 For a related discussion of the considerations relevant to determining whether a government should have the right to sell natural resources, see Leif Wenar, 'Property rights and the resource curse', *Philosophy and Public Affairs*, 36 (2008), 2–32.

24 For discussion, see Thomas Pogge, 'Achieving democracy', *Ethics & International Affairs*, 15 (2001), 3–23; Ashfaq Khalfan, Jeff King and Bryan Thomas, 'Advancing the odious debt doctrine', *Centre for International Sustainable Development Law* (working paper, McGill University, Montreal, 11 March 2003); Jonathan Shafter, 'The due diligence model: a new approach to the problem of odious debts', *Ethics & International Affairs*, 20 (2007), 49–67.

25 Given the fungibility of resources, speaking of what is done with 'the' resources made available through debt relief is problematic but I will ignore this complexity here.

26 Quoted in Andrew England, 'Concern grows over "no-strings" debt relief', *Financial Times*, 18 January 2006, <www.ft.com/cms/s/0/25fa7e76-87c8-11da-8762-0000779e2340.html>.

27 For arguments to the effect that many indebted countries lack such capacity, see William Easterly, 'Think again: debt relief', *Foreign Policy*, 127 (2001), 20–6.

28 These kinds of effects are widely recognised with respect to foreign aid flows, but tend to be neglected in discussions of debt relief.

29 Governments may of course also be required to make efforts to fulfil the human rights of those outside of their territory, for example by ceasing unjustified military aggression, advocating fairer international institutions, or providing assistance to countries unable to provide their people with an adequate standard of living.

30 For some reasons why this might be so, see Tony Killick, 'Principals, agents and the failings of conditionality', *Journal of International Development*, 9 (1997), 483–95.

31 Office of the Prime Minister, Government of Norway, 'The Soria Moria declaration on international policy', <http://www.regjeringen.no/en/dep/smk/documents/Reports-and-action-plans/rapporter/2005/The-Soria-Moria-Declaration-on-Internati.html?id=438515>. This view is widely endorsed by debt relief campaigns throughout the world.

32 As argued in Amartya Sen, *Development as Freedom* (New York: Knopf, 1999).

33 See, for example, Partha Dasgupta and Debraj Ray, 'Inequality as a determinant of malnutrition and unemployment: policy', *Economic Journal*, 97 (1987), 177–88; Ross Levine and David Renelt, 'A sensitivity analysis of cross-country growth regressions', *American Economic Review*, 82 (1992), 942–63.

34 See, for example, Dani Rodrik, *The New Global Economy and Developing Countries: Making Openness Work* (Washington, DC: Overseas Development Council, 1999). It has been argued that governmental enforcement of labour standards has created incentives for technological and organisational innovation and thereby enhanced economic growth in Europe and the United States. See, for example, Michael J. Piore's discussion of the nineteenth-century US textile

industry in 'International labor standards and business strategies', *International Labor Standards and Global Integration: Proceedings of a Symposium*, ed. US Department of Labor (Washington, DC: US Department of Labor, 1994), pp. 21–25.

35 See Vivien Collingwood, 'Aid with fewer strings attached', *Ethics & International Affairs*, 17 (2004), 55–67.

36 Examples include the National Labor Relations Board in the United States and comparable bodies in other countries, the WTO's Dispute Settlement Body (DSB), existing free trade agreements with labour provisions such as the US-Jordan Free Trade Agreement, the North American Agreement on Labor Cooperation, and the Canada-Chile Free Trade Agreement.

37 Robert E. Goodin, 'Support with strings: workfare as an "impermissible condition" ', *Journal of Applied Philosophy*, 21 (2004), 297–308.

38 Ibid., p. 301.

39 See Robert E. Goodin's comment, 'The ethics of political linkage', in Christian Barry and Sanjay Reddy, *International Trade and Labor Standards: A Proposal for Linkage* (New York: Columbia University Press, 2008), pp. 127–34. My discussion here draws on that work.

40 The conditions imposed on loans and debt relief by the IMF and World Bank have ordinarily been based on economic and fiscal performance, and do not (and may not) make explicit reference to human rights.

41 This proposal is outlined in Noreena Hertz, *The Debt Threat: How Debt Is Destroying the Developing World* (New York: Harper Business, 2004); Sony Kapoor, 'Unblocking the path to broader debt cancellation using trust funds', *Ethics and Debt Conference* (working paper, New School, New York, NY, November 2005).

7

Justice in the Diffusion of Innovation

Allen Buchanan, Tony Cole and Robert O. Keohane

Contemporary theorists of distributive justice do not make the mistake of thinking that the problem of justice is that of fairly dividing a fixed stock of goods. They acknowledge that what is available to distribute changes as our productive capacities develop, that what is produced and how much is produced are subject, within constraints, to choices that human beings make, and that these choices should be guided by principles of justice. To that extent, their views are at least *consistent* with a remarkable fact about modern society: the prominence of innovation in our lives, especially in the form of new technologies developed through the application of scientific knowledge. Yet the significance of innovation for justice—the opportunities for promoting justice that it creates, and the risks of injustice that it poses—has not been adequately appreciated by theorists of justice.[1]

In section I of this article, we explain why a theory of justice must take the fact of innovation seriously and focus attention on one important problem of justice in innovation: the fact that when powerful innovations do not diffuse widely, but are available only to some, this creates opportunities for domination and exclusion. In section II, we advance a proposal for a new international institution designed to ameliorate this problem. In section III, we strengthen the case for our proposal by comparing it both to the status quo and to a prominent proposal for international institutional change advanced by Thomas Pogge. Section IV explains how our proposal could be integrated into existing international law. Our aim is not to provide a

Political Theory Without Borders, First Edition. Edited by Robert E. Goodin and James S. Fishkin.
© 2016 John Wiley & Sons, Inc. Published 2016 by John Wiley & Sons, Inc.

full-blown theory of justice in innovation or a detailed blueprint for its institutional embodiment. Instead, it is to bring innovation to center stage in thinking about justice, to demonstrate that serious efforts to achieve justice in innovation will require institutional innovation, and to stimulate deeper consideration of the issues we address by articulating a concrete institutional proposal.

I. Toward a Theory of Justice in Innovation

A. The need for an account of justice in innovation

Innovation is significant from the standpoint of justice because it can have either positive or negative effects on justice. Depending on what is created and to whom it becomes available, innovation can worsen existing injustices or create new injustices, or it can lessen existing injustices. Justice in innovation is not restricted to the just distribution of *existing* beneficial innovations for two reasons. First, as the much-discussed case of essential medicines makes clear, the fact that vitally important innovations are *not* occurring can be a concern of justice. Because of lack of market demand in developing countries, medicines that could save the lives of millions of people in these countries, at relatively low cost, may not be developed. If justice implies a human right to healthcare (even of a rather limited sort), this situation is not merely unfortunate, but unjust. Second, if restricted access to important innovations resulted in unjust inequalities of political power or in other forms of wrongful domination, this may contribute to injustices of other sorts.

One final, less obvious connection between justice and innovation is worth considering. In extreme cases the effect of limited access to the innovation would be a concern of justice if those who lacked access were excluded from participation in the most important forms of cooperative interaction. To understand this possibility, consider the much-discussed possibilities of biomedical enhancements of normal human capacities, using an analogy with disability rights. The Americans with Disabilities Act requires that "reasonable accommodation" be made to the special needs of persons with disabilities. For example, in public buildings, such as courthouses, curb brakes and ramps must be provided so that persons in wheelchairs can have access. Suppose that the cumulative effect of a number of biomedical enhancements, including significant enhancements in cognitive capacities and capacities for communication and coordination, was to enable those who had them to interact with other 'enhanced cooperators' in a new, more complex, and extremely productive kind of economic cooperation. If most people became 'enhanced cooperators' but some did not, the unenhanced might be unable to participate, or only able to participate in a minimally competent way, in the most important forms of cooperation in their society. They would in effect be the newly disabled. If the exclusion of people with physical disabilities from important sites of interaction is a matter of justice—a question of their *rights*, not just a matter of charity—then exclusion due to lack of access to powerful innovations would seem to be a matter of justice as well.

Given these possibilities, it is clear that taking the fact of innovation seriously in theorizing about justice requires not only including the products of innovation as subject to principles of just distribution, but also efforts to influence which innovations occur. Such efforts may be needed both to prevent innovations that would worsen existing injustices or create new injustices, and to encourage innovations that would lessen existing injustices. Accordingly, we can define 'justice in innovation' as the conformity of both the distribution of the fruits of the processes of innovation, and of the character of the innovation process itself, to the requirements of justice. Justice in innovation may require a pro-active stance: that is, it may be necessary to shape the innovation process in the name of justice, either to try to avoid the production of justice-degrading new technologies or to harness the innovation process for the purpose of promoting justice.

B. How innovation can promote justice

To the extent that thinking about justice has focused on innovation, concern about the negative impact of innovation on justice has been prevalent. Some observers have worried that if biomedical enhancements of normal human capacities become available to some but not all, this will worsen existing injustices. For example, genetic enhancements are likely to be affordable, at least at first, only to those who already benefit from injustices in the distribution of social goods.[2] Similarly, "the digital divide"—the fact that some people lack access to computers—can itself contribute to political and social inequality and may also exacerbate existing injustices in the distribution of other goods, including wealth.

Less attention has been given to the potential of innovation for promoting justice. To correct this imbalance, we offer the following examples of technological innovations that may have significant justice-*promoting* effects. In each case the innovation in question could be seen as promoting justice by reducing unjust advantages that some people enjoy or by empowering individuals so that they can better exercise their rights.

1   Some cognitive enhancement drugs are most efficacious for the less bright; to the extent that existing social arrangements unfairly disadvantage those with lower intelligence or lower intelligence results in part

from socio-economic injustices, making such drugs available to the latter could be justice-promoting.[3] Such pharmaceutical cognitive enhancements might prove more cost-effective than some educational interventions.

2   Cheap calculators help "level the playing field" for those who are mathematically challenged, thus reducing injustices that may arise from the ways in which society rewards those with superior math skills, or penalizes those who lack them.

3   Medical innovations can remove disabilities that interfere with opportunities individuals ought to have as a matter of justice or that prevent them from exercising their rights.

4   Cell phones allow cheap, rapid coordination of economic and political activities; this can help people to lift themselves out of poverty and enable them to exercise their rights of political participation more effectively.

5   Internet access to medical information reduces knowledge asymmetries between physicians and patients and this in turn can reduce the risk that patients' rights will be violated.

6   Cell phone cameras provide checks on police behavior, thus helping to reduce violations of civil and political rights or at least facilitate remedial action when they occur.

C. Disagreement and uncertainty about justice

Each of the preceding six innovations appears to reduce certain *inequalities*, but not all inequalities are *injustices*. To know which inequalities are unjust, and hence whether particular innovations are impacting justice positively or negatively, one needs an account of justice. Theorizing about justice is notoriously afflicted, however, with both disagreement and uncertainty. There is disagreement between consequentalists and deontologists, between proponents of 'positive' rights and libertarians, between egalitarians, prioritarians, and sufficientarians, and among egalitarians as to what the 'currency' of egalitarian justice is (well-being, opportunity for well-being, or resources). In addition, there is uncertainty as to how to move from a given theory's abstract, highest-level principles to lower-level principles with clearer implications for policies and institutions. For example, even if one assumes one knows what the proper principles of distributive justice are for what Rawls calls the basic structure of society, it is not clear which principles of justice should guide particular policies or decisions about rationing scarce medical resources.[4] Given that there is no indication that this disagreement and uncertainty is likely to be resolved in the foreseeable future—how should thinking about justice in innovation proceed? How *can* it proceed in a principled way?

D. A provisional starting-point: The injustice of extreme deprivation

Most theories of justice converge on the belief that what might be called extreme deprivation is presumptively unjust, at least when it is undeserved and unchosen. People suffer extreme deprivation when they lack adequate food, shelter, safe drinking water, are afflicted with serious preventable diseases, and when their physical security is seriously compromised by the threat of violence, as in the case of civilians in war zones.

We proceed on the assumption that whatever else it should be concerned with, a theory of justice in innovation should treat extreme deprivation as a matter of concern, in two ways: It should provide guidance both for reducing the risk that innovations will produce or exacerbate extreme deprivations and for helping to ensure that the power to innovate will be harnessed to help ameliorate existing extreme deprivations. The strategy is to consider policies regarding innovation that address the concern about extreme deprivation, without waiting for a resolution of the disagreement and uncertainty that characterize current theorizing about justice. Surely there is enough agreement that some harms should be included to allow us begin to grapple with the problem of justice in innovation.

E. Exclusion and domination

To focus *only* on extreme deprivation, however, is too restrictive, for reasons already indicated: it overlooks the fact that innovation can be a concern of justice when limited access to innovations results in unjust exclusion or domination. The analogy with disability rights shows that unjust exclusion can occur without severe deprivation and that these are distinct injustices. Even if a person with mobility limitations is not impoverished and leads an otherwise comfortable life, she may rightly complain of injustice if she is barred from access to public buildings.[5]

Political inequalities can also be unjust even when they do not result in extreme deprivation. The fact that women in the U.S. lacked the right to vote until 1920 was an injustice, apart from whatever contribution it made to the extreme deprivation that some women suffered. Similarly, if some innovation in electronic communications conferred advantages in influencing national political processes, in ways that are incompatible with the commitment to broad effective political participation embodied in democratic institutions, this would be an injustice, even if those who were disadvantaged suffered no extreme deprivation.

Some inequalities in political power are inevitable even in the most democratic societies; and some inequalities in political power are not unjust, including those that result from special excellence in the qualities of political leadership. But under modern conditions, in which the State wields such great power over our lives, inequalities in political power have the potential to exacerbate existing injustices and undermine justice where it exists.[6] So political inequality is a proper *concern* of justice even if the people involved are integrated into the society and political inequality is not in itself unjust.[7] Both instrumental considerations grounded in the strategic nature of political inequalities and views according to which political equality is valuable in itself converge on the conclusion that political inequalities are a proper concern of justice, independently of their propensity to create or sustain extreme deprivation. For brevity, we will use the phrase 'basic political and economic inequalities', not to refer to just any unequal distribution but only to (a) seriously unjust inequalities in political power and (b) lack of access to important sites and forms of social cooperation that is of comparable consequence to the exclusion suffered by persons with disabilities in societies that do not take disability rights seriously. Our suggestion is that an account of justice in innovation should not be limited to a concern about extreme deprivation, but should also address the potential impact of innovation on 'basic political and economic inequality' understood in this way.

It could be argued that the impact of innovation on extreme deprivations is a higher priority, from the standpoint of justice, than the impact on basic economic and political inequality. Whether or not that is so may depend upon the resolution of deep disputes in the theory of justice—in particular whether some form of prioritarianism is the correct view. We have already explained why we think it is appropriate to avoid attempts to resolve such disputes before embarking on an attempt to develop a principled practical response to the issues of justice in innovation.

From the standpoint of many persons in developing countries, the main concern about innovation is its potential impact on extreme deprivation, but for most of those who live in developed countries the impact on basic political and economic inequalities may be more pressing. Given that this is so, there are two reasons to include basic economic and political inequality, not just deprivation, in our provisional conception of justice in innovation. First, it is a *legitimate* concern for people generally, regardless of whether they live in developed or developing countries, even if deprivation is the more serious moral concern. Second, practical thinking about justice in innovation must take the problem of political feasibility seriously, and generally that requires engaging the interests of the better off. An approach to justice in innovation that focuses not only on deprivation but also on basic social and political inequalities is more likely to gain the support of those who are critical for its success.

The threads of the argument thus far can now be pulled together. Because of the prominence of innovation in modern life, thinking about justice should take seriously the potential of innovations both to worsen injustices and to ameliorate them. We begin with undeserved and unchosen severe deprivation, but expand this narrow focus to encompass 'basic political and economic inequalities'— seriously unjust inequalities in political power and exclusion from the most important sites and forms of productive cooperation.

F. Types of institutional strategies

There are three basic types of institutional strategies for the pursuit of justice in innovation: (1) *prohibition* of innovations that would worsen existing injustices or create new injustices; (2) *creation* of innovations to ameliorate existing injustices; and (3) *diffusion* of innovations in order to avoid injustices that would arise from differential access to them or to promote justice by ameliorating or removing existing unjust disadvantages.

i. Prohibition   Voluntary abstention from the development and diffusion of valuable innovations would likely fail, due to familiar free-rider and assurance problems, and is also in tension with the scientific ethos of discovery. Regulation (coercively-backed prohibitions) to try to stop development and/or diffusion of innovations thought to have unjust inequality-increasing effects is hardly more promising, for at least two reasons. First, the innovation process is by its nature highly unpredictable and the effects of an innovation on justice, whether for good or for ill, may be especially hard to predict. Consequently, a coercively-backed prohibition strategy might deprive us of valuable innovations that would turn out to be consistent with the demands of justice or which might even promote justice. Second, if a certain line of research and development is prohibited in one country or regional governance regime (such as the European Union), it is likely to be taken up in less regulated locales, as has happened across a wide range of cases, including gene therapy and human embryonic stem cell research. For a number of reasons, including the lack of regulatory capacity in many countries, an effective, world-wide scheme of regulatory prohibition, while conceivable in principle, is unlikely in the foreseeable future.

ii. Creation   There are many examples of private and government efforts to spur innovations of various sorts, such as research grants, government contracts, and public and private prizes. Few of these efforts are explicitly directed toward issues of justice in innovation. An exception may be the U.S. Orphan Drug Act, which provides research grants and extended patent life for drugs developed to treat serious diseases that afflict small numbers of people. One plausible interpretation of the purpose of this legislation is that it is designed to ameliorate the unfairness of a situation in which the direction of drug research and development is determined by market demand rather than need, to the life-threatening disadvantage of those with rare diseases. Several more recent proposals to ameliorate the "essential medicines" problem, including one by the philosopher Thomas Pogge which we consider in detail below, can also be seen as efforts to stimulate the creation of drugs for the purpose of promoting justice. We will use the term "the Creation Problem" to refer to obstacles to the creation of innovations designed to address injustices, including unprofitability under standard market conditions.

iii. Diffusion   Limited or slow diffusion of a beneficial innovation can be problematic from the standpoint of justice for either or both of two reasons: once created, innovations do not mitigate problems of inequality unless they are diffused widely to the disadvantaged; and if diffusion is too limited or occurs too slowly it may actually produce new injustices, either by giving unacceptable advantages in political power to those who do have access to them or in excluding those who lack access to them from important sites or forms of economic cooperation. For convenience, we will use the term 'the Diffusion Problem' to refer to both of these phenomena.

A wide range of existing programs, projects, and organizations can be seen as exemplifying the strategy of promoting the diffusion of technologies in order to avoid or mitigate injustices due to lack of access or to promote justice by removing existing unjust disadvantages. An illustrative list might include the following.

1   Private and government efforts to bridge the "digital divide" by providing subsidized or free computers, high-speed and/or wireless internet service, etc.
2   Private and government programs designed to diffuse more widely the extremely valuable cognitive enhancement technology commonly known as literacy.
3   Vaccine delivery programs in less developed countries, where infectious diseases are still a major contributor to childhood mortality.
4   Donation or reduced pricing of "essential medicines" through arrangements between governments and pharmaceutical companies (in particular, anti-retroviral HIV-AIDS medications).
5   'Compulsory Licensing', as recognized by the WTO's Doha Declaration on TRIPS and Public Health, which acknowledges the right of States to grant licenses for producing essential medicines without the permission of IPR-holders, if certain standards are met.

These examples of diffusion policies are not part of an overall strategy formulated in response to the articulation of goals of justice in innovation.

Instead, they reflect an uncoordinated, piecemeal approach. In the next section, we outline a systematic proposal for promoting justice in innovation that emphasizes the Diffusion Problem, but also does something to address the Creation Problem. The core of this proposal is a new institution—the Global Institute for Justice in Innovation. The proposal focuses on one important impediment to diffusion: the monopoly pricing that results from the current intellectual property rights (IPR) regime.[8] Our proposal is to modify the IPR regime in a way that preserves its valuable functions while remedying or at least significantly ameliorating its institutional failures.

II. The Global Institute for Justice in Innovation

The Global Institute for Justice in Innovation (GIJI) would be an international organization designed to construct and implement a set of rules and policies governing the diffusion of innovations, on the basis of a sound set of principles. It would operate under conditions of accountability, according to rule-governed procedures, and would seek gradually to inculcate norms that specified appropriate behavior with respect to the diffusion of innovations.[9] The GIJI would be created by a multilateral treaty, with permanent staff, and international legal authority to make decisions that would not automatically be incorporated into the domestic law of its member States, but would only become enforceable as a result of political and constitutional processes undertaken by each Member State. In this sense, the GIJI would be similar to the World Trade Organization (WTO), the rules of which are directly effective only on the international level, rather than the European Union, which requires as a condition of membership that certain rules be directly applicable in domestic legal proceedings. Such an arrangement would limit the sovereignty costs of the GIJI.

A subsidiary activity of the GIJI would be to encourage the creation of useful innovations, for example through prizes and grants for justice-promoting innovations and through offering extended patent life for innovations that have a positive impact on justice. But its major efforts would be directed toward the wider and faster diffusion of innovations in order to ameliorate extreme deprivations and reduce their negative impact on basic political and economic inequalities, as defined in section I above.

The GIJI would actively promote diffusion entrepreneurship, that is, efforts by NGOs and others to accelerate the diffusion of justice-promoting innovations. Indeed, the GIJI could give awards or prizes to firms that had consistently exceeded its diffusion standards, thus providing the firms with reputational benefits.[10] Its most important asset, however, would be what we will term a "licensing option," under which the GIJI would authorize compulsory licensing on a country-by-country basis of innovations that are diffusing too slowly. "Too slowly" here means that the innovations are failing to realize their potential for making significant gains in promoting justice or are exacerbating existing injustices, in the form of extreme deprivation or basic political and economic inequalities.

Member governments of the GIJI would enact legislation authorizing the relevant domestic authorities to initiate administrative actions to issue compulsory licenses for intellectual property as authorized by the GIJI. Since this proposal to allow centrally-directed compulsory licensing of intellectual property in these cases is, to our knowledge, a new idea, we will focus on it in what follows.

A. The licensing option

Licenses would be granted to firms or other entities selected by the GIJI free of charge or for nominal fees, and would be distributed so as to reduce the price of the innovation to competitive levels. Thus, if the current slow diffusion of the product is due to monopoly pricing, freely distributing the license would accelerate diffusion. Some innovations, however, diffuse slowly because they are of little value. This is why the GIJI would have a licensing *option*. It would only act where there is evidence that the obstacle to diffusion would be removed by authorizing compulsory licenses and creating a competitive market for the innovation in question.

It is important to understand the political implications of the GIJI's authorization option. Without imposing supranational authority over governments, such authorization would render mandatory licensing by a developing country internationally legitimate. In view of the broadly representative nature of the authorizing body, to be discussed in more detail below, it would be hard for companies, in such a situation, to claim unfairness. The GIJI would therefore greatly strengthen the bargaining position of countries that had well-founded claims of insufficient diffusion. At the same time, however, it would protect firms against attempts by opportunistic governments to abuse compulsory licensing by seizing private property. This proposal, therefore, does not try to suppress or avoid politics (a quixotic venture in international relations) but to shape politics in desirable ways.

If the GIJI's threat to authorize mandatory licensing has sufficient credibility, and imposes sufficiently high threat of loss on the firm, exercise of the GIJI licensing option should be a rare event. The threat of mandatory licensing would deter producers from exercising the capacity for monopoly pricing that intellectual property rights (IPR) confer. Producers would know that they can keep their full IPR by refraining from monopoly pricing in the case of innovations whose slow diffusion would have a negative impact on justice. Producers would know that they could avoid the negative publicity of being warned about mandatory licensing, and could receive public praise and reward (through the prizes and grants policy), if they act in ways that promote justice. Over time, this array of incentives could help foster the norm of taking justice into account in the innovation process.

B. Stages of intervention

Exercise of the licensing option would be a last resort. The GIJI would construct a "watchlist" of innovations that warrant scrutiny from the standpoint of inadequate diffusion. Producers of innovations on the "watchlist" would be notified, without public announcement, that they are on it and that if diffusion does not improve, a *publicized* warning of potential liability to mandatory licensing will be issued in due course. If there is no significant improvement or evidence of significant efforts on the part of the producer to bring about improvement, the GIJI would initiate its internal process for authorizing mandatory licensing and announce that it was doing so. Such authorizations would be both (1) time-limited and (2) area-specific. Compulsory licensing would be authorized for a limited time period only, say from one to as much as ten years, depending upon projections as to how long it would take to achieve a significant increase in diffusion, and the time required for the licensee to receive an adequate return on its initial investment. If the diffusion problem were limited to certain less developed countries in which access to the innovation is critical (as is the case with medicines to combat malaria, for example), then the innovator would lose IPR only with respect to that market. After the GIJI had authorized compulsory licensing, there would be another period in which the firm whose products were under scrutiny could change its policies to promote diffusion, providing another opportunity for compromise before mandatory licensing was imposed.

We have to consider the likelihood that firms and States supporting them might use this opportunity not to adjust their own policies but instead to put pressure on weaker States not to exercise their authority to invoke compulsory licensing. To reduce this risk, several measures would be necessary. There would have to be a clear legislative statement of observable "pressuring" actions that were inappropriate in conjunction with a GIJI process for compulsory licensing, and of the period of time in which they were inappropriate (any time after the GIJI started considering compulsory licensing for a given product in a given country). Inappropriate actions would include any actions that would be reasonably interpreted as a punishment or threat toward a country that utilized a GIJI authorization for compulsory licensing. Such actions would include: withdrawing products from a country's market or raising prices/royalties on them except as part of a general policy applying to a set of similar countries, or threatening to do so; threatening the withdrawal of other forms of international aid, or of support on an unrelated issue in another forum. On a complaint by a State against a company or another State, a GIJI process would be set in motion involving conciliation, an arbitral panel, and the GIJI's Appellate Tribunal, as necessary.

If a State or company were found responsible for such actions, it would be put on probation. Complaints against companies or States on probation would be put on a fast track, bypassing the conciliation stage and short-ening time periods for each stage in the process, while nonetheless remain-ing within the limits of due process. Lists of States and companies on probation would be published, and penalties for repeat offenses would be steeply increased. Such a process would strongly discourage coercive inter-ference with a State's decision to utilize the GIJI's authorization of com-pulsory licensing, while not violating due process or mixing judicial with legislative functions.

Given that compulsory licensing would be time-limited and area-specific, and that the option need rarely be exercised for its purpose to be realized, this proposal can be properly characterized as a modification of existing IPR, not a radical over-turning of them.

C. Compensation

With respect to the crucial question of compensation, we can imagine a continuum, at one extreme of which there would be no compensation. Such a policy would have the advantage of deterring monopolistic practices and would enable the Institute to operate on a relatively small budget. But there are three decisive objections to a no-compensation policy. First, innovation would be discouraged, especially innovations designed to help poor people in poor countries, since it is precisely these innovations that would be subject to GIJI authorization of compulsory licensing. Second, significant alterations would be necessary to many contemporary international agreements, including TRIPS and numerous bilateral investment treaties, which require that some level of compensation be paid upon the compulsory licensing of a patent. Third, it is virtually unimaginable that such a policy would be endorsed by wealthy countries that are home to the most innovative firms in such fields as pharmaceuticals and electronics, and whose ratification of a Treaty for Justice in Innovation would be essential for the GIJI to have a meaningful impact.

At the opposite extreme of this continuum would be a policy guaran-teeing full market-value compensation. If credible, such a policy would not significantly discourage innovation and would generate support from powerful firms. However, such a policy would essentially use public funds to pay monopolistic prices to private firms. This would be unpopular with democratic publics, and it would be difficult to raise sufficient sums to finance many such licenses. Furthermore, it would not deter monopolistic behavior—quite the contrary, it might encourage it.

It seems clear that neither zero compensation nor compensation at the full (monopolistic) market value of the innovation is satisfactory. Hence some middle ground will have to be found. A "fair price," representing a substantial but not exorbitant rate of return for the company, would have to be paid. In our view, current theorizing about justice does not ground a unique determination of "fair price" here; instead, there is probably a range of reasonable alternatives. One of the first actions of the GIJI would be to devise a set of procedures through which a fair price would be determined. The trick is to pick a pricing system that creates the right incentives, given the goals the licensing option is designed to promote, and avoids any clear unfairness to any of the parties concerned. Since anything less than paying the monopoly price could somewhat discourage innovation, the GIJI might find that its diffusion strategy would be more effective if combined with subsidies for the creation of promising drugs, compensating for the speculative but sometimes alluring prospect of very large monopolistic profits in the long run.

Compensation would be paid directly by the GIJI, rather than through the traditional approach of the payment of royalties from sales of licensed products, in order to avoid the price increases that would result from royalties designed to pay the "fair price" determined by the GIJI. Such an approach would be consistent with the GIJI's goal of increasing diffusion of innovations, as a lower price would maximize the number of individuals able to afford the innovation in question.

D. Political decision-making by the GIJI

One of the major functions of the Global Institute for Justice in Innovation would be to assess the justice implications of the pace at which useful innovations were diffusing to disadvantaged people, either those suffering severe deprivation or those laboring under burdens of basic economic and political inequalities. Carrying out this function would be contentious and large amounts of money could be at stake, so the GIJI's decision-making arrangements need to be carefully designed. We only sketch one possible design here, to suggest the feasibility of our proposal and to promote discussion.

The GIJI would have an administrative unit with analytical competence and the authority to propose exercise of the Institute's licensing options and other actions. The model here is something between the WTO, the Secretariat of which is relatively small and definitely subordinate to the membership, and the World Bank or the International Monetary Fund, which are operated by much larger administrative organizations that make many decisions with only general supervision from their boards. The Executive Head of the GIJI could not order licensing of IPR on her own, but could propose licensing to an Assembly of the GIJI.

The Assembly, which would meet annually, would be composed of representatives of developed and developing countries, NGOs with substantial records of service to disadvantaged people (such as Save the Children and Oxfam), and firms holding patents. Participating NGOs would have to satisfy familiar requirements of transparency, financial integrity, independence from governments and corporate interests, and responsiveness to the preferences and needs of those individuals and groups they claim to represent or on whose behalf they claim to act.

Each of the four constituencies would elect its representatives at the Assembly. As in the Montreal Protocol Fund, governments of developed and developing countries would have equal numbers of representatives, elected separately from these constituency groups. One possibility would be an Assembly of 32 representatives, consisting of eight industrialized countries, eight developing countries, eight NGOs, and eight innovation-producing firms. It is important that the numbers not be too large; the Montreal Protocol Fund body, with fourteen members, has operated much better than the unwieldy universal bodies involved in the Kyoto Protocol and post-Kyoto negotiations.

Decisions by the GIJI Assembly to authorize compulsory licensing would require a super-majority for immediate action, coupled with a majority of the votes in three of the four categories of representatives. Demanding immediate action, NGOs and developing countries could not join with one or two industrialized countries to exercise a licensing option; on the contrary, they would have to get a majority of either industrialized countries or firms. There could be a provision for relaxing this requirement after a delay (say, of one year) in order to give IPR-holders and others time to voice disagreement. The idea is to promote deliberation and compromise, but not to give any one group (such as major drug companies supported by the United States) a veto.

E. Accountability

The basic structure and key procedures of the GIJI would be deliberately designed to promote accountability. The composition of the GIJI Assembly would ensure that the organization is accountable, not just to the states that ratify the treaty which creates it—both with developed and developing economies—but also to various publics whose interests are represented by NGOs, and to the community of innovators. Furthermore, accountability would be enhanced by the stipulation that all major organizational actions, including acquisitions and changes in operating rules, are subject to administrative due process.

Proposals to authorize compulsory licensing could only be made under a set of rigorous due process requirements. First, the Executive Head of the

GIJI would have to make a public announcement of intention to propose compulsory licensing of a specific set of intellectual property rights in a specific country for a specified period of time, and the GIJI would have to provide clear means for comments and discussion. This procedure would be similar to the 'notice and comment' procedures of US administrative law, which require Federal agencies to publish potential rules, allow time and opportunity for interested parties to complain and make suggestions, and require a reasoned response from the agency proposing the rules. After the required period of perhaps 45 or 60 days has elapsed, the GIJI would have to re-issue its proposed order for compulsory licensing, at which point it would formally be put on the docket of the Assembly. Decisions of the GIJI could be reviewed for conformity to due process standards by an Appellate Tribunal, roughly modeled on the Appellate Body of the World Trade Organization.[11] That is, there would be a public set of procedures that encouraged compromise but provided for rulings by expert panels that could be appealed to the Appellate Tribunal, composed of judges selected for relatively long terms. The Appellate Tribunal would hear cases in public and issue public decisions providing reasons, which could serve as precedents to develop a body of GIJI law.

F. Funding

The GIJI's funding would come chiefly from member States, on a sliding scale, according to ability to pay. On the model of the World Bank subscription system,[12] countries would commit funds as necessary in large amounts—funds that would be essential to ensure that IPR holders subject to compulsory licensing received fair compensation.[13] As noted above, the GIJI would pay compensation directly, subsidizing diffusion of the innovation. Having funds readily available would enhance the credibility of the GIJI's warnings that it was intending to order compulsory licensing, and contribute to its deterrence of monopolistic pricing.

G. Is the proposal a morally unacceptable modification of existing IPRs?

This proposal does not assume that innovators are morally responsible for injustices that result from inadequate diffusion of their products. On the contrary, we do not believe that innovators have any special moral obligation to promote justice through the diffusion of their products.

The GIJI's ability to order compulsory licensing only assumes that the moral rights innovators have regarding their creations do not preclude the very limited form of interference with existing legal IPR that properly-exercised compulsory licensing entails. At any rate, our proposal is directed toward those who view the existing IPR regime as roughly within the bounds of the reasonable and the morally acceptable, not toward radical natural rights views that ascribe extremely broad, indefeasible 'natural' moral rights to innovators. Moreover, our argument is *comparative*: given a reasonable construal of the existing IPR regime as an instrument designed to serve a plurality of widely held values, our proposed modification of it does a better job of balancing those values. It ameliorates a very troubling side-effect of monopoly pricing without an unacceptable decrease in incentives for innovation.

H. Is the proposal politically realistic?

One could expect the Global Institute for Justice in Innovation to be greeted with at least cautious enthusiasm by developing countries and NGOs. Of course, their bargaining strategies will temper their public support, since they will be working for more favorable terms; but in fact they have much to gain and little to lose from the proposal. The proposal will not be as attractive to powerful developed States and the innovation-creating firms based in these states. If the GIJI is to work, it will require the support of these States, including especially the United States and Japan, and the European Union; and at least acceptance by major firms—which might itself be a necessary condition for support by powerful States. Without making unrealistic assumptions of altruism, what incentives would powerful States have to help create and to sustain the GIJI?

Before focusing on the positive incentives, it is important to note that the GIJI does not threaten the constitutional sovereignty of States: that is, their legal supremacy and independence.[14] States would retain their ability to make final decisions on issues of importance to them. All member States would retain the ability to determine for themselves how much control to deliver to the GIJI, and would also retain the right to decide whether to take up any authorizations they received. The GIJI's rulings would not have direct effect within domestic jurisdictions, and could not override domestic laws. Moreover, States could withdraw from the organization, with due notice.

Like the WTO, the GIJI would constitute an *exercise* of sovereignty by States. Members of the GIJI would be publicly committed not to thwart the purposes and actions of the organization—for instance, by threatening retaliation against the GIJI for ordering compulsory licensing of IPR owned by their own firms, if these acquisitions were judged by the Appellate Body to have been carried out in conformity with its rules and procedures. Like all international legal agreements the GIJI would limit the legal freedom of action of States, but it would not affect their constitutional sovereignty: their fundamental right to make decisions for themselves.

There are four major positive reasons for developed countries and their firms to support the GIJI. The first and most general is that more rapid diffusion of innovations would accelerate economic development worldwide—a long-term goal of developed countries, as it is in their interests to enhance both prosperity and the chances for a peaceful and more democratic world order. Wide diffusion of innovations would create conditions facilitating the creation of more innovations in more diverse ways, some of which would almost certainly rebound to the advantage of people in developed countries.

Since appeals to general interests are often not persuasive to firms or governments, we rely more heavily on three more self-interested reasons to support the proposal. The most concrete of these three reasons is that the GIJI's role in evaluating patents for potential compulsory licensing could reduce the potential arbitrariness of current compulsory licensing procedures. Decisions at the GIJI would be reached within a system in which both developed countries and IPR producers themselves are active participants. Developing countries would retain the power to order compulsory licenses without sanction by the GIJI. However, any decision to order a compulsory license that either had previously been rejected by the GIJI or was never submitted to the GIJI would be difficult to defend in the public arena, and arguably inconsistent with claims that it was being pursued for the public good.

The third and fourth reasons are both reputational. The GIJI would provide significant reputational advantages to IPR holders involved in disputes about alleged monopolistic pricing that harms disadvantaged people. At present, these disputes take place in an open public sphere, in which interest groups with the best sound-bites and the media play a large role. Major drug companies were quite bruised, for example, by the campaigns against them at the beginning of the millennium with respect to pricing of AIDS drugs—campaigns that often portrayed the companies as rapacious profit-seekers unconcerned about the welfare of poor AIDS sufferers in Africa. The GIJI would give the companies and their supporters a forum for their own defense: if a GIJI that was regarded as legitimate by attentive world publics ruled in favor of the company, this would provide compelling support for its reputation.

The fourth reason concerns the reputations of countries rather than firms. By supporting the GIJI the developed countries would be making a powerful symbolic statement at relatively low cost to themselves. The reputation of the rich countries for being willing to help poor ones has been badly damaged by their reneging on promises in the Uruguay Round of trade negotiations (1987–1994) to reduce trade barriers to agricultural products. While the various agricultural lobbies in rich countries may make fulfillment of those pledges impossible, moving ahead with a Global Institute for Justice in Innovation could demonstrate good faith. There is no denying that the

GIJI would be a 'hard sell' for drug companies and other patent-holders whose business plans count on monopolistic returns on successful innovations to compensate them for huge up-front investments, many of which yield no commercial products. However, the ability of the GIJI to authorize licensing on a national basis, rather than globally, would mean that patent-holders would retain their IPR in countries in which diffusion was indeed adequate, these being the countries in which current revenue from the innovation in question would predominantly come. Public pressure and attention to the problem of innovation diffusion, in industrialized democracies, would be essential for this proposal to gain sufficient traction to be politically feasible. But in the end, this is a modest proposal that would not fundamentally disrupt the activities of innovation-creating companies, and that might induce them to devise ways to accelerate diffusion of their innovations in ways that rebounded to their long-term benefit.

III. The Comparative Merits of the Global Institute for Justice in Innovation

A plausible case for institutional innovation must be comparative in two ways: it must show that the proposed institution is superior both to current efforts to solve the problem it addresses and to the best developed rival proposal currently on the table. The current response to this problem is the provision in international legal agreements for compulsory licensing of essential medicines through domestic legal systems. The best-developed proposal for an alternative system is that of Thomas Pogge for a new drug patent system that would be responsive to the global disease burden.

A. Compulsory licensing as currently employed

Existing compulsory licensing does not fare well in comparison with our proposal for a Global Institute for Justice in Innovation for several reasons. First, although existing compulsory licensing is supposed to be accompanied by compensation, there are no provisions for ensuring that States actually render fair compensation or indeed any compensation at all. While failure to do so might technically give rise to the possibility of a claim at the WTO, this will only happen if the IPR holder's home State is willing to publicly insist upon payment for the company in question. However, political concerns mean that it is highly unlikely such a claim will be brought where the State undertaking compulsory licensing was one of the poorer developing countries attempting to ensure the availability to its citizens of an essential medicine or other important innovation. Moreover, even if a claim were brought, the dispute resolution process would be formally controlled by the

IPR holder's home State, with the IPR holder itself having only indirect influence over how the dispute is argued, or whether a given settlement offer should be accepted. In contrast, the GIJI would provide fair compensation without the need of intervention from the IP holder's home State, and all dispute resolution processes undertaken at the GIJI would be engaged in directly by the IPR holder itself. As noted above, these processes operate in accordance with due process, including the possibility of appeal with review by the Appellate Body.

Furthermore, existing compulsory licensing is unilateral, at the discretion of a single State, with no accountability mechanism, whereas a decision by the GIJI to authorize compulsory licensing would occur through the operation of a multilateral institution, with credible provisions for accountability not only to States, but to other stake-holders as well. Lack of accountability might seem to advantage weak States that are most likely to need to exercise the option of compulsory licensing. However, weak States are subject to powerful pressures from strong States (where most IPR are held) to not exercise this option. Since GIJI authorization of licensing is multilateral, with robust accountability, it would provide opportunities for weaker States to benefit from initiatives with respect to diffusion without having to resort to politically risky efforts to invoke compulsory licensing on their own authority. Multilateralism provides some protection for weak States that act as part of, or on behalf of, a larger group.

B. Pogge's 'Patent 2' proposal

In several influential papers, Thomas Pogge has offered an institutional proposal designed to address both aspects of the 'essential medicines' problem: the lack of access to life-saving drugs that millions of people suffer because of monopoly pricing under the current IPR system, and the failure to develop drugs that would be of great benefit to millions of people. Both of these deficiencies derive from the lack of market demand resulting from poverty. Pogge proposes to leave intact the existing IPR system (what he calls the Patent 1 option) but to create an alternative: innovators could opt for Patent 2, which requires them to make public all information about their innovation and forgo all regular IPR, but which makes them eligible to be rewarded by disbursements from an international fund in proportion to the positive impact of their innovation on the global burden of disease.[15]

Pogge has made a major contribution by emphasizing the moral importance of the issue of the diffusion of life-saving drugs and by putting forward an ingenious proposal that is responsive to firms' interests and the many incentive problems that arise in this area. We see his proposal as a very valuable prod to discussion, rather than as an attempt to provide the 'last word', and in that spirit we offer criticism and defend our alternative in comparison to his Patent 2 proposal.

Our proposal for a Global Institute for Justice in Innovation is in one sense much broader than Pogge's Patent 2 proposal, which is limited to one kind of innovation, namely patentable drugs, and is designed only to address one aspect of justice in innovation, namely, the problem of extreme deprivation. In contrast, the GIJI takes into account the relevance of innovation to justice more generally and identifies legitimate interests in justice—namely, the concern about basic economic and political inequality—beyond the preoccupation with extreme deprivation. This difference, however, is not critical. In principle, Patent 2 could be instituted as part of a broader effort on innovation, with adaptations of Pogge's ideas to other types of innovation that might affect basic economic and political inequality more than extreme deprivation.

A key feature of Pogge's Patent 2 proposal is that its exercise is entirely voluntary. This voluntariness may seem to be an advantage of Pogge's scheme over ours: no potentially intrusive institution would be created under Patent 2, and opposition by firms to a legal regime providing for it would presumably be muted by the voluntary adherence provision. Drug companies could decide, case-by-case, whether to invoke Patent 1 or Patent 2 protections. However, the voluntary nature of Patent 2 is a double-edged sword, since firms might never invoke the Patent 2 option. Never invoked, Patent 2 would be like unfinished monuments in the desert: testimonies to failed ambition. The big question about Patent 2, therefore, is whether firms will invoke it.

Whether they will do so depends upon how credible the promise of reward is. For the promise to be sufficiently credible to induce drug producers to forgo the known benefits of the Patent 1 option, two things must be true. First, drug producers must have confidence that the promised funds will be available, perhaps many years in the future. We call this the *funding assumption*. Second, the firms must have confidence that the procedure for identifying the disease burden reduced by a drug, and therefore the patent 2 rewards due to drug companies, will be reliable and fair. Call this the *reliability assumption*. In our view, both of these assumptions are so problematic as to threaten the credibility and therefore feasibility of Pogge's proposal.

The problem with the funding assumption is that it is inconsistent with what is known about the trustworthiness of international funding pledges. The most notorious of these pledges is that made in United Nations General Assembly Resolution 2626 (1970), adopted without a vote. This resolution pledged that "Each economically advanced country will progressively increase its official development assistance to the developing countries and will exert its best efforts to reach a minimum net amount of 0.7 per cent of its gross national product ... by the middle of the Decade."[16] Thirty-seven years later, only five small European countries exceeded that target, and U.S. aid stood at 0.16% of Gross National Income.[17] Looking at this track record on the most publicized commitment in the world political economy over the last 40 years, it is very unlikely that any drug company would rely on any promises about long-term funding for the Patent 2 scheme. Providing public funds to drug companies is unlikely to be politically popular: competing demands will always seem more urgent and desirable.

The reliability assumption is also problematic because of the difficulty of obtaining agreement, even among experts, on reliable measurements of the impact of a particular drug on the global burden of disease. One source of difficulty is the fact that in many cases the decline in the incidence of a particular disease will be the result of a number of factors, including the decline of other diseases, in cases where co-morbidity is prominent, and the cumulative effect, over many years, of a combination of medical, environmental, and cultural changes. Furthermore, the assessment authority would have an institutional incentive to understate the value of a patented innovation, in order to reduce the payment that it needs to make. Given the complex causation and the inherent negative bias of the assessment institution, it seems unlikely that drug producers will forgo the well-trod path to profits in exchange for an unpredictable outcome in a very problematic process for determining who gets rewarded and how large the reward is.

We conclude that although Patent 2 does not require any restriction of existing intellectual property rights and thus might be thought to be superior to the GIJI on this count, this advantage will be nullified if drug producers have insufficient incentives to take up the Patent 2 option in the first place. *The central problem with Pogge's proposal is that neither the funding assumption nor the reliability assumption is credible.* Due to the weakness of these essential assumptions, Patent 2 is very unlikely to be implemented in its current form.

In contrast, both the funding and reliability requirements of the GIJI's policies are much less demanding. The resources required by the GIJI on an annual basis are moderate, to cover administrative costs. On the other hand, in the event of compulsory licensing, the GIJI would indeed have to pay substantial compensation from the fund provided by the contingent State commitments described in Section II F above. That is, the GIJI does require a "war chest" of contingent resources provided by States, but the existence of the IMF and World Bank demonstrates that such contingent commitments are feasible. Moreover, while the compensation paid should be fair, it need not equal or even approximate the income IPR holders would generate from monopoly pricing, and the deterrent effect of authorized compulsory licensing, and provisions for consultation, should ensure that the provisions are rarely exercised. Consequently, the level of funding required for the GIJI will be significantly lower than that required for Patent 2. The GIJI does require a 'war chest' of contingent resources from governments, but the existence of the World Bank demonstrates that making large contingent commitments is feasible. Although the GIJI does include a provision for prizes and grants, its main focus is not on rewarding those who create products that the market would not otherwise produce, but rather on making sure that what does get produced becomes widely available, rapidly enough, to promote justice or at least not to worsen injustices.

It is important to understand why the poor track record on international financial commitments is a debilitating problem for Patent 2 but not for the GIJI. For the GIJI's threat of internationally authorized compulsory licensing to provide an effective incentive for innovators to lower prices or take other measures to accelerate the diffusion of their products, it only needs to make credible claims of a much more limited sort than those required under the Patent 2 scheme. Innovators must believe that they are at risk of authorized compulsory licensing if their product is diffusing so slowly that it is likely to be perceived by the GIJI to be contributing significantly to existing injustices or to be failing to make a significant contribution to ameliorating a significant injustice. Generally speaking, the risk that one may completely lose one's monopoly for a highly valued innovation would seem to concentrate the mind more effectively than the speculation that one could be rewarded—and continue to be rewarded – decades from now, if states hold fast to their pledges to create and sustain a reward fund.

Pogge might reply that it counts heavily in favor of his proposal that it includes a powerful Creation Strategy as well as a Diffusion Strategy, while the GIJI focuses only on the latter. In other words, he might argue that the GIJI's inclusion of provision for prizes and grants is an insufficient response to the fact that drugs that would have a large positive impact on justice are not being created due to the inadequate incentives provided by the existing IPR system. This is a fair point in the sense that institutional proposals that would stimulate the creation of new innovations would certainly be welcome; but if, as we have argued, Pogge's proposal would be a dead-letter, it does not count in favor of his scheme. In any event, no institution can reasonably be expected to do everything. It is true that the distinctive thrust of the GIJI, the licensing option and free licensing authority, is directed toward the Diffusion Problem, not the Creation Problem. Revisions of Pogge's Patent 2 proposal that made it institutionally more credible for helping to solve the Creation Problem would be welcome. Indeed, if our proposal for a Global Institute for Justice in Innovation effectively resolved the Diffusion Problem, the task of designing an institution to solve the Creation Problem might be easier to fulfill. Its designers would no longer have to address both problems simultaneously with one instrument—a job that in institutional design, as in economics, is often difficult or impossible.

The problem of inadequate diffusion of innovations is of sufficient importance to warrant consideration in its own right, independently of the problem of essential medicines. Many innovations that could have an important impact on justice are *not* like anti-malarial drugs: access to them will be beneficial not just to those in less-developed countries, but to virtually everyone, and the problem they present for justice is not that they are unlikely to be produced by the market. Consider, for example, biomedical technologies that extend years of vigorous life or that augment the immune system, or drugs that enhance important cognitive skills. The problem here is not that there is insufficient market demand to stimulate research and development; rather, it is the risk that these valuable innovations will not be available except to the better off or that they will not become available to most people quickly enough to avoid significant injustices.

IV. The Status of the Global Institute for Justice in Innovation Under International Law

While there are a number of international agreements that would potentially affect the actions of the Global Institute for Justice in Innovation, attention here will be paid only to the two most important types: (1) the WTO's TRIPS Agreement, and (2) Investment treaties.

A. TRIPS

As a mandatory agreement for all WTO Members, TRIPS has a far-reaching global impact, and thus the degree to which the GIJI and its actions would conform to the requirement of TRIPS is extremely important. The following discussion will explain why a WTO Member State that grants a compulsory license as a result of a decision by the GIJI would not be in violation of its obligations under TRIPS.

While there have previously been questions raised regarding the acceptability of compulsory licensing under TRIPS, its acceptability as well as the freedom of States to decide the reason for compulsory licenses being granted was explicitly confirmed in the 2001 Doha Declaration on the TRIPS Agreement and Public Health. Moreover, while TRIPS does specify some reasons for which compulsory licenses might be granted under domestic law, these are not stated to be exclusive. Consequently, so long as compulsory licensing under the GIJI operates in a manner consistent with the constraints on compulsory licensing enunciated in TRIPS, no WTO liability would attach to any appropriate action taken in accordance with a GIJI compulsory licensing decision.

Compulsory licensing restrictions under TRIPS are predominantly found in Article 31, which lists 12 procedural standards that must be met in order for any grant of a compulsory license to be TRIPS-consistent. For the purposes of discussion of the GIJI, four are particularly important, and thus will be discussed here.

Under Article 31(a), decisions to grant a compulsory license must be made on an individualized basis. That is, licenses cannot be granted for all products of a particular type, such as "all pharmaceuticals". Rather, each individual product must be considered for compulsory licensing on its own merits. As the GIJI process specifically involves evaluation of innovations on an individualized basis, this provision clearly presents no obstacle to the GIJI.

Under Article 31(b), an attempt must be made prior to compulsory licensing to obtain authorization from the patent holder to license the patent on reasonable commercial terms and conditions. Exceptions exist to this rule, including where a national emergency or other urgent circumstance exists. However while in some circumstances the GIJI may indeed need to rely upon this "national emergency" exception, it will usually not be necessary. The GIJI is institutionally designed to ensure that direct discussions with patent holders occur for a reasonable time prior to any decision to order a compulsory license. Consequently, unless a "national emergency" makes a rapid compulsory licensing order necessary, the requirements of Article 31(b) will be met—and if a "national emergency" has occurred, Article 31(b) will not be applicable.

Under Article 31(h) the patent holder must receive "adequate remuneration" to compensate it for any losses due to the compulsory license. While there is no clear agreement regarding the meaning of "adequate" as used in this provision, the goal of the GIJI to pay "fair" compensation, at a rate higher than the 2-5% royalty rate conventional in compulsory licensing, would seem to ensure that the compensation paid by the GIJI will indeed be more than "adequate".

Under Articles 31(i) and (j), the compulsory licensing decision must be subject to review by an authority superior to the body making the original decision. While appeals may not be available within the domestic legal system in which compulsory licensing was ordered, this requirement is clearly met by the incorporation within the GIJI of an Appellate Tribunal.

The GIJI, then, is designed in a manner that would make enactment of its compulsory licensing decisions consistent with the TRIPS obligations of the GIJI Member State concerned. Ideally, to remove any doubt, this would be reflected through the enactment of a special amendment to TRIPS clarifying that no grant of a compulsory license taken in accordance with a GIJI decision could give rise to a claim for violation of WTO obligations. However, even if such an amendment were not able to be passed at the

WTO, an additional protection exists for developing countries enacting GIJI-ordered compulsory licenses, in the form of the dispute settlement system of the WTO.

As TRIPS is a WTO text, any claim that a State was in violation of its TRIPS obligations in enacting a GIJI-ordered compulsory license would have to be resolved through State-to-State arbitration, rather than through individual patent holders directly bringing a claim against the GIJI Member State in question. However, Members of the GIJI will find it politically enormously difficult to justify bringing a WTO case against a State that has merely implemented a GIJI decision, when the complaining State itself had previously agreed by becoming a Member of the GIJI that the GIJI's procedures were fair. Non-Members of the GIJI would, of course, face no such obstacle. However, as already argued, there is no reason to believe that any compulsory licensing decision made by the GIJI would result in WTO liability even were a claim brought.

B. Investment treaties

An enormous number of investment treaties now exist around the world, and a great number of them explicitly include reference to IPR as constituting a form of "investment". Consequently, it is possible that the granting of a compulsory license by a developing country, in accordance with a decision by the GIJI would give rise to a claim for compensation under an investment treaty.

While investment treaties all contain a variety of grounds on which an investor can claim compensation from a State, those based on the manner in which an investment has been treated, such as "fair and equitable" treatment, would be very unlikely to serve as the basis for a claim for any action taken in accordance with a GIJI decision, due to the procedural safeguards included in the design of the GIJI. In addition, the traditional claim for "expropriation", made when a State takes the property of a foreign investor, could not be made with respect to compulsory licensing done in accordance with a GIJI decision, as the investor would retain the patent in question, but would merely be required to allow others to produce licensed versions of the product in question.

Compulsory licensing could, however, give rise to a claim of "indirect expropriation", which occurs when a State regulates an investment in a manner that leaves formal ownership of the investment with the foreign investor, but effectively takes away the benefits of the investment. While arguments would be available to any GIJI Member State forced to defend such a claim, the unresolved nature of contemporary international investment law regarding indirect expropriation means that it is impossible to be certain that a compensable indirect expropriation would not be found.

Moreover, the structure of investment treaty dispute resolution means that the patent holder would have the right itself to institute arbitration in order to secure compensation for its alleged losses. Thus, unlike at the WTO, developed States would not be able simply to reject claims for compensation by their investors who have allegedly suffered losses as a result of a GIJI decision.

Nonetheless, while investors control their own claims under an investment treaty, it is important to remember that the treaty is nonetheless between the two States, with the investor itself having no direct role in its implementation or interpretation. As a result, the risk of claims being raised under investment treaties as a result of a GIJI compulsory licensing decision could be significantly reduced merely by requiring States joining the GIJI to sign a declaration that no compulsory licensing granted in accordance with a GIJI decision would give rise to a claim under any investment treaty to which it was a party.[18] Alternatively, even greater protection could be gained if individual agreements were signed by GIJI Member States that were parties to investment treaties stating that compulsory licensing granted in accordance with a GIJI decision would not give rise to a claim under the specific treaty in question.

This would, of course, not be a complete solution, as claims could still be made under investment treaties involving non-GIJI Member States. Moreover, investment arbitration tribunals have recognized the right of investors to qualify as an "investor" under a specific treaty merely by undertaking the formalities of incorporation in a State party to the treaty, so long as the treaty itself permitted this. Consequently, the risk of an investment treaty claim could not be entirely eliminated by such agreements.

Nonetheless, the possibility of a compensation order being made by an investment arbitration tribunal against a developing country due to a GIJI decision could be adequately addressed by having such claims paid by the GIJI itself where the State acted in accordance with GIJI rules and instructions. In this way the burden would be spread amongst all GIJI Members, thus minimizing the financial burden on any individual State.

V. Conclusion

One of the morally unacceptable features of the contemporary world is that innovations that would be of immense value to severely deprived people, and that would ameliorate unjust economic and political inequalities, are not widely available even though the marginal costs of providing them are low. One source of this problem is the patent system, which stimulates innovation by giving monopoly rights to patent-holders. Monopoly pricing by patent-holders combines with lack of resources by those who need the innovations the most to generate deprivation and inequality. The *diffusion of innovation* is blocked by the features of dominant institutions.

Since this is an institutional problem, we propose an institutional solution: a Global Institute for Justice in Innovation. This Institute would offer prizes and other incentives for innovation, but its major task would be to promote the diffusion of existing justice-impacting innovations through a multi-step process. Quiet encouragement of more rapid diffusion could be followed, when unsuccessful, with public 'naming and shaming' of firms that restricted access to their products through monopoly pricing or other means. But the Institute would also have a standing compulsory licensing option for intellectual property rights whose owners were not sufficiently promoting diffusion to disadvantaged people. If informal measures did not succeed, the GIJI could authorize states to issue compulsory licenses for innovations that were not diffusing at a sufficiently rapid rate. Such proposals would have to be accepted by supermajority vote of an Assembly in which developed countries, developing countries, NGOs and firms holding intellectual property rights would be equally represented. Fair compensation, according to previously publicized procedures and guidelines, would be paid by the GIJI, drawing from funding by its member States. Finally, in applying any authorized measures, the GIJI would be subject to procedures of global administrative law, including oversight by an independent Appellate Tribunal.

We anticipate that many of these elaborate procedures would not need to be invoked. We expect that the mere threat of compulsory licensing would accomplish a great deal, without its frequent exercise. Much good would therefore be done, at low cost and without incursions on state sovereignty or frequent use of coercion.

Our proposal is indebted to the pioneering work of Thomas Pogge, who has emphasized the importance of access to new drugs—a major part of the innovation diffusion problem—and has made an institutional proposal of his own. In our view, however, his Patent 2 proposal has institutional flaws inherent in the lack of credibility of long-term promises by States fairly to assess the value of drugs in relieving the global disease burden, and on that basis to provide an adequate flow of royalties to drug firms. What we deem both Pogge's *reliability assumption* and his *funding assumption* highly problematic. We argue that our proposed Global Institute for Justice in Innovation would be more credible and more effective, and accomplish enormous good at very low cost. It would not solve the problem of creating new innovations—for which a revised version of Pogge's proposal might be valuable—but it could go a long way toward solving the Diffusion Problem, which currently is the source of so much unnecessary misery and unjust inequality in the world.

Notes

1 An important, though as we shall argue, partial exception is the work of Thomas Pogge in his Patent 2 proposal, which we consider in some detail in section III of this article.

2 See, for example, Francis Fukuyama, *Our Posthuman Future* (New York: Farrar, Straus and Giroux, 2002), pp. 9–10.

3 Anders Sandberg, Nick Bostrom, "Converging cognitive enhancements," *Annals of the New York Academy of Science*, 1093 (2006), 201–27. Nick Bostrom, "Smart policy: cognitive enhancement in the public interest," *Reshaping the Human Condition: Exploring Human Enhancement*, ed. Leo Zonneveld, Huub Dijstelblowem, and Danielle Ringoir (The Hague/London: Rathenau Institute and British Embassy, Science & Innovation Network, and Parliamentary Office of Science and Technology, 2008), pp. 29–36.

4 Allen E. Buchanan, "The right to a decent minimum of health care," *Philosophy & Public Affairs*, 13 (1984), 55–78. Normal Daniels, "Justice, health, and healthcare," *The American Journal of Bioethics*, 1 (2001), 2–16. Dan W. Brock, "Ethical issues in the use of cost-effectiveness analysis for the prioritization of health care resources," *Making Choices in Health: WHO Guide to Cost-Effectiveness Analysis*, ed. T. Edejer et al. (Geneva: World Health Organization, 2003), pp. 289–312.

5 The Americans with Disabilities Act and the international Convention on the Rights of Persons with Disabilities both recognize this point.

6 Michael Walzer, *Spheres of Justice: A Defense of Pluralism and Equality* (New York: Basic Books, 1983), ch. 1.

7 According to some democratic theorists, what might be called basic political equality—having secure standing as an equal participant in the most fundamental political processes in one's society—is itself a requirement of justice, because it is required for a proper public recognition of the equality of citizens. On this view, inequalities in political power that are incompatible with or that tend to undermine this fundamental equality are unjust, independently of their tendency to produce other bad effects, including extreme deprivations, violations of particular civil and political rights, or distributive unfairness. See Thomas Christiano, *The Constitution of Equality: Democratic Authority and Its Limits* (Oxford: Oxford University Press, 2008).

8 It should be noted that when "monopoly pricing" is referred to in the current article, this includes the partial or complete refusal to sell in a given market by an IPR holder, as this refusal is based upon an inability to receive the monopoly prices insisted upon.

9 On institutions see Stephen D. Krasner, ed., *International Regimes* (Cambridge, MA: MIT Press, 1983), introduction; Robert O. Keohane, *International Institutions and State Power* (Boulder, CO: Westview, 1989). On accountability see Ruth Grant and Robert O. Keohane, "Accountability and abuses of power in world politics," *American Political Science Review*, 99 (2005), 29–43.

10 Geoffrey Brennan and Philip Pettit, *The Economy of Esteem* (Oxford: Oxford University Press, 2004).

11 The combination of notice and comment procedures with judicial review of due process is a feature of administrative law, as developed in the United States since the Administrative Procedures Act of 1946, and now spreading to international organizations. See Benedict Kingsbury, Nico Krisch, and Richard Stewart, "The emergence of global administrative law," *Law and Contemporary Problems*, 68 (2005), 15–62.

12 Article 5 of the Articles of Agreement of the International Bank for Reconstruction and Development, the largest unit in the World Bank Group, provides that twenty percent of the subscription of each member is subject to call when needed for ordinary obligations of the Bank, and eighty percent is basically held in reserve to guarantee loans issued by the Bank. For the Articles of Agreement, see: ⟨http://siteresources.worldbank.org/EXTABOUTUS/Resources/ibrd-articlesofagreement.pdf⟩.

13 This should include the possibility of extra payment necessary to secure the cooperation of IPR holders in cases in which the IPR-holder possessed non-public information essential for the manufacture of the licensed product.

14 Hedley Bull, *The Anarchical Society* (New York: Columbia University Press, 1977), p. 8.

15 Thomas W. Pogge, "Human rights and global health: a research program," *Metaphilosophy,* 36 (2005), 182–209.

16 Michael A. Clemens and Todd J. Moss, "Origins and relevance of the international aid target," Working Paper Number 68, Center for Global Development, September 2005, p. 8.

17 Anup Shah, "US and foreign aid assistance," ⟨http://www.globalissues.org/article/35/us-and-foreign-aid-assistance⟩, last updated April 13, 2009.

18 Naturally, the language used to describe the declaration is only intended to convey the substance of the declaration, and the precise wording of the document itself would need to be different.

8

From Migration in Geographic Space to Migration in Biographic Time
Views From Europe*

Claus Offe

From a global perspective, two facts are worth noting from the outset. First, a person's place of birth is the single most powerful predictor of that person's lifetime income and other components of overall welfare.[1] Second, this distributional pattern is largely unrelated to the person's decisions, effort, ambition, or productive contribution, as one's place of birth is of course entirely beyond one's control and, in most cases, beyond the control of one's parents as well. The vast majority of people inherit the citizenship of their birth place. As a result, the acquisition of citizenship and the privileges and disadvantages tied to it have been described as a giant "birthright lottery."[2] Some, if born in the advanced societies of the global West and North (which includes some prosperous societies of the Asia-Pacific region), benefit from the infrastructural and civilizational accomplishments that have accumulated in these regions over many generations. Others, born into countries where such accumulation has not taken place (or perhaps was even prevented from taking place as a consequence of colonialism), have mostly to accept and live with the conditions that prevail in the global South, that is, much of Asia, Africa, and Latin America. In both cases, inherited citizenship is, on average, highly consequential for a person's life-long well-being and is arguably one of the most consequential assets or liabilities of a person.

Political Theory Without Borders, First Edition. Edited by Robert E. Goodin and James S. Fishkin.
© 2016 John Wiley & Sons, Inc. Published 2016 by John Wiley & Sons, Inc.

There can be no doubt that these conditions constitute a challenge for normative political theorists, in particular theorists of global justice. These theorists try to devise arguments for the definition of (and methods to arrive at reasonable consensus about) *obligations*[3] that apply to *agents* (such as states, NGOs, and individuals) in the wealthy North. Such obligations would apply to their relations with people and political entities of the largely impoverished global South. Over the last 30 years or so, the normative theory of distributive justice in general, and that of liberal egalitarians with their keen awareness of "morally arbitrary" factors in particular, has been focused on the question of how the luck component and the effort component of distributional outcomes can be separated, and the former effectively neutralized, *within* the wealthy liberal societies of the West.[4] This challenge is even greater if we look at the interpersonal distribution of life chances on the global scale.

My aim in this article is much narrower, however. It consists in finding out whether and to what extent the *migration regimes* of the EU and its member states can be conceived of as contributing to the fulfillment of obligations of global justice, and which interests and normative principles they are designed to accommodate. One important difference between a normal lottery and the "birthright lottery" is that the latter involves (limited) options of *corriger la fortune*, that is, of changing the lottery's outcome in beneficial ways. This can happen through migration, change of citizenship, the acquisition of additional citizenship(s), and the acquisition of (legal or irregular) residence status in countries with preferable overall life chances. Given vast inter-regional differences in prosperity, there are strong incentives for individuals to make use of one or more of these options. These options are shaped by the legal *conditions of exit* from countries which people want to leave and the *conditions of entry* which are established by the *migration regimes* of receiving countries.[5]

What I am trying to arrive at in this article is a minimum moral standard for migration policy and migration regimes. Receiving ("host") societies have rights and duties in their relation to migrants (and persons with a "migration background"). We want to find out the nature of arguments that can serve as foundations for such rights and duties. Yet this is a modest position that stands back from larger substantive claims about the moral duties of migrants and host societies alike; from considerations of global justice (to the extent they can be promoted through migration policy); from group rights of migrants and non-migrants; from the moral qualities of multi-culturalism, cosmopolitanism, and sovereignty; from the impact migration policy may have on the overall level of trust and solidarity in receiving societies[6] and so on. Instead, this minimal moral standard will stick to formal and procedural rules such as: keep promises; honor implicit contracts; stick to international conventions; do not reify the "identity" of groups; practice the art of abstraction and "color-blindedness"; remain consistent with existing legal norms and constitutional principles; provide ample institutional space and time for deliberation and reconciliation; refrain from using majoritarian rules in relation to minority issues; do not waste human resources, talent, and life time; for democratic reasons, do everything that is legal and effective to minimize the status gap between permanent residents and fellow citizens by urging and incentivizing the former to join the status of the latter; and most generally, be aware that you cannot get rid of problems by "keeping them out" or "exporting" them. Rather, problems have to be addressed "here," from "now" on, and in the light of far-sighted considerations. Most importantly, perhaps we need to realize that the rights of migrants and their descendants apply to them not because they are migrants or foreigners but because they are human beings and bearers of human rights, who often suffer from specific vulnerabilities which are due to the fact of having migrated. If we were to introduce special rights for migrants, there would be no stop to introducing further discriminatory distinctions such as white versus non-white, male versus female, or desirable versus non-desirable migrants.

I. Types of Migrants and Their Legal Status

The very concept of "migrants" is a highly ambiguous one and requires considerable sharpening to be useful for statistical purposes. One of most encompassing versions of the concept is the one employed by the German Statistical Federal Office. It defines "migrants" as the resident population with a "migration *background*." This includes (a) foreign-born persons who have migrated to the country after 1949 (since 1990, this includes the unified territories of the Federal Republic and the former German Democratic Republic); including ethnic Germans who were born abroad (for example, those belonging to large German minorities in Romania, Kazakhstan, and so on, who have migrated to Germany). It includes (b) all those born in Germany and who have at least one parent belonging to category (a). This broad definition yields a share of the total population with a "migration background" of almost a fifth—19 per cent in 2005.[7] In contrast, the term "foreigner" (*Ausländer*)—a term that is recently on the retreat from legal and statistical language—refers to persons who are (long-term) residents in the territory of a state, are foreign-born or children of foreign-born persons and not naturalized. It is a term with exclusionary ethnic, religious, linguistic, and phenotypical connotations. Also, it is a term that is exclusively used by *non*-foreigners, as those labeled as "foreigners" by the latter will of course refer to themselves as Croats, Turks, Pakistani, etc. "migrants" rather than "foreigners."

The broad statistical category of people having a migration background can be subdivided into six major categories, according to the main purpose or circumstances of their being "here" and the legal status granted to them. In the following brief profiles of these categories, I will also include normative considerations which arguably apply to their claims and conditions, as well as current policies that (re)define their status.

A. Irregular migrants

Beyond entry *rights* that are granted by states, there are vast *factual* conditions of entry which, however, do not take the form of a legal permit to enter and to reside. This is the path that "irregular" or "undocumented," "unauthorized" migrants ("*sans papiers*," "*clandestinos*") take outside the migration regime of the state they enter and in violation of its border or visa regime. Given modern means of transportation, communication, and organization,[8] neither national border control technologies nor Europe-wide ("*Schengen*") controls are capable of effectively sealing their borders from irregular migrants.[9] For irregular migrants in Continental Europe, it seems to be relatively easy to come in (either individually or through people-trafficking organizations; either by overstaying on a tourist or study visa, or through forging a visa), while states encounter difficulties in keeping irregular migrants out or returning them to their country of origin (these are legal, logistic, and political[10] difficulties, including states of origin refusing to re-admit their own citizens, provided that the state of origin can be found out after passports may have been discarded by migrants). The result is the accumulation of a stock of migrants without any legal residence status, who make a living as cleaning and care workers, agricultural workers, in the tourism and catering industries, and as sex workers. Being illegal and undocumented residents, once they are in the country they are subject not only to state repression, but also to sometimes extreme forms of dependency and exploitation. They typically work in low skilled, highly insecure, short term, low paid jobs, often in the informal economy and often that belong to the 3D category ("dangerous, difficult, dirty").[11]

Not only is this virtual *de facto* openness of borders something that states find difficult to control, but additionally, apprehended violators are difficult to sanction in ways that would trigger individual and general prevention. If people's determination to come and to stay is strong enough, and if their willingness to accept the risks and deprivations involved is equally strong, then the chances are good that they will succeed. Joppke speaks of "the states' sheer incapacity to keep [irregular] migrants out."[12] But beyond that incapacity, and even though virtually all EU member states are facing domestic waves and movements of what Joppke calls xenophobic "populist restrictionism,"[13] the governments of liberal states on the European continent and in Scandinavia (with the exception of Denmark) seem to have been somewhat reluctant to actually employ the limited means they have to either prevent irregular migration or to return irregular migrants to where they came from (*refoulement*). This reluctance may partly be explained in terms of (for example, agricultural) employers' interest in cheap labor and the states' complicity with that interest. Yet Joppke makes a rather convincing argument that, in addition to such interest-guided considerations, there is also a principled stance of major segments of Western political elites which he terms a liberal "antipopulist norm."[14] The idea here is that under the soft pressure of constitutional and human rights jurisprudence, governments become forced to make concessions concerning the rigor of their border regimes that they would *not* make for the sake of popularity with their voters. The anti-populist norm would, in policy terms, call for opening up some option of regularization of irregulars.

B. Refugees and asylum seekers: Humanitarian migration

Some measure of freedom of entry is provided by humanitarian international conventions which target *refugees* (from repressive regimes and from international and civil wars) and *asylum seekers* (who make a case before specialized administrations that they are threatened by violent discrimination, repression, and political prosecution in their country of origin).[15] While the term "refugee" describes the conditions for which people leave, the term "asylum" describes the status they (seek to) acquire after having arrived. The rights to enter and to remain (in case asylum is actually granted) are qualified, however, by restrictive conditions such as exclusion from economic activity, discrimination, coerced internal immobility, material need, and high levels of overall uncertainty. We can say that "free entry" (together with its very restricted freedoms *after* entry) is granted only in those cases where it follows upon an "*unfree* exit," that is, an exit that is necessitated by extreme conditions of threat and risk. It is also associated with precarious legal and material conditions with which beneficiaries of "free entry" have to content themselves. Given these empirical conditions, the question appears more and more open as to whether intervention on the place of origin—through "sending food and medical aid or intervening to remove a genocidal regime from power"[16]—is not the morally preferable (if costlier) way to proceed, compared to granting at least temporary[17] entry rights to the lucky few who may make it to "our" shores. The latter option may even have been adopted in some cases as an excuse to avoid the level of costs and engagement the former would require.

Also, European nation states have adopted in recent years a rich variety of sophisticated policies to prevent, deter, or discourage refugees from actually applying for the asylum to which they are also entitled under the Geneva

Convention on the Status of Refugees (1951) and the Protocol (1967). Asylum seekers must demonstrate, in the face of strong suspicions concerning the evidence they produce, that they *are* in fact persecuted in their countries of origin on the basis of their race, nationality, religion, political opinion, membership and participation in associations, or gender. Any asylum granted thus implies that state A is officially passing a negative judgment concerning the human rights situation prevailing in state B, the refugee's country of origin. Such judgment may or may not be fitting with diplomatic interests. Moreover, as asylees are perceived to be a burden, EU member states are interested in minimizing such burdens by either keeping potential claimants out, by seeing to it that other (member) states share the burden equitably, by increasing the hurdles which refugees have to pass in order to actually become asylees, or by returning those whose asylum-worthiness has been denied at the end of states' administrative procedures. One such strategy, now widely adopted, is the establishment of a list of allegedly safe countries. When one of the countries on that list[18] has been transited by a refugee on the way to her chosen destination, such transit implies an automatic denial of even the right to apply in the latter. Probably the most serious violation of the intended humanitarian function of the Convention and the Protocol, by now adopted as law by around 150 UN member states, is the denial of physical access to places at which they are entitled to apply for asylum.[19] As a consequence, the illegal crossing of borders has become the most common access road to places in which the procedure of applying can be started.

One rather obvious normative standard applying to refugee and asylum policies is that rights must be made accessible, and effectively so; otherwise, they remain entirely nominal. Another normative consideration is that the collective action problem of fair burden sharing must be solved through harmonization at the European supranational level.[20] Concerning the trajectory from accessing the procedural right of initiating an application to the actual granting of asylum status, there exist vast differences between European states. The most generous granting of that status occurs in the Netherlands, Denmark, and Switzerland, where around 48 per cent of applications were successful in 2009, compared to just 1.1 per cent in Greece and 7.8 per cent in Spain. Prospects of success (as well as other features of countries that make up their overall perceived desirability as destinations) seem in turn to feed back into steering the inflow of refugees, with the most generous asylum-providers thus predictably becoming flooded by applicants. Whereas, according to Eurostat data, generous Switzerland received 2065 applicants in 2009 per million residents, and Norway and Sweden (reputed as generous for other reasons) had to deal with even larger numbers of applicants (3570 and 2610, respectively), Spain got away with just 65 applicants per million.

As far as asylum seekers are concerned, and keeping in mind that the vast majority of asylum seekers access the point at which they can claim asylum as irregular migrants, there is a Europe-wide package of rights and claims evolving out of the member states' constitutional and statutory rules, and several rounds of European "harmonization" efforts. The latter were framed by the EU's competence in the fields of visa, asylum, immigration and other policies related to the free movement of persons.[21] This package consists of social, economic, and legal rights of asylum seekers such as: subsistence level transfers, basic health services, entitlements to some kind of accommodation (often in "homes"), the right to appeal decisions in court, and protection of children from being returned to the country of origin. On the other hand, there is a (temporary) ban from labor market participation, limited mobility rights, and the threat of being arrested for deportation (for widely varying lengths of time) in the case of those whose asylum claims have been denied. EU harmonization efforts are intended to preclude (through a data base of finger prints) multiple or sequential asylum claims and to equalize the relative attractiveness of destinations. The latter, however, is undermined by two conditions. First, the generosity of the rights and claims of migrants remains a matter of national sovereignty, not European legislation, due to the principle of *subsidiarity*. Second, *geography*, together with the rule that claimants must apply in the member state where they first enter the EU, plays a big role in determining outcomes. Taken together, these factors have caused a mounting migration pressure on the Mediterranean member states (Spain, Malta, Italy and, in particular, Greece), while Germany, being one of the few member states (Luxemburg is another) that is completely[22] surrounded by other member states, cannot possibly be a country of *first* entry[23] and is thus allowed to return arriving asylum seekers to the country that they have passed through en route. To make things even more complicated, the disadvantages of its geographic location, together with its extreme fiscal conditions and highly restrictionist popular attitudes and policies,[24] have made conditions in Greece (and, to an extent, Italy) so unacceptable by standards of human dignity that courts in Germany, Sweden, and Norway have ruled that migrants may not be returned to Greece *even if* they demonstrably have entered Europe through that country. (Incidentally, Greece is the only EU member state that did not have a common border with any of the others until 2007, when Bulgaria acceded, and which is located on the South-Eastern margin of Europe where migration pressure from Asia and also Africa is greater than in the member states to the North.)

C. Family migration

There is a *soft force of normative consistency* that becomes evident if we look at why European states are relatively generous in allowing for the immigration of third nation citizens (TNCs), that is, those from outside current member states of the EU, for the sake of family formation and reunification. Family migration includes the three sub-cases of family formation, family unification, and the legal status of children immigrating with their parents. Yet national migration and residence laws, which typically regulate these cases in much detail, seem to be inspired by three suspicions. First, is the marriage for which (mostly) women migrate a voluntary act—or are women *forced* to enter into an arranged marriage by parents or relatives? Second and inversely, does the immigration genuinely take place for the sake of the marriage or is the marriage *just a cover* for getting easy access to long term residence rights? Third and less importantly, is the residential space of the resident partner (and hence his *income*) big enough for accommodating a couple and family?

Today, after the period of guest worker migration ended around 1973 and the homecoming of external ethnic minorities is exhausted in most places (except for Greece, Hungary, and Poland), migration for the sake of family formation and unification constitutes a major proportion of the annual inflow of migrants across the outer borders of the EU. Yet family migration is not popular. Nor is it desirable from a functional economic point of view, given that the labor market participation rates of female migrants tend to be far below those of domestic populations and also given that ethnically homogeneous parents can be strong hindrances to the integration of the next generation, especially in its linguistic dimension (which is of course strongly contingent upon the language spoken at home). At the very least, ethnic homogeneity in family formation is bound to increase the efforts made by educational institutions in terms of linguistic integration. But there are limits to the extent to which liberal states can dispense themselves from observing family rights, and these rights (as, for instance, proclaimed in article 6 of the German constitution) apply to human beings, not just to national citizens. The core of family rights is the right to enter into a partnership, to do so voluntarily, and to have children. These rights opened the door to residence and even citizenship rights for foreign-born family members, including prospective husbands or wives. Joppke sees a case here of "the independent workings of moral obligations,"[25] which follow a judicially enforced logic: since we originally allowed first-generation guest workers to stay (rather than to return home with the end of the post-war boom, as we had expected most of them would), nothing can prevent them from doing so, as their trust in a future as permanent immigrant residents must be honored; if they do stay (even without becoming citizens), their grown-up children enjoy the right to marry; and unless this right to marry is combined with residence rights (and in the case of a naturalized resident spouse: citizenship rights), their constitutional right to marry would be significantly injured.

This yields a general normative rule, or an answer to the question of what host states owe their migrants and migrants' offspring. *We owe them what we have given them reasons to expect.* Such expectations are reasonable and hence legitimate if they are built not so much on migrants' assessment of risks and opportunities, but upon the legal order of the receiving states and the normative commitments made by them.[26] These commitments differ widely across member states and across categories of migrants. The readiness and ability of states to protect the human rights of non-citizens is generally contingent upon constitutional guarantees of the rights of migrants and the extent of their enforcement, which in turn are affected by the configuration of three factors: forces of international public opinion; humanitarian political pressures coming from civil society initiatives within states; and the strength of restrictionist, populist, and xenophobic political forces.

To continue with the normative argument: since "we" have actually invited immigrants to trust us and to build life plans on that trust, be it through acts of commission or omission (for example, through our failure to fix termination points in contracts with migrant workers), this trust (which can be roughly supposed to grow with the length of stay and certainly with the transition from one generation to the next) must be honored. "They," the migrants and their descendents, have become legitimate stakeholders whose well-being depends on being socially incorporated.[27] Claims deriving from this status are to be granted—and not just for their sake, but for ours as well. The latter applies not just because "we" have entered into an implicit or "quasi-contract"[28] with them, which we supposedly want to honor as a matter of moral consistency, but also for the consequentialist reason that there will be massive fiscal costs if we fail to assist long term foreign residents and their children in the process of integration and the acquisition of economic self-sufficiency.[29]

At the same time it is well known that, particularly in the case of migrant minorities with an Islamic background, the three types of social relations that occur in families—relations between husband and wife, relations between parents and children, relations between male and female siblings—often (though far from consistently) tend to deviate, for reasons of religious culture, from what a liberal understanding of the human rights of family members would suggest. In spite of the fact that the core family rights specified above must be held sacrosanct and are thus beyond the reach of legislators, the *actual use* family members make of their (marital and educational) rights may not be beyond such reach. In both Germany and France, a debate is emerging on the role of family structures and practices in the process of integration, that is, on the extent to which the paternal authority of fathers over wives and children (as well the presumed authority of brothers to regiment sisters in the name of "family honor") can and must be curbed. Respective policy proposals include the introduction of mandatory kindergarten and pre-school programs for all residents beginning at year one (that is, at the beginning of the process of language acquisition and primary socialization). Also, special integration courses for parents (*de facto* mostly mothers) have been initiated by the German migration authority. Furthermore, the right of parents to decide whether or not their children participate in gym classes or school excursions is categorically denied. Instead, parents are fined if they fail to send their children to school and make them participate in the entire school curriculum. In order to prevent residential segregation (with its obvious implications for the ethnic composition of the student body of schools), pupils can either be allocated to schools through administrative measures (such as "busing") or, arguably more effectively, the ethnic "mixing" of neighborhoods can be promoted through targeted housing subsidies and regulatory measures.[30] The media and civil society organizations of migratory *milieux* can be encouraged and challenged to launch change-oriented discourses concerning male and female, as well as adult and adolescent, identities and role models. At any rate, the integration of the next generation of migrants is increasingly seen as a problem whose solution cannot exclusively focus on the young. The solution must also address parents through comprehensive programs of family services which are designed to curb and redefine educational family rights.

D. European mobility

With the mobility rights deriving from EU citizenship coming into full effect in 2014 at the latest, TCN labor migration (though not TCN illegal, human-itarian, and family migration) may decline—except, perhaps, at the highest levels of skilled labor, for which a global labor market keeps unfolding. The Irish case provides an illustration of this substitution effect (and of the overall Europeanization of labor markets): while the inflow of migrant workers coming from the 12 accession countries (the Baltics, Central Europe, South East Europe plus Slovenia plus one and a half small Mediterranean islands) rose from 9,000 in 2002 to 127,700 in 2006, the number of workers arriving from countries outside of the EU fell, less dra-matically, from 38,700 in 2002 to 34,100 in 2006.[31] In Austria, Belgium, Denmark, and Germany, more than half of all immigration is intra-EU migration.[32] It is too early to assess the nature of integration problems caused by *intra*-EU labor migration, with the overall experience of Polish labor migration to Britain, Ireland, and Sweden (often ending in return migration) providing a favorable outlook. It is also worth keeping in mind that some of the richest EU member states have experienced a noticeable decline in the inflow of foreign nationals (both from within the EU and from outside) since 2005, with the decline from 2005 to 2006 alone amounting to 18 per cent in Austria; while a dramatic increase (118 per cent) occurred only in Portugal (mostly due to family unification inflows from Ukraine) and, to a lesser extent, the Slovak Republic, Sweden, Ireland, and Denmark.[33]

Germany has experienced a recent decline in its overall resident population as a combined effect of declining immigration, increasing remigration, and increased emigration of nationals.

E. Third country nationals' labor mobility

In many EU member states, policy makers, as well as the public in general, still need to realize that third country nationals constitute a "stock" problem (of integrating those who are "here" already) much more than a "flow" problem of new arrivals (if we abstract from the problem of irregular migration, discussed above). If anything, the dynamics of change have shifted market sides, from supply-push to demand-pull. The stock problem, as I have argued, cannot be solved in space by incentivizing remigration, to say nothing about deportation. It can only be solved in time—the time that is needed for complex and contested processes of integration to which both sides (people who do have a migratory background and those who do not) must equally contribute. Even if borders could be effectively sealed to the flow of newcomers, the stock of residents with foreign roots and their integration would remain as the major challenge for public policy.

F. Ethnic kin state mobility

This type of migration, which accounted for hundreds of thousands of new arrivals after the fall of the Iron Curtain, does not play a significant role any more after the two waves of Eastern Enlargement in 2004 and 2007. The only countries in which this type of ethnically privileged migration is still significant are Greece, Hungary, and Poland, while Germany has the greatest proportional stock of co-ethnic migrants (called *Aussiedler* or "re-settlers").

How do these different types of migrants relate to each other in quantitative terms, that is, as components of the whole? In many EU countries, *regular* labor migration from third countries (which could, in principle, be stopped by negative admission decisions) has dropped below 10 per cent of the overall flow of immigration. In contrast, and looking at the OECD world as a whole, 44 per cent of all immigration was family related and only 14 per cent labor market related, with the second largest proportion, humanitarian migration of asylum seekers, varying widely between OECD member states.[34]

II. The Configuration of Interests

The *interests* that shape the migration transaction are located at the *individual* and *immediate* level of *persons* and at the *collective* and *long-term* level of *states* (as well as, in between the two, at the intermediate level of *organized interests*, at least in the receiving countries). These interests can be roughly summarized as follows. They are being pursued on the two liberal normative grounds of *individual* self-determination of people and *collective* self-determination of states.

First, the interests of *individual migrants* from countries of emigration. Most emigration is from the less developed to the richer countries.[35] Depending upon his or her level of marketable skills, the income prospects corresponding to those skills, perceived labor demand in the country of destination, and the (lack of) economic opportunities available at home (or through domestic migration within the country of residence), there will be strong economic incentives to migrate—be it legally or in irregular ways, permanently or temporarily. These incentives can become even more urgent if there are family members to support through remittances. At the aggregate level, these interests constitute a "supply push" causing "migration pressure." There are not just anticipated gains migrants can expect from migrating, however, but also costs. Migrants need to accept and cope with the conditions of leaving their homes, local networks, and families. They must accept the costs and risks of migration, the burdens and uncertainties of adjustment, and possibly discrimination and exposure to exploitative economic power relations at the place of destination. Considering these costs, one can only agree with Brian Barry's view that "an ideal world would be one in which the vast majority of people were content with conditions in their own countries"[36] and thus could afford *not* to migrate. Yet from a normative perspective, it seems easy to agree, at least under liberal presumptions,[37] that the right to emigrate (temporarily or for good) should not be denied to people who want to do so after assessing the net utility of the move. If they "want" to do so, however, because they feel the need to flee from economic misery or political repression (or both), the issue emerges of whether regimes that are causally responsible, be it through acts of omission or commission, for the conditions that people feel compelled to flee, should be allowed to get away with an appeal to the liberal principle of "freedom of emigration" rather than providing them with acceptable conditions at home—an alternative that applies with particular force to sending countries. The backwardness of these must at least in part be attributed to the impact of former colonial rule of the very same countries that are now receiving countries.

Second, the collective and long-term interests of the sending *states*. Here, there is a strong prospect of improving their overall economic situation, through the export of labor power[38] that yields private revenues in the form of remittances[39] and thus unburdens whatever funds for poor relief and unemployment benefits would otherwise have to be made available domestically. That provides a strong positive incentive to facilitate and even actively encourage labor emigration, be it for the sake of economic benefits or for the related sake of expatriating sources of social and political conflict.[40] They may also be interested in building bilateral ties to particular destination states as a result of migration. But there is a dilemma here. Sending states become increasingly aware that they are at risk of demographic distortions and losing labor through the (permanent) *brain drain* that results from emigration, given the increasingly selective skill-focused strategies that receiving countries apply. Yet sending states' options for restricting their citizens' right to emigrate are strictly limited by national and international law.[41] Some of them (for example, Poland within the EU) have therefore begun to incentivize the return migration of workers, particularly of those who have upgraded their skills through work experience abroad (*"brain gain"*). Others make it mandatory for students who receive fellowships from their governments for studying abroad to return after they have graduated. If they fail to do so, they are contractually bound to pay back the entire amount of the stipend they have received. From a normative perspective, states should probably be required not only to grant freedom of exit rights, but also to take into policy consideration the long-term effects of emigration upon those who stay. Such consideration cannot result in an illiberal individual, much less a collective, denial of the right to emigrate as it existed under state socialism. But it may well lead to targeted policies which incentivize potential emigrants to stay or return. It also may justify claims for compensation for brain drain losses, addressed to receiving states.

Third, individuals and interest groups within *receiving* countries. Public opinion in most of the old EU-15 member states is clearly restrictionist as regards the granting of permanent residence rights and certainly citizenship rights, with Greece, followed by Austria and Denmark, being consistently the most migration-averse country. Only in Spain and Finland were *less* than half of the populations surveyed found to be immigration averse.[42] These restrictionist attitudes are inspired by a fear of *economic* consequences of migration (loss of jobs, wage depression, adverse effects upon the welfare state), the fear of *politically* motivated violence (including "terrorism"), and the fear of *cultural* incompatibilities and resulting conflicts. On the other hand, employers and their associations often advocate a stepped-up inflow of (skilled) labor, and middle class private households make extensive use of unskilled and cheap foreign labor employed in cleaning, taxi transport, and caring functions. This indicates, in many countries and regions, an evolving de-facto ethnic division of labor with considerable elements of "brain *waste*" (as when, for instance, a professional history teacher from Cameroon works as an office cleaner in Paris). The pattern of demand for migrant labor that results from these diverse interests on the receiving side is typically "hour glass shaped"[43] in terms of skills and education. As I shall argue in more detail later, there is no obvious normative argument against individuals and organized social categories pursuing their interests concerning both the quantity and quality of inward migration. The only moral requirement here, or so I shall argue, is (a) to honor the terms of the "quasi-contract"[44] between local populations and those who have been allowed in *already* and who have formed legitimate expectations on the basis of this contract and (b) to act truthfully, that is, to submit motivating counterfactuals (of the form: "if more people come in, the boat is going to sink"[45] to rigorous deliberation. Morally, we may also be required to recognize that (c) the challenge of integration is one that imposes demands not just upon migrants, but on non-migrants as well. The latter demands will have to be met, in part, by a reorientation of public attitudes and behavior. Societies will of course undergo changes as the result of immigration. At the very least, these changes should not be resisted by non-migrants at the expense of migrants and their integration.

Finally, *political elites and governments* of *receiving* countries. They are also typically caught in a dilemma: on the one hand, they need to respond to restrictionist sentiments within their own constituencies; on the other hand, a sizeable inflow from both the new member states and, in particular, of TCN migrants is something that cannot be avoided under European law and in any case is positively needed to compensate for the distorted demography of aging EU societies (for financing their fixed benefits and pay-as-you-go pension systems, as well as filling labor supply gaps).[46] Moreover, there is an emerging international market for highly skilled labor from third countries, in which EU member states try hard to improve their competitive position as demand side actors, for example, through the proposed introduction of Canadian/Australian style point systems. Some European countries—notably Britain and Germany, being the greatest losers of emigrating skilled human capital in absolute terms—need to attract trained professionals from outside of the EU in order to compensate for their net losses of skills. In order to avoid what I have called "brain waste," highly complex legislative and administrative initiatives are currently under way to validate and recognize occupational and academic credentials earned abroad. In general, the core dilemma of migration policy-making within the EU (and in particular its old member states of EU-15) consists in a constellation of time-inconsistency: elites find it hard to persuade mass constituencies "now" to accept and support policies that are highly desirable as to their medium term demographic and economic effects. Yet given the ongoing transition of an aging society into a "knowledge-based" economy, both increased rates of immigration and a more effective integration of immigrants' children and grandchildren must be considered as *imperative* as they are *unpopular*. Restrictionist attitudes and resulting policies are typically based upon—or rationalized by reference to—one or more of the following propositions: (a) "more" migration jeopardizes democratic stability and increases the risk of "terrorism" or, for that matter, rightist populist mobilization; (b) it undermines the socio-economic viability of the welfare state; (c) it hinders the integration of the stock of migrants who are "here" already.[47] Elite strategies to escape from or circumvent this dilemma have included: pro-natalist family policies, with an emphasis on policies affecting the female and male work/life balance; an appeal to "growing skills at home" (rather than importing them via migration) through better education (which would also reduce the costs of integrating the descendents of migrant families); and the largely symbolic upgrading of the status of citizenship through the adoption of courses, tests, and ceremonies which are mostly designed to signal to national constituencies that citizenship status is nothing that is to be acquired easily and cheaply.[48] In addition to this kind of time-inconsistency, there is an inverse dilemma, known from the days of guest-worker migration in the 1950s and 1960s, between the concentrated benefits of migration "now" and the diffuse incidence of costs "later."[49] What are the normative implications here that could be addressed to governments and party elites? This question should probably be answered in terms of an institutional (re)design of migration policy-making that is capable of reconciling short-term and long-term concerns, or reconciling the often conflicting democratic virtues of *responsiveness* (to current popular preferences) and *responsibility* (to foreseeable future needs and conditions). In addition to public attitudes and behavioral patterns, much of the normative quality of host societies will depend upon the far-sightedness and "anti-presentist" capacity of institutional migration regimes.

III. The Nature and Dynamics of Migration Regimes

Migration regimes are complex institutional arrangements, still mostly emerging from national legislation, which specify four items in substantive and procedural terms. First, they specify *who* is legally allowed to *cross borders* for what purposes and which procedural requirements (such as visas) apply to those who intend to do so. Second, they specify the regulation of *residence rights* (for example, residence duration, internal mobility rights, threat of termination and coerced repatriation) of categories of people who have arrived from abroad (ranging from tourists to applicants for naturalization). Third, migration regimes specify the rights and other resources migrants are endowed with or granted a claim to, duties they are supposed to fulfill, and efforts they are expected to make, in order to "earn" extended residence rights by achieving a gradual *integration* into the receiving polity and society (for example, through learning the language of the society into which they immigrate). Finally, the migration regime stipulates the procedural and substantive conditions under which migrants, typically after an extended period of continuous residence, are granted access to the full incorporation (or "naturalization") into *citizenship* (including time-limited or

unlimited dual or multiple citizenship), and hence full and equal membership in the polity of the receiving society.

According to a standard model, these four matters that a migration regime
regulates are conceived of as a system of consecutive filters: admission →
residence → integration → naturalization. Yet inversions within that
sequence are also to be found. For instance, *family migration* (that is, immigration for family formation or family unification) can be made conditional
upon the success of *prior* integration through, for example, language courses
taken in the country of origin (as in the German and Dutch cases). This
means that a core component of integration, namely basic linguistic skills,
must *precede* admission. Similarly, integration is supposed to take place
prior to admission in cases where citizenship is granted to members of
external co-ethnic minorities, and often (as in the cases of Germany,
Hungary, and Greece) almost automatically so, with ethnic belonging taken
as a valid indicator of integration.[50] Another inversion occurs when the process does not *culminate* in naturalization but when the granting of (partial,
for example, local voting) citizenship rights is conceived of as a *catalyst
towards* further integration. In such cases, the stages of naturalization and
integration are inverted relative to the standard model. Nor need the chain
from the initial entry through admission to eventual naturalization be completed. For many migrants it ends, quite intentionally from their point of
view, with the stage at which they have acquired permanent residence rights
and (partial) integration, as they are not interested in proceeding to full
citizenship. Others, such as business men, managers, or professionals,
provided that they import capital or earn high incomes, enjoy the privilege
of being excused from any integration requirements. Still others, namely
persons coming from *EU member states* and enjoying the mobility rights
associated with EU citizenship, may well be in need of integration without
having "migrated" beforehand, as their citizen rights apply EU-wide and
access and residence rights are available to them upon request. As far as *refugees* and *asylum-seekers* are concerned, the process ends after the second
step since, contingent upon improvements in their country of origin, they
are expected and often mandated to return home. Lastly, *irregular migrants*,
being subject to a generalized negative admission decision (which, however,
remains largely unenforceable) by the state in which they are physically
present, may (hope to) gain residence rights through some procedure of
re-regularization and the long-term official toleration of their presence.

Finally, a rule of prudence is recommended by many theorists and practitioners of migration regimes. This rule refers to a desirable balance between
stages one and three of the model, that is, a balance between the quantity
and quality/origin of people being admitted at the *present* point in time and
the *ongoing* and effective integration efforts the receiving state and its citizens are able and prepared to make. This balance can be tilted in two ways:

either the available *programs and institutions* of integration are inadequate to absorb incoming migrants and their offspring or the *numbers and characteristics* of the latter overburden those programs and institutions. Both these frames involve pragmatic policy conclusions concerning the action parameter that can best be used to tackle integration problems. Here my thesis is that only the first of these frames and its policy implications actually makes sense, both morally and pragmatically, under present European conditions. That is to say, since numbers and characteristics of migrants are largely beyond the control of public policies (as most of the migrants and their offspring are irreversibly "here" already), any balance must be achieved through the supply of adequate programs and institutions, which is to say: not in space but in time.

What is actually going on in policy terms is a drift of migration regimes and their ongoing reform that follows two principles. First, residence status and also citizenship is made easier to acquire through migration and citizenship reforms adopted by most member states during the first decade of the century.[51] Second, the increased permeability of borders is accompanied by policies of "migration productivism" (even "eugenic" migration regulations[52]), that is, a selective emphasis put on the long term productive contribution migrants can make to the receiving economy and the capacity of migrants to support themselves. The first message is: "you are welcome, wherever you come from." And the second: "you are welcome, as long as you are a self-supporting net asset for 'our' economy and as long as your presence does not raise concerns about 'security.'"

In contrast to a normal contract into which two parties freely enter (supposedly after each having carefully considered their preferences, the alternative courses of action available to them, and the costs associated), decisions to migrate and to allow migrants to enter is a phenomenon full of uncertainties, collective action problems, and problems of myopia. Nor can the decision of migrants to exit their country of origin be taken as typically a "free" decision, since comparatively undesirable economic and political conditions can, and often do, necessitate a move that may well be regretted at a later point. Similarly, the governments of receiving states may be unable or unwilling to assume the responsibilities involved in a liberal regime of immigration. We can therefore conclude that interests, as the standard starting point of "realist" political theory,[53] are unhelpful in explaining and prescribing the design of a migration regime, as these interests are unusually hard to define in the policy area of migration and its regulation. What is needed, instead, is ultimately a yardstick that allows us to distinguish between *morally legitimate* interest and others.

Nor are economic and political interests (including the interests of political elites to appease politically destabilizing mass sentiments and their impact upon party competition) the only causal factors that drive migration policy and the ongoing overhaul of migration regimes both at the member state and EU levels. The growing parts of the migration that is actually taking place are governed by intra-European mobility rights anyway, as well as international conventions (regarding the admission and residence rights of refugees and asylum seekers) and national constitutional law (regarding family rights and the mobility of (prospective) family members). Moreover, there is an unknown but substantial number of *irregular* migrants whose movement is exclusively guided by an individual calculus of gains and risks/ losses that escapes regulation through the interests and policies of actors in both sending and receiving countries.

IV. Dimensions of "Integration"

Of the four terms making up the standard model of migration (entry, residence, integration, citizenship) the term "integration" is by far the most elusive. It is a social construct that is a composite of two dimensions: the (normative) dimension of what members of a migrant minority *must* do in order to reach the status of actually being "integrated" (comprising the *demands* imposed on migrants by authorities and citizens of the receiving state), and their perceived *capacity* to comply with these expectations and to *supply* the expected behavioral contributions to the process of becoming integrated. In other words, migrants and their descendents are coded by actors in receiving societies in terms of what they *must* do (demand) and what they *can* and are typically willing to do (supply). Together, these two dimensions constitute types of implicit "integration theories" that inform policies.

Again, there are four analytically distinguishable cases.[54] If both demand and supply are held to be high, we arrive at a notion of integration that is *assimilationist*: migrants need to comply with *high* standards of conformity with the norms of the majority, and there is *no* reason to assume that, being reasonable and adaptable human beings, migrants (wherever they may come from) are categorically unable to do so, provided they are adequately guided and assisted in the process. The adoption of this type of integration theory logically involves the need to develop a fairly explicit and uncontroversial description of the distinctive normative foundations that "all of us" share as a collective identity, that is, the non-migrant majority; for this is the standard to which migrants will eventually have to conform. While such self-description can arguably be achieved in the case of French republicanism, it has manifestly failed in the case of attempts to canonize a German "lead culture" (*Leitkultur*); and it borders on the ridiculous when migrants are expected to adopt distinctively "Dutch values."

If we move to the opposite end of our two dimensions we arrive at the *multiculturalist* integration theory: as virtually all people are born into and essentially confined by a cocoon of religious and other cultural identity[55] and hence cannot assimilate without a painful loss of that protective shell, it would be seriously unfair to expect them to conform to standards of the majority culture, which in its turn is likely to benefit from (and eventually also to come to appreciate the gains it derives from) the rich diversity of identities that it comprises.

Thirdly, integration can be conceptualized by making high demands in terms of what migrants *must* do while simultaneously *denying* that they will and *can* (ever) live up to those requirements, for reasons that are ultimately rooted in their "cultural genes" (if not their biological ones). This configuration is essentially—or serves as a pretext for—a *racist* construct, as it insists on a notion of integration that is largely premised upon an essence of ethno-nationalist purity to which foreigners cannot have full access (certainly not all kinds of them).

Its opposite is a *pluralist* concept of integration, which combines moderate adjustment demands addressed to migrants with cautiously optimistic assumptions concerning the ability and willingness of migrants to adopt—over the course of two or three generations—patterns of cultural, political, and economic behavior and capabilities that are compatible and ultimately may converge with those of the majority population (which itself is bound to undergo changes in the process). The starting point of this open-ended and bilateral process is the recognition, on the part of long-term residents and naturalized citizens *and* on the part of the non-migrant majority population, of basic constitutional values and procedures. In the spirit of a highly abstract "constitutional patriotism,"[56] these values and procedures can then be employed in the ongoing negotiation of the terms of cultural and socio-economic co-existence. Within the framework of the pluralist integration theory, the viability of its concept of integration is contingent upon two conditions: first, that the majority population is willing to live with and actively adjust to the condition of diversity that is brought about by migration, that is, to integrate *itself* into conditions of ethnic, religious and cultural pluralism. Second, that public institutions (foremost the education system, social services, the media, labor market institutions, and civil society associations such as sports clubs and faith-based organizations) adopt—and effectively deliver on—their responsibilities of helping the integration of migrants and their descendants and the overall management of diversity.

All of these four semantics (as well as the political pragmatics implied) of what is meant by "integration" coexist. They jointly form the background of fluid and fluctuating, often event-driven and resentment-driven public (as well as not-so-public) discourses in a European Union which is soon to face the condition of unrestricted mobility that *European* citizenship involves. With it will come a new wave of migration-induced ethnic and linguistic[57] diversity—the legal category of "migrants" will become obsolete as a descriptor for citizens of any of the 26 member states being present in any other of them; instead, they will turn, legally speaking, into European fellow citizens.

Of the four ideal-typical integration theories just distinguished, only the last can lay claim to normative validity as well as to practical feasibility. Assimilationism amounts to the imposition of a cognitive frame according to which the ethnicity, phenotypical markers, religion and other dimensions of minority cultures are condemned to insignificance and ignored in the name of official color-blindness. This frame does not work in practice and, on the contrary, nurtures a backlash of identity politics. The "micro-communitarianism" of multicultural migration regimes fails in the opposite direction, as it is plainly not conducive to any gradual approximation of a shared concept of cultural, socio-economic and political citizenship. And the "macro-communitarian" discriminatory approach of ethno-nationalist purity, while in some countries successfully appealing to large political constituencies, is normatively unacceptable as it verges on the categorical denial of human, civil, and social rights to migrant minorities and their descendants. After these simple steps of subtraction, what remains, in both normative and practical terms, is a version of the pluralist approach to integration that emphasizes complementary rights and duties on both sides of the migrant/domestic divide, while conceiving of the problem of integration as a long-term one that must be dealt with over several generations.

In Europe, the major difficulty with this pluralist (or "accomodationist") approach derives from the fact that European nation states are made up of majority populations the members of which tend to claim for themselves some superior historical legitimacy, both in relation to minority nation(alitie)s and in relation to migratory minorities. "Titular" nations think of themselves not just as majorities, but as *historically validated, dignified* and *privileged* majorities, since "we" have "always" been here, which supposedly entitles "us" to unilaterally set the terms that govern the presence of others as a matter of collective self-determination.[58] In contrast, populations of the classical countries of immigration in the Americas and Australia are, as it were, constitutionally aware of the fact that "all of us" (except for the largely marginalized "native" or "aboriginal" populations) are (descendants of) migrants who have arrived at some point in historical time. Although the linguistic (and some legal, cultural and religious) legacies of Portuguese, Spanish, Dutch, French, and, most importantly, British colonialism are clearly visible in these classical immigration countries, these legacies have been largely neutralized through successful movements of independence in which *new* nations were constituted. They consist, from the beginning, of ethnically diverse populations of which no part can lay a valid claim to greater historical and political rights compared to others who have migrated.

Where everybody is a (descendant of a) migrant, the very category of being a migrant (or of having a "migratory background") loses much of its significance as a frame of potential legal discrimination.[59] Lacking the opportunity to develop an ethnically-based patriotism, settler societies have comparatively easier access to a "constitutional" version of patriotism, while European nation states are still in the conflict-ridden process of transitioning from a "national" to a post-national or "constitutional" understanding of patriotism and citizenship. This admittedly highly stylized difference between the European and the (North) American/Australian contexts can also explain why issues of the cultural/religious compatibility of migrant minorities are still dominant in the former case, while in the latter the migration regime is unashamedly utilitarian, that is, focused on the balance of human capital gains and integration costs of migrants.

Integration is commonly understood as a process that results in something becoming a constitutive part of (or included in) a whole of which it originally was not a part. Starting with this intuition, we may ask: *into what* are migrants asked to integrate themselves by cooperating with the integration efforts of receiving societies? Answers differ widely according to the type of integration theory that is being used. Six commonly employed categories of integration criteria can be distinguished.

1   The ability to understand and speak the *local language* is a widely shared priority, on both sides of the migrant/non-migrant divide. It can be argued for as an encompassing precondition of employability and *economic* life, of a minimum of *cultural* assimilation, and of the ability of *all* migrants (not just linguistically homogeneous sub-groups of them) to develop *political* voice capacities in the polity they now inhabit (rather than the one they—or their parents—migrated from). Failure to read, understand, and speak the local language would thus count as a serious integration deficit, after an appropriate period of presence in the country and provided that formal learning opportunities (language courses, informal encouragement by native speakers) are available.

2   Successful participation of migrants and their children in formal *education* (itself premised upon language acquisition) is another measure of integration, which is in turn contingent not just upon the quality of pre-school and school services provided to them, but also upon low levels of—long term—urban segregation of migrant communities and upon effective limitations that can be imposed on the role of parents in the primary and secondary socialization of their children. Integration can certainly be said to be deficient if parents either fail to send their children to public (or state recognized) schools or if they cause children to boycott parts of the school curriculum (for example, co-ed gym classes). Other educational indicators of failed integration are ethnically specific

drop-out rates and the underrepresentation of migrants in the student body of secondary and tertiary education.

3 A standard by which the degree of integration can be usefully measured is the "conduct" of soul and body. The former refers, again on both sides of the divide, to recognition of the positive *and negative* freedom of religion of fellow citizens (including adolescent family members), and to respect for the precedence of secular over religious law. The latter refers to styles of dress, food and food preparation, gender and sexual relations and attitudes, and inter-generational authority relations and conduct. It is in these areas of (nominally "private") everyday life that cultural conflicts over the public use of identity signals are amazingly severe and persistent.[60]

4 A further measure of the degree of integration is law-abidingness and a rudimentary cognitive familiarity with the legal order and the principles on which the political system is built (while the basic contents of civic education, for example, knowledge about how laws come into being and so on, are required only for the last stage of the migration regime, naturalization). Group specific crime rates and the presence of ethnic criminal organizations are strong negative indicators in this area.

5 Majority populations usually also take a strong interest in defining integration in economic terms, that is, the ability of migrants to support themselves and their families rather than relying on social assistance and unemployment benefits. Negative indicators are disproportionately low enrolment in and graduation from vocational training programs, as well as differential rates of unemployment.

6 Strong positive indicators of integration are membership in civil society organizations (for example, sports clubs) of a *non*-ethnic nature, as well as the absence of strong ethnic preferences in the formation of friendships, partnerships, and marriages.

Note that the first segment of a migration regime—the rules regulating the legal crossing of the border of a state—is the only one that takes place in *space,* while the three subsequent stages (residence rights, integration, and naturalization) take place in *time*. In space we can move back and forth, which is trivially not the case with time: what happened in the past cannot be undone. The right to *entry* is largely unproblematic to the extent that exit, after a relatively short period of time, can be expected to take place spontaneously[61] or otherwise can be effectively enforced. What *is* problematic is the right to *stay*.[62] The temporal structure of the migration regime is not just shaped by statutory limitations and extensions of the duration of residence rights, or by the length of residence required for naturalization, but most significantly by the temporal chronology of the human life cycle itself: people are born, go to school, learn a trade, earn a living, move to other places, form marriages and partnerships, have children, grow older, retire, and die. In the process, they join associations, enter into all kinds of contracts, practice religious beliefs, fall sick, experience and cope with problems of social and economic insecurity, and participate in political life. All of this is not only what they actually do; it is what they *expect* (and must be expected by others) to do, accordingly make plans about, and build preferences and normative claims about, usually long before they actually do it. They reflexively form life plans. From the beginning of the life cycle (should Muslim women be granted the demand to be assisted by female obstetricians only?) to its end (should deceased Muslims be allowed to be buried without a coffin, with the dead body just wrapped in a cloth?), institutional adaptations and policy decisions need to be negotiated between representatives of the domestic majority and migrant minority or minorities. Apart from the micro-chronology of the human life cycle, there is also a macro-chronology of public policies and the polity as a whole: constitutions are adopted with the intention of making their basic principles irreversible, parties and coalitions of social forces are formed and become entrenched, institutions are built and policies adopted, the collective past is selectively remembered and appropriated, the future anticipated and shaped according to current preferences, and so on.

Along the time line representing the life cycles of successive generations, there is an important distinction between the first generation of migrants who actually crossed a border and later generations who were born to migrants yet never migrated themselves. Since the former (except those that had to flee their country) have made a *decision* to migrate, presumably weighing risks and opportunities, they can be, to an extent, *held responsible* for having made a *right* decision in doing so. Should it turn out (to them) that it was not the right decision, they can, we may assume, eventually return, as their relation with the country of origin can still be fully reactivated. Therefore, arguably, they have less of a claim against the government of the receiving country to be assisted and promoted in their process of integration, than do their children and grandchildren. This is so because the latter had *no* choice as to their place of birth and upbringing. Chances are that they do not have a realistic option to return, for instance because they no longer speak the language of their parents or grandparents, or because they lack social networks, or because job prospects and welfare state benefits are absent or inferior in the country from which their ancestors emigrated, so that there are strong interests that speak against even considering the option of returning. For all practical purposes, they are "trapped" and have become rooted in a place where they have not chosen to live. As a consequence, the responsibility of the receiving country for their integration and favourable development is much greater than with the first generation. An analogous difference between generations obtains in the intensity of affiliation with the culture of origin. While someone who arrives as an adult has been exposed to, and exclusively shaped by, the culture of his or her country of origin, that does not apply to the next generation(s). If the problem were one of migration in geographic space, it could be responded to by closing borders. But that is not the case, as the problem is of a "longitudinal" nature, unfolding in biographic time and the sequence of generations whose members are here already and who can neither be forced nor effectively incentivized to return. Retroactive "spatial" options of getting people out who were allowed to settle are no longer available, and neither is the option of closing borders to EU nationals. The only way to cope with the problem of integration—which, among other aspects, is a massive economic and social policy problem of wasting or underutilizing the talents and labor of poorly integrated descendents of migrants[63]—is to improve the arrangements of integration for those whose parents or grandparents originally "earned" the residence rights of which later generations cannot legally be deprived.

People who have themselves migrated made a *decision* to do so and remain *connected* to the society of their origin. In contrast, their children and grandchildren have not made such decision and mostly cannot even consider returning after adolescence. These two differences suggest the following normative guideline: members of the first generation cannot legitimately be expected to adopt the cultural norms (including gaining linguistic proficiency) of the country where they have arrived as adult persons. On the other hand, their claims on the host country in which they have chosen to settle are limited. Thus in both directions mutual claims from the "quasi-contract"[64] are relatively "thin." They are much thicker, for the reasons just spelled out, in the case of members of the second and later generations. At the end of their adolescent years, they can legitimately be expected not to have fully "assimilated" into the dominant culture, but to be fluent in its language and to have arrived at an amalgamated synthesis of cultural styles, social norms, and traditions of both the migrant minority and the domestic majority. Yet this synthesis does not emerge automatically; it must be cultivated, assisted, encouraged, and promoted through institutions of formal education, family services, the media, work organizations, urban conditions, associative life, and religious and artistic practices. This process of a gradual approximation across generations can succeed, or it can fail. Whatever the outcome may be (with the qualifiers "success" and "failure" themselves being to a large extent a matter of debate), it is hard to disentangle whether "they" or "us" and our institutions are causally responsible for either of these outcomes. If the second generation of migrants turns out to be *more strongly* or exclusively rooted in their parents' culture of origin than the latter, or if their levels of skills and employability are *inferior* to those of their parents, then clearly something went wrong—be it that parents and migrant communities were affected by the mechanism of *strengthening* their and their children's identity definition in reaction to the diaspora situation, or be it that "our" schools and other institutions failed to play their proper role in the process of integration.[65]

The normative standard that an acceptable migration regime must fulfil can thus be derived from the *pacta sunt servanda* rule. Once migrants have been given reasons to believe[66] that their presence in the receiving country can eventually be turned into a durable one, the life plans that they make on the basis of this assumption must be honored, and their realization adequately assisted. The problem is not one that derives from the fact that migrants have *come* from some *place* outside of the EU; the problem is the conditions under which they *stay* and pursue their life plans across biographic *time*.

Most importantly, an ongoing and fair process of decision-making must be established concerning the claims both sides can raise against each other. More precisely, there should be three reasonably institutionalized discourses and corresponding procedures. First, the discourse *within* migrant communities where issues of identity, religious and cultural norms, and the political as well as socio-economic demands of these communities are negotiated, within a framework of fair representation of gender and age categories. The presence of such an institutionalized discourse would help to overcome the sectarian fragmentation we can often observe within minorities of migrants, which tend to be divided between "orthodox" currents, with symptoms of seclusion and self-marginalization, versus liberal, even strongly assimilationist, tendencies. Second, there must be a discourse within the *receiving* society, which is typically also divided between, on one side, restrictionist social and political forces and resentments, and on the other, more open-minded ones, with the latter being partly motivated by demographic and labor market concerns and partly by multiculturalist ones. Both of these internal discourses aim at a critical assessment of what are, respectively, "our" histories, traditions, identities, and needs. Third, these two discourses and their shifting priorities must feed into an overarching deliberative process in which the terms of coexistence between migrants, their descendents, and non-migrants are to be continuously negotiated. The key characteristics of this process are the emphasis on mutual respect, the generation of mutually acceptable reasons, and the absence of majoritarian claims to the effect that the preferences of the domestic population must be taken for granted and must prevail. Institutions that have tried to approximate these ideals are the German *Islamkonferenz* and the French *Haut Conseil à l'Integration*. They represent a method of building norms and establishing insights that differs sharply from the conventional methods of majoritarian elections, parliamentary legislation, and the processing of conflicts in courts. As such, it can be appreciated on both sides as a welcome challenge to probe into one's own understanding of identity, history, and one's normative essentials, thus contributing to the formation of a political culture that is shaped by a continual exercise in abstraction and reflection. Max Weber's famous "feeling of belonging together" (*Zusammengehörigkeitsgefühl*),[67] which he considered the ultimate foundation of national statehood, would become the result rather than the premise of such reflection. Yet note that we have not arrived at any substantive answer to the (probably unanswerable) question of which moral rights and duties an ideal migration regime should entail. What we have arrived at, instead, is a *meta*-norm concerning morally desirable procedures according to which the previous question should be answered in a given situation and context.

V. The Acquisition of Citizenship

Let us next look at the last stage of the migration model: the acquisition of citizenship, or naturalization. Migrants and their descendants who hold full residence rights, and thus are potential candidates for naturalization, are legally *entitled* (after waiting periods that vary widely between European countries and categories of migrants) to *apply* for citizenship, but they can hardly be *forced* to actually do so and become citizens, least of all if that would imply that they give up (or automatically lose, according to the laws of their country of origin) their original *ius sanguinis* citizenship. On the other hand, political commentators and philosophers have always converged on the view that it is highly desirable, for the sake of the *democratic* quality of the polity, that all of those (adult) citizens to whom the law applies, including long term residents, have (and actually make use of) equal political rights in the making of the law. The political incorporation of long term residents is deemed desirable because the greater the quantitative difference between the universe of citizens and the universe of permanent residents becomes, the closer we would move from democratic equality to a kind of majority despotism, defined as a political system where a majority enjoys the exclusive entitlement to make the laws that bind *all*, including long-term resident denizens.[68] It is therefore also in "our" interest that foreign-born long-term residents and their descendents do actually adopt the citizenship of their country of residence, as that will presumably build loyalties to the country and also will prevent them from "importing" political causes and conflicts from their country of origin. Yet as naturalization cannot be mandated or enforced, it needs to result from a free decision on the part of those who are legally entitled to apply. Such decision is, on the part of potential candidates, likely to be shaped by two considerations. First, what do "I" *gain* by transforming myself from a mere long term resident ("denizen") into a citizen of the country in question? Second, to what extent would I *feel* "at home" in the country of my new citizenship, and feel recognized and respected by relevant segments of the majority society as a fellow citizen?[69] If that is right, the decision to join the political community would be driven by perceived individual *interests* and *emotions*.

The acquisition of citizenship by holders of a foreign citizenship is a transition that is nowhere automatic, as it is when it is acquired through birth by *ius sanguinis* or *ius soli*. In contrast, it always depends upon an explicit decision, initiative, and formal application by persons after they have met certain requirements (such as duration of legal residence and so on). The specific interests of migrants to actually opt for the transition from long term resident status to that of full citizenship are, as a rule, not particularly compelling; as their social and economic rights, having been acquired at an earlier stage of the migration sequence, often do not depend upon being a full citizen. For even without being citizens of their country of residence, they are entitled to vote in local elections (and, in addition, European elections if they hold the citizenship of an EU member state). Thus the first thing that naturalization provides access to is active and passive voting rights at the national level. Secondly, some member states exclude non-citizens from some social services and non-contributory social assistance ("welfare") transfers,[70] although such discrimination is more often contingent upon the duration of legal residence than it is on the citizenship status. Thirdly and most importantly, only national citizens (and in some countries also EU citizens) have access to public sector employment. Finally, failure to become a citizen involves marginally more limited mobility rights within the EU. Summing up these conditions, we might say that migrants who are not particularly interested in the politics of their country of residence, are not poor, earn a living in the private sector, and do not intend to relocate within the EU have at best very limited interest-related reasons to naturalize. Additionally, the acquisition of citizenship is not costless. Not only does it cost the time and effort to attend naturalization courses and pass the respective tests. It also involves in most cases the renunciation of one's own original (or, in the case of the second and third generation, one's parents') citizenship—a move that can be experienced as costly in material and immaterial terms as it involves at least symbolically severing ties to the legal system and the national culture of the country of origin.

Insofar as emotions are concerned, the sense of being excluded or discriminated against, and of being deprived of opportunities and recognition, will certainly not contribute to the readiness to acquire citizenship. The readiness for and the subsequent act of "citizenship acquisition can serve as a rough measure of integration."[71] If this is so, it should be food for policy makers' thought that just over a third of Turks in Germany have actually adopted German citizenship, and that the number of Turks who have chosen to make use of their legal entitlement to do so declined from 83,000 in 2000 to just 25,000 in 2009.

In addition to interests and feelings, the readiness to acquire citizenship status can also be driven by a *rational understanding*[72] and appreciation of the institutional order of the country in which long-term resident migrants and their offspring are to be incorporated as citizens. The acquisition of the cognitive prerequisites of civic competencies can take place through mandatory courses and tests, the introduction of which has been a major institutional innovation in the migration regimes of many EU member states[73] during the first decade of the century. At the same time, not all citizens, but only migrants and their descendants, are mandated to attend naturalization courses and to pass tests, and never is the citizenship of a native born at risk of being lost as a consequence of poor grades they receive in civics classes. This can lead to the perception of discrimination and stigmatization, deriving from a generalizing background assumption that all migrants suffer from symptoms of civic incompetence and ignorance. To the extent that values are taught and the adoption of these values is tested, such procedures invite the objections that (a) what is tested is not the actual adoption of values but rather the adroitness in paying lip-service to them and (b) that immigrants are asked to express value commitments that their domestic-born future fellow citizens have never been formally asked to make, thus amounting to a practice that Joppke has termed discriminatory and "illiberal liberalism" In other words, if you want to become a citizen, then you need to be a citizen that is better than and morally superior to everyone else—which is a blatant violation of standards of political equality. These three objections—stigma, lip-service, unfair demands—can be countered only by designing naturalization courses in analogy with what is taught in civics courses at public schools of the country of immigration. In this way participants, to the extent they are first-generation immigrants, are provided with the opportunity to "make up" for lessons that they missed as children and youths due to reasons that were beyond their control. Also, tests must be designed to check knowledge and understanding, not attitudes and values. And, almost needless to say, the courses (and, if need be, their repetition in case of failed tests) must be free of charge—just like ordinary public schools.

David Miller has asked the core question of the whole debate.[74] The question is "whether *citizenship alone* is a sufficiently strong cement to hold together a democratic welfare state, whose successful working depends upon relatively high levels of interpersonal trust and cooperation or whether it is also necessary for the citizens to share a cultural identity of the kind that common nationality provides."[75] In several of his earlier writings, he leans towards the second alternative, arguing in essence that diversity (ethnic, linguistic, cultural, religious, "racial fractionalization" in the US) will demonstrably undermine the functioning of the democratic welfare state. But that argument is a move that I would label "premature empiricism." For the alleged causal link between diversity and distrust (with which the non-migrant majority addresses migrants and their descendents) is mediated by the attitudes and practices of people of whom it is, to say the least, not categorically inconceivable that they might be able to *change* their habits and, as a consequence, render the causal link between diversity and distrust less forceful. Also, there are arguably *other* causal mechanisms (such as, in Europe, population aging, persistently high levels of unemployment, competitive disadvantages of EU economies under the impact of market-making "negative integration," austerity responses to the financial market crisis, and the transformation and subsequent defeat of social democracy) that play a greater role in weakening popular confidence in both democracy and the welfare state. Regardless of the answer to that question, I see the greatest weakness in Miller's argument in the clearly implied assumption that the second alternative, the one that ties citizenship to national culture, is still viable and feasible. Should that assumption be wrong, we are compelled to try to cope with the fact that citizenship is the *only remaining kind of cement* that is still at our disposal.

My thesis is that citizenship is a good that is being traded in what used to be a sellers' market (that is, the terms of the transaction of becoming a citizen were determined by receiving states) yet is currently being transformed into a buyers' market. Once upon a time, states were able to make the granting of citizenship rights contingent on all kinds of conditions, beginning with ethnic belonging and a ban on dual citizenship. Such demanding and exclusionary conditions are no longer legitimately feasible. As I have tried to show in my review of interests, emotions, and reasons for acquiring citizenship, the status of being politically incorporated in a particular nation state has lost much of its unequivocal attractiveness, and particularly so under conditions of derivative European citizenship. In contrast, what *is* valuable is the status that permits permanent residence and hence access to labor and other markets. It follows that, in order to transform migrants into fellow citizens, much will depend on facilitating their identification with (and their feeling at home in) the political community that *invites* them to join.

Immigration, if all goes well, will not just solve demographic and labor market problems. Moreover, it will provide all involved—migrants as well as "us", the non-migrants—with a welcome and durable challenge to practice the art of abstraction, which allows us to form and live in a kind of political community that is reasonably robust even in the absence of a much-mystified ethno-cultural "cement" of identity-based fellow-feelings. This challenge will exert an ongoing pressure to think about who "we" are and how our self-identification must be revised and upgraded so as to make it compatible, within the framework of constitutional patriotism, with an equally reflexive self-definition of others and their rights. It is this persistent challenge that would be responded to in the system of three negotiating tables I have suggested above.

VI. The Disanalogy Between Exit Rights and Entry Rights

After the end of the Cold War and the Iron Curtain, four human rights norms governing across-border mobility have clearly gained validity and recognition. First, the norm that states are not permitted to summarily "arrest" their own population (for example, by building a border wall with armed guards). Citizens are, as a matter of their human rights,[76] free to leave their country of citizenship; they enjoy *exit* rights. If exit rights of citizens are curtailed in particular cases (think of defendants under criminal prosecution), legal arguments must be provided according to standards of rule-of-law and in view of the individual case. Second, the norm of protection from *coerced* exit. It stipulates that states are not permitted to expel or deport their own citizens beyond state borders (as in cases of ethnic cleansing that occurred in the post-Yugoslav wars). As a corollary, states are obliged to allow the *re-entry* of individual citizens as well as expelled minority groups returning from abroad.[77] The right of *free* exit, in other words, means that the act of exiting must not be paid for by the price of its irreversibility. The horrors of the post-Yugoslav wars and practices of ethnic cleansing have given rise to a categorical revision of the doctrine that was considered valid, throughout the 20th century, that states have the right to determine the composition of their own populations through the expulsion or coercive deportation of minorities or the implantation of settlers who are brought in to replace them.[78] It seems that as a result of the evolution of human rights doctrines and international conventions, nation states have lost much of their competency to select and manage the composition of their populations.

To summarize, exit-related human rights—the right to leave one's country, the right to give up one's nationality, the right to do so voluntarily rather than due to being individually or collectively coerced, and the right to return and to resume full citizen rights (in case nationality has not been given up, be it explicitly or by implication[79])—seem all firmly entrenched. Yet in a world whose land is virtually fully covered by territorial states with their borders, every exit from one state is bound to imply an entry into the territory of another state. This being so, the freedom to exit can be rendered entirely nominal by the absence of the complementary right, the freedom to *enter*.[80] The absence of the latter freedom would thus appear to limit the extent and value of the former. States that limit the right to enter across their own borders can be said to diminish the exit options of an unspecifiable number of potential inward migrants. Without entry rights, somewhere, exit rights are meaningless. The same applies for immigration rights of one state without emigration rights granted by all other states. Yet the complementarity that exists between exit rights and entry rights, or so I wish to argue, is a highly *asymmetrical* one. For the two categories of rights differ in four respects. First, exit rights involve just *negative* duties of a respective state (at least if we disregard the trivial positive duty to provide travel documents), while entry rights imply *positive* duties of the receiving state (for example, duties to provide police and basic health protection even to short term visitors, at the minimum). Secondly and closely related, exit is a single event that takes place at one *point* in time, while entering another country can cause a whole *chain* of events, and the more so the more durable the stay is. To put it differently: granting access to immigrants involves an embryonic contractual relationship between immigrant and receiving state, while granting exit effectively terminates, at least for the time being and until a possible return, any contractual relation. Third, the loss (or gain) of (human) capital that exit can cause to the sending country can normally only be measured at the level of aggregate externalities, that is, the loss depends on *how many* people leave within a period of time; while the gain (or loss) that occurs in the receiving country can be attributed to concrete individuals and their interaction in local settings at their point of arrival. Finally, the duty to grant exit rights to would-be emigrants applies unambiguously to the state of residence/nationality alone, while the duty (if any) to grant entry rights is shared among all potential countries of destination. Therefore, if a person is denied exit rights, she or he is severely deprived of *all* rights to cross-border mobility; whereas, if denied entry rights by a particular state, there remain others, though perhaps less attractive ones, to turn to for admission. If that is so, denial of access to immigrants amounts to a comparatively lesser violation of rights than denial of exit.[81]

This would be different, and hence the complementarity of exit and entry rights would be more symmetrical, if either of the two following conditions were to apply, one objective and one subjective. The objective condition is that the world consists of just two countries, A-land and B-land, which means that the refusal of A-land to receive migrants from B-land amounts to the categorical *denial of exit rights* to citizens of the latter. The subjective condition applies when in a multi-country world a preference order exists (across all potential migrants) of the form: admission to country A > stay in country of residence > admission to countries {C, ..., N}. In this case, the denial of admission to country A would amount to the cancellation of the *desire* of inhabitants of country B to *make use* of their exit rights. As these two constructs are evidently of a nearly absurdly counterfactual nature, the above claim of asymmetrical complementarity holds.

I propose to conclude from these considerations[82] that entry rights granted to immigrants are, in morally perfectly legitimate ways, more qualified and restrictive than are exit rights granted to emigrants. As a consequence, (long term) migrants' liberty to leave is more extensive than their liberty to arrive, to stay, and to be incorporated into their desired country of destination. Correspondingly, states' duties to let people go are more binding than receiving states' duties to let people come and stay. This having been said, we need to determine what *justifies* the gap between the extent of exit rights and that of entry rights and how a fair balance between the two, or an *appropriately* asymmetrical complementarity, can be designed.

Rephrasing the problem in terms of the two core norms of liberal political theory—individual self-determination through rule of law and collective self-determination through representative democracy and external non-interference with the "internal" affairs of states—we get the following result: in the (typically rich) destination countries of migrants, collective self-determination trumps the individual self-determination of individual migrants, while the opposite is the case in (typically poor) sending countries with their strictly limited rights to restrict individual emigration moves in the name of their collective and long term interests. This configuration of priorities clearly favors the rich countries of destination, as it maximizes their options to "harvest" global labor power and talent according to criteria that they remain perfectly free to determine without any significant outside interference. This asymmetrical interdependence between the two types of countries calls for normative standards and practical measures that can restore a measure of symmetry and fairness.

Let us first look at countries of emigration. As we have seen in the rough account of interests given earlier, the typical case of poor sending nations is the combination of a long term individual interest and also, though ambiguous, a long term state interest in letting people emigrate. The ambiguity results from the fact that among the people who leave will be some who are (or will soon be) urgently needed for building the country and maintaining its infrastructure. Their absence causes a negative externality at the aggregate level (in the form of a shortage of human capital and skills), though that may be partly offset by positive externalities at the micro level of families who receive remittances from income earned abroad. If the negative externalities are seen to exceed the positive ones, sending countries suffer a net damage. As a consequence, governing elites may be tempted to make the emigration of skilled workers legally more difficult for them and thus to interfere with their exit rights, particularly given the fact that the skilled strata of the domestic work force are those increasingly in demand abroad. But outright violating the exit rights of skilled workers—building the equivalent of a Berlin Wall, as it were—is not the only way to control emigration. *Incentives* can be used (and are in fact widely used in contexts as different as soccer clubs and universities) to make people refrain from *using* their right of exit while, *as* a right, it remains fully intact. Another option for controlling emigration without undermining the right to emigrate consists in the *contractual* abrogation of the right for a specified period of time, with contractual penalties being imposed on violators. The same applies if some international regime were to be set up which imposes restraints on the hiring of skilled labor from poor countries. Still another option is to establish an exchange mechanism such that receiving countries assume the responsibility to send, within the framework of a mandatory or voluntary service program for young people[83] set up by these countries, one "man-year" worth of development aid in return for every man-year worth of foreign labor admitted.[84] Such services could be rewarded by partial tuition waivers for returning students, who would also benefit from the experience. Finally, similar compensation could take the form of granting fellowships for college and university study (with contractually mandated return clauses) for student migrants from a country in proportion to the foreign labor (legally) employed that originates from that country. I mention these options just to demonstrate that the greater stringency and extent of exit rights compared to entry rights, if it involves burdens such as a brain drain for states obliged to grant exit rights, can and should be mitigated by means other than the denial of exit rights.

Now, the immigration countries and their (qualified) obligations to grant entry rights. The argument so far has been that their obligations to grant rights to entry (and stay) are more limited than the obligations of sending countries to grant exit. That proposition, however, does not yet answer the subsequent question: what are morally *un*objectionable *reasons* to design admissions in ways that are selective and restrictive?

The discriminatory granting of entry and residence rights can be positive and negative, as well as quantitative and qualitative. In either case, discrimination is not to be morally excluded, provided that such discrimination can be justified—and if so, not just to local constituencies, but to the hypothesized figure of the "neutral spectator." *Negative quantitative* discrimination (limiting the quantity of people allowed in) can be justified with reference to an existing discrepancy of flow and stock. That is to say: we, the host state, have admitted so many migrants in the past that admitting more of them now would threaten the prospects for integrating those who are here already and who therefore, because they have developed a legitimate "stake" in living here, deserve to be given preference. Yet this justification would lose much of its validity if it could be demonstrated, in response, that the country in question has short-sightedly failed to provide migrants with the appropriate arrangements within the educational, housing, and labor market systems which are prerequisites for their successful integration. *Negative qualitative* discrimination occurs when it is based upon assumptions and suspicions about the cultural incompatibility of categories of migrants (for example, by religion, by gender, by country or region of origin), or upon the anticipated costs and frictions resulting from their presence. The logic of this attempted justification is what I have called "racist." The only respectable argument that could be made here would refer to the manifest failure or unwillingness of migrants to learn and use the local language. Such linguistic failure, however, would manifest itself only *after* an extended period of exposure to the language community in question. Furthermore and happily, the ability to learn a particular language and to use it, at least at an elementary level, is known to be a universal human capacity.[85] The analogous objection of "it remains to be seen" (and cannot be presumed *ex ante*, at least not at the individual level) applies to the closing of borders to those who are deemed unable to support themselves and their families. Whether or not they in fact are unable will turn out only after they have entered.

Qualitative and *positive* variants of discrimination use two criteria. First, capital, in particular scarce human capital, and second, ethnic or regional affinity of migrants with the prospective host society. The first is taken as a token of the economic assets the migrant represents, often assessed by using a point system; the second as a token of the "integration costs" (including ascribed security risks) the migrant and her or his offspring will cause. As far as the first is concerned, it is likely to cause damaging externalities on the human capital pool of the country of emigration; if so, these effects can be morally defended if compensatory mechanisms are in place of the kind I have mentioned when discussing them as alternatives to the limitation of exit rights.

Finally, the quantitative and positive combination is not really a variant of discrimination, but an expansionist strategy that is motivated by the need of host countries to stabilize and improve their demographic structure. Take the example of Germany. It is the most "polyethnic" country in Europe, with nearly 20 per cent of the resident population having a "migration background" of various sorts.[86] Among all experts on the matter, there is virtually no disagreement concerning the prognosis that by the year 2050 the resident population of Germany will have fallen from 82 to 69 million people, or by nearly 16 per cent—unless, that is, a massive wave of new immigration is allowed in. Thus a rational policy response would seem to be to avert this "sudden" shrinking and aging of the population, together with the associated crisis of production and (intergenerational) distribution, by opening borders as widely as possible and providing for more effective integration and human capital formation. Given this demographic emergency, there should remain little leeway for discriminatory admission practices.

This instrumental and consequentialist policy orientation should certainly trump all restrictionist qualifications of the right to entry, as I have just discussed them. In reality, however, it turns out that this unequivocally rational expansionist policy approach is, in its turn, trumped by what might be called "democratic myopia." Given the overwhelmingly restrictionist attitudes and preferences of constituencies (which, in their turn, are nurtured by poor integration results), policy elites feel that they simply cannot afford to act rationally without risking being punished by voters. Compared to the 1950s and 1960s, the logic of "democratic myopia" has remained the same, with just the algebraic signs inverted. In the earlier period, the post-war boom caused policy makers, largely responding to employers' interests, to permit a *great* influx of "guest workers" without providing for appropriate integration arrangements that (quite foreseeably) would be needed for them in the medium term. In the present period (and largely responding to popular resentment and the fear of populist mobilization), an overly *restrictionist* approach is maintained in spite of the foreseeable negative consequences of this approach for the demography and the political economy of European welfare states, their labor markets, and pension systems.

VII. Conclusion

I conclude with a negative proposition concerning the normative foundations of migration regimes: it is unpromising to make an argument for open borders that is based on a concern for *distributive global justice*. To be sure, migration regimes can be designed so as to provide protection to (some of) those who come as refugees and apply for asylum. But the question "would open borders lead to an international redistribution of wealth that benefits the globally worst off?"[87] must clearly be answered in the negative. First, it is not the worst-off in the sending countries who migrate in the first place, as these typically lack the material means and other resources they would need to migrate.[88] Second, open borders would withdraw human resources from the countries of origin which would be needed in order to improve the economic, as well as the political, conditions in these countries. If global inequality is what is to be remedied by an appropriately designed migration regime, it would have to be a regime that (a) is sharply selective as to the countries whose citizens are allowed in and that (b) entails strong conditions of mandatory and definitive remigration to the country of origin, as well as mandatory remittances. Both of these conditions are unlikely to be adopted and enforced in a liberal polity. If we want to heal the injustices of global distribution, designing a migration regime is neither a promising nor a realistic place to start.[89] Yet if the promotion of global justice is clearly too demanding a normative standard to which migration regimes must comply, seemingly less demanding ones—such as procedural fairness, non-majoritarian modes of conflict resolution, the non-discriminatory provision of labor market and educational opportunities, and the curbing of some educational family rights—remain normative challenges to which European migration regimes still need to fully and adequately respond.

Notes

* The author is grateful to David Abraham, Jim Fishkin, Bob Goodin, Micheline Ishay, Ulrich K. Preuss, and Lea Ypi as well to an anonymous reviewer for helpful comments on earlier versions of this article. I dedicate this article to my friend and colleague Faruk Birtek, with whom I have been discussing citizenship issues for decades.

1 Herbert A. Simon has observed that "any causal analysis explaining why American GDP is about $25,000 per capita would show that at least two thirds is due to the happy accident that the income recipient was born in the US" (quoted in van Parijs 2001, p. 131). Miller (2005, p. 197) says similarly, "A person's life prospects depend heavily of the society in which she happens to be born."

2 Shachar 2009. That is mostly in cases where it is acquired according to the *ius sanguinis* logic of descent, but also in cases where a strict *ius soli* logic applies (nowhere in the present-day EU). A pure *ius soli* regime of citizenship means that one's citizenship in a state is acquired by being born in the territory of that state, regardless of the citizenship, residence status, or origin of one's mother or parents. The pure version of *ius sanguinis* stipulates that the citizenship of one's mother or parents is transmitted through birth, regardless of where the birth takes place. Mixed arrangements are possible, such as making *ius soli* citizenship contingent upon length of legal residency in the relevant country of at least one parent.

3 Sen (2009) presents a rich and complex state-of-the-art account of this debate, as well as a compelling contribution to it.

4 Dworkin 2000. Roemer 1998. Beckert 2008.

5 In the case of the EU, a sharp distinction must be drawn between international migration to and from member states (which, by 2014 at the latest, will have turned into virtually unlimited mobility rights of persons as well as other economic items, despite the nominal autonomy of member states to set up their own citizenship laws and migration regimes) and the inward migration of *third nation citizens* (TNCs) from outside the EU. What migration, integration, and naturalization policies are concerned with in Europe is overwhelmingly TNC migration, not within-EU mobility.

6 Cf. Abraham 2010. Pevnick 2009.

7 There is a certain arbitrariness in this conceptualization. Suppose we were to take the year 1900 instead of 1949 as the retrospective limit in time and three generations instead of one as the prospective limit. We would easily arrive at a majority of the resident population having a "migration background." Needless to say, this concept does not apply to temporary residents such as foreign students, foreign diplomats, *au pair* persons, seasonal workers, and tourists.

8 cf. Jandl 2007.

9 According to an Italian study (quoted in OECD 2008, p. 39), "about 60 to 65 per cent of unauthorized immigrants are overstayers, another fourth persons who entered with fraudulent documents and the remainder persons who entered illegally, by sea or across [land] borders". In 2005, the EU has equipped itself

with a special border police force by the name of FRONTEX which is mandated to guard the EU's external borders.

10 In many EU member states, there are active and vocal NGOs putting pressure on governments not to expel apprehended irregular migrants.

11 cf. Triandafyllidou 2010.

12 Joppke 1998, p. 266.

13 Ibid., p. 268.

14 Ibid., p. 270; cf. Freeman 1995.

15 The Universal Declaration of Human Rights (1948) grants the human "right to seek and to enjoy in other countries asylum from prosecution." (art. 14.1).

16 Miller 2005, p. 303.

17 After the civil war in Kosovo has become a matter of the past, and after most EU member states have recognized Kosovo as a new political entity in Europe, there are no valid legal reasons any more to grant asylum status to people who have fled the region half a generation ago or more; yet given the fact that Kosovo neither has legal provisions nor the fiscal means to accommodate returnees and to provide them with jobs or social transfers, sending those people "home" (together with their foreign born children who, as a rule, speak neither Albanian nor Serbian, but rather German or French or so on) clearly amounts to an act of deliberate deprivation that seems impossible to justify in moral and political terms.

18 The French version of that list, adopted in 2005, includes "safe" countries such as Benin, Capo Verde, Ghana, Mongolia, Georgia, and Bosnia.

19 McBride 2009. Löhr 2010.

20 Such harmonization has in part happened through the Dublin II agreement of 2003, which specified which state is in charge of which asylum seeker arriving where. In contrast to asylum migration, labor migration will always leave the choice of destination countries to migrants themselves.

21 These are referred to by the names of cities where complex and short-lived agreements on asylum programs were reached at the EU level, such as Tampere (in 1999), Dublin (in 2003), The Hague (in 2004), Stockholm (in 2009).

22 With the exception of Switzerland, to which, however, the same applies.

23 By surface travel, that is; yet the presence of tight airport controls and respective regulations of airlines guarantee the truth of this proposition.

24 Greece is the only EU member state that has neither signed nor ratified Protocol 4 of the European Convention of Human Rights (1950); its Article 4 prohibits the *collective* expulsion of foreigners.

25 Joppke 1998, p. 287.

26 But note that the two are not fully independent. According to an estimate of the EU Commission, there were up to eight million irregular migrants residing in member state territories. Of these, around 400,000 were arrested in 2007, and less than 180,000 were eventually deported to their countries of origin, amounting to some 2 per cent of the "stock" of irregulars (Busse 2008). The legal and administrative practices that are reflected in these figures can ground the expectation of (irregular) migrants that their prospects for establishing themselves in the country of destination (including being regularized at a later point) are not altogether negligible.

27 Bauböck 2009, pp. 22–28.

28 Miller 2008, p. 371.

29 In economic terms, the implicit contract between the domestic population and migrant communities can be understood as an investment: only if the "stock" of the migrant population is "managed" wisely, a positive "return" in terms of demographic and economic benefits will occur. If not, the fiscal costs resulting from failed integration, in particular educational and labor market integration, will exceed positive results. As a German journalistic account has put it bluntly: "It's a disturbing trend for Germany. The country needs immigrants because Germans aren't having enough children. The population is shrinking and aging and its productivity is in danger. If the immigrants, who tend to have more children, are poorly educated and can't find jobs, they'll end up costing the state money rather than supporting it. A study by the Bertelsmann Foundation estimates that failed immigration is already costing the country up to €16 billion per year" (Elger et al. 2009).

30 As Hartmut Häussermann has argued in unpublished work, the problem of managing urban ethnic segregation can best be approached by, again, thinking in temporal rather than spatial terms. That is to say, in the *short run* ethnically homogeneous segregation will be legitimately preferred by migrants because it provides a "bridgehead" where newly arriving migrants gain access to material, cultural, and political resources derived from the homogeneity of neighborhoods. Yet in the *medium range* of their presence in the host society, migrants should be encouraged to move to non-segregated parts of cities. In this way, segregated *neighborhoods* would persist, while their *residents* would move in and out.

31 OECD 2008, p. 38.

32 Ibid., p. 35.

33 Ibid., p. 29.

34 Ibid., pp. 36–7.

35 Kleven 2002, p. 79. See also ibid., p. 85: "Seven of the world's richest countries (the United States, Germany, France, the United Kingdom, Italy, Japan and Canada) with less than one eights of the world's population, had about one third of the migrant population."

36 Barry (1992, p. 279). This notion of an ideal world applies to the supply side of sending states. A reciprocal demand-side ideal of conditions in receiving states is what Bauböck (2009, p. 2) describes as "states have no more reason to restrict admissions because the political and economic disparities between them that currently trigger refugee flows have been flattened out."

37 In contrast, strong republican presumptions would require migrants to weigh their individual interests against obligations they have towards their fellow citizens at home.

38 In the trade of countries such as Turkey or Mexico, labor power has been at or near the top of their export items.

39 Not much is known, at least to this author, about the distributional impact of remittances, either across the social structure of countries of emigration or across time.

40 These incentives play a role even among EU member states. When in August 2010 the French president Sarkozy launched a campaign threatening sanctions against the 15,000 Romanian Roma legally residing in France under the

European norm of free mobility of citizens of member states (Anon. 2010), the Romanian president Basescu expressed his sense of "gratitude" to his fellow-nationals abroad "for what they are doing for our country"—namely claiming social assistance payment in France rather than at home. "Imagine what would happen," he added, "if the two million Romanians [currently working in other EU member states] would return home and claim unemployment benefits here, given the fact that our unemployment fund runs a deficit already." (Schmidt 2010.)

41 The International Covenant on Civil and Political Rights grants the right to leave except "when necessary to protect national security, public order, public health or morals or the rights and freedoms of others." (Art. 12.3)

42 For these and further data, cf. Howard (2009, ch. 3). See also Boeri et al. 2002, ch. 5.

43 "Most recent South-North migrants have education levels significantly below host-state medians, but a minority of them—highly skilled/professional migrants—are more educated that host-state citizens" (Cornelius and Rosenblum 2005, p. 103).

44 Miller 2008, p. 371.

45 *Nota bene*: There is no doubt that boats *can* be full. But that needs to be truthfully demonstrated, and the resulting burdens of scarcity, if any, fairly distributed. If the boat is actually overcrowded, people can be asked to leave—or a bigger boat can be provided.

46 To be sure, an alternative to promoting immigration in order to fix demographic imbalances would be to increase the internal labor force utilization rate by making more people work longer per life, which was the implicit preference of the largely failed European Employment Strategy (EES) of 2000. As such measures of "activation" are known to be highly unpopular on the European continent (as they run up against the resistance of the growing cohorts of the elderly and near-elderly), promoting inward migration of workers may be considered by elites a slightly lesser evil. Also, from the point of view of business interests, (first generation) migrants have the considerable advantage of being flexible in space, as they do not have the rootedness and resulting stickiness of much of the domestic work force. Cf. Boeri et al. 2002, pp. vii–xiii.

47 Such propositions can and must be subjected to rigorous plausibility tests.

48 Joppke (2007, p. 11) speaks of the symbolic dimension of courses and tests which he sees as serving the function of "appeasing anti-immigrant publics."

49 Freeman 1995, p. 885.

50 Not all states have a full-blown migration regime. When an exclusive *ius sanguinis* criterion for the acquisition of citizenship applies (as in Japan and Israel), only co-ethnic categories of people and descendents of ethnic citizens can be naturalized.

51 Howard 2009. Bauböck et al. 2006a; 2006b; 2009.

52 Some German Christian Democratic MPs have proposed introducing mandatory IQ tests for arriving migrants. See, for example, Anon. 2010.

53 Hendrickson 1992.

54 Cf. Offe 1996.

55 For an effective critique of this most rigid version of multiculturalism, see Phillips (2007, ch. 1).

56 For a discussion of constitutional patriotism in the context of migration, see Müller (2007, ch. 3).

57 The EU-27 recognizes 23 official languages, many of them linguistically as remote from each other as Portuguese and Estonian, or Hungarian and Dutch.

58 If the status of a titular nation is contested and there is more than one nation in a state making claim to the status of titular nation, the state is likely to fall apart. European examples are Czechoslovakia, Yugoslavia, Cyprus and (perhaps soon) Belgium.

59 Needless to say, this logic does not apply to those whose ancestors have "migrated", yet not voluntarily so, and who, on top of that, are phenotypically recognizable as belonging to that group, namely the descendants of former African slaves in the US. And neither does it apply to those who (in historical time) never migrated, but constitute a "native" or "aboriginal" population.

60 Cf. Joppke (2009) as a comparative study of headscarf policies in Europe.

61 This applies to tourism, business trips, and foreign students. It was also (wrongly) assumed to be the case in guest worker programs of the 1950s and 1960s.

62 Hendrickson 1992, p. 222.

63 For a documentation and statistical analysis of the cost of failed integration in Germany, see Woellert et al. 2009.

64 Miller 2008.

65 To *welcome* such persistence of culturally inherited patterns is the point at which multiculturalist ideologies turn openly cynical, as they discount the socioeconomic and cultural marginalization that victims of such persistence will have to experience.

66 In France, residence rights are explicitly contractualized. Immigrants are mandated to sign a contract in which they agree to the performance of legal, economic and educational duties on which the duration of their residence rights is made contingent.

67 Similarly, Michael Walzer (1983, p. 62) speaks of the national political community as a "community of character."

68 "On democratic grounds, it appears wrong for someone whose interests are chiefly impacted by the policies of a particular state to have no say in determining those policies." (Miller 2008, p. 377).

69 Note that there is one seemingly insurmountable discrepancy between the majority of *ius sanguinis* citizens and newcomers. While the former form a political community, defined as having a common future *and a common past*, including the memories and responsibilities deriving from that past, newcomer citizens share only a common future. For instance, what sense, if any, should a Ukrainian born German medical doctor make of the standard phrase of German political elites that, given the facts of history, Germany bears a special responsibility for the state of Israel?

70 Howard 2009, pp. 6–7.

71 Ibid., p. 8.

72 In a "thin" Weberian sense, "rationality" is a quality of all matters that can be learnt and taught, rather than emanating from revelation, intuition, habitus, or affect.

73 Pioneered by the Netherlands, mandatory integration and citizenship courses are now standard routines in Austria, Finland, Germany, France, Denmark and the United Kingdom.

74 Cf. also Abraham 2010.

75 Miller 2008, p. 378 (my emphasis).

76 According to the United Nations Universal Declaration of Human Rights (UDHR) both the physical exit from one's country (Art. 13 (2)) and the legal exit from the nationality of one's country (Art. 15 (2)) are guaranteed.

77 This norm against expatriation that was violated in spectacular and highly consequential ways by the GDR government in 1976 when it denied re-entry to the dissident poet Wolf Biermann when he was trying to return home from a trip to West Germany.

78 The UN Human Rights Commission unanimously adopted, in 1997, a "Draft Declaration on Population Transfers and the Implantation of Settlers." Its formal ratification by the UN is, however, still pending. As it was first stipulated in the Dayton agreement of 1995, wherever such dislocations of people have taken place, victims have the right to return and states the obligation to facilitate and desist from obstructing such return.

79 "Implicit" abdication occurs when second generation *ius sanguinis* citizens live abroad and relinquish their rights and duties from being a citizen. To them applies a negative *ius soli*, as they no longer have a stake in the country from which their parents have emigrated.

80 People were "walled *in*" by the border and its guards that the GDR government erected around West Berlin in 1961 and that crumbled in 1989; up to 200 people where shot dead during those 28 years by border guards when they tried to cross the wall to enter West Berlin. In contrast, the fences and border control arrangements that the US government installed on the Mexican border were designed to "wall *out*" illegal migrants from the south. Among those who try to cross anyway, an estimated 350 die every year (Pevnick 2009, p. 160)—though not from being shot, but from other causes such as dehydration and accidents. It seems worth reflecting upon the vastly different attention the two cases receive, and also on the fact that "walling in" and "walling out" are not opposites, but amount to the same condition—except that the latter can more precisely be described as "walling in from the outside" rather than by the government of those whose movement is obstructed. Remarkably, the "walling out" of people seems to be a much more justifiable practice than that of walling them in, although the former can cause the same (or greater) amount of human suffering and death. The answer may be that if state A blocks the entry of citizens of state B, they remain free to try it at the border of states {C, ..., N}, whereas such freedom does not apply if state B walls in its own citizens.

81 This asymmetry manifests itself in the generalization that "emigration does tend in practice to be far freer than immigration, which is highly controlled by most countries." (Kleven 2002, p. 73.)

82 This is in contrast to attempts to establish a strictly symmetrical (or "consistent") relation between exit and entry rights (cf. Goodin 1992; Ypi 2008).
83 US examples are AmeriCorps and Peace Corps.
84 This idea was suggested to the author by Micheline Ishay.
85 Here is a problem of circularity: if the right to stay is made contingent upon some linguistic proficiency, this may stimulate learning efforts; it may also *demo-tivate* them, as the anticipation of having to leave may make such efforts appear in vain.
86 At the same time, incidentally, the country is one of the least "multinational" ones in Europe, having the smallest autochthonous population—just about one per cent—with recognized ethno-linguistic minority status.
87 Bauböck 2009, p. 4.
88 Miller 2005, p. 198.
89 That does not preclude efforts of, in particular, BRIC countries to benefit from student (re)migration. For instance, the idea of attracting back "home-grown but overseas-nurtured" talent is incorporated as a major policy objective in the 11th Chinese five-year plan. This idea illustrates the fact that remittances can take the form of both monetary transfers and human capital transfers.

References

Abraham, David. 2010. Immigration and social solidarity in a time of crisis: Europe and the US in the new century. University of Miami: unpublished paper.

Barry, Brian. 1992. The quest for consistency: a sceptical view. Pp. 279–87 in B. Barry and R. E. Goodin eds. *Free Movement: Ethical Issues in the Transnational Migration of People and of Money*. University Park: Pennsylvania State University Press.

Bauböck, Rainer, Eva Ersboll, Kees Groenendijk and Harald Waldrauch, eds. 2006a. *Acquisition and Loss of Nationality: Policies and Trends in 15 European Countries*. Volume 1: *Comparative Analyses*. Amsterdam: Amsterdam University Press.

Bauböck, Rainer et al., eds. 2006b. *Acquisition and loss of nationality: policies and trends in 15 European countries*. Volume 2: *Country Analyses*. Amsterdam: Amsterdam University Press.

Bauböck, Rainer et al., eds. 2009. *Citizenship Policies in the New Europe*. Amsterdam: Amsterdam University Press.

Bauböck, Rainer. 2009. Global justice, freedom of movement, and democratic citizenship. *Archives Européennes de Sociologie*, 50, 1–31.

Beckert, Jens. 2008. *Inherited Wealth*. Princeton, NJ: Princeton University Press.

Boeri, Tito, Gordon Hanson, and Barry McCormick, eds. 2002. *Immigration Policy and the Welfare System*. Oxford: Oxford University Press.

Busse, Nikolas. 2008. EU: Einwanderung besser regeln. *Frankfurter Allgemeine Zeitung*, June 18, 2008.

Cornelius, Wayne A. and Marc Rosenblum. 2005. Immigration and politics. *Annual Review of Political Science*, 8, 99–119.

Dworkin, Ronald. 2000. *Sovereign Virtue*. Cambridge, MA: Harvard University Press.

Elger, Katrin, Ansbert Kneip and Merlind Theile. 2009. Einwanderung: für immer fremd, *Spiegel Online*, January 29, 2009, <http://www.spiegel.de/spiegel/0,1518,603321,00.html>.

Freeman, Gary P. 1995. Modes of immigration politics in liberal democratic states. *International Migration Review*, 29, 881–902.

Goodin, Robert E. 1992. If people were money.... Pp. 6–22 in B. Barry and R. E. Goodin, eds. *Free Movement: Ethical Issues in the Transnational Migration of People and of Money*. University Park: Pennsylvania State University Press.

Hendrickson, David C. 1992. Political realism and migration in law and ethics. Pp. 213–31 in B. Barry and R. E. Goodin, eds. *Free Movement: Ethical Issues in the Transnational Migration of People and of Money*. University Park: Pennsylvania State University Press.

Howard, Marc Morjé. 2009. *The Politics of Citizenship*. Cambridge: Cambridge University Press.

Jandl, Michael. 2007. Irregular migration, human smuggling, and the eastern enlargement of the European Union. *International Migration Review*, 41, 291–315.

Joppke, Christian. 1998. Why liberal states accept unwanted immigration. *World Politics*, 50, 266–93.

Joppke, Christian. 2007. Beyond national models: civic integration policies for immigrants in Western Europe. *West European Politics*, 30, 243–73.

Joppke, Christian. 2009. *Veil: Mirror of Identity*. Malden, MA: Polity Press.

Kleven, Thomas. 2002. Why international law favors emigration over immigration. *Inter-American Law Review*, 33, 69–100.

Löhr, Tilman. 2010. *Schutz statt Abwehr. Für ein Europa des Asyls*. Berlin: Wagenbach.

McBride, Jeremy. 2009. *Access to Justice for Immigrants and Asylum Seekers in Europe*. Strasbourg: Council of Europe.

Miller, David. 2005. Immigration: case for limits. Pp. 193–206 in Andrew I. Cohen and Christopher Heath Wellman (eds), *Contemporary Debates in Applied Ethics*. Malden, MA: Blackwell.

Miller, David. 2008. Immigrants, nations and citizenship. *Journal of Political Philosophy*, 16, 371–90.

Müller, Jan-Werner. 2007. *Constitutional Patriotism*. Princeton, NJ: Princeton University Press.

Organisation for Economic Co-operation and Development (OECD). 2008. *International Migration Outlook*. Paris: OECD.

Offe, Claus. 1996. Modern "barbarity": a micro-state of nature? Pp. 17–40 in A. Heller and S. Puntscher Riekmann (eds), *Biopolitics: The Politics of the Body, Race and Nature*. Aldershot: Avebury.

Parijs, Philippe van, ed. 2001. *What's Wrong with a Free Lunch?* Boston: Beacon.

Pevnick, Ryan. 2009. Social trust and the ethics of immigration policy. *Journal of Political Philosophy*, 17, 146–67.

Phillips, Anne. 2007. *Multiculturalism without Culture*. Princeton, N.J.: Princeton Univeristy Press.

Roemer, John E. 1998. *Equality of Opportunity*. Cambridge, MA: Harvard Univeristy Press.

Sen, Amartya. 2009. *The Idea of Justice*. Cambridge, MA: Harvard University Press.

Shachar, Ayelet. 2009. *The Birthright Lottery: Citizenship and Global Inequality*. Cambridge, MA: Harvard University Press.

Triandafyllidou, Anna, ed. 2010. *Irregular Migration in Europe: Myths and Realities*. Farnham: Ashgate.

United Nations High Commission for Refugees. 1951. *Convention Relating to the Status of Refugees*. <http://www.unhcr.org/protect/PROTECTION/ 3b66c2aa10.pdf>.

United Nations High Commission for Refugees. 1967. *Protocol Relating to the Status of Refugees*. <http://www.unhcr.org/protect/PROTECTION/ 3b66c2aa10.pdf>.

United Nations Human Rights Commission. 1997. *Draft declaration on population population transfers and the implantation of settlers*. Appendix II in Mr. Al-Khasawneh, *Freedom of Movement: Human Rights and Population Transfer*, UN doc. E/CN.4/Sub.2/1997/23, <www.unhchr.ch/Huridocda/Huridoca.nsf/ (Symbol)/E.CN.4.Sub.2.1997.23.En?Opendocument>.

Walzer, Michael. 1983. *Spheres of Justice*. New York: Basic Books.

Woellert, Franziska, Steffen Kröhnert, Lilli Sippel and Reiner Klingholz. 2009. *Ungenutzte Potentiale. Zur Lage der Integration in Deutschland*. Berlin: Berlin Institut für Bevölkerung und Entwicklung.

Ypi, Lea. 2008. Justice in migration: a closed border utopia? *Journal of Political Philosophy*, 16, 391–418.

Friedrich Schmidt. Sicherheitsoffensive für die Wahl 2012. *Frankfurter Allgemeine Zeitung*, August 6, 2010, <http://www.faz.net/s/RubA24ECD630CAE40E483841 DB7D16F4211/Doc~EDD98155D916A4CFBA56C359CD95AC3BC~ATpl~ Ecommon~ Scontent.html>.

Xenophobia: casting out the un-French. Editorial. *New York Times*, August 6, 2010, p. A22.

Anon. Unionspolitiker fordern IQ-Test für Zuwanderer, *Sueddeutsche Zeitung*, June 6, 2010, <www.sueddeutsche.de/politik/einwanderungspolitk-unionspolitiker-fordern-iq-test-fuer-zuwanderer-1.966379>.

9

On Citizenship, States, and Markets*

Ayelet Shachar and Ran Hirschl

This article brings to center stage the debate that is currently absent in larger discussions about citizenship and immigration: the reality that state and market forces are becoming increasingly intertwined in shaping migration selection criteria and membership-allocation priorities. The bulk of academic debate has understandably focused on the "restrictive turn" witnessed in recent years with respect to ordinary immigration and naturalization applicants, such as those who enter on the basis of a family reunification claim or for humanitarian reasons.[1] We will argue, however, that equally important lessons about the current state of citizenship can be learned by examining *who* is given the red-carpet treatment, and on *what basis*. In today's global knowledge economy, those who can shore up the human capital reserve of the nation while bolstering its international reputation as a talent magnet are in high demand. Who is fast-tracked in the visa and citizenship line is no less revealing of the qualities we value in others and seek to incorporate into our political communities, than who is pushed to the back of the line or denied access altogether.

From the ultra rich to successful entrepreneurs to top scientists, elite athletes, and world-class artists, we increasingly find well-off countries facilitating specialized entry tracks and expedited naturalization for those "high value" migrants they seek to attract. Governments are now willing to go so far as to reconfigure the boundaries of political membership to allow faster and smoother access to citizenship for exceptionally talented individuals they covet as prized assets, often with the expectation of return—reputational or otherwise.[2]

Political Theory Without Borders, First Edition. Edited by Robert E. Goodin and James S. Fishkin.
© 2016 John Wiley & Sons, Inc. Published 2016 by John Wiley & Sons, Inc.

As the demand for the "best and brightest" (a term of art used by immigration policymakers worldwide) has intensified, a global race for talent has emerged. It has taken the form of recruitment of those with extraordinary skills and achievements—whether in the sciences, arts, or sports—as well as the intuitively more questionable practice (we return to this key point later) of permitting the ultra rich a fast-track to citizenship based on specialized cash-for-passport programs open exclusively to high-net-worth individuals. Such programs have proliferated in recent years from the United Kingdom to Australia, Portugal to Malta, France to the United States. Either way, these privileged migrants now have more destination countries from which to choose, with each country offering its own set of benefits and incentives, chief among them is an expedited access to membership in the body politic.

These developments, which we generically label *Olympic citizenship*, have received only scant attention in academic circles, despite their growing prominence in the real world of immigration policymaking and their contribution to larger processes of redrawing the boundaries of (selective) inclusion into the political community. This new trend poses major legal and ethical puzzles, telling us something significant about the fusion of market logic and national interests in the early decades of the twenty-first century.

Our discussion highlights the practice of governments "picking winners" through targeted and occasionally strategic grants of citizenship to those with extraordinary talent or conspicuous wealth, entrenching new inequalities and stratifications in the process. After identifying these dramatic yet under-theorized developments, we explore the conceptual transformation associated with the rise of Olympic citizenship, and how it may erode the ideal of citizenship as a political relation grounded in equality rather than competition.

We will further argue that, although specialized skills-based and investor-based migration programs both instantiate the rise of Olympic citizenship, from a normative perspective it is important to distinguish between recipients of citizenship who are given specialized treatment on the basis of their *human* capital from those who gain citizenship merely in exchange for a hefty bank wire transfer or a large stack of cash. Although John Rawls famously held that the distribution of natural talents and endowments is arbitrary from a moral point of view (one cannot be said to "deserve" to be born with athletic prowess or an outstanding ability in math), we here side with Charles Beitz's position that the *choice* to develop one's natural or raw talent—and the significant effort that goes into cultivating one's human capital—is bound up with identity and can be said to be protected by considerations of personal liberty.[3] This position is compatible with the recognition that societal conditions are crucial for allowing any one of us to refine and improve his or her human capital. Even the most brilliant athlete, scientist, or innovator needs a community in order to succeed; or to paraphrase a familiar proverb, it takes a village to raise an Olympian. The more significant point for the purpose of our discussion is, however, that raw talent is *not* a sufficient condition for achieving the extraordinary level of accomplishment expected of those who benefit from Olympic citizenship.

In the context of talent migration, the concern with favoring the best and brightest is not moral arbitrariness. On the contrary, Olympic citizenship provides the most elaborate model on offer of what a carefully-calibrated merit-based admission policy that falls under the discretionary migration category might look like. The normative difficulties lie elsewhere and broadly fall into three categories: 1) arguments grounded in fairness (which analytically can be broken into distinct subcategories: fairness to other would-be immigrants, to the population of the admitting country, and to those who stay in the country of origin); 2) the equation between human capital and capital per se, which we will challenge in this article; and finally 3) the concern that government-facilitated transactional visions of citizenship may ultimately erode the ties that bind and what it means to belong to a political community. Throughout the discussion, we will draw upon comparative examples from the citizenship and immigration laws and policies of core participants in the global race for talent to explore how the more instrumental logic of Olympic citizenship may irrevocably transform the ideal of political membership—as a relation grounded in equality and participation—by morphing civil and political goods into more calculated and strategic transactions.

By focusing on the highly skilled, the new breed of "desired" migrants that competitive states wish to attract and admit, we offer what we hope is a fresh perspective on the depth and direction of these legal, ideological, and institutional shifts, including their growing affinity with certain aspects of market-oriented thinking—a conceptual turn that our conventional theories of citizenship and migration have regrettably not taken up.

The discussion advances in four steps. We begin by explaining the logic and political economy of talent migration. In today's stratified international mobility market, the focus is not on closing the gates of admission, but on opening them *selectively*. Next, we chart the main legal strategies adopted by leading countries engaged in the global race for talent, strategies that are increasingly used to set human capital criteria for selecting whom to admit. In so doing, desired destination countries are signaling their preference for a particular class of immigrants. This empirical foundation will later serve as the backdrop for our inquiry into the legitimacy of adopting skills-based criteria, and more controversially, investment-based schemes, both of which exemplify the rise of managed and selective migration regimes.

In the third part, we juxtapose the normative implications of these two related yet separate practices: recruiting the highly skilled on the basis of their human capital, and admitting the ultra rich by virtue of their temporary or permanent financial contribution or investment in the passport-issuing country. The former grants political membership to those with extraordinary achievements as part of a selective recruitment strategy that sees skills-based migration as a mechanism for human capital accretion. This process can only succeed when talented migrants settle in the recruiting nation and generate positive externalities in their interactions with others in that community. The latter, by contrast, is based merely on the transfer of capital—in large quantities—without necessarily requiring the investor to ever set foot in the recipient country. In some cases, the capital investment—ranging from a minimum of $1 million ($500,000 for specially defined areas) in the United States, to at least £1 million in the United Kingdom, to $5 million under the significant investor stream in Australia—is eventually returned back to the investor after a fixed number of years. These fast-tracked gateways offer migrant millionaires who may never reside in the country or participate in its society a share and vote in the political community in return for a portion of their wealth. The transacted monies in effect serve as a time-limited "collateral" for securing the grant of citizenship, and with it, a new passport under which to travel. It is not surprising that such cash-for-passports programs are proving popular among the world's moneyed elite with a desire or need for global options and a backup passport. More puzzling is the willingness of governments—our public trustees and legal guardians of citizenship—to engage in processes that, in some cases, cannot be described as anything but the sale and barter of membership goods in exchange for a hefty bank wire transfer or a large stack of cash.[4] Rapid processes of market expansionism have now reached what for many is the most sacrosanct non-market good: membership in a political community. Placing a price tag on citizenship is, we will argue, qualitatively different and ethically more disturbing than selectively focusing on the extraordinary talent and track record of those entering the country through designated skills-based, talent-for-citizenship exchanges.

We conclude by suggesting that expanding the scope of comparative citizenship debates beyond the traditional focus on those who are *excluded* to instead consider those who are given priority and fast-tracked in the immigration and naturalization line, reveals equally important yet under-studied insights about the transformation of citizenship regimes, present and future.

I. The Legal Framing of Talent Migration

Although some predicted that globalization would lead to the demise of state control over borders and membership boundaries, states have proven more resilient and creative than anticipated.[5] Operating alone or in concert with other countries (and increasingly with private sector actors as well), governments and enforcement agencies at the local, national, and supranational level have not abandoned migration and citizenship control.[6] Instead, they have launched sophisticated and multidimensional efforts to "*manage* migration"—the new catchphrase and paradigm favored by policymakers worldwide. Accepting that human mobility across borders is here to stay, and that previous zero-migration approaches have reached the end of the line, this new paradigm at its core is: "managerial, economistic, and [instrumental], focusing on the potential economic and social contributions by immigrants to host societies."[7]

The actual design and implementation of managed migration policies differs across countries and regions, but the underlying commonalities are hard to miss. On the contraction side, we find states reinventing their ability to control their membership boundaries by shifting borders, (re)introducing cultural and linguistic prerequisites to naturalization, authorizing often precarious temporary migration programs, erecting extraterritorial barriers to prevent the entry of unsolicited and "unwanted" migrants, and implementing new obstacles that make it increasingly harder for those seeking refuge and asylum to even reach the shores of what were once the promised lands of migration. On the expansion side, countries keen on recruiting the new breed of desired migrants—the highly skilled, the entrepreneurial innovators, the creative class, and in some places, the ultra rich—are engaged in a high-stakes competitive scramble to attract and retain them.

Those with an ear to the ground have not completely failed to notice these new trends. Think tanks, lawyers and human-rights advocates with an interest in migration policy and practice have reasonably focused their scarce resources on "objecting to a country's practice of excluding outsiders" and revealing the dire human consequences of the contraction dimension of today's managed migration control measures.[8] Far less attention has been paid, however, to the expansion side. Here, the focus is not on closing the gates, but on opening them *selectively*, especially for the crème de la crème— the fast-tracked recipients of Olympic citizenship on the basis of their specialized skills and talents—be they acclaimed scientists, technology wizards, innovative entrepreneurs, elite athletes, or brilliant artists. (We bracket for now the discussion of investor-based categories, which focus exclusively on attracting the ultra rich, a topic that is taken up in Part III). While at first blush the rise of selective and targeted admission routes designed to attract the best and brightest may appear to contradict the idea that states are attempting to "regain control" by restricting entry to those perceived as too different, risky, costly (or all of the above), it is, in fact, the other side of the same coin. Both contraction and expansion measures make visible the undercurrents and tensions informing the emerging narratives of who is welcome within the political community and who is not.

This makes the study of managed and selective migration regimes ever more vital. Debates about migration and globalization can no longer exclusively revolve around the dichotomy between open versus closed borders. Countries simultaneously engage in *both* opening *and* closing their borders, but they do so selectively—by indicating quite sharply who they desire to bring in (namely, those with specialized skills and talent, or, as we shall later see, deep pockets) and erecting higher and higher legal walls to block out those deemed "unwanted" or "too different."[9] In this stratified international mobility market, membership goods, including fast-tracked access to permanent residence and the promise of eventual citizenship, are turned into instruments for gaining a relative advantage in a competitive inter-jurisdictional scramble for "brainpower." In this global race for talent, no country is an island, and none wants to be left behind.[10]

By setting human capital criteria for selecting *whom* to admit, desired destination countries are signaling their preference for a particular class of immigrants. For governments faced with growing public sentiment in favor of restrictive immigration policies, the focus on productive, highly-skilled migrants allows them to convey a message of control, while internationally signaling to those with high-demand skills and extraordinary talent that they are "wanted and welcome."[11] Legal strategies to recruit the highly skilled play a vital role in this larger process of redesigning membership categories and regaining control over borders, by turning such ideational shifts into actionable plans. At the same time that would-be immigrants who seek admission on the basis of family ties or humanitarian causes are becoming subject to increased scrutiny and control, highly skilled migrants are facing more attractive admission offers than ever before. Those who fit the new category of talent migration now have more destination countries from which to choose—each country offering its own set of targeted membership and mobility benefits.

Citizenship and immigration are conventionally understood as identity-laden and domestic-centered policy arenas, steeped in questions of member-ship and belonging and a commitment to certain national narratives and values. In today's spiraling race for talent, however, the legal measures adopted by *other* countries influence how we shape the entry doors to our membership communities. We are witnessing a pattern of interdependent causality whereby, in developing their own strategies to attract the highly skilled, countries factor in the already-tested policies or projected responses of their major international competitors. Policymakers who specialize in targeted migration regimes routinely engage in transnational "borrow-ing"—or simply "importing"—of the innovations of their counterparts.[12]

This competitive emulation is not the result of a coordinated interna-tional effort to harmonize immigration or to delegate authority to technocratic global-expert bodies—as we have seen in other policy arenas, such as the regulation of international trade by the World Trade Organization. Rather, the race for talent results from *non*-cooperation by nations arising from the perception that in the knowledge-based global economy, "the resource that is in greatest scarcity is human capital." Counter-intuitively, and under conditions of uncertainty, national immigration agencies (and increasingly local and regional officials, too) reassert themselves as significant players in the global market for the highly skilled. They do this by developing the logic of competitive immigration regimes, maintaining tight control over their power to govern legal entry, and offering membership goods to attract highly skilled migrants perceived as "assets." The last of these is especially significant. In today's age of globalization and privatization, full membership in the political community remains the only good that even the mightiest economic conglomerate cannot offer to the skilled migrant. Only governments can allocate the legal status and prized reward of citizenship to those not born as members—and with it, they allocate not just the dignity and ability to exercise political power, but also the security and opportunity that come with full and equal membership.

It is useful to provide a brief legal "guide to the perplexed" as the backdrop to our critical analysis of the proliferation of such skills-based migration programs adopted by some of the world's most desired destination countries. There is plenty of anecdotal evidence about the crème de la crème, those at the top of the "talent pyramid," who receive the red-carpet treatment. From Russian-born opera star soprano singer Anna Netrebko, who was granted fast-tracked Austrian citizenship for "her special merits as one of the world's most distinguished singers" (without having to pass the nationality test that most applicants are required to take); to fashion models of "distinguished merit and ability" qualifying for a special occupancy visa in the United States; to examples from Italy (the host of the Torino Winter Olympics 2006), where expedited citizenship grants were used to build up the Italian Olympic squad. No fewer than ten of Italy's national hockey team players were Canadian hockey players who had not made the cut on their home team and held only the flimsiest ties to Italy; some of them had never visited the country nor did they speak its language. In another instance, former President Bush signed a congressional bill that included a special provision for granting citizenship to "aliens with extraordinary ability," just in time to allow ice dancer Tanith Belbin, born and raised in Canada, to join the American squad and represent the United States in the Torino Winter Olympics, where Belbin and her partner secured an Olympic medal. Harboring similar hopes, Russia recently granted citizenship by presidential decree to Korean three-time gold medalist short-track speed skater Ahn Hyun-Soo, who competed for Russia under the name Viktor Ahn in the Sochi Winter Olympics.

But skills-based migration is far from limited to a few extraordinary cases. In Canada, home of the influential point-system selection matrix, which assesses applicants by assigning them a score based on combined factors such as level of education, professional experience in high-demand occupations, age, linguistic ability, and adaptability (with bonus points increasingly awarded for job offers as well), the skilled/economic migration stream consistently accounts for more than half of newly admitted permanent residents per annum.[13] In Australia, this has been the case for the past few decades.[14] The United Kingdom also witnessed a spike in the recruitment of talent from across the world until the recent governmental decision to reduce net migration to the country. And even there, the new Tier 1 "exceptional talent" category is explicitly designed to attract, as the official guidelines put it, "exceptionally talented individuals in the fields of science, humanities, engineering and the arts, who wish to work in the UK." American immigration law, too, explicitly designates extraordinary achievement as a recognized admission category. The O-1 visa (often referred to as the "genius visa") targets individuals who possess "extraordinary ability in the sciences, arts, education, business, or athletics." In addition, the employment-based first-preference category (EB-1) offers a privileged path to a green card for those with "extraordinary ability in the sciences, arts, education, business, or athletics" who can demonstrate "sustained national or international acclaim." Evidence of such truly extraordinary ability, as explained by U.S. Citizenship and Immigration Services, includes receipt of internationally recognized prizes or awards, such as a "Pulitzer, Oscar, [or] Olympic Medal." In the United Kingdom, the criteria for demonstrating exceptional talent include "a nomination for an Academy Award, BAFTA, Golden Globe or Emmy Award in the five years before applying."

In 2000, European leaders reached agreement on the Lisbon Agenda, committing the European Union to the goal of becoming "the most competitive and dynamic knowledge-based economy in the world" and particularly to "the competition for people."[15] The race for talent has accelerated further in recent years in part because the more dynamic Asian economies, such as Singapore, which brands itself as a "talent capital," as well as Hong Kong, South Korea, and Taiwan, have begun to recruit globally. China and India, the emerging economic giants, are also weighing in. India is tapping its extensive diaspora abroad and relaxing its citizenship laws at home to allow successful emigrants to hold an "overseas citizenship of India," a status that grants them significant opportunities to maintain ties with and invest in the homeland. China, for its part, has adopted a multipronged strategy, a key feature of which is tremendous government investment in basic sciences and their commercial applications. As part of its One-Thousand-Talent program, China is aggressively using financial, taxation, and membership perks to attract high-caliber international scholars and returning Chinese citizens "to lead key laboratories, projects and disciplines in China." These changes in policy and in attitude, along with stronger growth prospects in emerging markets, have contributed to a pattern of skills-based and entrepreneurial "return migration" from the United States and other developed countries to the rest of the world.

The inter-jurisdictional dynamics and competitiveness of the global race for talent mean that it is no longer necessarily tied to, or motivated by, cyclical domestic skills shortages and short-term economic pressures. Rather, it is about "building a future through well-managed entry and settlement of people."[16] To draw upon the terminology favored by international relations theory, the global race for talent now operates as a multiplayer, multilevel game informed by domestic and international inputs, in which immigration policymaking by competing jurisdictions reflects growing interdependence, characterized by a mixture of employer and government-led initiatives.[17] At times there is much ferment and fervor as recruiting nations seek to respond to (and preferably preempt) the "offers" other countries make to secure what is perceived as a scarce and coveted resource—namely, extraordinary talent.

Challenging prevalent theoretical approaches that have predicted the demise or "retreat" of control over citizenship and immigration in a globalizing world, as well as those focusing almost exclusively on identity-and-difference to the exclusion of non-cultural factors, the recent changes identified here illuminate a more nuanced and complicated picture.[18] By and large, globalists and postnationalists have underestimated the resilience of states and their inventiveness in "retooling" migration regulation and control. Political theorists, for their part, have focused much of their attention on identity-and-recognition claims, and have largely failed to foresee or respond to these more market-oriented variants of citizenship. Neither school of thought has established the vocabulary and analytical tools required to explain the dramatic surge in managed and selective migration regimes, with their unmistakable tendency to give preference and priority to those perceived to have the potential to contribute economically and integrate rapidly. Clearly, the extensity, intensity, and velocity of today's multifaceted globalization processes have generated a more competitive environment for the cross-border recruitment of the highly skilled.[19] The crucial point, however, is that *governments*, as they have been constantly fine-tuning and recalibrating their skilled migration streams in response to (or in preemption of) their counterparts in the global race for talent, have come to treat potential gains from highly skilled migration as an important element of new economic, innovation, and growth policies, and in the process have allowed market-based rationality and valuation to influence how they make what are arguably quintessentially social and political decisions about "who belongs," or ought to belong, to the political community.

In this new world order, recruiting nations are willing to go as far as redrawing their membership boundaries to allow faster and smoother access to citizenship for those talented individuals they covet as prized assets, while at the same time making full and equal membership harder to secure for applicants who are perceived as a "threat" to national identity or a drain on social services and the public purse. This is the charged and fraught terrain of the new political economy of membership and mobility: it is a bifurcated regime of scrutiny and restriction on the one hand, and proactive recruitment on the other.

Scholars and human rights activists are hard at work to map the contours of the *contraction* side of these developments and are determined to explore possible responses to them, ranging from compliance to legal challenge to strategic manoeuvring to finding alternative routes of entry. But our focus here is on the *expansion* side and the market-oriented conceptual shifts associated with it. The basic thrust is this: competitive states grant skilled migrants privileged access not on the basis of a shared cultural affinity or linguistic heritage, but on the strength of their human capital, proven professional track record, and potential future achievements. Managed migration is the new policy *bon ton* and it is also seen as more palatable for voters; it is perceived as inserting into an otherwise tired and conflict-ridden debate over immigration policy more objective and selective standards. This occurs in a political climate where different streams of migration appear to be rationalized and socially constructed in strikingly different terms of discourse. Whereas the "unwanted" are pejoratively presented as exhibiting immutable differences that make them unassimilable, quintessential "Others," skilled migration is treated functionally and technocratically as a measure to advance the country's economic, reputational, and scientific advantage. Managed migration programs are therefore promoted as the vindication of merit, dynamism, and innovation in the face of diverging values and competing conceptions of the good.

II. Setting Human Capital Criteria for Selecting Whom to Admit

We can think of the new political economy of membership and migration as based on a "scale of attractiveness" according to which the more desired the immigrant is, the faster she will be given an opportunity to lawfully enter the country and embark on a fast-tracked path to its membership rewards. This is part of a subtle, yet potentially dramatic, recalibration of citizenship that is interconnected with the rise of a more calculated, market-oriented "value added" conception of migration and membership. This raises the question of whether it is legitimate for governments—our public trustees of citizenship—to strategically use membership goods as incentives to draw in "desired" migrants in order to boost their relative advantage in the fiercely competitive global environment. To some extent, this practice resembles the pre-modern world's notion of patronage, whereby monarchs, dynasties, and empires of past days recruited extraordinary talent to aggrandize and cement (ideally for eternity) their legacies. However, today, unlike the past, we live in a world in which citizenship is infused with ideals of equality and participation, not of noble privilege and patronage. It is these political ideals that are now placed under pressures by the growing influence of instrumentalized, managed migration regimes, and the kind of efficiency and merchant values that undergird them.

Alas, from a national welfare perspective that is in tune with the rise of managed and selective migration regimes, things look different: the whole "business" of immigration policymaking is to determine priorities and preferences. If there is more supply than demand, then by definition not everyone will get in. Surprisingly, the political philosophy of immigration provides little guidance here. The core debates in the field are mainly couched in terms of what equality to immigrants requires, when compared to the rights and protections afforded to those who already hold full and equal membership—namely, citizens. In such discussions, the focus is on immigrants who have already arrived and settled. Regrettably, only scant attention is paid to the core questions that concern us here: how to justify immigrant or naturalization priorities, and on what basis.[20] Yet these are the hardest tasks at the heart of the actual institutional design of immigration law and practice: how to define which priorities and preferences should inform the system, and which considerations could legitimately guide its design.

We can trace the outer limits, as currently defined by domestic and international law. We know, for example, that states bear a legal and moral obligation to admit refugees, and that other humanitarian causes represent a special and compelling case. States are also obliged to minimize statelessness. There is also a consensus that ascriptive factors, such as race and gender, are illegitimate considerations and are prohibited grounds for denial of admission. It is also widely agreed that there is no obligation on a political community to admit non-citizens who pose either a threat to public safety (because of a criminal record or for another reason) or to national security (however difficult it remains to define this category). These inadmissibility grounds must be subject to judicial review and fair treatment requirements, and arguably, proportionality as well, but recall that we are concerned here with would-be entrants, whom even Joseph Carens, otherwise an enthusiastic advocate of immigrants' rights, aptly describes as "*potential* immigrants who have no specific moral claim to admittance."[21] Beyond this narrow area of consensus, significant disagreement exists as to the extent of state discretion in otherwise selecting prospective members.[22]

In practice, we know that "many seek to enter and few are chosen."[23] The question of *whom* to admit therefore requires states to develop their selection criteria. We earlier saw that certain negative restrictions are placed on states, but there are no correlating guidelines defining which positive standards to adopt. Under current international law, each country is free to determine its priorities and preferences, and then arrange and implement its admission categories accordingly. Typically, admission categories include a combination of family-based, humanitarian, and employment-based migration streams.[24] The highly skilled squarely fall into the employment stream, but in practice they are often entitled to bring in their immediate family members (spouses and children) as prospective citizens too, effectively creating a blend of the employment and family-based categories in what is ostensibly a very difficult-to-enter, "talent only" category.

The emphasis on preferring "those with the kind of skills and attainments which make the admission advantageous to our society" (as U.S. President Lyndon D. Johnson once famously stated) dates back to the earliest major development of the current global race for talent: the United States' overhaul of its immigration law and policy in 1965. These amendments ushered in the modern legislative architecture of favoring family ties, skills, and humanitarian considerations over considerations of race, ethnicity, and national origin.[25] In signing the amendments into law, President Johnson changed the course of U.S. immigration policy for the decades to follow, and articulated a vision for the future of immigration that now reads as a precursor to the rise of competitive immigration regimes: "immigrants should not be judged on their country of origin, but by what contributions they could make to the [destination country] because of their skills."[26]

Fast-forwarding to today, American immigration law, despite its well-known complex and often cumbersome structure, nevertheless permits those with extraordinary talent and the kind of "skills and attainments which make admission advantageous to [U.S.] society" to qualify for a green card on the strength of their achievements through specialized gateways that fast-track their admission. These include the "aliens of extraordinary ability" classification, which in the technocratic terminology of American immigration law and policy falls within the "first-preference employment-based category." Note the language here: the system explicitly indicates preferences and priorities among potential migrants and entrants. It reserves the highest-preference, fast-track-admission category for those with the greatest potential to make a positive contribution to society. The "second-preference" employment-based category is open to talent migrants who are merely "exceptional" (rather than "extraordinary") in their fields, and to those who fall short of the legal standard for both extraordinary and exceptional talent, but wish to apply for a "national interest waiver" in order to escape the ponderous labor certification and employer sponsorship requirement. Yet another option open to outstanding migrants is to apply for a premium designation such as that offered by the "outstanding professor and researcher" category, which is reserved exclusively for academics with an internationally recognized track record of exceptional merit and excellence in their academic field.

Even this brief review of the subcategories of talent migration reveals the prevalence of selective admission in the actual design of immigration law and policy and demonstrates the careful calibration informing decisions about who is fast-tracked and when to use membership goods as a competitive tool to attract the world's best and brightest. In the global race for talent, the ease with which a migrant can gain access to permanent residency as a stepping stone to citizenship (the green card in the U.S., the landed immigrant status in Canada, and so on) has come to serve as a measure of the perceived benefit and "value" that the skilled migrant can bring to her new society.[27]

Those occupying the upper echelons of the talent pyramid—those the law recognizes as "extraordinary," "exceptional," "outstanding," and so on— are perceived by the competing nations in the global race for talent to have a choice of destination. As savoir-faire professionals in high demand, they hold an enviable position: they are perceived to "know where they are wanted." For this reason, they can vote with their feet, which increases the pressure on recruiting nations to provide them with attractive settlement packages.[28] At this top level, the proactive recruitment of talent across borders by competitive states comes very close to resembling corporate headhunting practices, turning once-passive immigration officials (with some help from other governmental agencies and authorized private sector actors) into enterprising recruiters of talent.

III. The Trouble with Cash-For-Passport Programs

A close look at the emerging citizenship-by-investment market that thrives alongside the global race for talent may help us identify other branches of the rise of Olympic citizenship (beyond skills-based migration), as we seek to unpack the ethical conundrums that follow. If we think of a country's immigration law and policy as a porous membrane that in part reflects and discloses the qualities it values in its members-to-be, then the rise of managed and selective migration regimes tells us something important about the state of citizenship today and the direction in which we may be heading. As we have just seen, in this brave new world, an instrumental understanding of "value added" underlies the political economy of wanted-and-welcomed migration. Priority is given to those with marketable skills and employability over those with vulnerabilities and needs. And we have deliberately bracketed until now the investor categories that crudely permit the actual "purchase" of an entry visa for a hefty price (US $1 million for conditional green card in America, €1 million in Germany, and in the UK, a minimum investment of GBP £750,000 in British stocks and the holding of additional funds of GBP £250,000). Recent years have also seen the introduction of unfettered cash-for-passport programs, where citizenship is literally offered "for sale" to the world's moneyed elite, creating dangerous liaisons between wealth and access to political membership. The public act of naturalization— of turning a non-member into a citizen—has always borne an air of legal magic, with the result that it is the "most densely regulated and most politicized aspect of citizenship laws."[29] Everybody knows that at stake is the regulation of the most important and sensitive decision that any political community faces: how to define who belongs, or ought to belong, within its circle of members. Less well known is the fact that governments are now proactively facilitating faster and smoother access to citizenship for those who can pay.

Consider the following examples. In 2012, Portugal introduced a "golden residence permit" to attract real estate and other investments by well-to-do individuals seeking a foothold in the EU. Spain recently adopted a similar plan. In Cyprus, affluent foreign investors were offered citizenship as "compensation" for their Cypriot bank account deposit losses (the value of which was set at €3M in the aftermath of the EU bailout). Malta recently approved amendments to its Citizenship Act that put in place a new individual investor legal category that will allow high-net-worth applicants to gain a "golden passport" in return for €650,000. Government officials in Malta have made clear that applicants can expect an expedited treatment, meaning that they will not have to "stand in the queue" like everyone else. Under these cash-for-passport programs, many of the requirements that ordinarily apply to those seeking naturalisation, such as language competency, extended residency periods, or renunciation of another citizenship, are waived as part of an active competition, if not an outright bidding war, to attract the ultra rich. Portugal, for example, offers a fast-track for qualified applicants that entitles them to a 5-year permanent residence permit, visa-free travel in Schengen countries, the right to bring in their immediate family members, and ultimately the right to acquire Portuguese citizenship and with it the benefits of EU citizenship. This package comes with a hefty price tag: a capital transfer investment of €1M, a real estate property purchase at a value of €500,000, or the creation of local jobs. The investment itself must remain in Portugal for the program's duration. However, the individual who gains the golden permit bears no similar obligation. Simply spending seven days in Portugal during the first year and fourteen days in the subsequent years is enough to fulfil the program's requirements. Malta's program goes a step further and waives residency requirements altogether, just as it removes any other "genuine link" prerequisites. Instead, it makes the grant of citizenship conditional upon the applicant's wallet size. Once the hefty fee is paid, the paper citizen obtains a Maltese passport—and access to European citizenship—immediately. So much for the conclusion of the International Court of Justice, in the 1955 *Nottebohm* decision, that "real and effective ties" between the individual and the state must undergird the grant of citizenship.

The citizenship-by-investment programs that we have just described fall into the category of brute and unfettered cash-for-passport exchanges. No *"jus nexi"* linkage or connection between the country and passport grantee is required; only the investment monies must remain in the country, either temporarily or permanently, depending on the program.[30] This is to be distinguished from more traditional programs, themselves the subject of perennial critique, under which multimillionaires can receive an admission visa through a designated business-investment stream, but would then have to more or less comply with standard residency and naturalisation requirements.[31] As mentioned earlier, such programs are found in, among other places, the United States and the United Kingdom. Both kinds of program raise serious ethical quandaries, but the unfettered cash-for-passport programs are far more extreme and blatant than the traditional investment programs. They contribute to some of the most disturbing developments in 21st-century citizenship, including the emergence of new forms of inequality and stratification. Instead of retreating to the background as some theorists had forecasted, states are proactively creating and exacerbating inequalities through their selective and managed migration policies, setting up easy-pass citizenship for some, while making membership more restrictive and difficult to achieve for others. This new world order reveals tectonic pressures and introduces urgent dilemmas about the proper scale, scope, and relations of justice and mobility, citizenship and (selective) openness. These developments also have a profound impact on immigration law and policy on the ground, since they entail processes through which the boundary between state and market is constantly tested, eroded, and blurred.

Legally, the sovereign prerogative to issue a valid and recognized passport is reserved in our international system to states alone. As mentioned earlier, governments and only governments—not markets—can secure and allocate the precious legal good of membership in the political community. But what happens when the logic of capital and markets infiltrates this classic statist expression of sovereignty? The proliferation of such unfettered cash-for-passport programs is a dramatic example of this pattern at work and it invites our critical scrutiny, especially since governments that use these programs often do so in the name of advancing their country's national interest and collective pride, while paradoxically setting up dangerous connections between money and access to citizenship, possibly to the detriment of basic egalitarian and democratic thrust of political membership, as we currently know it. These developments raise major quandaries. Why are states putting citizenship up for sale? And what precisely is wrong with easy-pass naturalisation along the lines of the cash-for-passport programs? Is it the queue jumping? The attachment of a price tag to citizenship? The erosion of something foundational about political membership itself? Or, perhaps, all of the above?

Surely, zealous free-marketeers will enthusiastically defend such programs as freeing us from the shackles of culture, nation, and tradition and moving citizenship forward to a new and more competitive global age of transactional contracting in which, as Nobel Prize laureate Gary Becker once put it, a price mechanism substitutes for the complicated criteria that now determine legal entry.[32] As much as Becker would like to deny it, though, these programs have something of a "whiff of scandal" not only due to frequent accusations of money laundering and fraud, but also because of something deeper and more profound. Citizenship as we know it (at least since Aristotle) is comprised of *political* relations; as such, it is expected to both reflect and generate a notion of participation, co-governance, and a degree of solidarity among those included in the body politic. It is difficult to imagine how these values could be preserved under circumstances in which insiders and outsiders are distinguished merely by the ability to pay a certain price. The objection here is to the notion that *everything*, including political membership, is "commensurable" and reducible to a dollar value. This is what makes cash-for-passport exchanges, even if they account for only a limited stream or quota of entrants per year, deeply problematic and objectionable. The sale and barter of citizenship, even if initially reserved only for a small stream of recipients, nevertheless sends a loud message in both law and social ethics about whom the contemporary market-friendly state gives priority to in the immigration and naturalisation line and whom it covets most as future citizens. This expressive conduct and the new grammar of market-infused valuation it entails indicates the volatile state of citizenship today, and the direction in which we may be heading.

Although economists will be quick to note that cash-for-passport programs can create a hefty stream of revenue for governments, this is hardly a strong enough justification to endorse them. The desire to enlarge their coffers may, as a matter of real-life experience, *explain* why some countries offer these programs. As a normative matter, however, such an exchange threatens to corrupt the good that is put on sale: what changes when we "sell" citizenship is not just the price tag of membership, but its substantive content as well. If political relations that are valued in part because they are *not* for sale become tradable and marketable, the ramifications may prove far-reaching, affecting not only those directly engaged in the transaction but also broader societal perceptions of how we value these relations.[33] This is because laws do not only guide action. Markets do not only allocate goods. They also "express and promote certain attitudes toward the goods being exchanged."[34] Turning the ability to pay into a condition for citizenship risks undermining the very concept of political membership. It may in turn erode the civic bonds and practices that allow a democratic society not only to survive, but to thrive. As it plays a more and more important role in the countries' immigration and naturalisation policies and priorities, citizenship-for-sale may also gradually reshape the greater class of those who are likely to enjoy political membership. Reliance on a price mechanism alone, to the exclusion of other important considerations, would not only prevent the vast majority of the world's population from ever gaining a chance to access citizenship in well-off polities. Taken to its logical conclusion (as *reductio*) it might also lead, corrosively and over time, to a world where *anyone* included in the pool of members must pay up, or risk "falling helplessly to the wayside."[35]

Several scholars have taken up the task of imagining how our world might look were the market—rather than the state—to govern access to, and the acquisition of, political membership. As one study explains, "[i]f we take the basic incidents of citizenship to be protection of members and participation in modes of governance, the market for citizenship could form around offer of and demand for these services. Indeed, the offer of broader packages of citizenship services would be the basis for product differentiation."[36] "Product differentiation," it should be noted, is a euphemism for providing lesser rights and services in exchange for lower fees.[37] Farewell, then, to the hard-earned ideal of equal citizenship with its emancipatory thrust of inclusion of those once excluded and disenfranchised.[38] In its absence, auction mechanisms and supply-and-demand rules may well replace our (however imperfect) procedures for ensuring some degree of accountability and collective decision-making on what it means to belong to a political community, how to obtain a secure legal status of citizenship, and on what conditions.

Even staunch defenders of the market approach to citizenship understand that theirs is a hard sell. Becker, for one, admits that "people object to the sale of permits because, as they say, 'citizenship is not to be for sale,'" and this is a moral intuition that runs deep.[39] The reasons are many. As just mentioned, the transactional vision of citizenship relies on the assumption that everything can be put on sale; it leaves no room for the idea that there are moral limits to markets and that certain political relations are hollowed out when "bought and sold." Such a move prefigures the conflation of the political and ethical with the economic and calculative. It may also undermine membership bonds grounded in co-authorship and cross-subsidisation of risk, as well as cause harm to the vision of citizenship as grounded in long-term relations of trust, participation, and shared responsibility. At present, citizenship involves making collective decisions and translating those decisions into binding commitments, in the context of a political project that is far larger than oneself, and extends well beyond the lifespan of each generation of members. Such a political project will be extremely hard to sustain under a membership regime strictly guided by strategic "wealth buys citizenship" transactions. We can reasonably predict that those with the flimsiest of ties to the community (other than a purchased real-estate asset or bank account deposit box) will likely dispense with the investment or seek to recoup it and move in search of a more secure business environment in times of need or crisis. This is not a particularly solid foundation upon which to build a country or sustain a polity. By legitimizing a transactional variant of citizenship, states risk further eroding the willingness of members who habitually contribute to the civic fibre of these societies to continue to do so vigorously when others free ride on their efforts.

From a normative perspective, turning citizenship into a money-based prize also contradicts any Walzerian-like notion of complex equality according to which advantage in one sphere (here, wealth) cannot be legitimately transferred to another (in this case, membership).[40] This makes the idea of selling membership unnerving for anyone who objects to the ultimate triumph of economics over politics, the reduction of our public life and ethics into mere pecuniary transactions, or the imperialistic idea that "trades" occupy the full terrain of human value and meaning.[41]

There are also complex questions about *to whom* (beyond its own citizenry) the transacting government is obliged to provide justificatory reasons concerning its cash-for-passport initiatives. In the context of supranational citizenship, as in the derivative structure of European citizenship, need it justify itself to other member states? To the Commission of the European Union? To would-be entrants who might have had a shot at admission through standard migration streams (family, employment, and humanitarian) but who are priced out of the advantage given to those who can afford a "golden passport"? From a global perspective, citizenship-by-investment programs clearly exacerbate pre-existing inequalities rather than alleviate them. Should the sedentary populations of the emigrants' countries of origin, which are typically less stable or poorer than the destination countries, get to weigh in as well? Or, if an expansive all-affected-interests principle is applied, perhaps anyone at all who may be unfairly and arbitrarily affected should have a voice in these decisions.[42] And what about migrants who are already settled in the country, but ineligible to benefit from naturalisation schemes that require no knowledge or familiarity with the political structures, main civic institutions, history or language of the country, and who are subject instead to ever more demanding civic integration requirements? If civic integration is a required precondition of bestowing full membership (as restrictive citizenship tests increasingly indicate), how can this demand only apply to some and not to others?

After all, there is no rational connection between delivering a stack of cash or sending in a bank wire transfer and establishing the kind of participation and equal standing among fellow citizens that the political bonds of membership are meant to represent and foster. From this vantage point, the very trading in citizenship, even if carefully regulated and implemented by monopolistic governments or their authorised delegates, should be prohibited. Taken to its dystopian extreme, this approach may lead to a situation whereby the size of their wallets, and nothing else, distinguishes suitable from unsuitable candidates for initial entry and eventual citizenship. This kind of transaction, as lawyers and philosophers like to put it, is value-degrading: the trading in citizenship "taints," "degrades," or outright "corrupts" (in the moral sense) its value as a good.[43] We might, in the same vein, say that these cash-for-citizenship programs detrimentally affect the "character of the goods themselves and the norms that should govern them."[44] As critics of commodification have been at pains to clarify in other contexts, it is not that €1M is too high or too low a price, but that placing a "for sale" tag on citizenship, no matter what amount is written on it, has a corrosive effect on non-market relations, eroding the ties that bind and altering our view of what it means to belong to a political community.[45] Just as we should be critical of granting citizenship according to nothing but the fortuitous and arbitrary circumstances of station of birth, we must resist, with even greater force, the notion that money can buy "love of country"—or secure membership in it.[46]

Turning back to highly skilled migration programs, a similar conclusion is not warranted. We have already established that the focus of such programs is on the *human* in "human capital" (not capital per se)—the unique and irreplaceable individual in which "extraordinary," "exceptional," or "outstanding" talent is encapsulated.[47] Skills-based selective migration programs are distinct from money-based investor categories: the latter depend on the alienability and transferability of purely fungible funds, the former focus on the distinctive skills, talents, or abilities "encapsulated" in the recruited migrant herself who moves to the new country. The individual's human capital, the reason for granting that *particular* immigrant access to the new political community, is non-transferable and non-alienable; it is part of the self.

It is time to take stock of the argument. While categorically opposing the notion of selling citizenship for all the reasons discussed above, we wish to clarify that strict prohibition cannot be the answer to the question of whether states may legitimately select migrants on the basis of merit-centered criteria. Competitive states may, and occasionally do, expedite the citizenship applications of medal contender athletes, acclaimed artists, and world-renowned scientists, potentially causing a stir. But so long as these provisions remain exceptional and the collective interest in doing so is transparent and sufficiently convincing, these programs cannot be said to breach any prohibited grounds. Such transactions are permissible, from a normative point of view, if the recipients are expected to establish real and genuine connections to their new home country, just like any other category of migrant seeking naturalization. The problem, we believe, lies not in the selection of *some* migrants to join our political committees based on their extraordinary talent or potential to generate reputational gains and positive externalities. The different selection criteria for admitting newcomers—family based, humanitarian, and employment-based— serve different purposes and follow distinctive logics. There is no principled reason to presuppose that any of them, standing alone, can respond to the full spectrum of human motivation for mobility. The danger lies elsewhere: in the *totalizing* impact of turning talent and human capital into the make-or-break criteria for cross-border mobility, and the consequent emergence of a more stratified perception of membership goods as "Olympic laurels" to be awarded by competitive nations only to those they covet most.

These developments, which are only now beginning to gain wider scholarly recognition, are ripe for critical exploration, especially given their connection to larger transitions in and recalibrations of the ways in which countries draw their membership boundaries in a globalizing world. The effects of "picking winners" become particularly evident when we focus on those in the top echelons of the talent pyramid, where the extent of the membership goods that talent-hungry nations are willing to barter has become a clear metric for the perceived value of the recruited migrant to the admitting nation. Echoing larger processes of stratification, the surge of selective and managed migration regimes also reflects a vision of an ideal citizen who is productive and contributory, and who has been able to maximize her talent and turn herself into a "net benefit" to her new society.[48] Those without the desired traits in the global race for talent are increasingly classified as "costs."[49]

This is the context in which we find ourselves. At the dawn of the era of Olympic citizenship, managed and selective migration regimes have spread rapidly with little democratic or deliberative input by the governed. In today's era of "market triumphalism" or "market fundamentalism," as Michael Sandel and Joseph Stiglitz have respectively observed, the economic logic of "buying and selling no longer applies to material goods alone."[50] Now, that logic is infiltrating the semi-sacrosanct political realm of citizenship, a realm that we might have thought of as the last bastion of the sovereignty of *non*market norms and values. Thus, the global race for talent, with Olympic citizenship at its apex, offers us a rare window to explore the most foundational tensions and questions about the future of citizenship in a world marked by mounting pressures of competitive global markets and blatant commercialization. It tests our deepest intuitions about the meaning and content of the relationship between the individual and the political community to which she belongs. It compels us to take a hard look at how these more calculated and strategic migration priorities are becoming ever-more-aligned with market-oriented value-enhancing criteria of success, and how these new forms of valuation may turn membership bonds into far more instrumental bargains.

It is important to acknowledge, however, that Olympic citizenship is *not* adverse to membership. Rather, it offers fast-tracked, privileged access to the social and political goods of citizenship, goods which *both* states *and* immigrants clearly perceive as highly valuable. Emigrants from poorer and less stable countries regard the promise of citizenship, or the grant of a predicable path to achieve it, as a major draw.[51] And we saw earlier that even the ultra rich are willing to dish out significant sums to obtain the benefits that flow from the acquisition of citizenship and a freshly-minted passport. No less puzzling is the realization that a core motivation for competitive states to engage in the global race for talent, and to do so with the zeal and fervor they have exhibited to date, is to *enhance* their national interest and position relative to their counterparts. There is therefore a great paradox at work: government officials are willing to expedite citizenship for certain migrants in order to enhance the collective pride, international reputation, and competitive standing of the political community—but that community is tied together by the very membership bonds that Olympic citizenship may unwittingly erode.

This is a delicate and complex (and perhaps unrealistic) equilibrium that recruiting nations are trying to achieve. Such government-initiated "flexibilization" and "mercantilization" of the concept of political membership may advance the short-term interests of states and may indeed grant them a competitive advantage. In the long term, however, it may erode something deeper—citizenship itself—by reshaping the defining characteristics required to establish a *political* (here understood as deontological and not merely functional or utilitarian) bond between the individual and her political community. This is what makes the study of Olympic citizenship so urgent and captivating. It is high time to explore the core ethical and distributive ramifications that it portends.

IV. Conclusion

As we have seen, human capital is the new mobility currency. For the millionaire migrant, it is the commensurability of money and its stealth impact in realms of public life once thought to be sheltered from direct commodification that have opened up new pathways to literally purchase citizenship. The emphasis on skills and talent is certainly preferable to using the size of applicants' wallets to determine who to bring in and who to keep out. Still, human capital—especially the refined and rarefied kind of talent that recruiting nations seek—is not possessed equally by all. Indeed, it is a perception of scarcity—of exuberant demand and systemic under-supply— that is fuelling the flames of the global race for talent.

Importantly, Olympic citizenship and the various admission categories that flow from it are officially and unapologetically blind to color, race, gender, and national origin. This is no minor point given the long and troubling history of discrimination and exclusion in citizenship and immigration world- wide. Although formally open to anyone, anywhere, so long as they exhibit the requisite "extraordinary," "exceptional," or "outstanding" talent to unlock the golden gates of admission, this emerging political economy of mobility and membership is anything but stratification-free. In Olympic citizenship we thus find a unique blurring of state and market influences, of allegiance and interest, and perhaps most puzzling of all, of national pride and neoclassical economic principles that treat human capital as a factor of production able to generate tangible and reputational gains for the recruiting nation relative to its competitors, with traceable impact on the global stage.

Curiously resembling the space race before it, Olympic citizenship— today's fast-paced race to recruit the world's most creative and brightest minds—represents the frontier of a new era: the upsurge of a more calcu- lated approach to citizenship grounded in a desire to be great and to make a lasting mark: a desire as old as recorded human history. Today, greatness is no longer measured only by the size of a nation's armed forces, the height of its pyramids, the luxury of its palaces, or even the wealth of its natural resources. Governments in high-income countries and emerging economies have come to subscribe to the view that in order to secure a position in the pantheon of excellence, something else is required: it is the ability to draw human capital, to become an "IQ magnet," that counts.

This desire for greatness, in the context of the global race for talent, privileges those who have perfected and honed their skills. It does not reward raw talent per se (which is morally arbitrary), but instead captures elements of "cultivation" of such talent in a social context that rewards determination, hard work, and adaptability: traits that some countries' highly-skilled point-system selection matrix explicitly values.[52] This model does not stand in tension with perfectionist conceptions of citizenship, but it may pose serious moral hazards to liberal-democratic and egalitarian notions which at least formally assign membership to individuals *irrespec- tive* of how innovative, talented, or accomplished they are (although the latter suffer from the other ills, such as scrambling to legitimately justify bounded membership in the first place, or to provide persuasive reasons for blindly perpetuating birthright privilege in the automatic assignment of citizenship according to nothing but station of birth).[53]

Set as they are against the backdrop of a growing public sentiment against multiculturalism and immigration, the investment-based and merit-based admission categories and fine-grained selective migration regimes that we have discussed in the previous sections are unlikely to go away any time soon. It is precisely the reliance on the language of efficiency, voluntary exchange, and innovation that allows talent or investment to seem neutral and unobjectionable as criteria for selection. For this reason, the study of Olympic citizenship can help us identify and critically evaluate some of the most foundational and pressing challenges to membership and mobility that are taking place in the world around us, but that our established approaches have failed to adequately register.

The ideal of equal citizenship has been inflicted with many wounds over the past decades, especially as the rollback of the welfare state has picked up over the past decades. It has always been more of an aspiration than a reality. However, the danger of increasingly frequent links between wealth and privileged access to political membership threatens not only the implementation of the ideal, but the ideal itself.

Notes

* We would like to thank Bob Goodin, Jim Fishkin, Rogers Smith, Cristina Rodriguez, Craig Mullins, Eric Monkman, and the anonymous reviewers for insightful comments on earlier drafts. We also benefited significantly from the responses of the audiences at the American Society of International Law Annual Conference, the Columbia Political Theory Workshop, the Yale Legal Theory Workshop, and the Max Planck Institute for Tax and Public Financing in Munich. This study was generously supported by the Canada Research Chair Program.

1 Shamir 2005; Joppke 2007; Orgad 2010; Goodman 2012.

2 With the advent of dual nationality, gaining a freshly minted passport in an affluent and rule of law society no longer extracts a potentially prohibitive cost (from the emigrant's perspective) of severing her membership ties with the country of origin. She can hold both, simultaneously.

3 The constitutive connection between talent development and the self is discussed in Beitz (1999, pp. 138–9).

4 In this increasingly commodified migration regime, not only state agencies are involved, but also various third-party intermediaries. For example, elite global law firms now discretely offer their multi-million-dollar-worth individual clients advice on "citizenship planning," much like international tax experts explore offshore investment strategies for their wealth management portfolios.

5 There is a rich literature on the debate between statists and globalists regarding the "demise" of borders and migration control, or the lack thereof. The full list is too long to cite. For examples of this vibrant debate, see: Sassen 1996; Andreas and Snyder 2000; Guiraudon and Lahav 2000.

6 Government agencies are increasingly sharing, delegating, or outsourcing the authority and responsibility of regulating and controlling international human mobility to various private sector actors, from airline companies whose frontline agents regularly screen travelers' passports and entry visas on sanction of heavy

penalties if they allow unauthorized migrants to reach desired destination countries, to multinational corporations providing border control equipment and various migration management tasks, raising weighty questions about the human rights consequences and public accountability of the "migration industry." For further discussion, see: Guiraudon and Lahav 2000; Gammeltoft-Hansen and Sørensen 2013.

7 Menz 2008, p. 2.

8 Wellman and Cole 2011, p. 151. With tightening regulation of borders and growing pressures to escape desperate political or economic circumstances, the line between volitional and forced migration is constantly being tested, leading to the coining of the term "survival migration" (Betts 2013). This development falls beyond the scope of this article.

9 Joppke 2007; Orgad 2010.

10 For a detailed discussion of the competitive dimension of the global race for talent, see Shachar (2006).

11 This term is drawn from a collection of essays with the same title: Triadafilopoulos (2013).

12 On policy emulation and diffusion in international political economy, see Simmons and Elkins (2004). On competition and inter-jurisdictional borrowing in the context of highly skilled migration, see Shachar (2006).

13 In 2012, the latest year for which official statistics are available, skilled migrants (and their immediate family members) constituted sixty five percent of Canada's annual intake of new permanent residents. See Canada 2012, p. 5.

14 The proportion of skill-stream migrants to Australia in 2012 was sixty-eight percent reflecting the extraordinary emphasis placed on the selective recruitment of migrants who can integrate quickly, as part of the impetus to admit those who can provide the greatest economic and reputational returns. See Australia 2013, Table 2–1.

15 Florida and Tingali 2004, p. 12.

16 Australia 2011.

17 Putnam 1988.

18 The emphasis on identity, culture, and recognition has been criticized as potentially distracting attention from distributive concerns within the body politic. See Fraser 1997; Fraser and Honneth 2003. Scholars in other disciplines have looked at how different cultural perceptions and mobility experiences may inform individuals' and families' perception of citizenship as a transnational asset. See Ong 1999. Our focus is on the re-conceptualization of citizenship, not on the relationship between recognition and redistribution, whether domestically or internationally.

19 Held et al. 1999, pp. 14–28.

20 A rare exception to the lack of attention paid to actual priorities in immigration policy is found in Carens (2013) and Offe (2011).

21 Carens 2013, p. 179 (emphasis added).

22 See e.g.: Benhabib 2004; Miller 2007; Wellman and Cole 2011.

23 Carens 2013, p. 179.

24 As mentioned above, democratic states prohibit racial, ethnic, and other ascriptive barriers to admission, something which is taken for granted today, although it is of surprisingly recent vintage. For most of its history, immigration law and policy was steeped in racialized and gendered hierarchies and exclusions.

25 The 1965 modern architecture of American immigration law and policy eventually privileged family-based migration over skilled-based and humanitarian migration, and the current legislative debate in the United States is partly about rebalancing these priorities.

26 Despite these commitments, the vast majority of immigrants to the United States, as a percentage of that country's overall admission priorities, enter through family-based categories, or preferences, as they are known in American immigration law and policy. In terms of absolute numbers, however, the United States receives the biggest share of skilled migrants worldwide.

27 This can be seen as a new twist on the classic Lockean labor theory, where manual or agricultural labor is replaced with sophisticated knowledge economy equivalents, and applied to the acquisition of membership status in the state rather than of property in cultivated land.

28 The choice of destination for these migrants is, of course, neither unlimited nor necessarily determinative. It is likely that language, networking, family ties, and post-colonial channels of migration play a role in shaping the directionality of human mobility. See Van Parijs (2000), on the unfair distribution effects of factors such as linguistic dominance in the international "market" for the highly skilled in academia.

29 Bauböck and Goodman 2010, p. 1.

30 For a discussion of the "jus nexi" principle, see Shachar 2011. Others have referred to related notions of a stakeholder society, or the importance of social membership in determining access to citizenship. See Bauböck 2005; Carens 2013.

31 For an overview of such policies and a profile of the recipients, see: Dzankic 2012; Ley 2010.

32 For a classic exposition, see Becker 1992.

33 For a relational critique of markets, see Satz 2010.

34 Sandel 2012, p. 9. On the expressive function of law, see Sunstein 1996.

35 Spiro 2008, p. 34.

36 Downes and Janda 1998, p. 55.

37 Jordan and Düvell 2003.

38 That the practice of citizenship does not always meet this ideal is not in itself a valid justification to depart from it.

39 Becker 1992. Borna and Stearns 2002, p. 197.

40 Walzer 1983.

41 Radin 1987; Sunstein 1997; Sandel 2012.

42 Goodin 2007.

43 For a distinction between fairness and corruption arguments, see Sandel (2012, pp. 111–3). For earlier discussions of "corruption" and "contagion" in the context of a normative critique of markets, see for example Lukes (2005, 303–9). For closely related ideas, see also Satz 2010.

44 Sandel 2012, p. 113.

45 On the corrosive effect on non-market relations in other contexts, see Cohen 2003.

46 For a critique of birthright citizenship, see Shachar 2009.

47 The longstanding debate about what "greatness" is, how people achieve it, is beyond the scope of this article, as is a discussion of the moral obligations owed to sending countries. On the current research evidence, see for example Kaufman (2013), which explores the legal categories of talent in the context of migration. See also Beitz 1999, 138–9.

48 For staunch critiques of these internal transformations of social citizenship and the imbalances of power in the American economic and political system, see e.g.: Sommers 2008; Hacker and Pierson 2012.

49 Jordan and Düvell 2003, pp. 91–5.

50 Sandel 2012, p. 6; Stiglitz 2003.

51 This assertion is based on naturalization data collected in Canada and the United States.

52 To establish the level of "talent" required by recruiting nations' point system selection matrix and other specialized immigration categories, an applicant must demonstrate the kind of qualifications (specialized training, education, and the like) and accomplishments for which an individual is arguably responsible and in this sense are not a matter of "thin luck" or "brute luck" (Hurley 2003; Dworkin 1981; Cohen 1989), but closer to "option luck" and what economists would define as the investments that lead to increased human capital.

53 For further discussion, see: Shachar and Hirschl 2007; Shachar 2009.

References

Andreas, Peter and Timothy Snyder, eds. 2000. *The Wall Around the West: State Borders and Immigration Controls in Europe and North America.* 2nd edn. London: Rowman and Littlefield.

Australia, Department of Immigration and Citizenship. 2013. *Australia's Migration Trends, 2011–2012.* Available at <www.immi.gov.au>.

Australia, Joint Standing Committee on Migration. 2011. *Inquiry into Multiculturalism in Australia.* DIAC: Submission no. 150.

Bauböck, Rainer. 2005. Expansive citizenship: voting beyond territory and membership. *Political Science and Politics*, 38, 683–7.

Bauböck, Rainer and Sara Wallace Goodman. 2010. *Naturalisation.* Florence: European University Institute Robert Schuman Centre for Advanced Study. EUDO Citizenship Policy Brief No. 2.

Becker, Gary. 1992. An open door for immigrants—the auction. *Wall Street Journal*, Oct. 14, 1992, A1.

Beitz, Charles R. 1999. *Political Theory and International Relations.* Rev. edn. Princeton: Princeton University Press; originally published 1979.

Benhabib, Seyla. 2004. *The Rights of Others: Aliens, Residents and Citizens.* Cambridge: Cambridge University Press.

Betts, Alexander. 2013. *Survival Migration: Failed Governance and the Crisis of Displacement.* Ithaca: Cornell University Press.

Borna, Shaheen and James M. Stearns. 2002. The ethics and efficacy of selling national citizenship. *Journal of Business Ethics*, 37, 193–207.

Canada, Citizenship and Immigration Canada. 2012. *Canada Facts and Figures 2012: Immigration Overview, Permanent and Temporary Residents.* Available at <www.cic.gc.ca>.

Carens, Joseph H. 2013. *The Ethics of Migration.* Oxford: Oxford University Press.

Cohen, G. A. 1989. The currency of egalitarian justice. *Ethics*, 99, 906–44.

Cohen, I. Glenn. 2003. The price of everything, the value of nothing: reframing the commodification debate. *Harvard Law Review*, 117, 689–710.

Downes, Daniel M. and Richard Janda. 1998. Virtual citizenship. *Canadian Journal of Law and Society*, 13, 27–61.

Dworkin, Ronald. 1981. What is equality? Part two: equality of resources. *Philosophy and Public Affairs*, 10, 285–345.

Dzankic, Jelena. 2012. The pros and cons of ius pecuniae: investor citizenship in comparative perspective. *EUI Working Papers*, RSCAS 2012/14. Florence: European University Institute.

Florida, Richard and Irene Tingali. 2004. *Europe in the Creative Age.* London: Demos.

Fraser, Nancy. 1997. *Justice Interruptus.* London: Routledge.

Fraser, Nancy and Axel Honneth. 2003. *Redistribution or Recognition?* London: Verso.

Gammeltoft-Hansen, Thomas and Ninna Nyberg Sørensen, eds. 2013. *The Migration Industry and the Commercialization of International Migration.* London: Routledge.

Goodin, Robert E. 2007. Enfranchising all affected interests, and its alternatives. *Philosophy and Public Affairs*, 35, 40–68.

Goodman, Sara Wallace. 2012. Fortifying citizenship: policy strategies for civic integration in Western Europe. *World Politics*, 64, 659–98.

Guiraudon, Virginie and Gallya Lahav. 2000. A reappraisal of the state sovereignty debate: the case of migration control. *Comparative Political Studies*, 33, 163–95.

Hacker, Jacob S. and Paul Pierson. 2012. *Winner-Take-All Politics.* New York: Simon & Schuster.

Held, David; Anthony G. McGrew; David Goldblatt; and Jonathan Perraton. 1999. *Global Transformations.* Stanford, CA: Stanford University Press.

Hurley, Susan. 2003. *Justice, Luck, and Knowledge.* Cambridge, MA: Harvard University Press.

Kaufman, Scott Barry, ed. 2013. *The Complexity of Greatness: Beyond Talent or Practice.* Oxford: Oxford University Press.

Joppke, Christian. 2007. Beyond national models: civic integration policies for immigrants in Western Europe. *West European Politics*, 30, 1–22.

Jordan, Bill and Franck Düvell. 2003. *Migration: The Boundaries of Equality and Justice.* Cambridge: Polity.

Ley, David. 2010. *Millionaire Migrants: Trans-Pacific Life Lines.* Wiley-Blackwell.

Lukes, Steven. 2005. Invasions of the market. Pp. 298–321 in Max Miller (ed.), *Worlds of Capitalism.* London: Routledge.

Menz, Georg. 2008. *The Political Economy of Managed Migration: Nonstate Actors, Europeanization, and the Politics of Designing Migration Policies.* Oxford: Oxford University Press.

Miller, David. 2007. *National Responsibility and Global Justice.* Oxford: Oxford University Press.

Offe, Claus. 2011. From migration in geographic space to migration in biographic time: views from Europe. *Journal of Political Philosophy*, 19, 333–73.

Ong, Aihwa. 1999. *Flexible Citizenship: The Cultural Logic of Transnationality*. Durham: Duke University Press.

Orgad, Liav. 2010. Illiberal liberalism: cultural restrictions on migration and access to citizenship in Europe. *American Journal of Comparative Law*, 58, 53–105.

Putnam, Robert D. 1988. Diplomacy and domestic policy: the logic of two-level games. *International Organization*, 42, 427–60.

Radin, Margaret J. 1987. Market-inalienability. *Harvard Law Review*, 100, 1849–937.

Sandel, Michael J. 2012. *What Money Can't Buy: The Moral Limits of Markets*. New York: Farrar, Straus and Girous.

Sassen, Saskia. 1996. *Losing Control? Sovereignty in an Age of Globalization*. New York: Columbia University Press.

Satz, Debra. 2010. *Why Some Things Should Not be for Sale: The Moral Limits of Markets*. Oxford: Oxford University Press.

Shachar, Ayelet. 2006. The race for talent: highly skilled migrants and competitive immigration regimes. *NYU Law Review*, 81, 148–206.

Shachar, Ayelet. 2009. *The Birthright Lottery: Citizenship and Global Inequality* Cambridge, MA: Harvard University Press.

Shachar, Ayelet. 2011. Earned citizenship: property lessons for immigration reform. *Yale Journal of Law & the Humanities*, 23, 110–58.

Shachar, Ayelet and Ran Hirschl. 2007. Citizenship as inherited property. *Political Theory*, 35, 253–87.

Shamir, Ronen. 2005. Without borders? Notes on globalization as a mobility regime. *Sociological Theory*, 23, 197–217.

Simmons, Beth A. and Zachary Elkins. 2004. The globalization of liberalization: policy diffusion in the international political economy. *American Political Science Review*, 98, 171–89.

Sommers, Margaret R. 2008. *Genealogies of Citizenship: Markets, Statelessness, and the Rights to Have Rights*. Cambridge: Cambridge University Press.

Spiro, Peter J. 2008. *Beyond Citizenship*. Oxford: Oxford University Press.

Stiglitz, Joseph E. 2003. *Globalization and Its Discontents*. New York: Norton.

Sunstein, Cass R. 1996. On the expressive function of law. *University of Pennsylvania Law Review*, 144, 2021–53.

Sunstein, Cass R. 1997. Incommensurability and kinds of valuation: some applications in law. Pp. 234–54 in Ruth Chang (ed.), *Incommensurability, Incomparability, and Practical Reason*. Cambridge, MA: Harvard University Press.

Triadafilopoulos, Triadafilos, ed. 2013. *Wanted and Welcome? Policies for Highly Skilled Immigrants in Comparative Perspective*. New York: Springer.

Van Parijs, Philippe. 2000. The ground floor of the world: on the socio-economic consequences of linguistic globalization. *International Political Science Review*, 21, 217–33.

Walzer, Michael. 1983. *Spheres of Justice*. New York: Basic Books.

Wellman, Christopher Heath and Philip Cole. 2011. *Debating the Ethics of Immigration: Is There a Right to Exclude?* Oxford: Oxford University Press.

PART III
Global Interventions

10

Colonialism as Structural Injustice
*Historical Responsibility and Contemporary Redress**

Catherine Lu

> During the battle, which lasted about fifty days, I did not see any women at all. I knew that as a result of (being without access to women), men's mental condition ends up declining, and that's when I realized once again the necessity of special comfort stations. This desire is the same as hunger or the need to urinate, and soldiers merely thought of comfort stations as practically the same as latrines.
>
> – Japanese 11th Army Signal Corps officer, 1945[1]

I. Introduction

Colonialism was officially repudiated as an international practice at the 947th plenary meeting of the United Nations General Assembly in its 1960 "Declaration on the Granting of Independence to Colonial Countries and Peoples." The declaration equated the "subjection of peoples to alien subjugation, domination and exploitation" to "a denial of fundamental human rights"; affirmed the principle of self-determination for all peoples in their political status and economic, social and cultural development; and condemned the 'standard of civilization' rationale for colonial rule by asserting that "inadequacy of political, economic, social or educational preparedness should never serve as a pretext for delaying independence."[2] This declaration constituted an official rejection by the society of states of the colonial history

Political Theory Without Borders, First Edition. Edited by Robert E. Goodin and James S. Fishkin.
© 2016 John Wiley & Sons, Inc. Published 2016 by John Wiley & Sons, Inc.

of international and transnational relations as it had been practiced for more than four hundred years.

Although half a century has passed since the declaration, the colonial past is still a raw and corrosive ingredient in contemporary international relations between former colonizing countries and their colonial subjects. In particular, fractious interstate politics over issues of acknowledgement and redress raise questions about historical responsibility for colonial injustice and how contemporary agents should respond to that past. Contemporary politics of redress in international relations are dominated by a state-centric approach that frames all questions about historical responsibility, rectificatory justice, or political reconciliation in terms of interactions *between* former colonizing and colonized peoples or states. Because colonialism involved states as perpetrating agents and peoples as subjects of alien domination, it is typical to "think of colonialism first and foremost as a wrong done by the colonizer to the colonized."[3] Historical colonialism, of course, did fundamentally entail colonizer states violating the self-determination of colonized peoples, through practices such as military conquest and political subjugation, enslavement and exploitation of subjugated populations, the annexation of territories, expropriation of property, and resource extraction.[4]

A state-centric interactional approach that focuses only on the responsibility of perpetrator states, however, cannot tell the whole story about historical responsibility for many colonial injustices. In this article I explore the implications of a "structural injustice" approach to thinking about responsibility for past colonial injustices.[5] Like most political, social and economic injustices that affect large groups of people, colonial injustices involved not simply wrongful acts by individual or state perpetrators. They also relied on social structural processes that enabled and even encouraged individual or state wrongdoing, and produced and reproduced unjust outcomes. Acknowledging colonialism as structural injustice does not displace assessments of individual or state liability for wrongful actions, but identifies other contributory agents in the production of colonial injustices, and raises the question of their remedial responsibilities. A structural analysis reveals that the international society of states, in enacting through its rules, customs and practices a colonial international system, bears some historical responsibility for the unjust international social structures that enabled state wrongdoing. In addition, a structural approach identifies the contributory role of structural injustices within colonized societies in the production of some colonial injustices, thus raising questions about responsibility *of and among* colonized peoples.

How should acknowledgement of the structural bases of colonial injustices—located in international society and the colonizer state as well as the colonized society—affect the way we think about reparative responsibilities for the harms and injuries produced by colonial injustices? In particular, what responsibilities do those who participated in unjust social structures but who were not direct perpetrators themselves have towards victims of structural injustices? And how do contemporary agents in the affected societies come to acquire any responsibility for repairing the damages caused by past structural injustices?

I will be concerned in this article primarily with the experience of Japanese colonialism in Korea (1910–45) and the divisive politics of redress that has marked contemporary Korean-Japanese relations.[6] With the normalization of political relations through the 1965 "Treaty on Basic Relations between the Republic of (South) Korea and Japan," leaders of both countries voiced hopes of establishing "future-facing permanent and friendly relations on which [they] can build a new respectful and prosperous history." Despite this common desire, and while the 1965 treaty "declares that all issues involving compensation and reparations claims are settled by the treaty, disavowing the possibility of future claims," the presence of an unsettled past is observable in several aspects of contemporary Japanese-Korean relations.[7] The politics of redress has been especially rancorous: while Japanese officials, starting in the early 1990s, have issued routine apologies on several aspects of Japan's twentieth century imperial and colonial record, activists in South Korea, more sensitive to efforts by Japanese conservatives to evade and displace liability for Japan's transgressions, have rejected statements of apology as "lip-service," and continue to press the Japanese government to offer a "clear-cut" apology and compensate victims.[8] In particular, since the 1990s, South Korean and transnational human rights activists have pursued redress for survivors of Japan's military comfort system, which used women, the majority of whom were colonial subjects from Korea, to provide sexual services to Japanese soldiers during the Asia-Pacific War.[9]

How should we think about historical responsibility for Japanese colonial injustices, and in particular, for the military comfort system? According to a structural injustice approach, assigning moral culpability to the leading figures of the Japanese state and military is appropriate, but insufficient, as such an accounting leaves unexamined the unjust social structural processes in international society, as well as within Korean society, that contributed to the production of specific patterns of harms and victims. Acknowledging colonial injustices as structural injustices generates a "political responsibility" to effect structural reforms that ought to be shared by Japanese and Koreans, as well as by the international society of states.[10] This political responsibility is met, and social structures can be considered adequately reformed, only when victims of colonial structural injustices achieve the necessary conditions for effective political and social agency within their respective societies. To the extent that this political responsibility is unmet and structural injustice persists, the political responsibility to effect just social structures and conditions is a legacy that those who contributed to the production of structural injustice pass on to their descendants.

II. Legal Colonialism and International Structural Injustice

The relative lack of accounting for injustices committed in contexts of colonial rule is striking. The settling of accounts after World War Two was aimed mainly at crimes against the peace and war crimes. Both the Nuremberg and Tokyo Trials focused on repudiating wars of aggression as the most serious violations of international law and order, and although the Trials saw the introduction of the category of 'crimes against humanity,' only such crimes committed in the context of interstate war were acknowledged. As Judith Shklar observed about Nuremberg, the Tribunal "decided to interpret crimes against humanity restrictively, limiting itself to those committed after 1939, and so assimilating them to the less controversial charge of war crimes."[11] Yuma Totani's comprehensive study of the Tokyo Trial shows that contrary to popular belief, the Trial recognized a wide variety of wrongful conduct by Japan in the war, constituting twenty "particular patterns of atrocities" for which the Tribunal held the Japanese government at the highest level to be accountable. Totani's examination of actual trial records also shows unambiguously that Allied prosecutors at the Tokyo Trial, especially the Dutch representative, Sinninghe Damste, presented evidence of "the Japanese commission of various forms of sexual violence including sexual slavery, targeted in principal at the Asian female population."[12] While there was some accountability for Japanese mistreatment of the colonial subjects of other colonizer states in the context of war, the Allied prosecutors did not pursue an accounting of Japanese mistreatment of its own Korean or Taiwanese colonial subjects. Evidently, Japan's treatment of its own colonial subjects was excluded from the mandate of the Tokyo Trial, which focused on Japan's war of aggression and war crimes against other colonial powers and *their* colonial subjects.

Resistance against acknowledging responsibility for injustices committed in the context of colonial rule, that were distinct from the injustice of aggressive war and crimes against humanity committed in contexts of war, has persisted. Thus, even in the case of the undisputed 1904 genocide of the Herero people in the context of Germany's colonization of German South West Africa (today's Namibia), the former German president Roman Herzog, in 1998, cited the absence of international legal reparative provisions for colonialism in the early twentieth century to support his government's decision not to pay reparations to Herero descendants.[13] As Sidney Harring has perceptively noted, the German politician framed the Herero genocide in the context of colonialism, and "for Herzog, colonialism was 'legal' in 1905 under international legislation, therefore ending the discussion of Herero reparations."[14] It is estimated that in Germany's campaign to colonize South West Africa, over three-quarters of the entire Herero population (60,000 out of a population of 80,000), as well as half of the Nama people, were killed, either in battle or due to harsh conditions imposed by German troops.[15] Germany did eventually apologize for the Herero genocide on 14 August 2004, but it has consistently refused to accept liability, and hence reparative obligations, to Herero descendants, "since the international rules on the protection of combatants and civilians were not in existence at the time that war crimes were being committed in Namibia."[16]

While the historical legality of colonialism cannot constitute an adequate moral defense of colonial practices, legal colonialism does not fit into a typical way of thinking about the nature and circumstances of wrongdoing, as an aberrant and willful violation of shared communal norms, laws or practices. As Iris Marion Young has observed, what usually "counts as a wrong for which we seek a perpetrator and for which he or she might be required to compensate, is something we generally conceive as a deviation from a baseline."[17] This standard model of wrongdoing assumes a just or morally acceptable baseline, against which individuals' wrongful actions constitute aberrations. Contemporary redress politics typically assume this model with states as the relevant moral agents. Colonial injustices are thus constituted by a state's wrongful acts against another state or nation, for which the perpetrator state ought to be held accountable through punishment of its leaders as well as through compensation to the victimized people.

This approach to accounting for colonial injustices, however, is vulnerable to the criticism that it inaccurately portrays the nature and circumstances of wrongdoing in the colonial case. Colonizer states' actions were typically not aberrant violations of international norms, customs or laws. The state-centric interactional approach has difficulty acknowledging the legal basis of many colonial injustices because its underlying model of wrongdoing and responsibility cannot grasp the nature of wrongs that are constituted in part by unjust baselines. In such circumstances, individuals' or states' wrongful actions typically conform to, rather than deviate from, a morally defective baseline.

Japan, for example, sought to negotiate its entry into a colonial international system characterized by European domination of non-European peoples in a way that would avoid the insecurity and vulnerability of all non-Europeans to be branded inferior—a prospect which rendered "a nation ripe for colonization."[18] According to Japanese leaders at the time, there seemed no better way of achieving recognition as a member of the family of civilized nations than to acquire colonial subjects and build a colonial empire.[19] The sociological reality was that in a colonial international system, Japan was not behaving like a deviant state, but was acting in accordance with prevailing international norms, if not international law, when it annexed and colonized Korea in 1910.[20] A compelling normative assessment of colonialism as a historical injustice must be able to acknowledge this fact of internationally *legitimated* (to be distinguished from morally *legitimate*) colonization prior to the 1960 declaration, and also explain in what way a legally sanctioned or socially legitimized practice can be considered wrongful or morally objectionable.

In their development of such an account, Jeppe von Platz and David Reidy have put forward a type of injustice characterized by "social contexts that are in some sense completely or pervasively unjust." In such forms of injustice, "a system of entitlements may be predicated on, may track and express, a morally corrupt or unacceptable desert- or value-basis." Colonialism, premised on an entitlement to conquer and subjugate other peoples based on a notion of racial or civilizational superiority, was such a structural or systemic historical wrong, in which there is a "manifestly unacceptable or morally corrupt desert- or value-basis underlying a rule-governed social practice, institution or system of entitlements."[21]

The work of von Platz and Reidy builds on an illuminating examination of structures and structural injustice developed by Iris Marion Young. Young defines "structures" as "the confluence of institutional rules and interactive routines, mobilization of resources, as well as physical structures such as buildings and roads." Structures provide "background conditions for individual actions by presenting actors with options; they provide 'channels' that both enable action and constrain" agency. The concept of structural injustice refers to social structures and processes—embodied in "institutions, discourses, and practices"—that are based on morally unacceptable values or belief systems.[22] The existence of structural injustice in a society perverts systems of norms and entitlement; enables, legitimizes and normalizes individual wrongdoing; and, depending on the social structures affected, may produce unjust outcomes ranging from unfair distributions of the burdens and benefits of social cooperation to mass violations of human rights against socially vulnerable groups. According to Young, "[s]tructural injustice exists when social processes put large categories of persons under a systematic threat of domination or deprivation of the means to develop and exercise their capacities, at the same time as these processes enable others to dominate or have a wide range of opportunities for developing and exercising their capacities."[23] Structurally unjust social processes based on class, disability, race, and gender, for example, produce and perpetuate social vulnerabilities for some and advantages for others.[24]

Young has also employed a structural injustice approach to account for inhumane or unjust labor conditions that result from transnational unjust structural processes of the global apparel industry; the harms produced by such structural injustices have "no isolatable perpetrator, but rather result from the participation of millions of people in institutions and practices." It is not the case, however, that the concept of structural injustice is only pertinent in cases of harms or injustices where there is no determinate perpetrator. In her reference to the Nazi Holocaust, Young observes that "the makers of genocidal policies and those that directly implement them are enabled and supported by wider social structures in which many participate." Structural injustice is thus an important constitutive component in the production of some injustices which have identifiable perpetrators and/or direct causal relationships between an agent and a harm. Most cases of social and political injustice, from inhumane labor conditions to sexual exploitation to genocide, should therefore "be analyzed on these two levels."[25]

While structural injustices as moral wrongs are analytically distinct from "the wrongful action of an individual agent" and "the willfully repressive policies of a state," structurally-based injustices can involve all of these types of wrongs. Colonial injustices, like most political, social and economic injustices that affect large categories of people, involve not simply wrongful acts by individual or state perpetrators, but rely on social structural processes that enable and even encourage individual or state wrongdoing, and produce and reproduce unjust outcomes. A state-centric interactional approach that focuses only on guilty states or guilty individuals thus cannot tell the whole story about historical responsibility for structurally-based injustices. A structural account of colonial injustice can acknowledge the legalization and normalization of colonial practices, and indeed, views colonial legality as a hallmark of the structural nature of colonial injustice, since typically, structural injustices occur "as a consequence of many individuals and institutions acting in pursuit of their particular goals and interests, *within given institutional rules and accepted norms*." A structural injustice approach highlights the contributory role of those who participate in rules, institutions and social practices at various levels that enable, encourage and produce "widespread and repeated" violations.[26]

Structural injustices in the colonial system of international law, for example, made Korean women more vulnerable to being recruited, often deceptively or forcibly, into Japan's military comfort system. Japan had signed international treaties banning traffic in women and girls in 1925, but Article 14 of the "International Convention for the Suppression of Traffic in Women and Children" allowed member states to exempt colonies from the application of the convention, and Japan, like many other colonial powers, exempted its colonies of Korea and Taiwan, as well as Kwantung.[27] While Japanese leaders were anxious about the recruitment of Japanese women for the comfort women system, they showed little prudential or normative regard for the recruitment of non-Japanese women. Thus Yoshiaki Yoshimi has documented that a notice distributed in February 1938 by the Japanese Home Ministry's Chief of the Police Bureau to each prefecture and metropolitan district in Japan contains the admonishment that recruiting Japanese women to serve as prostitutes for Japanese military personnel may be "contrary to the spirit of international treaties relating to the traffic in women and girls," but this admonishing notice was not distributed to (the Government-Generals of) Korea or Taiwan.[28] Just as international practice permitted the annexation and colonization of Korea, it also provided a legal loophole for Japan to mistreat its most vulnerable colonial subjects.

According to a structural approach, moral responsibility for wrongful acts can certainly be attributed to the colonizing state and culpable individuals, but some share of historical responsibility should also be attributed to all states, especially the dominant ones, that contributed to perpetuating the unjust social structures of a colonial international system. Acknowledging colonialism as structural injustice does not displace assessments of individual or state liability for wrongful actions, but identifies other agents that contribute to the production of colonial injustices, and raises the question of their remedial responsibilities. If colonizer states bear duties of redress for those who suffered harms and damages from their colonial injustices, a structural injustice approach should lead us to inquire about the responsibilities that all participants in international structural injustice may have towards victims of colonial injustice.

III. Domestic Structural Injustices under Colonial Rule: The Case of the Japanese Military Comfort System

In all societies, including those under colonial rule, individuals occupy different social positions that enable them to exercise different capacities for social agency as well as expose them to different kinds or levels of social vulnerabilities. Colonial rule introduced a racially-based structural injustice into the colonized society, but also at times reinforced or exacerbated other existing structural injustices within the colonized society. While the vulnerabilities attached to being colonial subjects were collectively shared, the operation of other structural injustices within colonized societies means that not all colonial subjects faced the same structural constraints on agency, nor experienced the same kinds or degrees of vulnerability to marginalization, domination or exploitation. Being a victim of colonial domination does not translate into equality of domination with all other members of the colonized society. In this sense, a state-centric interactional perspective on colonial injustice distorts the historical record about who were victims and who were perpetrators of colonial injustices. Young's account of structural injustices as social contexts that place "large categories of persons under a systematic threat of domination or deprivation of the means to develop and exercise their capacities, at the same time as these processes enable others to dominate or have a wide range of opportunities for developing and exercising their capacities," allows for a complex array of social positions that individuals and groups may occupy in the social structures that produce injustice.[29]

In other words, a structural analysis of colonial injustice is not likely to support a simplistic division of colonizers and colonized into perpetrator and victim roles. Among colonized populations, individuals and groups occupy different social positions in the structure of colonial domination, and some may use their relatively privileged position and resources to dominate others, and may even derive some benefits from participation in colonial enterprises at the expense of their more socially vulnerable compatriots. Another hallmark of structural injustice, then, is its propensity to produce victim-perpetrators: those in colonial positions of subordination (such as all Korean colonial subjects) nevertheless still occupied different social positions that enabled some (for example, private Korean entrepreneurs engaged in the commercial sex industry or human trafficking) to derive benefits at the expense of their more socially vulnerable compatriots (such as impoverished Korean women and girls). The complexity of structural injustice thus permits more nuanced as well as more expansive judgments about the agents who bear historical responsibility for specific patterns of injustice in colonial contexts. A state-centric interactional approach obscures the fact that colonial practices typically had differential impacts on those within colonial populations. Accounting for this differential impact requires some examination, not only of Korean collaboration, but also of domestic structural injustices operating in colonized societies. I will use the Japanese military comfort system as an illustrative case.

The anthropologist Sarah Soh has provided a comprehensive examination of the Japanese military comfort system as a historical institution "deriving from the dynamics of capitalism, militarism, and a sexual-cultural order." Her study shows that the Japanese military comfort system had three distinct and overlapping phases of development. A major part of the system operated as a commercial for-profit sex industry, in which women were paid for their sexual services and could leave after paying off their debts. Another phase of the system that developed as Japan became more deeply engaged in war operated as a paramilitary service organization, in which the enforced prostitution of women's sexual labor served the military objective of maintaining troop morale, thereby supporting the war effort, and preventing troops from committing sexual atrocities against civilians in occupied territories. Finally, some parts of the military comfort system, especially near the front lines in occupied territories towards the end of the Asia-Pacific war, amounted to a criminal sexual enterprise, involving forced abductions and sexual slavery.[30]

Soh's anthropological study shows that the Japanese military's recruitment of Korean girls did not typically involve large-scale forced abductions or slave-raids, but required the cooperation of the Korean colonial government and the collaboration of local Korean elites and entrepreneurs. According to Soh, survivor accounts support the conclusion that civilian "Koreans actually outnumbered civilian Japanese among those seeking profit by human trafficking, forcing prostitution and sexual slavery upon young female compatriots."[31] She and scholars such as Pyong Gap Min have demonstrated that "colonization, gender, and class were inseparably tied together" in producing the heightened social vulnerability of poor, rural and working-class Korean women to recruitment into the Japanese military comfort system. Min notes, for example, that because Japanese colonial economic policy devastated Korean agriculture, many young women in rural areas became vulnerable to pressures to leave home in search of profitable work, a situation exploited by Korean recruiters for the military comfort system. Indeed, the majority of the Korean comfort women (fifty-nine per cent) were "drafted through false promises of well-paying jobs in Japan."[32]

A structural injustice approach, by highlighting the differentiated suffering of Koreans, raises the thorny issue of Korean collaboration under Japanese colonial rule. If we regard the Japanese military comfort system in its entirety as one large, "consolidated wrong" that involved multiple wrongs—including deceptive and/or forcible recruitment methods; specific targeting of poor rural and working-class women; and enforced prostitution, rape, confinement, and/or sexual slavery—then the contributory acts of Korean colonial state officials and police, local elites and private entrepreneurs in the recruitment process can be viewed as partially constitutive of the wrong. Although they had no role in initiating the wrong, their contributions were central to the operationalization of the system.[33] In the terminology offered by Chiara Lepora and Robert Goodin, the Japanese military and state were the "plan-makers" but the Korean colonial government, local elites and private entrepreneurs contributed significantly as "plan-takers" to implementing the plan.[34]

It is unlikely in the Korean case that the field of those who bear moral culpability for their contribution to such injustices under Japanese colonial rule can plausibly be limited to a handful of politicians, as some nationalists claim, or in fairness be extended to "all those who at some point in time had been in touch with Japan."[35] While judging individual liability for actions committed under conditions of structural injustice is appropriate, the experience of contemporary international criminal tribunals shows that this is a difficult task. In cases of structurally-based injustices that involve organized intentional wrongdoing or mass participation in direct wrongdoing, the attribution of individual guilt is more complicated than in a standard case of individual interactional wrongdoing (where the individual's actions constitute isolated aberrations against a reasonably just background structural condition and violate shared norms, laws or practices).[36] Acknowledging contexts of structural injustice is thus important for making morally reasonable assessments of individual liability for wrongdoing. As Lepora and Goodin suggest, the culpability of plan-takers must be assessed individually, depending on factors such as their motives, their enthusiasm or reluctance in implementing the plan, the existence of excusing circumstances such as duress, and the availability of reasonable opportunities for pursuing alternative courses of action.[37]

The judgment of blameworthy collaboration bases guilt on the degree to which individual Korean agents willfully and intentionally participated in wrongdoing that was planned by their Japanese colonial masters. A structural approach, however, raises the question of how structurally unjust social processes within the colonized society might have contributed to producing the negative outcomes of unjust colonial policies. In the case of the military comfort system, gender- and class-based structural injustices within Korean society were central to producing the pattern of exploitation and abuse of impoverished rural and working class women. In one example, in 1941, the Japanese Kwantung Army requested the assistance of the colonial Government-General of Korea to recruit twenty thousand Korean women to provide sexual services to Japanese troops preparing to invade the Soviet Union. The colonial government, in turn, relied on local elites or heads of townships to meet the request. These elites proceeded by visiting poor households and persuading the parents "to send their unmarried daughters to work in Japan." This collaborative effort enabled the quick procurement of almost eight thousand recruits who were then sent to military comfort stations in northern Manchuria.[38]

The moral blameworthiness of the head of the township who recruited the women may be judged according to the factors mentioned above. His decision to approach only indigent households, however, was not unique; the concentration of victims in impoverished and working-class groups indicates that the practice was common, suggesting the influence of unjust social structural processes on the specific distribution of victims. In addition to assessing the moral culpability of individuals for their wrongful acts, acknowledging the role of domestic structural injustices within Korean society in this case raises the question of domestic Korean shared responsibility for those structural injustices. The contemporary politics of redress for the Japanese military comfort system, however, have left "little room for critical self-reflection in South Korean public discourse" on the historical responsibility of Koreans themselves.[39]

The 2000 Women's International War Crimes Tribunal on Japan's Military Sexual Slavery, organized by human rights activists from Japan, South Korea and the Philippines, is just one example of a major redress movement that concentrated on indicting Japan—most notably the late Hirohito, posthumously named Emperor Shōwa—for sexual violence against women during the era of Japanese colonialism and aggressive war, but neglected to make any wider assessments of international or domestic Korean responsibility. Christine Chinkin has noted that the Tribunal hoped to contribute to the "appropriate attribution of responsibility," away from the victimized women themselves, who were stigmatized, and towards the Japanese government.[40] The stigmatization of survivors, however, was most apparent in postcolonial Korea, where the gender inequalities of strong patriarchal traditions compounded the hardships endured by the women when they returned to Korea.[41] For many survivors, it was not their wartime sexual labor, but "the humiliation of social stigma and isolation in their postwar lives [in Korea] that made these women despair."[42] A broader structural approach to the question of historical responsibility for the Japanese military comfort system would have illuminated the operation of structural injustices that cut across the colonizer/colonized divide, and such an acknowledgement might have helped to prevent the instrumentalization of victims of sexual violence in ethnonationalist politics in South Korea.

Such instrumentalization, to the detriment of victim-survivors, was apparent in the controversy over the National/Asian Women's Fund (AWF), established in 1995 by Japan with "the aim of expressing a sense of national atonement from the Japanese people to the former 'comfort women,' and to work to address contemporary issues regarding the honor and dignity of women." Although the AWF reflected compromises between conservative and progressive forces within Japanese politics and society, and did not amount to legal state compensation to survivors, it was a "hybrid national public organization" (NPO), the operation of which was financed and administered by the Japanese government.[43] Instead of supporting such redress efforts as progress towards developing a greater sense of responsibility among Japanese for their colonial and wartime past, critics found fault with the AWF as a 'private' fund, through which the Japanese government evaded official and legal responsibility. The Korean Council for Women Drafted for Military Sexual Slavery by Japan (Korean Council), a nongovernmental activist organization, lobbied against the AWF and went so far as to denounce the seven Korean survivors who accepted AWF compensation in 1997. In addition, the Korean Council lobbied the South Korean government to offer special support payments to 140 survivors, "with the proviso that survivors sign a pledge not to receive AWF money."[44] What is remarkable about this latter effort is that it did not constitute any acknowledgement by the South Korean government, or society at large, of their responsibility to redress the harms suffered by survivors; rather, the payments instrumentalized the plight of victim-survivors in an ethnonationalist political contest. Not surprisingly, these redress efforts only produced "fissures among the communities of victim-survivors and their supporters."[45]

Observing these developments, Soh has criticized the partiality of the "paradigmatic story" of comfort women as a "sex slaves," a war crimes and crimes against humanity issue, which was put forward by both "a transnational women's human rights perspective and South Korean ethnonationalism." Her concern is that the human rights activists' "master narrative has glossed over the more complex, wider-reaching narratives of women's oppression and has thereby failed to generate a sense of societal responsibility among Koreans for their compatriots' lifelong suffering."[46] The critique that contemporary human rights discourse has obscured Korean domestic responsibility reveals a flaw in that discourse's understanding of how human rights violations were produced in a colonial context. Crimes against humanity in such contexts involve not only wrongful actions by colonizers, but also typically require various kinds and degrees of complicity among the colonized, as well as the existence of enabling unjust social structures shared by colonizer and colonized groups. Patterns of human rights violations in contexts of colonial rule may result not only from the unjust structural processes introduced by a colonizer state, but also from the operation of pre-existing structural injustices operating within colonized societies.

When Korean and transnational human rights activists focus their redress efforts only on getting the Japanese state to acknowledge its moral culpability, they miss an opportunity to examine and reform problematic Korean societal practices and structural processes, leaving unjust social structures in place that may contribute to recurrences of similar injustices. It is perhaps worth noting that in postcolonial Korea, the Korean military instituted its own comfort system, a practice that began in the early 1950s and ended in 1954 with the cessation of the Korean War. Soh notes the parallel rationales offered by Korea's armed forces and Japan's imperial forces: both considered comfort systems to be instrumental to raising troop morale, and a necessary evil to reduce the likelihood of military personnel committing sexual brutality against civilian populations. Although Korea was the victim of Japanese colonial ambitions, Korean society evidently shared with Japanese society debased views of women as sexual objects with only instrumental value for meeting soldiers' natural urges.[47]

A structural injustice approach to assessing historical responsibility for colonial injustices goes beyond the state-centric interactional approach, admitting a more expansive view of morally responsible agents, as well as a more complex view of the different kinds and degrees of responsibility that attach to individuals' wrongful actions and to their participation in background social structures that produced colonial injustices. Because responsibility for structural injustice is not zero-sum, clarifying the responsibility of the Japanese state or society does not disqualify others, including the Korean state and society, from also bearing some measure of historical responsibility.[48]

A structural approach exposes gender-based and class-based structural injustices in Korean society that enabled the targeting or vulnerability of poor women for recruitment into the military comfort system. Identifying the structural bases of colonial injustices, that were either shared by colonizer and colonized societies, or particular to the colonized society's historical development, reveals an illusion underlying contemporary nation-based politics of redress. In such politics, all Koreans can proclaim solidarity with the victims of the military comfort system, and may even come to view comfort women survivors as the symbols of Korean national victimhood under Japanese colonial rule. This solidarity, unfortunately, is illusory, and comes at the price of glossing over legitimate grievances and claims of redress that actual victims may hold against their own compatriots and society, as well as obscuring the need for critical collective self-reflection and reform of structural processes within Korean society.

IV. Responsibility for Structural Injustice and Reparations

A structural injustice approach reveals that many colonial injustices were enabled, supported or perpetuated by international, transnational and local structurally unjust social processes and background conditions. What implications does this have for thinking about responsibility for colonial injustices? With respect to individuals and states that are direct perpetrators of wrongdoing, this conclusion does not displace the requirement to assign moral blame for wrongdoing to them, although the structural context of wrongdoing is an important factor in assessing the blameworthiness of agents. For individuals acting in extreme cases of structural domination, such as that faced by interns in Nazi concentration camps, judgment may be impossible. Thus, as Primo Levi noted about judging prisoners who helped to run Nazi concentration camps and sometimes committed brutalities against fellow inmates, "[t]he condition of the offended does not exclude culpability, which is often objectively serious, but I know of no human tribunal to which one could delegate the judgment."[49] States acting under extreme cases of structural domination may also be denied the structural conditions of effective state agency and responsibility: for example, given that Korea was a colonized state of Japan and enjoyed no formal or effective sovereignty over its own internal and external affairs, it would be difficult to assign to it moral culpability as a perpetrator state, despite Korean human and material contributions to Japan's aggressive war efforts.[50]

In addition to complicating judgment about the moral culpability of direct perpetrators, be they individuals or states, a structural analysis raises the question of what kinds of responsibilities are incurred by agents who are not direct perpetrators in relation to a set of victims, but who participated in the production of unjust structural social processes that enabled or supported others' wrongdoing. At the level of international society, for example, states enacted and legitimated through their norms, laws and practices a colonial international system in which dominant (mainly European) states competed for colonial possessions, each pursuing dreams of empire by subjugating weaker states, peoples or territories. Korea fell victim to Japanese imperial ambitions, but do other state participants in a structurally unjust colonial international system bear any responsibilities in relation to Korea's victimization? More generally, what responsibilities do agents who participate in producing unjust structural conditions, but who may not be direct perpetrators of wrongdoing, have towards the resulting harms and damages suffered by vulnerable others?

In her account of responsibility for global structural injustice, Young proposes a "political" or "social connection" model of responsibility, whereby all those participating in a social structural process that produces, even indirectly and unintentionally, unjust outcomes, bear responsibilities to reform their activities, practices and institutions to prevent the reproduction of similarly unjust outcomes. Young distinguishes "political responsibility" from a "liability model" of responsibility. The function of the latter type of responsibility is chiefly to hold culpable individuals accountable for their wrongful actions, through punishment, redress or compensation, while the main function of the former type of responsibility is to stimulate collective action to transform social structures so as to avoid further injustices and injuries. Both types of responsibility are important in response to structurally-based injustices, but they are distributed differently.[51] Those who participate in unjust social structural processes are not morally liable for other individuals' wrongful acts, even if those acts were conditioned by those unjust structures. To accept political responsibility, therefore, is not to accept moral blame for the harms and damages caused by others' wrongdoing.

I argue, with Young, that non-culpable agents who contribute to the production of unjust structural conditions bear political responsibility to reform their social practices so that they produce more just outcomes. Young, however, seems to think about compensation for victims only within the framework of a liability model of responsibility, and argues that her conception of political responsibility "seeks not to reckon debts, but aims rather to bring about results," namely, structurally just social relations and conditions. She also argues that political responsibility avoids blaming agents, and is mainly concerned with mobilizing "collective action for the sake of social change and greater justice."[52] My argument, however, makes the concept of political responsibility more controversial, because the justness of the outcomes or social conditions that result from structural reform must include the elimination of social disadvantages that identifiable victims may suffer as a result of past injustice.

What is the relationship of contemporary descendants of colonizing and colonized societies to this political responsibility? After all, contemporary descendants are not morally blameworthy for the wrongs committed by their ancestors, nor were they participants in the social structural processes that produced unjust outcomes. What basis is there, then, to assign to them any responsibility at all for past structural injustices?

One thing to note is that there is a distinction between acts of injustice being past and structural injustice being a thing of the past. Even if unjust acts or policies end, for example, through defeat of perpetrators in a war, unjust structural processes and conditions may persist. To the extent that structural injustices are inherited, the political responsibility to reform them is a legacy that those who contributed to the production of structural injustices pass on to their descendants. Political responsibility thus continues to exist for present and future generations until their social structures become reasonably just.

At the level of international society, some might argue that this political responsibility has been met by the society of states through measures such as the 1960 "Declaration on the Granting of Independence to Colonial Countries and Peoples." Such changes in the formal rules of international law and society, while promising, are not adequate for meeting my or Young's conception of political responsibility. According to Young, structural injustice refers not only to unjust formal laws, but is characterized mainly by unjust social processes and practices that bring about certain unjust social conditions, such as inhumane working conditions for factory workers, or a disproportionate percentage of single mothers living under the poverty line. Young describes structural injustice as involving "large categories of persons" being dominated or deprived, while others enjoy benefits in the form of greater opportunities to develop and exercise their capacities, and as "structural social processes *with unjust outcomes*."[53] A political responsibility to correct structural injustice is thus concerned with changing the formal laws and societal norms underlying social institutions and practices, but political responsibility is fulfilled only when these changes bring about or realize just structural or social conditions.[54]

In the context of international society, just social conditions in the aftermath of colonialism would, at a minimum, require not only formal, but also effective, equal sovereignty for previously colonized states. Although colonialism has been repudiated in international law, we are still far away from a world in which all previously colonized peoples enjoy effective equal sovereignty. Thus, contemporary international society continues to bear political responsibility for reforming international social structures, institutions and practices in ways that would result in a fairer and more inclusive international order, especially for previously colonized peoples. One might understand this political responsibility as similar to John Rawls's "duty of assistance" to "burdened societies,"

the aim of which is to enable peoples to develop the appropriate social structures and conditions necessary for exercising effective political and moral
agency. My view of this political responsibility to assist previously colonized
peoples, however, differs from Rawls's account by noting that one source of
burdened societies' "unfavorable conditions" is past international structural
injustices, such as colonialism.[55] While legal changes can go a long way
toward establishing just social conditions, reparations for victims who continue to experience disadvantages resulting from past structural injustices is
also necessary for realizing, in practice, the patterns of social relations that
define a just international society. In a political responsibility framework,
the ground for providing reparations to victims is not that contemporary
agents are liable in a morally culpable way for historical colonial injustices.
Rather, contemporary agents bear political responsibility to correct inherited structural injustices, and reparative measures that enable former victims
to exercise effective political and social agency constitute one requirement
for social structures to be considered just.

Applied to Korean society, the political responsibility of contemporary
Koreans to reform their own society's unjust structural processes similarly
requires, in addition to broad societal changes to combat gender-based and
class-based structural injustices, helping those who were directly damaged by
colonial injustices to achieve the necessary conditions for effective democratic
citizenship.[56] Special reparative measures are required because, as Kok-chor
Tan has noted, historical injustices produce "spillover unjust effects in an
indirect way … by tainting present relations that make justice between the
affected parties difficult to achieve."[57] Although Tan is referring to relations
between colonizing and colonized peoples, his observation is also pertinent
to thinking about the relationship between victimized Koreans, such as survivors of the Japanese military comfort system, and their own state and
society, given that their injuries and subsequent suffering resulted in part
from structural injustices that involved Korean political and social institutions and practices. Those who experienced political and social injustices
may develop a profound sense of mistrust of and alienation from political
and social institutions that linger even after general political and social transformations. Reparations, in a political responsibility framework, constitute
measures to clear out "an undergrowth of disrespect and distrust" left by
historical structural injustice, "so that trusting relations can take root."[58]

Some might find the assertion that Korean victims of a Japanese colonial injustice are entitled to reparations from Korean society to be absurd
or perverse. The President of Senegal rejected reparations claims for
slavery on the basis of the claims' implications for his own responsibility,
given his ancestors' involvement in the slave-owning business: "If one can
claim reparations for slavery, the slaves of my ancestors or their descendants can also claim money from me because slavery has been practiced

by all people in the world."[59] Once slavery is viewed as a structural injustice, however, it makes moral sense to think more seriously about how all those whose historical relations involved unjust social processes that supported the institution of slavery may need to make amends to identifiable victims as part of their political responsibility to realize just social relations and conditions.[60]

V. Conclusion

Frantz Fanon has argued that one of the aims of contemporary societies marked by a colonial past must be "to move away from the inhuman voices of their respective ancestors so that a genuine communication can be born."[61] If this is the correct future-oriented normative aim of dealing with a colonial past, it exerts demands on the colonized as well as the colonizer nation to engage in the difficult tasks of critical self-reflection and transformation. In some ways, one must surpass oneself, or what one has known about oneself, as well as what one thinks or knows about others, in order to give birth to a new form of politics and relationship. The willingness of former colonized peoples to become partners with their former colonizers in new political relationships defined by mutual respect and justice may depend on their willingness to acknowledge not only their victimization but also their agency and political responsibility.

A structural injustice approach to historical responsibility should lead us to be critical of contemporary practices of redress that enforce a simplistic moral coherence on the past in order to stabilize contemporary national identities or shore up internal political legitimacy. In reflecting on what duties contemporary individuals and societies have in relation to past injustices, Judith Shklar wrote, "[p]erhaps the best intellectual response is simply to write the history of the victims and victimizers as truthfully and accurately as possible."[62] Such a history requires more than an accounting of what individuals or nations did to each other; it must also inquire into the history and social contexts of their relations, especially the structural processes that shaped social agency and its outcomes. When participants who share a history of structural injustice engage properly in the quest for such a truthful accounting, the process will most likely be a deeply unsettling and disorienting one. If a new politics of mutual respect and friendship is the goal of those societies sharing a colonial past—as colonizer or colonized—it will only be born through a painful labor that forsakes ancestors, avoids soothingly self-serving narratives, and faces the unpleasant, humbling, and complicated, but agency-sensitive and thus potentially liberating, truths revealed by understanding colonialism as a structural injustice.

Notes

* The author wishes to thank Arash Abizadeh, Ashok Acharya, Christian Barry, James Fishkin, Pablo Gilabert, Bob Goodin, Mark Kramer, Lorenz Lüthi, Colleen Murphy, Alan Patten, Makoto Suzuki, Timothy Waligore and an anonymous referee for their helpful discussions and/or written comments. She would also like to thank Kristin Rawls and Janine Pietsch for their research assistance. A shorter, earlier version of this article appeared in a Korean language translation: "Colonialism as structural injustice and implications for responsibilities of repair," *The Journal of Asiatic Studies*, 53 (2010), 33–54. Later versions of this article benefited from discussions at the Canadian Political Science Association annual meeting (May 2010) at Concordia University; the Society for Applied Philosophy annual meeting (July 2010), at St. Anne's College, Oxford University; and in a Comparative Theory seminar (December 2010) at the Developing Countries Research Centre at the University of Delhi. The author is grateful to the Social Sciences and Humanities Research Council of Canada, as well as the Alexander von Humboldt Foundation, for their financial support of this work.

1 Quoted in Yoshiaki Yoshimi, *Comfort Women: Sexual Slavery in the Japanese Military During World War II*, trans. Suzanne O'Brien (New York: Columbia University Press, 2000), p. 199.

2 United Nations, "Declaration on the granting of independence to colonial countries and peoples," Resolution 1514 of the United Nations General Assembly, 1960, <http://www.un.org/Depts/dpi/decolonization/declaration.htm>.

3 Lea Ypi, Robert E. Goodin and Christian Barry, "Associative duties, global justice, and the colonies," *Philosophy and Public Affairs*, 37 (2009), 103–35 at p. 133.

4 See Daniel Butt, *Rectifying International Injustice: Principles of Compensation and Restitution Between Nations* (Oxford: Oxford University Press, 2009), p. 5. Butt provides a lucid theoretical treatment of the rectificatory duties owed by contemporary states to non-nationals for violations of principles of "just international interaction" from an "international libertarian perspective."

5 For development of the concept of structural injustice, I will draw mainly from the work of Iris Marion Young, "Responsibility and global labor justice," *Journal of Political Philosophy*, 12 (2004), 365–88; "Responsibility and global justice: a social connection model," *Social Philosophy and Policy*, 23 (2006), 102–30; "Taking the basic structure seriously," *Perspectives on Politics*, 4 (2006), 91–7; "Structural injustice and the politics of difference," *Contemporary Debates in Political Philosophy*, ed. T. Christiano and J. Christman (Malden, MA: Wiley-Blackwell, 2009), pp. 362–83.

6 In addition to using Korean women in its military 'comfort women' system, a case that will be analyzed in detail in this article, Japan's colonial injustices include subjecting large numbers of Koreans, mainly men, to forced labor in mines and factories, or to conscription in the Japanese imperial army. It is estimated, for example, that between 6,500 and 10,000 Korean forced laborers were killed in the atomic bombings of Hiroshima and Nagasaki. See John W. Dower, "The bombed: Hiroshimas and Nagasakis in Japanese memory," *Hiroshima in History and Memory*, ed. Michael J. Hogan (Cambridge: Cambridge University Press, 1996), p. 140. In addition, Koreans lost not only political autonomy under

colonial rule, but also faced an attempt by Japan to obliterate their cultural identity, through measures such as forcing Koreans to adopt Japanese names, imposing Japanese as the official language of education, and requiring Koreans to take an oath as imperial subjects. Typically, Korean comfort women were assigned Japanese names upon arrival at a military comfort station. See Yoshimi, *Comfort Women*, p. 153.

7 Alexis Dudden, *Troubled Apologies Among Japan, Korea and the United States* (New York: Columbia University Press, 2008), pp. 44 and 94.

8 Martin Fackler, "Japan apologizes to South Korea on colonization," *New York Times*, August 10, 2010, <http://www.nytimes.com/2010/08/11/world/asia/11japan.html?ref=southkorea>. For an account of the struggle between conservative and progressive forces in Japan over collective memory of the imperial and colonial past in post-war Japan, see Kiyoteru Tsutsui, "The trajectory of perpetrators' trauma: mnemonic politics around the Asia-Pacific war in Japan," *Social Forces*, 87 (2009), 1389–422.

9 It is estimated that the Japanese military comfort system involved between 50,000 and 200,000 women (of Korean, Chinese, Taiwanese, Filipino, Indonesian, Malaysian, Burmese, Dutch and Japanese origin). See C. Sarah Soh, *The Comfort Women: Sexual Violence and Postcolonial Memory in Korea and Japan* (Chicago: University of Chicago Press, 2008), p. xii; Pyong Gap Min, "Korean 'comfort women': the intersection of colonial power, gender, and class," *Gender and Society*, 17 (2003), 938–57.

10 My account of political responsibility is drawn mainly from Young, "Responsibility and global labor justice," pp. 374–83.

11 Judith N. Shklar, *Legalism: Law, Morals, and Political Trials* (Cambridge, MA: Harvard University Press, 1964), p. 165.

12 Yuma Totani, *The Tokyo War Crimes Trial: The Pursuit of Justice in the Wake of World War II* (Cambridge, MA: Harvard University Press, 2008), pp. 184 and 179.

13 Jeremy Sarkin and Carly Fowler, "Reparations for historical human rights violations: the international and historical dimensions of the Alien Torts Claims Act genocide case of the Herero in Namibia," *Human Rights Review*, 9 (2008), 331–60 at p. 355.

14 Sidney L. Harring, "German reparations to the Herero nation: an assertion of Herero nationhood in the path of Namibian development?" *West Virginia Law Review*, 104 (2002), 393–417 at p. 406.

15 Sarkin and Fowler, "Reparations for historical human rights violations," p. 333.

16 Allan D. Cooper, "Reparations for the Herero genocide: defining the limits of international litigation," *African Affairs*, 106 (2006), 113–126 at p. 117.

17 Young, "Responsibility and global justice: a social connection model," p. 120.

18 Alexis Dudden, *Japan's Colonization of Korea: Discourse and Power* (Honolulu: University of Hawai'i Press, 2005), p. 1.

19 Disastrously, Japanese colonial and imperial politics culminated in fifteen years of war and devastation in Asia and the Pacific (1931–45).

20 Although the legality of the annexation is hotly disputed, there is no question that the dominant Western powers of the international system accepted Japan's annexation of Korea in 1910, having themselves engaged in similar practices

(the United States in the Philippines, Germany in East Africa, Britain in Egypt, France in Madagascar). See E. Taylor Atkins, *Primitive Selves: Koreana in the Japanese Colonial Gaze, 1910–45* (Berkeley: University of California Press, 2010), p. 14; Dudden, *Japan's Colonization of Korea.*

21 Jeppe Von Platz and David Reidy, "The structural diversity of historical injustices," *Journal of Social Philosophy*, 37 (2006), 360–76 at pp. 364 and 366.

22 Young, "Responsibility and global justice," pp. 111–2; "Basic structure," p. 95.

23 Young, "Responsibility and global justice," p. 114.

24 See: Young, "Structural injustice and the politics of difference."

25 Young, "Responsibility and global labor justice," p. 377.

26 Young, "Responsibility and global justice: a social connection model," pp. 114 (my emphasis), 115.

27 United Nations, "International Convention for the Suppression of Traffic in Women and Children," 1921, <http://untreaty.un.org/English/CTC/CTC_04.asp>.

28 Yoshimi, *Comfort Women*, p. 155.

29 Young, "Responsibility and global justice: a social connection model," p. 114.

30 Soh, *Comfort Women*, p. 115 and pp. 107–142.

31 Ibid., p. 140.

32 Min, "Korean 'comfort women': the intersection of colonial power, gender, and class," pp. 940, 945 and 951. See also: Soh, *Comfort Women*, p. 116.

33 For an account of measuring an agent's causal and moral responsibility based on chronological primacy, impact, and multiple causation, see Robert Stover, "Responsibility for the Cold War – a case study in historical responsibility," *History and Theory*, 11 (#2) (1972), 145–78 at pp. 166–7.

34 Chiara Lepora and Robert E. Goodin, "Complicity and its conceptual cousins," unpublished paper, pp. 18 and 29, <http://philrsss.anu.edu.au/people-defaults/goodinb/Lepora-Goodin_Complicity_3-11-10.pdf>.

35 Koen de Ceuster, "The nation exorcised: the historiography of collaboration in South Korea," *Korean Studies*, 25 (2001), 207–42 at p. 230. De Ceuster provides an insightful historiography of the collaboration issue in South Korea, from its taboo status during authoritarian rule to its instrumentalization by a nationalist paradigm in the early period of democratization. Deepening democratization by the late 1990s has allowed for historical scholarship on the collaboration issue, at least, to be less hysterical and politicized, and more historically contextualized and fair to individual narratives.

   The public struggle over historical memory and judgment of collaborators, however, remains painful and divisive within South Korea. See Choe Sang-hun, "Colonial-era dispute agitates South Koreans," *The New York Times*, April 4, 2010, <http://www.nytimes.com/2010/04/05/world/asia/05poet.html>.

36 See Mark Osiel, *Making Sense of Mass Atrocity* (Cambridge: Cambridge University Press, 2009), for an attempt to improve current legal frameworks for judging individual guilt for mass atrocities such as genocide. These frameworks have been criticized for "missing the collaborative character of genocidal massacre, the vast extent of unintended consequences, and the ways in which 'the whole' conflagration is often quite different from the sum of its parts" (Osiel, *Making Sense of Mass Atrocity*, p. 2).

37 Lepora and Goodin, "Complicity and its conceptual cousins." Stover, "Responsibility for the Cold War."

38 Soh, *Comfort Women*, pp. 138–9.

39 Ibid., p. 237.

40 Christine M. Chinkin, "Editorial comments: Women's International Tribunal on Japanese Military Sexual Slavery," *American Journal of International Law*, 95 (2001), 335–41 at p. 341. Chinkin provides an example of a human rights perspective on the experience of women in the Japanese military comfort system: "[o]nce confined in the facilities, the women were subjected to lives of utter misery, fear, and brutality" (Chinkin, "Editorial comments," p. 337). Her characterization of the comfort women experience seems particularly appropriate for the criminal enterprise elements of the comfort system, but arguably does not capture counter-narratives of women's experiences in the other phases of the military comfort system. On counter-narratives and their significance, see Soh, *Comfort Women*, pp. 175–196.

41 Min, "Korean 'comfort women': the intersection of colonial power, gender, and class," p. 948.

42 Soh, *Comfort Women*, pp. 140 and 148.

43 See C. Sarah Soh, "Japan's National/Asian Women's Fund for 'comfort women,'" *Pacific Affairs*, 76 (2003), 209–233 at pp. 218, 210 and 221. The AWF distributed a letter of apology from the Japanese Prime Minister and two million yen to each of 285 former comfort women from the Philippines, Korea and Taiwan. Of this number, only seven Korean women received the letter and compensation, and four others later received "medical welfare support." The AWF also provided 750 million yen from Japanese government funds for "medical welfare support" to affected women in these countries as well as in the Netherlands. In Indonesia, the AWF committed 380 million yen over ten years to build facilities for senior citizens and to support NGO projects and facilities for former comfort women. See Tomiichi Murayama, "The statement by President of the Asian Women's Fund at the final press conference," *Digitial Museum: The Comfort Women Issue and the Asian Women's Fund*, <http://www.awf.or.jp/e3/dissolution.html>.

44 Soh, "Japan's National/Asian Women's Fund," p. 229. Furthermore, the eleven women who accepted AWF compensation or medical support were denied the right to apply for South Korean government funds.

45 Ibid., p. 218.

46 Soh, *Comfort Women*, pp. xiii and 237.

47 Ibid., pp. 215–6.

48 Similarly, Henry Louis Gates has pointed out that the role of some African leaders in slavery has recently surfaced as a complication in the slavery reparations debate in the United States: "Advocates of reparations for the descendants of those slaves generally ignore this untidy problem of the significant role that Africans played in the trade, choosing to believe the romanticized version that our ancestors were all kidnapped unawares by evil white men, like Kunta Kinte was in 'Roots.' The truth, however, is much more complex: slavery was a business, highly organized and lucrative for European buyers and African sellers alike." See his Op-ed, "Ending the slavery blame-game," *New York Times*, April 22, 2010, <http://www.nytimes.com/2010/04/23/opinion/23gates.html?emc=eta1>. Thanks to Yashar Saghai for bringing this case to my attention.

49 Primo Levi, *The Drowned and the Saved*, trans. Raymond Rosenthal (New York: Vintage International, 1989), p. 44.

50 The judgment that Korea as a state was not morally culpable does not preclude judgments of culpability against Korean individuals whose collaboration with Japan's aggressive war aims might have been blameworthy. For example, while most Koreans conscripted to fight for the Japanese were victims of circumstance, South Korea's governing elites before democratization in the 1980s included more blameworthy collaborators, with some having risen to officers in the Imperial Japanese Army. See Atkins, *Primitive Selves*, p. 191.

51 Young, "Responsibility and global justice: a social connection model," p. 118.

52 Young, "Responsibility and global labor justice," pp. 379, 381.

53 Young, "Responsibility and global justice: a social connection model," pp. 114, 118 (my emphasis).

54 As Miriam Ronzoni has argued, "a basic structure is just not when each of its institutions (whatever they are) respects certain principles, but when, taken as a whole, it brings about certain social conditions." See Ronzoni, "What makes a basic structure just?" *Res Publica*, 14 (2008), 203–18 at p. 205.

55 John Rawls, *The Law of Peoples* (Cambridge, MA: Harvard University Press, 1999), §4.1, p. 37 and §15.1, p. 106. Even if one does not subscribe to a robust egalitarian ideal for international society, discharging the political responsibility to assist former colonies in achieving effective equal sovereignty entails reducing global distributive inequalities, to the extent that such inequalities undermine autonomous political decision-making and fairness in international bargaining procedures. See Charles R. Beitz, "Does global inequality matter?" *Metaphilosophy*, 32 (2001), pp. 95–112.

56 I discuss the relationship between reparations to victims and retributive, democratic and distributive justice in "Delivering the goods and the good: repairing moral wrongs," *Calling Power to Account: Law, Reparations, and the Chinese Canadian Head Tax Case*, ed. D. Dyzenhaus and M. Moran (Toronto: University of Toronto Press, 2005), pp. 147–64.

57 Kok-Chor Tan, "Colonialism, reparations and global justice," *Reparations: Interdisciplinary Inquiries*, ed. J. Miller and R. Kumar (Oxford: Oxford University Press, 2007), 280–306 at p. 287.

58 Leif Wenar, "Reparations for the future," *Journal of Social Philosophy*, 37 (2006), 396–405, at pp. 403 and 404. A structural injustice approach thus stimulates a moral concern for political reconciliation not only between former colonized and colonizer societies, but within and among each of these societies.

59 Quoted in Butt, *Rectifying International Injustices*, p. 1.

60 See Ypi, Goodin and Barry, "Associative duties, global justice, and the colonies," p. 134, for an argument that distributive justice obligations among those sharing a past colonial relationship may also not be unidirectional (from colonizer to colonized) but multilateral.

61 Frantz Fanon, *Black Skin, White Masks*, trans. Richard Philcox (New York: Grove Press, 1952), p. 206.

62 Judith N. Shklar, *Ordinary Vices* (Cambridge, MA: Harvard University Press, 1984), p. 23.

11

The Judging of Nations
Some Comments on the Assessment of Regimes in the New States

Clifford Geertz

I

Like prophecies, revolutions restart time, and the distance between l'An I and l'An X is greater than any other decade in history. After that, or a little bit more, things seem to slow down, not because less happens but because less happens for the first time. The 'infinite grandeur of beginnings' fades, a certain possibility disappears from things. Attempts may be made to prolong the excitements of setting out. Pillars are erected in squares, purification movements launched in schools, guerilla styles imitated in offices. But all this soon becomes parody, the sort of thing V.S. Naipaul memorializes, as the ordinariness of life reasserts itself. This is where the New States are now, and their study as well, and it is an awkward point for both.

The readiest reaction, in the countries themselves and in the world observing them, is cynicism and despair. Too much having been expected at the start, too little is expected later, and a chorus of disappointment dressed up as realism appears. Within, this takes the form of careerism, a resignation to the private politics of everyday; without, it takes that of the flourishing of a bitter pragmatism, hard to distinguish from pique, and harder yet from selfishness. As independence has not transformed the New States, or not in the directions anticipated, the suspicion, derided earlier as reactionary, that it is but a prelude to regression, reappears in a more analytical guise. It is no longer Nehru who is taken for the Third World's augur, but Amin.

All this is not wholly to be condemned. Calling tyranny by its rightful name has much to be said for it, and anything that lessens the sentimental

Political Theory Without Borders, First Edition. Edited by Robert E. Goodin and James S. Fishkin.
© 2016 John Wiley & Sons, Inc. Published 2016 by John Wiley & Sons, Inc.

cant that has so often surrounded the excesses and worse of New State governments—'they are still young'—can only be to the advantage of every-body save those who live from it. There has been too much apologizing in terms of imagined necessities or past oppressions already, and reading backward steps as devious routes to progress, as a kind of cunning of tradition, is wearing thinner as the progress fails to materialize. But however that may be, the new disenchantment has not much more to offer the understanding than did the old enchantment. The replacement of the best case view of the New States by a worst case one is a mere change of emotional sign. The central obstacle to assessing developments in the post-colonial world from a perspective more than arbitrary—namely, the enormous difficulty in deter-mining what can reasonably be expected—is left wholly untouched by it.

This issue, constructing a norm of behavior against which to measure New States' actions, has haunted the study of them from the outset, no less among scholars seeking objectivity than ones frankly pressing a political case. Relativists have sought to derive such a norm from the history and culture of the states themselves; liberals, Marxists, and others have attempted to draw it from one or another strain of Western political thought; and vacillators, the majority, have tried to do a little of both and mumble past the problem. But whether discussing one-party systems, army rule, personal autocracy, ethnic infighting, religious education, or the role of traditional authorities, there has always lurked somewhere in the background (and not always in the background) the troubling question: what, in fact, may one properly hope for? Relativism, in its degenerate form, might adopt a to-understand-is-to-forgive view, excusing Sukarno as an expression of Javanese aestheticism or Algerian fundamentalism as a return to authentic personality. Westernism, in its degenerate form, might dismiss the whole against the standard of Aristotle, Burke, Lenin, or the Federalist Papers. But generally, matters have looked too complicated for such mechanical conclu-sions, and judgment has consequently been equivocal to the point of evasion, a difficulty the passage of time has more deepened than assuaged. Seeing the New States steadily and whole seems even harder now than when they were founded, and as each surprise emerges (Indira Gandhi's suspension of Indian democracy, Yakubu Gowon's overthrow, Shiekh Mujib's murder, the resto-ration of military rule in Thailand) our inability to decide whether it is a necessity or a catastrophe, a breakthrough or a ripple in a steady current, reveals that whatever we have learned about the New States since 1945—and it has been a great deal—has not yet given us a ground for maintaining a stance toward what goes on in them.

Nor is this concern a merely academic one; it is one the inhabitants of the New States share with the scholars of them. They too are puzzled as to what they can expect from their governments and from themselves. After early hopes for rapid social and economic improvement, 'takeoffs' of various sorts, the settling into a situation rather less dynamic, and certainly less linear, naturally leads to a malaise. But this is not so much because the millennium has failed to arrive (that was always less believed in than platform rhetoric made it seem); it is because it is difficult to assess the present in terms of any pattern of progress at all. People do not know whether to congratulate themselves for what they have achieved given the obstacles they have faced or condemn themselves for having squandered the possibilities they have had. And how can one come to a conclusion about a leadership that seems both imprisoned in circumstances beyond anyone's power to affect and the major element making of circumstances a prison? Despite the ideological screaming that still goes on, the sense for the true dimensions of social possibility is as confused within the New States as it is outside of them.

It is the task of the social scientific study of the New States to provide an empirical grasp of these dimensions so that judgment will be neither baffled by the mere strangeness of things nor issue out of some arbitrary moral or ideological stance. The reaction against normative political theory of the traditional sort was not a reaction against the impulse that theory served—the desire to formulate propositions about the rational conduct of collective life; it was a rejection of the notion that such propositions could be formulated effectively in independence of detailed knowledge of how such life was in fact conducted. Empirical investigation—systematic, comparative, and oriented to capturing the subjects' own sense of what they were about—was not supposed to replace philosophical reflection but to provide a base for it beyond what formal reasoning and familiarity with Western classics could afford. This is what, indeed, Edward Shils promised the world on our behalf at the end of his introduction to *Old Societies and New States* when he saw us 'proceeding along the lines of Max Weber [to] bring to fruition what was begun by Aristotle and Cicero'. It would be pleasant to be able to say that this has happened, or even begun to happen. But, as I have said, not only has it not but the whole prospect seems less imminent now than it did then.

Those who never thought very much of the scientific turn in political analysis in the first place would say this was because of a lack of acquaintance with approved writings and a positivist approach to reality, and they are back preaching high culture, first principles, and the history of ideas. But the real cause has lain in the difficulty of distinguishing the accidental from the characteristic in states just in the process of putting themselves together. So much effort has had to be expended determining what was going on that not much time has been left for reflecting upon it; and until some more stable image of what was going on could be constructed such general reflection seemed unlikely to be profitable. The years since our book was published have been the years of the monograph—country-oriented books concerned to trace out particular processes, supplemented with the development of concepts (of which 'modernization' is only the most famous) designed to characterize those processes and compare their dynamics—plus now and then a treatise devoted to an anatomization of the concepts. The struggle to get a descriptive and analytical hold on social and political systems in which the generic and the ephemeral looked very much alike has proved so difficult that meditative thought has hardly known where to begin.

Yet, now that the period when almost everything seemed unprecedented has passed and the New States are starting to have a history properly their own, it should be possible to find a few points upon which such ruminative reflection might fasten. If it is true that the end of the heroic period in the New States has left them even less easily summed up than before, it is also true that time has now had time enough to accomplish what analysis has been unable to: the beginning of a sorting of the abiding from the transient. Some features of the New States are now beginning to emerge as more than accidental characteristics of them, as products of the sort of thing they are rather than of the immediate circumstances in which they find themselves. Pondering these, as scattered and still unsubstantial as they are, some progress might now be made toward—to quote Shils' promissory note again—'the schooling of judgment', the ability to come to evaluative conclusions about developments in this or that New State, or in the body of them as a whole, which are more than facts turned into apologies or civics lessons into denunciations.

There are three such characteristics of the New States, collectively and separately, that look to me settled enough to be taken as objects for such discriminative thought: nationalism, autocracy, and what, to have a suitably ugly name for it and because it has none of its own, I will call Singaporization. I shall discuss each in turn, not to come to any firm conclusions—the point is to start debate, not to pre-empt it—but to suggest that they are suitable matters for reflective consideration, that they have for the most part not gotten it, and that together they form a useful place to begin to construct a conception of the New States within which the assessment of events, neither evaded nor abandoned to the vagaries of sentiment, can proceed rationally.

II

Nationalism, commonly a radical, intransigent nationalism, was, of course, the most prominent feature of the New State phenomenon from the start. Indeed, at the start, it was almost the whole of it. Indonesia, India, or Nigeria were ideas as Germany, Italy, or Hungary once had been. One would have expected that scholars from a civilization, 'the West', which had very nearly been destroyed by such ideas over a half century or so would be at best ambivalent in their reaction to the appearance of them across most of the rest of the globe. But the desire to see the end of colonial domination inhibited, as it did among New State intellectuals themselves, any consideration of what the wildfire spread of what Elie Kédourie once called 'The European Desease' might mean for the societies in which it appeared, or for general political order. The desire was reasonable and the inhibition understandable; but its continuance, now that Independence has been gained and autonomous regimes established, is neither, whatever overhangs of past domination—and they are considerable—remain. The uneasy attitude toward intense assertions of national identity, that should naturally have arisen as the Independence movements did, needs finally to emerge now that those movements have turned into powers.

The role of nationalism, as well as the impetus for it, was to give a definable personality to projected political entities which had little else to give them one. Whether the problem was severe, as in Nigeria or Pakistan, or relatively mild, as in the Philippines or Morocco, the invention of new polities implied the invention of new peoples. (The sudden appearance of a nationality called 'Sehaoui'—i.e., 'Seharawi'—in the Spanish Sahara as it becomes a candidate for de-, or perhaps only re-, colonization, shows the process is even now not wholly completed). By scholars this was sometimes called 'nation-building', a term which, like 'bodybuilding', had a virtuous and optimistic tone; but what really got built was a theory of political legitimacy—*viz.*, authority rests on a cultural congeneracy of ruler and ruled—whose implications for the sort of States the successors to His Majesty's Possessions or France d'Outre-Mer are going to be have yet to be systematically considered.

One thing blocking such consideration has been the confusion between this principle—'like over like', as indirect rule theorists had more bluntly put it—and one more familiar to Western scholars, the consent of the governed. New State nationalism spoke, and still speaks, in democratic and populist accents, quoting Jefferson or Thomas Paine; but it has had a great deal more to say about the intolerability of being governed by foreigners for foreigners' interests than the intolerability of being governed without being consulted. What was illegitimate about colonial regimes was less that they were arbitrary than that their loyalties lay outside the field of their operations. Decolonization was a matter of domesticating authority, not—despite a certain amount of rhetoric about the people's will being heard—democratizing it. The rhetoric indeed blurred the distinction for all but a few of the more Western-oriented New State politicians, who in any case were quickly elbowed from the scene, and it blurred it for the bulk of foreign scholars as well. Replacing foreign elites with local ones and replacing oligarchies with representational elites came to look like very much the same thing. 'Better to be ruled like hell by Filipinos than like heaven by Americans', Osmena is supposed once to have said. It is a hard sentiment to argue with, but a hard one, too, to live with over any extended length of time.

It is for this reason—that nationalism has mainly functioned to legitimize domestic elites—that some of the things that, given the European experience, might have been feared from its advent have not much occurred. The Pakistan-India conflicts and Sukarno's short-lived confrontation with Malaysia aside, hegemonic ambitions have not appeared, and not one of the New States can really be said, so far at least, to be expansionist. Nor, though internal nationalisms have been troublesome to the point of civil war in Nigeria, and separatist, or quasi-separatist, conflicts continue elsewhere, only with Bangladesh, a rather special case because of the lack of a colonial precedent for Pakistan's existence, have they led to significant redrawings of the boundaries of established states. Both these accompaniments of nationalism elsewhere, expansionism and balkanization, may still occur, especially as some countries and parts of countries develop more rapidly than others. But until now and for what seems like the foreseeable future, the energies of nationalism are mainly being directed toward providing an answer to that most immediate of political questions: who are you that I should obey you?

Its importance in this connection is only the greater given the progressive elimination of competing answers: hereditary right, constitutionalism, and historicist notions of a revolutionary vanguard. The right to rule is justified almost everywhere in the New States, whatever poor remnants of these alternative conceptions manage to persist, in terms of a particular fidelity to national traditions, national sentiments, and national interests. Morocco still has a king, Malaysia a functioning parliament, and Vietnam a Leninist cadre, but there too (as the tensions between Vietnam and Cambodia, or Hassan's nativism, only demonstrate) the real basis for the regime's legitimacy is its ability to represent itself as the authentic expression of Moroccan, Malaysian, or Vietnamese culture. Nor does the imposition of military rule change this; the colonels claim to be more efficient or more honest, but hardly—Burma, Libya, Uganda, Indonesia, Zaire— more cosmopolitan. The governments of the New States are representative in the sense that symbols represent, not in the sense that delegates do; they stand for the idea that their peoples are distinctive, a category of man appropriately set off in a frame of borders. If they fail to do this, or fail to seem to do it, they don't persist, however properly born, properly chosen, properly ideological, or even properly armed they may be.

All this has some fairly familiar, but not always accurately understood, results. One is the intense sensitivity to foreign and especially Western influence, or as it is more commonly, and even vaguely put, 'interference'. This sensitivity has, if anything, and to some minds paradoxically, increased since the revolutionary period. India is only the most striking case of the failure of the expectation that it would moderate as the state became more firmly established and self-confident, and the colonial period receded; the phenomenon, if perhaps not universal (Tunisia seems to be one exception,

Singapore another), is quite general. The anti-Japanese riots in Jakarta in January of 1974, the expulsion of Indians from Uganda in 1972, and the tremendous growth of the C.I.A. as an all-purpose explanation for unto-ward political developments (a status the Agency has, indeed, done more than a little to earn) are all witness to the fact that age has not withered nor custom staled the belief that external influences are threats not just to national well-being but national existence. Such influences of course exist and are growing stronger as the New States become integrated into the post-colonial world economy (a point I will return to). But it is less mere realism that prompts the deepened nationalism—some of those who most encourage the influence most encourage the nationalism—than the increasing difficulty in maintaining a culturalist legitimacy in an acculturating world.

Or rather, a partially acculturating world. For as the elites of the New States become fixed in place they enter into a closer connection with the modern world, become in fact part of it, at the same time as the mass of the people do not, and in fact in many cases re-traditionalize. The gap, there from the beginning, but now widening, between dominant groups projected, or projecting themselves, more and more into an emerging political and economic world order and the separate populations of peasants, traders, laborers, craftsmen and so on enclosed in local life, produces an intensifica-tion of nationalist ideologizing to bridge it. The causes of the cultural estrangement of the rulers from the ruled may indeed come in good part from without, but (as the passionate reaction, hard to account for in terms of power realities, of 'essentialist' movements—Hindu in India, Muslim in Indonesia, tribal in Uganda—demonstrates) its impact is mainly felt within. The difficulty with a like-over-like theory of legitimacy is that as society differentiates its self-conception may not.

III

Fifteen years ago, scholarly writings on the New States, including our own, were full of discussions of parties, parliaments, and elections. A great deal seemed to turn on whether these institutions were viable in the Third World and what adjustments in them—single party systems, tiered elections, quota parliaments—might prove necessary to make them so. Today, nothing in those writings seems more *passé*, relic of a different time. Marcos, Suharto, Ne Win, al-Bakr, Sadat, Gaddafi, Boumedienne, Hassan, Houphouet, Amin, Mobutu may be doing their countries good or harm, promoting their peoples' advantage or oppressing them, but they are not guiding them to democracy. They are autocrats, and it is as autocrats, and not as preludes to liberalism (or, for that matter, to totalitarianism), that they, and the governments they dominate, must be judged and understood.

Western scholars, and American ones especially, have had a particular reluctance to do this, partly because their own preference for popular democracy has made sorting between various forms of authoritarian government seem like abandoning principle and consigning the New States to a lesser order of political possibility; partly because a conscious or unconscious evolutionism has led them to see New State autocracy as a stage on the way to something else, whether Sweden, Switzerland, or the Soviet Union; and partly because their own intellectual background has provided them with precious little means for doing so. If Balewa was preferable to Nkrumah, Lee Kwan Yu to Sukarno, U Nu to Bandaranaike, or Bourguiba to Nasser, then it must be because they were less autocratic, though on the fact of it this would be a very difficult thing to have to prove. And now that the few figures who seem to have had a more than tactical belief in liberal government—Sjahrir, Nehru, Busia—have disappeared from the scene, comparisons on such a scale seem academic altogether. One would do better with quiet and noisy, wary and impetuous, or ascetic and self-indulgent.

The reluctance is anyway unnecessary; recognizing the simple fact that New State governments are virtually all authoritarian and look to remain so for some time to come is not to applaud the situation, nor for that matter to curse it. It is but to acknowledge the existence of what, if one is going to do any discriminative applauding or cursing at all (as opposed to philosophical outbursts of enthusiasm or rage), one is going to have to do it about. It probably never was entirely legitimate to lump the New States into a single category—the Third World, the Underdeveloped Countries, the New States—toward which to have a single response; but whatever justification it had in the years immediately following Independence it has now lost. And if that necessitates making distinctions between various forms of autocracy—as empirically it does—and doing so in terms other than their relative promise for democratic evolution or susceptibility to totalitarianism—as conceptually it does—then political pieties will have to be put aside. The Whig view of history, or its reciprocal, whatever the one held by Karl Wittfogel, P.T. Bauer, and Barrington Moore should be called—the Leviathan?—are as distorting applied to the present as they are to the past.

The main dimension upon which the autocracies of the Third World seem to vary—other, that is, than the personal characteristics of the autocrats—is the degree to which they reduce the country's elite to a collection of individuals separately dependent upon its leader, a personal entourage, or allow it to preserve a sense of being, however dependent, a social entity. Even fairly high-handed styles of government—Bourguiba's or Hussein Onn's for example—can maintain a degree of responsiveness if the relation between the central authority and those who serve it is that of a prince to notables; even fairly undemanding ones—Ne Win's and Hassan's for example—can harden into rigidity, if it is that of a prince to courtiers. It is not the power of the dominant figure, which can be as great in the one case as in the other, that is the critical factor; it is the extent to which he confronts any thoughts not his own. The degree of political solipsism—'all tongue and no ears', as used to be said of Sukarno—distinguishes one New State authoritarianism from the next: whatever difference Sadat's Egypt shows from Nasser's, Nyerere's Tanzania from Mobutu's Zaire, or even Mrs. Gandhi's India of 1970 from Mrs. Gandhi's India of 1976 lies far more in that than in the comparative democracy of their rule.

Estimating the degree to which the various New State regimes have, to use another image, imploded, fallen in upon themselves to become dissociated from the society they ostensibly govern, and seeking for the factors that encourage or impede their doing so, is not a task to lift the spirits. But it seems a more practical activity than trying to describe the qualifications and determine the conditions for a settled republicanism that never comes to be. Especially now, a couple of decades into Independence, the varying element seems not to be the intensity with which various regimes are attempting to bring their populations into the political process but the skill with which they are manœuvering to keep them out of it. From the Philippines and Indonesia, to Egypt and India, to Kenya and Nigeria, the watchword is not the mobilization of the populace but its depoliticization. Where a dozen years ago the New States seemed to be classifiable according to the energy with which their governments were trying to rouse their people to collective assaults on historic tasks—'development', 'modernization', 'nation-building', 'The Alburmalian Road to Socialism' or whatever—they seem to be classifiable now according to the deliberateness with which those governments (some of them the same governments) are trying to contain their people within the boundaries of local concerns.

The left-wing foreign policy of so many of the New States is not in contradiction to this but in support of it. 'Epochalist' radicalism, and especially unremitting attacks on countries, such as the United States, regarded as working to continue imperialist domination, shifts the hope for revolutionary change, as well as the forces impeding it, to the wider world, leaving the domestic scene, once represented as almost infinitely dynamic but now as decelerated by forces external to itself, in a kind of ideological limbo. African states, both northern and sub-saharan—Algeria and Zaire—are the classical instances of this neutralization at home through polarization abroad; but it is quite general (though, again, variable in force), and has given rise to the rhetorical Jacobinism of the General Assembly that Western observers have been better at deploring than they have at comprehending. The radical idiom in foreign affairs does not arise out of an upsurge of Marxian populism in the New States nor, an even stranger idea, the power there of Fabian theories of social paternalism, but out of the privatization of government, the depoliticization of the populace, and the drawing in (I shall come to this in a moment) of modernizing ambitions to a small sector of the society. The idea of revolution is projected ideologically outward in an effort to account for its weakening inward, an effort to make a perplexing situation—the progressive implosion of public life—a natural effect of a general situation. It may, of course, in fact be such an effect. But it is the idea's convenience that recommends it to a Boumedienne, a Mobutu, or an Indira Gandhi—and will shortly to an Ahmad or a Marcos—not its accuracy.

The degree to which New State elites have or have not been reduced to courtiers, the degree to which New State leaders have or have not sealed themselves into a prison of self-regard, and the degree to which New State ideologies have or have not married internal immobilism to external radicalism are thus interconnected and are at the core of any attempt to evaluate New State autocracy as opposed to merely decrying it or apologizing for it. Differential assessment is no less possible here than with regular governments, nor does it demand a theory of benevolent despotism. There are one and two (well, one-and-a-half)-cheer autocracies as there are one and two-cheer democracies, even if the cheers are hollower, uneasier, and marked with a certain despair.

IV

The battle cry for the fifties and sixties, the one that replaced independence after that was won, was of course development: the sixties were even supposed to be the 'Development decade'. Take-off, balanced and unbalanced growth, import replacement, incremental capital output ratios, backward and forward linkages, factor proportions, absorptive capacity, sectoral planning, backward bending supply curves, entrepreneurship were the common coin of discussion. Since then, though not very much as a result of the discussion, a fair amount of economic advance has indeed occurred (and in some places—Libya, Singapore—a striking amount), at least if *per capita* income is taken as the measure. And even where *per capita* income has not much increased there has been, a few especially hard cases (Chad, Bangladesh) aside, at least a gross expansion. Jakarta looks like Tokyo now, down to the smog, and Casablanca like Marseilles, complete to the yacht clubs. But what was not foreseen then, or not very clearly, was the degree to which development could take place without involving the mass of the population in the countries where it occurred, the degree to which it could produce modern islands in unmodern seas.

The mistake was in assuming that because the industrial revolution had convulsed the whole social order of northern and western Europe and the United States, and had done so in, as historical change goes, a startlingly short time, it would do the same in the New States. As all but a few peripheral groups in Europe had been caught up, at one level or another—turned into businessmen, turned into workers, turned into farmers or turned into clerks connecting the three—in the great sweep of mechanization after 1850, so all but a few of the more remote or traditional would be transformed by the introduction of modern techniques of production, organization, marketing, and calculation into countries as yet unconscious of them. There was fear on the Left that this would lead to exploitation, in the center to destabilization, and on the Right to *dirigisme;* but that significant economic growth could occur which would leave just about everything beyond its immediate confines just about as it was is not something that much occurred to anyone. Yet, unless one equates mass disturbance with mass change or treading water with movement, that to a very large degree is what has happened. The Third World is dotted with free-working city states, enclave economies busily disengaging from their stranded hinterlands.

It is perhaps unfair to call this phenomenon 'Singaporization' simply because history, geography, and the Chinese capacity to focus effort have conspired to make that island a peculiarly clear example of the set-apart growth pattern. But despite its empirical specialness, and indeed to some degree because of it, Singapore provides a useful image of the way things are pointing elsewhere: toward a detachment of the dynamics of modern commercial and industrial life from local contexts and its integration into an international structure of trade and production. That Singapore has actually managed to do what is a practical impossibility for Manila, Jakarta, Delhi-Bombay, Algiers, Rabat-Casablanca, Dakar, Lagos-Ibadan, Kinshasa, Nairobi or, most tragically, Beirut—politically remove itself from any wider social entity at all—only brings out into full view a process that, through other devices and less openly and completely, is taking place generally. Development has turned out to be a far more encapsulatable process than 'the Great Transformation' of agrarian Europe led us to expect.

The main reasons why this has been so seem to me to be three: modern modes of production tend by-and-large to make less of an employment impact than their early-modern predecessors; much of the income growth in the New States has been occasioned more by alterations in world market conditions than by economic innovations; insofar as there have been economic innovations—technical, managerial, or financial—they have largely come from abroad, that is, the U.S., Japan, and (some inputs from Czechoslovakia, East Germany, and the Soviet Union aside) Western Europe. The relative importance of these factors varies from place to place as does their collective impact; Niger is not Nigeria. But together they add up to the pattern we are seeing more and more: a restricted group of nationals of each New State rather thoroughly integrated into the most advanced sectors of the modern world economy, and becoming more so all the time, while the mass of the people are even less directly touched by it than they were in the

Colonial Period when labor-intensive plantations, mines, and infrastructural constructions were the main product of contact between the developed world and the undeveloped. It is at least arguable that the impact of the West upon the foundations of social existence of the mass of the people in the New States was more profound and extensive in the two decades or so that culminated in Independence than it has been in the two decades or so that have issued from it, and that the shift from direct exploitation to selective incorporation has a good deal to do with the change.

However that may be, the economic differentiation of the Third World (now advanced enough to lead to the spinning out of new distinctions, between the third and fourth worlds, or between the less developed countries and the least developed, which reflect the event without doing anything to clarify it) is taking place less in terms of the emergence of Marxist classes—a bourgeoisie, a proletariat, a rabble, and a peasantry—than in terms of a separation between a small group—managerial, laboring, and lumpen alike—caught up into a modern form of life and a much larger group thrashing about, sometimes violently, more often dispiritedly, in a half-traditional, half-detraditionalized steady state. There are no names for these two groups, except perhaps the encapsulated and the unencapsulated, and their relative size and sharpness of separation varies from place to place. But almost everywhere, the relation between them is an increasingly critical issue, the true center of domestic (and sometimes, as in the Gulf States, extra-domestic) politics. Like nationalism and autocracy, Singaporization is the name of a question the New States raise, not a pit into which they have fallen.

Looked at this way, the dramatic developments in the oil producing countries— some of which, like Saudi Arabia, have relatively manageable hinterlands (unless Egypt contrives to make itself part of them), others, like Nigeria, relatively unmanageable ones—are thus but the most extreme examples of a quite general process: a narrow-focus prosperity built on a labor-economizing technology, favorable changes in the international price structure, and integration into a world-wide system of corporate organization—OPEC, the various state monopolies which comprise it, the oil multinationals, many of which are quasi-state enterprises themselves. Elsewhere, with less peculiar commodities, less special technologies, and less comprehensive organization, the situation is less advanced, but whether it is phosphates in Morocco, tourism in Tunisia, rubber in Malaysia, sugar in the Philippines, transit processing in Singapore, or multinational manufacturing all over the place, it takes the same sort of form and poses the same sort of problem: what to do with the rest of the population—the overwhelming bulk of it —which is not occupationally connected to such modern, semi-modern, or hyper-modern activity. J.H. Boeke, trying in the thirties to imagine an industrialized Egypt, asked: if ninety percent of her income were generated by ten percent of her people, what would happen to the ninety percent of her people who produced the ten percent of the income? Things have not quite come to that yet; but it is the way, in the New States as a body, and in most of them individually, they are moving.

How this problem is handled, how the relationship between the two parts of the bifurcated economy is managed is thus also a variable across the New States with respect to which differential judgment may be exercised. In some cases, where the government is particularly repressive (Uganda), where it is particularly weak (Bangladesh), or where the problem has not yet become acute (Mauritania) it may simply be ignored at the cost of ascending governmental terror, a cacaphony of unfocused mass disorder, or the loss of irreplaceable time. More commonly, it is dealt with by a varying mix of military force, 'welfare' type income transfers, appeals to national unity, promises of a better future and more or less serious efforts to broaden the base of development and involve the mass population in it. From a Tunisia or Malaysia, where enclave development is at least confronted as an issue and policies to ameliorate it projected, through Morocco or Indonesia, where it is accepted as a fact of life and the situation stabilized through a combination of police activities and trickle down expenditures ('even the peasants now wear sun glasses'), through Zaire or Thailand, where elite corruption and popular disorder interact to generate a rising spiral of tension, there is obviously a scale along which discriminations can be made which are neither arbitrary expressions of Western ideals nor relativistic apologies for non-Western evils. Coping with the narrowed social focus of contemporary development in countries, most of which are neither Kuwait nor Singapore (and they may soon find the anomalousness of their situations catching up with them too) but have unincluded populations, usually massive, to worry about, is a critical task for virtually all New State governments. How those governments go about that task is a useful measure of their approximization to regimes toward which one can have some warmth and for which some hope.

V

It is clear, a quarter century after the great wave of decolonization first began, that the New States are moving in courses quite other than those envisaged for them at the outset. To some this may seem like a betrayal of a revolution; but it is more than the correction of a mistaken idea of what sort of revolution it was. Its central aim, indeed almost its only aim, was the destruction of governmental forms which drew legitimacy from one people and exercised authority over another, and in that it has been quite successful. That this success should have set in motion organizing forces of its own, and that those forces should have produced regimes which test the limits of our capacity to evaluate them, ought not to be surprising. The categories of political judgment are not independent of its objects; when the practical world changes, the moral does also.

The ideals—supranationalist, populist, developmental—current on the post-war scene provided the necessary vocabulary of the struggle for Independence in that time and in that place; but the ethic actually animating it grew not out of them, part of the Euro-American effort to revive hope after catastrophe, but out of the intense desire of Asians and Africans to establish states whose leaders would be racially, linguistically, and culturally akin to those they led. Much was expected from this change—material advance, decreased inequality, spiritual renaissance, world respect; but above all, and as the cause of these, what was expected was a more empathic relation between mass and elite, a new consonance of outlook and sensibility between those at the center of society and those away from it. The degree to which this relation has in fact come into being, or, on the contrary, the center has redetached itself to become another sort of social island, varies enormously behind the seemingly uniform facade of Third World nationalism. Having claimed power on the principle that rule that is not inwardly connected to the life around it is not just, the elites of the New States can now be judged by it.

It is not whether parliaments are real or sham, elections free or rigged, or courts independent or politicized that are the best indices of what sort of polity a New State is and what sort of leadership it has got; one tends to get the same readings on these variables just about everywhere now. It is whether nationalism is a state-orchestrated mystique of cultural originality or a popular sense of self-regard; whether autocracy is a personalized, favor-of-the-sovereign, solipsism or a high-handed, interest-conscious administrationism; whether development is a name for an attempt to separate the fates of the leading and trailing edges of society or to link them. Comparing measures on such scales—and others like them—is an unsatisfactory business, full of part-approvals and half-damnations ('Anarchy yes, but not so much', as a sign in that most unexpected New State, Portugal, recently said). But as they are the scales that are available, they are the ones even those who hope for more must learn to use.

Political philosophy has always been more a response to the appearance of novel political arrangements—the Greek city state, the Roman imperium, the Renaissance principality, the Enlightenment republic—than a free exercise of systematic reason. Reflections on government need governments to reflect on if they are not to descend into academic exercises. At a time when general questions of justice, equality, liberty, and authority are coming back into fashion in the form of deductive theories based on psycho-moral axioms, or supposed such, not the least contribution the study of the New States, as they age, diverge, and organize their ambitions, can make is to rescue such questions from scholastic answers. Whether or not anything comparable to Aristotle, Cicero, Machiavelli, or Madison emerges from it we shall merely have to wait and see. But in the meantime we will profit more by cultivating their sense for the actual than by imitating their claim to finality.*

Note

* This article was originally prepared for a conference held at the University of Chicago in the fall of 1975. It was sponsored by the Committee for the Comparative Study of New Nations and the Ford Foundation, and was designed to review the issues raised by the Committee's collective study, see C. Geertz (ed.), *Old Societies and New States* (New York, Free Press, 1963) a dozen years further on. As the conference was dedicated to the memory of one of the founders and former chairmen of the Committee, L. A. Fallers, so also is this article. I am grateful to Albert Hirschman, Francine Frankel, and Fernando Henrique Cardoso for comments on an earlier draft, although, especially since I have frequently resisted what they have said, they are in no way responsible for the views expressed.

12

From Humanitarian Intervention to the Responsibility to Protect*

Gareth Evans

What should be the response of the international community when faced with situations of catastrophic human rights violations within states, where the state in question claims immunity from intervention based on longstanding principles of national sovereignty? When, if ever, it is right for states to take coercive action, in particular military action, against another state for the purpose of protecting people at risk within it?

These issues, the centerpiece of international debate for most of the 1990s, have not gone away, despite current preoccupations with a new post-9/11 slate of concerns: global terrorism, externally directed Islamist extremism, energy security, nuclear proliferation, and resurgent nationalism. They are intellectually right at the intersection point of international relations, law, policy, ethics, human rights, and human security. And in practice they keep coming to haunt us: most obviously, currently, in Darfur, where over the last three years at least two hundred thousand people have died, over two million have been displaced, and five thousand more are dying each month from war-related disease and malnutrition as well as from continuing outright violence; and where international peacekeeping efforts have been manifestly inadequate, political settlement talks have been floundering, humanitarian relief is faltering, and the overall situation is again deteriorating.[1]

The good news is that the international community is much closer to consensus now than it ever has been on the proper conceptual response to the questions in issue. What we have seen over the last five years is the emergence, almost in real time, of a new international norm, one that may ultimately become a new rule of customary international law with really quite fundamental ethical importance and novelty in the international system. The evolution away from the discourse of *humanitarian intervention*, which

Political Theory Without Borders, First Edition. Edited by Robert E. Goodin and James S. Fishkin.
© 2016 John Wiley & Sons, Inc. Published 2016 by John Wiley & Sons, Inc.

had been so divisive, and toward the embrace of the new concept of *the responsibility to protect* has been a fascinating piece of intellectual history in its own right.

The less good news is that the story is incomplete. With the forces of resistance to the idea of the responsibility to protect still quite strong in the international community, for a variety of reasons, which are understandable if not acceptable, there is a critical need to maintain the momentum of this conceptual evolution. And there is an even more critical need to translate such theoretical consensus as does now exist around this principle into effective practical action whenever cases arise that cry out for its application.

I. The Birth of a Doctrine

In understanding how far we have come, but have yet to go, the best place to begin is with the UN Charter of 1945. The UN founders were overwhelmingly preoccupied with the problem of states waging war against each other, and the charter produced a really quite stunning innovation to the extent that it outlawed, across the board, the use of force, the only exceptions being self-defense in confronting an attack[2] and authorization by the Security Council,[3] a new international institution given unprecedented authority to act in cases of threats to international peace and security. On the question, however, of external force being applied in response to an internal catastrophe, the charter language, if anything, pointed the other way with a clear statement of the principle of non-interference in Article 2(7): "Nothing contained in the present Charter shall authorize the United Nations to intervene in matters which are essentially within the domestic jurisdiction of any state."[4]

The inclination to read the charter as very limited in its reach was reinforced not only by the Cold War, which commenced almost immediately after the UN began, but also by the large increase in UN membership during the decolonization era. States, all newly proud of their identity and conscious in many cases of their fragility, saw the non-intervention norm as one of their few defenses against threats and pressures from more powerful international actors seeking to promote their own economic and political interests. This was extremely inhibiting to the development of any sense of obligation to respond in an effective way to situations of catastrophic internal human rights violations.

One big agreed exception to the non-intervention principle was the Genocide Convention of 1948.[5] But it was almost as if, with the signing of this convention, the task was seen as complete. Nothing much was done throughout the Cold War years to give practical force and effect to the plain terms of the Genocide Convention itself, even in situations where legal arguments about lack of provable intent and so on were simply not in issue. The starkest case was Cambodia under Pol Pot in the mid-1970s. Although there were, even here, technical problems in applying the convention (in this case because the people being massacred and starved were overwhelmingly of the same nationality, ethnicity, race, and religion as those doing the killing), the world did come to accept this as a catastrophic genocidal situation. But far from being praised after crossing the border to displace the Khmer Rouge, Vietnam received widespread international condemnation. While Hanoi's motives may have been neither pure nor humanitarian, its intervention did stop the génocidaires in their tracks. Nonetheless, all the international pressure was on the interveners rather than those perpetrating the horror to begin with.

Other relevant instruments emerged during the Cold War period, including the Universal Declaration of Human Rights[6] and the 1966 conventions on civil and political rights as well as economic, social, and cultural rights.[7] But in terms of practical implementation and commitment, the world remained at the level of grandiloquent rhetoric, and non-interference in domestic affairs still led the list of unbreakable commandments so far as international discourse was concerned.

With the arrival of the 1990s, the end of the Cold War, and the new era of apparent cooperation between formerly warring parties, it seemed there was new hope for a newly active and effective international security system. The international defense of Kuwait against Iraq's invasion in 1991 was a classic example of the international system working as it was intended to in response to acts of interstate aggression. But the euphoria about a rules-based system emerging, or re-emerging, did not last long.

The quintessential problem of the 1990s became that of intrastate conflict, civil war, and internal violence perpetrated on a massive scale. With the break-up of various Cold War state structures, most obviously in Yugoslavia, and the removal of some superpower constraints, conscience-shocking situations repeatedly arose, but old habits of non-intervention died very hard. Even when situations cried out for some kind of response and the international community did react through the UN, it was too often erratic, incomplete, or counterproductive. So we had the debacle of the intervention in Somalia in 1993, the pathetically inadequate response to the genocide in Rwanda in 1994, the lamentable failure to prevent murderous ethnic cleansing in the Balkans, in particular in Srebrenica, in 1995, and also the Kosovo situation in 1999 when the international community did in fact intervene, as it probably should have, but did so without the authority of the Security Council in the face of a threatened veto by Russia.

All this generated very fierce debate about what came to be called humanitarian intervention.[8] On the one hand, there were those who argued fiercely for "the right to intervene"—the *droit d'ingérence* for which Bernard

Kouchner of Médecins Sans Frontières made the battle cry;[9] on the other hand, equally strong claims were made about the primacy and continued resonance of the concept of *national sovereignty*, seen as a complete inhibitor to any such coercive intervention. The debate was a fierce one and, throughout the 1990s, utterly unresolved in the UN or anywhere else. Battle lines were drawn and trenches were dug.

This led UN Secretary-General Kofi Annan to make his agitated plea to the General Assembly in 2000, bringing the issue to a very public head, which continues to resonate to this day: "[I]f humanitarian intervention is, indeed, an unacceptable assault on sovereignty, how should we respond to a Rwanda, to a Srebrenica—to gross and systematic violations of human rights?"[10] Secretary-General Annan's own initial solution to this problem was to say that in these situations national sovereignty had to be weighed and balanced against individual sovereignty.[11] But this formulation, in truth, did little more than restate the basic dilemma: When exactly *did* individual sovereignty claims take primacy over state sovereignty? How does one identify the point at which the former should override the latter?

That same capacity to state a core issue elegantly but not resolve it in any very compelling way characterized the influential report in 2000 of the Independent International Commission on Kosovo, chaired by Richard Goldstone and Carl Tham.[12] Wrestling with the problem of the NATO intervention in 1999 that had not been authorized by the Security Council, the report described the intervention as "unavoidable" because "diplomatic options had been exhausted, and two sides were bent on a conflict which threatened to wreak humanitarian catastrophe."[13] The commission concluded that "the intervention was legitimate, but not legal."[14] They recognized the need "to close the gap between legality and legitimacy" and recommended that the General Assembly adopt a "principled framework for humanitarian intervention which could be used to guide future responses to imminent humanitarian catastrophes."[15]

The task of drafting such a framework—and meeting the challenge laid down by Annan—fell to the Canadian government-sponsored International Commission on Intervention and State Sovereignty (ICISS). The ICISS, which I had the privilege of co-chairing with the Algerian diplomat Mohamed Sahnoun, presented its report, entitled *The Responsibility to Protect*, to the UN Secretary-General at the end of 2001.[16] The report made four main contributions to the international policy debate, which, it seems fair to say, have been resonating ever since.

The first, and perhaps ultimately the most politically useful, was to invent a new way of talking about humanitarian intervention. We sought to turn the whole weary debate about the right to intervene on its head and to re-characterize it not as an argument about any *right* at all but rather about a *responsibility*[17]—one to protect people at grave risk—with the relevant perspective being not that of the prospective interveners but, more appropriately, of those needing support.[18] This new language clearly has been helpful in taking a good deal of the heat and emotion out of the policy debate, requiring the actors to change their lines and think afresh about what the real issues are. The commission's hope—and so far, broadly what our experience has been—was that entrenched opponents would find new ground on which to more constructively engage, just as relations between developers and environmentalists improved after the Brundtland Commission introduced the concept of *sustainable development*.[19]

The second contribution of the commission, and perhaps the most conceptually significant, was to insist upon a new way of talking about sovereignty: we argued, influenced in particular by the work of Francis Deng,[20] that its essence should now be seen not as *control* but as *responsibility*. The UN Charter's explicit language emphasizes the respect owed to state sovereignty in the traditional Westphalian sense, but actual state practice has evolved in the six decades since the charter was signed, with a new focus on human rights and, more recently, on human security, emphasizing the *limits* of sovereignty.[21]

We spelt out the implications of that change by arguing that sovereignty implies responsibilities as well as rights: to be sovereign means both to be responsible to one's own citizens and to the wider international community.[22] The starting point is that any state has a primary responsibility to protect the individuals within it.[23] But that is not the finishing point: where the state fails in that responsibility, through either incapacity or ill will, a secondary responsibility to protect falls on the international community, acting primarily through the UN.

The third contribution of the commission was to make it clear that the responsibility to protect was about much more than intervention and, in particular, military intervention. It extends to a whole continuum of obligations:

The responsibility to *prevent*: to address both the root causes and direct causes of internal conflict and other man-made crises putting populations at risk;[24]

The responsibility to *react*: to respond to situations of compelling human need with appropriate measures, which may include coercive measures like sanctions, international prosecution, and, in extreme cases, military intervention;[25] and

The responsibility to *rebuild*: to provide, particularly after a military intervention, full assistance with recovery, reconstruction, and reconciliation, addressing the causes of the harm the intervention was designed to halt or avert.[26]

Of these three dimensions to the responsibility to protect, the commission made very clear its view that prevention was the single most important.[27]

But, that said, the question of military action remains, for better or worse, the most prominent and controversial one in the debate. Whatever else it encompasses, the responsibility to protect implies above all else a responsibility to react—where necessary, coercively, and in extreme cases, with military coercion—to situations of compelling need for human protection.

The fourth contribution of the commission was to come up with guidelines for when military action is appropriate—going both to its legality and legitimacy, in terms of the language of the Kosovo Report.[28] The effectiveness of the global collective security system, as with any other legal order, depends ultimately not only on the legality of decisions but also on the common perception of their legitimacy—their being made on solid evidentiary grounds and for the right reasons, morally as well as legally.

As to legitimacy, we identified five criteria that we argued should be applied by the Security Council—and be used by the world at large—to test the validity of any case made for a coercive humanitarian intervention. All five have an explicit pedigree in Christian just war theory, but their themes resonate equally with other major world religions and intellectual traditions. They are as follows:

1   Just Cause: Is there "serious and irreparable harm occurring to human beings, or imminently likely to occur, of the following kind:
    A   Large-scale loss of life, actual or apprehended, with genocidal intent or not, which is the product either of deliberate state action or state neglect, inability to act, or a failed-state situation; or
    B   Large-scale ethnic cleansing, actual or apprehended, whether carried out by killing, forced expulsion, acts of terror, or rape."[29]
        The bar for military intervention here has been set deliberately high and tight and excludes many kinds of unconscionable behavior (e.g., imprisonment and torture of political opponents or overthrow of a democratically elected government) that would certainly justify other forms of coercive response (e.g., targeted sanctions).
2   Right Intention: Is the primary purpose of the proposed military action to halt or avert human suffering, whatever other motives may be in play?[30]
3   Last Resort: Has every non-military option for the prevention or peaceful resolution of the crisis been explored, and are there reasonable grounds for believing lesser measures will not succeed?[31]
    This guideline was not intended to mean that every non-military option must literally have been tried and failed. Given that there will often be simply no time for that process to work itself out, what is necessary is that there be reasonable grounds for believing, in all the circumstances, that these other measures would not have worked.

4 Proportional Means: Is the scale, duration, and intensity of the planned military action the minimum necessary to secure the defined human protection objective?[32]

5 Reasonable Prospects: Is there a reasonable chance of the military action being successful in meeting the threat in question, and are the consequences of action not likely to be worse than the consequences of inaction?[33]

This last balance-of-consequences test is, and should be, a very important constraint. Apart from anything else, it effectively rules out military action against any one of the five permanent members of the Security Council—e.g., against Russia over Chechnya or against China over some imaginable course of events in Xinjiang—even if all other conditions for intervention were to be met. The same is true for other major powers—which is why Indonesia's permission was required for the East Timor intervention. That permission was given only very reluctantly and under much international pressure, but it *was* given; the case was, accordingly, not one of coercive humanitarian intervention at all. All this raises the familiar question of double standards to which the only answer can be this: the reality that interventions may not be able to be mounted in every case where there is justification for doing so is no reason for them not to be mounted in any case.

The ICISS was not naïve about these criteria of legitimacy. We recognized that there was no push-button inevitability about their application and that for the Security Council to adopt them could not guarantee that the objectively best outcome would always prevail. But we argued that the existence of agreed criteria would change the nature of Security Council debate: Maximize the possibility of achieving council consensus around when it is appropriate or not to go to war; maximize international support for whatever it decides; and minimize the possibility of individual member states bypassing or ignoring it.[34]

There remained to address the problem of legality. What if, taking into account all five criteria of legitimacy, a very clear case could be made for coercive intervention, but the Security Council—under the UN Charter the *only* source of authority for the use of military force except in cases of legitimate self-defense—simply would not vote to authorize it? This was exactly the issue that had to be confronted with Kosovo in 1999 when all the elements of a horrific new ethnic cleansing operation were falling into place, but Russia made clear it would veto any military intervention.[35]

In these cases a very real dilemma arises as to which of two evils is the worse: the damage to international order if the Security Council is bypassed or the damage to that order if human beings are slaughtered while the Security Council stands by. The commission's response to this dilemma was not to try and establish some alternative basis for the legality of interventions in these situations.[36] We saw the need as not to find alternatives to the Security Council as a source of authority but to make it work better. We opted for a clear political message: if an individual state or ad hoc coalition steps in, fully observes and respects all the necessary criteria of legitimacy, intervenes successfully, and is seen to have done so by world public opinion, then this is likely to have enduringly serious consequences for the stature and credibility of the UN itself.[37] That is essentially what happened with the United States and NATO intervention in Kosovo, and the UN cannot afford to drop the ball too many times on that scale.

II. The Evolution of a Doctrine

It is one thing to develop a concept of this kind but quite another to get any policy maker to take any notice of it. Everyone's bookshelves are full of barely opened reports by blue ribbon commissions and panels. The most interesting thing about the *Responsibility to Protect* report is the way its central theme has continued to gain traction internationally, even though it was almost suffocated at birth by being published in December 2001, in the immediate aftermath of 9/11, and by the subsequent massive international preoccupation with terrorism rather than internal human rights catastrophes.

For a start, the responsibility to protect concept was embraced enthusiastically by Secretary-General Annan, who acknowledged, very graciously, that it had rather more potential to bridge the sovereignty versus intervention divide than his own earlier attempt to find consensus around the idea of balancing state sovereignty against individual sovereignty. It began to be embraced, importantly, in the doctrine of the newly emerging African Union. And over the next two to three years, it won quite a constituency among academic commentators and international lawyers, a number of whom were prepared to accept, to a greater or lesser extent, the commission's own rather heroic assessment of the responsibility to protect as an emerging international norm that might, in due course, become accepted as customary international law. The responsibility to protect during this period even acquired that ultimate measure of recognition and acceptance, a now almost universally used acronymic abbreviation, *R2P*.

In international law, being the rather odd beast that it is, capable of evolving through practice and commentary as well as through formal treaty instruments, these embraces and acknowledgments are to some extent self-fulfilling. But that is only the case if the momentum is maintained. If the R2P concept was to really catch hold and become the primary frame of reference within which catastrophic human rights violations were assessed and responded to in the future, its acceptance had to become considerably more visible and universal.

A great deal of effort has been going into maintaining that momentum, and several big milestones have now been passed. First, the High-level Panel on Threats, Challenges and Change, whose report *A More Secure World: Our Shared Responsibility* was submitted to the Secretary-General in December 2004, squarely adopted the whole concept in these words:

> We endorse the emerging norm that there is a collective international responsibility to protect, exercisable by the Security Council authorizing military intervention as a last resort, in the event of genocide or other large-scale killing, ethnic cleansing or serious violations of international humanitarian law which sovereign Governments have proved powerless or unwilling to prevent.[38]

The High-level Panel also effectively endorsed the criteria of legitimacy which the ICISS had insisted must be a basis for any resort to military action. The only difference was that the panel recommended that these criteria be applied by the Security Council when considering whether to use military force in any context whatsoever, not only in internal humanitarian intervention situations.

The second milestone passed was the embrace of these recommendations by the Secretary-General himself in his own proposals for reform published in March 2005 as *In Larger Freedom: Towards Development, Security and Human Rights for All*, the basic working document for the World Summit scheduled in September last year in the context of the UN's sixtieth anniversary.[39] After repeating, in effect, the language of the High-level Panel, he went on to say: "While I am well aware of the sensitivities involved in this issue, I strongly agree with this approach. I believe we must embrace the responsibility to protect, and, when necessary, we must act on it."[40]

The third milestone passed, and by far the biggest, was the unanimous embrace of the responsibility to protect principle by the General Assembly, meeting as the World Summit itself.[41] The Summit outcomes overall were, from a UN reform perspective, deeply disappointing, certainly when measured against the breadth of the Secretary-General's *In Larger Freedom* proposals, which reached across the whole spectrum of development, security, human rights, and management issues, and against some of the hopes and expectations that had been generated by the preceding debate.[42] The endorsement of R2P, in this context, was a very major achievement and one of only a small handful of real achievements from the whole occasion (along with the creation of the Peacebuilding Commission and the agreement to replace the dysfunctional Commission on Human Rights with a new Human Rights Council).

That this endorsement happened was anything but inevitable. Nearly all the negotiation on the Summit Outcome Document took place in the notoriously difficult environment of the UN diplomatic corps rather than at a political leadership level in nations' capitals. A fierce rearguard action was fought almost to the last by a small group of developing countries joined by Russia that basically refused to concede any kind of limitation on the full and untrammeled exercise of state sovereignty, however irresponsible that exercise might be. What carried the day in the end was not so much the consistent support from the United States and EU countries, which was not particularly helpful in the prevailing post-Iraq environment in meeting these familiar sovereignty concerns. Rather, it was the persistent advocacy by sub-Saharan African countries led by South Africa; the clear—and historically quite significant—embrace of limited-sovereignty principles by key Latin American countries; and some very effective last minute personal diplomacy with major wavering-country leaders by Canadian Prime Minister Paul Martin.

The language of the summit outcome document was quite strong, including these critical passages:

> Each individual State has the responsibility to protect its populations from genocide, war crimes, ethnic cleansing and crimes against humanity. This responsibility entails the prevention of such crimes, including their incitement, through appropriate and necessary means. We accept that responsibility and will act in accordance with it. ...

> The international community, through the United Nations, also has the responsibility to use appropriate diplomatic, humanitarian and other peaceful means, in accordance with Chapters VI and VIII of the Charter, to help to protect populations from genocide, war crimes, ethnic cleansing and crimes against humanity. In this context, we are prepared to take collective action, in a timely and decisive manner, through the Security Council, in accordance with the Charter, including Chapter VII, on a case-by-case basis and in cooperation with relevant regional organizations as appropriate, should peaceful means be inadequate and national authorities are manifestly failing to protect their populations from genocide, war crimes, ethnic cleansing and crimes against humanity.[43]

Bearing in mind the almost pitched battles fought in the General Assembly not very long before on the intervention-sovereignty issue, to get such language endorsed unanimously by the whole international community, in that same global forum, was a considerable achievement. From any view, the evolution in just five years of the responsibility to protect concept from a gleam in a commission's eye to what now might be described as a broadly accepted international norm, creating in the process the context for a far more effective response to conscience-shocking situations than the international community has managed in the past, is an extremely encouraging story.

But it's not the whole story. The recognition of the responsibility to protect as a principle is one thing—its practical implementation, quite another. There are quite a number of problems that remain to be overcome in this respect, and I shall briefly describe them in turn as the problems of buy-in by the Security Council, false friends, capacity, and will.

III. The Implementation of a Doctrine

A. The problem of Security Council buy-in

A General Assembly resolution is helpful in identifying relevant principles, but the Security Council is the institution that matters most when it comes to executive action. And here a problem has already become apparent, even just at the level of generalities rather than specifics, in the context of an attempt after the World Summit to get the council itself to endorse the R2P language of the General Assembly's resolution. Debate on a thematic resolution on the protection of civilians in armed conflict, which incorporates this language, has been dragging on inconclusively since it was introduced by the United Kingdom presidency in December 2005, with Russia and China arguing, in their usual studied gravity, that the whole issue should first be addressed in more detail by the General Assembly. The cause is by no means lost, but the exercise has been instructive for anyone who would too readily assume that a new spirit of responsibility is abroad.[44]

The Security Council problem has been compounded by the unwillingness of almost anybody to buy into what was—for the ICISS, the High-level Panel, and the Secretary-General in his own report—an integral part of the R2P package, viz. the set of criteria addressing the legitimacy of using military force. The General Assembly resolution itself, quite apart from any Security Council follow up, omitted any language on these principles, whether in a specific R2P context or more generally.[45] Although the five criteria of legitimacy originally spelt out by the ICISS had managed to survive all the way through the earlier debate, they fell at the last hurdle: caught, in effect, in a pincer movement between, on the one hand, the hostility of the United States, which very definitely did not want any guidelines adopted that could limit in any way the Security Council's—and by extension, its own—complete freedom to make judgments on a case-by-case basis, and on the other, the hostility of a number of developing countries who argued, with more passion than intelligibility, that to have a set of principles purporting to limit the use of force to exceptional, highly defensible cases was somehow to encourage it.

B. The problem of false friends

The biggest inhibitor of all to the ready acceptance of R2P as an operating principle has been the misuse of that principle in the context of the war on Iraq. The initial rationales for military intervention in Iraq were cast not at all in R2P terms: the issue was Iraq's presumed possession of weapons of mass destruction, or at least the capacity to make them, and its perceived dissimulation in that respect to the international community, supplemented by the less plausible suggestion that Saddam Hussein was hand-in-glove with international terrorists. But as these rationales fell away, the argument came to be cast ever more specifically, particularly by the United Kingdom, but with Washington not far in the rear, in terms of Saddam's tyranny—the human rights violations he had perpetrated on his own people and the need to protect them from further abuse. The genocidal massacres of the Kurds using chemical weapons in the 1980s and of the Shiites in the early 1990s— to both of which the West had turned a blind eye at the time, but no matter— were surely proof, it was suggested, that this was a suitable case for R2P treatment and of the most coercive kind.

But of course, it was nothing of the kind. The rationale for coercive humanitarian intervention is not punishment for past sins, however grotesque, but to avert, here and now, threats to large numbers of people which are actually occurring or imminently about to occur. It is not to allow a regime with a bloody past to be attacked by others at a time of their choosing: as Ken Roth of Human Rights Watch has put it, "'Better late than never' is not a justification for humanitarian intervention."[46] And even if a prima facie case could be made for going to war on this threshold issue of the seriousness of the security threat to Iraq's own people, the case for actually doing so depends on multiple other criteria being satisfied, not least that the results of military action will not be worse than taking no action. There are not too many people outside the inner core of the Bush administration who would confidently have made that judgment at the time, and no one, I suspect, who would make it now.

The key issue here (not only for developing-country-sovereignty addicts but also for writers like David Rieff) is that the ideals of liberal interventionism captured in the R2P principle—which should have been carried through in Rwanda and Srbrenica but weren't, and were carried through but with incomplete authority in Kosovo—are all too easily capable of misapplication by neo-conservatives and others to justify unjustifiable military adventures such as Iraq.

This false friends problem is compounded when absolutely genuine, principled supporters of R2P decide to use it as a springboard for other forms of adventurism. Anne-Marie Slaughter and Lee Feinstein embarked on this path when in a *Foreign Affairs* article in 2004 they sought to build upon the foundations of R2P (to which they paid gracious homage) a new edifice, which they called "a duty to prevent."[47] This concept is currently getting a new lease of life, although I am not sure this is to both authors' present taste, in the current debate about Iran's nuclear ambitions, not least with the just-released new 2006 National Security Strategy restating this administration's determination to "if necessary, act preemptively in exercising our inherent right of self-defense."[48]

There was much to admire in Slaughter and Feinstein's enthusiasm for better preventive strategies for inhibiting nuclear proliferation but much to be alarmed about in their argument that ultimately military force could be used preventively (not just preemptively when attack was imminent) and not solely when the Security Council endorsed it against regimes whose "absolute power ... past behavior, and ... expressed intentions," as they put it, seemed to justify this course.[49] When one is trying to carefully build an international consensus where none has previously existed, of a kind which will actually mobilize real-time action to prevent real-time genocide and other atrocity crimes, it is not an enormous help to be told that preventive strikes against putative nuclear weapons states are a natural corollary of the R2P principle.

C. The problem of capacity

This is a further real-world problem of grave dimensions, which arises most acutely in the context of the use of military force. Even with complete agreement, in some last resort situation, about the legality and legitimacy of military intervention and the best will in the world to deploy military force, there may just not be the capacity to do so or at least a capacity to deploy force of the kind required.

The problems here are all very familiar ones. Those countries with apparently massive capacity—in terms of both personnel numbers and equipment—are often preoccupied with battles and deployments elsewhere or have the wrong kind of troop configurations and equipment to do the fast and flexible jobs most often required. Throughout Europe in particular, in country after country, the number of troops operationally deployable at any given time is a tiny percentage of the men and women in uniform. Elsewhere in the world, there may be no apparent shortage of boots able to go on the ground, but there will be issues of training, command, control and communications capability, transportability, and general logistic support. And for any proposed multinational deployment, there will be issues of planning, mission control, and field command—who is responsible for what and interoperability.

The present situation in Darfur is a classic demonstration of the problem of military implementation of the international responsibility to protect.

This is not a case where I would argue that external military forces should fight their way in whatever the resistance of the national government: if nothing else, the fifth criterion of legitimacy, the balance of consequences, would argue against that. But it is obviously a case for a major international protective response in which resources are committed to the resolution of an internal man-made catastrophe and on a scale that really will make a difference. At least twelve thousand fully mandated troops—desirably many more, but this number at a minimum—are, in the International Crisis Group's judgment, needed on the ground right *now* to protect villages against further attack or destruction, protect the displaced against forced repatriation and intimidation, protect women from systematic rape outside IDP camps, provide security for humanitarian operations, and neutralize the government-supported militias who continue to prey on civilians.[50]

At present, under the current African Union Mission in Sudan (AMIS), there are only some seven thousand inadequately mandated, insufficiently mobile, and otherwise militarily incapable personnel on the ground. And there are no firm plans to increase this number, although there is now some acceptance of the desirability of the UN taking over the operation in six months' time. The extra five thousand troops that are needed, at a minimum, are presently nowhere to be seen: no individual African country has that number available, and none are being volunteered by the European countries or NATO countries or other developed countries which could, on the face of it, make a difference. They are presently very comfortable sheltering behind the African Union's unwillingness to accept outsiders, particularly non-Islamic northerners, into the fray, but the truth of the matter is that they are neither able nor willing to provide the necessary resources. What they are best configured to supply, and most comfortable negotiating, as Kofi Annan has been heard to ruefully say, is some quick in-and-out heavy lift or other logistical support, a handshake, and a photo opportunity.

D. The problem of political will

Even if the capacity to react in the way required is there for the taking, there will always be a problem in R2P situations of mobilizing the necessary political will. This is true not only of the most extreme form of coercive reaction, the use of military force, but also of non-military coercive action, like the application of sanctions or the bringing of atrocity crime suspects before international criminal courts. (There has been some good recent news in that respect with the final establishment of the International Criminal Court—and less unyielding opposition to it by the United States, at least in the context of Sudan—and also with the bringing to justice of Charles Taylor before the UN Special Court for Sierra Leone; but the problem of absent political will remains starkly apparent with the continued failure of

Serbia to cooperate in bringing the indictees Radovan Karadzic and Ratko Mladic before the International Criminal Tribunal for the former Yugoslavia.) The need for political will is also there even with the use of utterly non-coercive preventive action, which may nonetheless involve expensive resources and the commitment to apply them effectively.

The problem of finding the necessary political will to do anything hard or expensive or politically sensitive is just a given in public affairs. The evident absence of such will should not be a matter for lamentation or despair but mobilization—even in a current environment where, as Philip Stephens put it recently in the *Financial Times*, "on both sides of the Atlantic, the impulse to engage is giving way to an inclination to retreat."[51] For every Indian Ocean tsunami that generates a massively sympathetic international human response and an outpouring of material support, there is a Pakistani earthquake, just about as horrendous in its human consequences, that does not. We have to live with these vagaries in the human psyche and our various body politics and work on ways of overcoming them.

The ICISS made the point that mobilizing political will is not only a matter of intelligently using the institutional instruments at hand—everything from CNN's cameras to the power of the "[UN] Secretary-General under Article 99 of the UN Charter to 'bring to the attention of the Security Council any matter that in his opinion may threaten the maintenance of international peace and security.'"[52] It is also a matter of intelligently and energetically advancing good *arguments*, which may not be a sufficient condition but are always necessary for taking difficult political action.

> Those arguments may be *party interest* arguments designed to consolidate a government's vocal domestic base (always an important element in the Bush Administration's interest in Sudan); *national interest* arguments (much easier to make now in relation to "quarrels in far away countries between people of whom we know nothing," in Chamberlain's terms, because of what we do know now about the capacity of failed states, in this globalised world, to be a source of havoc for others); or *financial* arguments (in terms of a million dollars worth of preventive action now saving a billion dollars worth of military intervention later). And if all else fails, they can even be *moral* arguments (given that however base politicians' real motives may be, they always like to be seen as acting from higher ones).[53]

There are, in short, many problems that remain if the principle of the responsibility to protect is to be consolidated, further refined and developed, and above all practically implemented. But for all the problems that remain, some extraordinary progress has been made and within a remarkably short time period given the normal pace at which international norms and patterns of behavior change. We really are now well on the way toward building an international legal order that, despite all the challenges which continue to buffet it, will give us some grounds for optimism that we are not forever condemned to repeat the mistakes of the past. And that means not only the mistake of going to war when we should not, but also what can sometimes be the even bigger mistake of *not* going to war to protect our fellow human beings from catastrophe when we *should*.

Notes

*   Keynote Address by Gareth Evans, President of International Crisis Group and Co-Chair of the International Commission on Intervention and State Sovereignty 2001, to Symposium on Humanitarian Intervention, University of Wisconsin-Madison, Mar. 31, 2006. Gareth Evans is the current President of the International Crisis Group (ICG) and former Australian Foreign Minister (1988–96). He is a former member of the UN Secretary General's High-level Panel on Threats, Challenges and Change, the Zedillo International Task Force on Global Public Goods and the Blix Commission on Weapons of Mass Destruction.

1   *See* INT'L CRISIS GROUP, TO SAVE DARFUR, AFRICA REPORT 105, 1–4, n.9 (2006), *available at* http://www.crisisgroup.org/library/documents/africa/horn_of_africa/105_to_save_darfur.pdf.

2   U.N. Charter art. 51.

3   *Id.* arts. 39–51.

4   *Id.* art. 2, para. 7.

5   Convention on the Prevention and Punishment of the Crime of Genocide, G.A. Res. 260A(III), U.N. GAOR, 3d Sess., 179th plen. mtg., U.N. Doc. A/810 (1948), *entered into force* Jan. 12, 1951, *available at* http://www.unhchr.ch/html/menu3/b/p_genoci.htm.

6   Universal Declaration of Human Rights, G.A. Res. 217A, at 71, U.N. GAOR, 3d Sess., 1st plen. mtg., U.N. Doc A/810 (Dec. 12, 1948).

7   International Covenant on Civil and Political Rights, G.A. Res. 2200A (XXI), 21 U.N. GAOR Supp. (No. 16) at 52, 7th Sess., U.N. Doc. A/6316 (1966), *entered into force* Mar. 23, 1976, *available at* http://www.ohchr.org/english/law/ccpr.htm; International Covenant on Economic, Social and Cultural Rights, G.A. Res. 2200A, 21 U.N. GOAR Supp. (No. 16) at 49, 7th Sess., U.N. Doc. A/6316 (1966), 993 U.N.T.S. 3, *entered into force* Jan. 3, 1976, *available at* http://www.ohchr.org/english/law/ccpr.htm.

8   However, this terminology continues to be strongly resisted by humanitarian relief organizations, starting with the Red Cross, that have always hated the idea of juxtaposing or identifying the concept of humanitarianism with that of military force in any circumstances.

9   *See, e.g.*, Bernard Kouchner, *Establish a Right to Intervene Against War, Oppression*, LOS ANGELES TIMES, Oct. 18, 1999, at B7.

10   The Secretary-General, *Millennium Report of the Secretary-General of the United Nations, We the People: The Role of the United Nations in the 21st Century*, at 48, U.N. Doc A/54/20 (2000), *available at* http://www.un.org/millennium/sg/report/ch3.pdf.

11 *See* Kofi Annan, *Two Concepts of Sovereignty*, ECONOMIST, Sept. 18, 1999, at 49.

12 INDEP. INT'L COMM'N ON KOSOVO, THE KOSOVO REPORT: CONFLICT, INTERNATIONAL RESPONSE, LESSONS LEARNED (2000).

13 *Id.* at 289.

14 *Id.*

15 *Id.* at 10.

16 INT'L COMM'N ON INTERVENTION AND STATE SOVEREIGNTY, THE RESPONSIBILITY TO PROTECT (2001), *available at* http://www.iciss.ca/report-en.asp (follow "View Document (PDF)" hyperlink) (last visited Nov. 25, 2006).

17 *Id.* ¶ 2.4.

18 *Id.* ch. 2.

19 World Comm'n on Env't & Dev. [WCED], *Our Common Future*, ch. 2, U.N. Doc. A/42/427 (Aug. 4, 1987). The World Commission on Environment and Development is also known as the Brundtland Commission, named after its Chair, Gro Harlem Brundtland. The commission was convened by the United Nations in response to the 1983 General Assembly Resolution A/38/1961 and produced the report, *Our Common Future*, in 1987. *Id.*

20 *See, e.g.*, FRANCIS M. DENG ET AL., SOVEREIGNTY AS RESPONSIBILITY: CONFLICT MANAGEMENT IN AFRICA (1996); *see also* INT'L COMM'N ON INTERVENTION AND STATE SOVEREIGNTY, *supra* note 16.

21 INT'L COMM'N ON INTERVENTION AND STATE SOVEREIGNTY, *supra* note 16, ¶ 2.7.

22 *Id.* ¶ 2.27.

23 *Id.* ¶ 2.8.

24 *Id.* ch. 3.

25 *Id.* ch. 4.

26 *Id.* ch. 5.

27 *Id.* ¶ 7.15.

28 *Id.* at XII–XIII.

29 *Id.* at XII.

30 *Id.*

31 *Id.*

32 *Id.*

33 *Id.*

34 *Id.* ¶ 4.14.

35 *See, e.g., id.* ¶ 1.2.

36 *Id.* ¶ 8.4.

37 *Id.* ¶ 6.4.

38 The Secretary-General, *Report of the High-level Panel on Threats, Challenges and Change, A More Secure World: Our Shared Responsibility*, ¶ 203, *delivered to the General Assembly*, U.N. Doc. A/59/565 (Dec. 2, 2004), *available at* http://www.un.org.secureworld/report2.pdf.

39 The Secretary-General, Report of the Secretary General, In Larger Freedom: Towards Development, Security and Human Rights for All, delivered to the General Assembly, U.N. Doc. A/59/2005 (Mar. 21, 2005) [hereinafter In Larger Freedom], *available at* http://www.un.org/largerfreedom/contents.htm (follow "Report" hyperlink; then follow "Full Report" hyperlink).

40 *Id.* ¶ 135.

41 G.A. Res. 60/1, U.N. Doc. A/RES/60/1 (Oct. 24, 2005).

42 In Larger Freedom, *supra* note 39.

43 G.A. Res. 60/1, *supra* note 41, ¶¶ 138–39.

44 Since this was written the Security Council has specifically endorsed the responsibility to protect principle in Resolution 1674, and subsequently incorporated it by reference in Resolution 1706 on Darfur. *See* S.C. Res. 1674, U.N. Doc. S/RES/1674 (Apr. 24, 2006); S.C. Res. 1706, U.N. Doc. S/RES/1706 (Aug. 31, 2006). But effective operational implementation of the principle still remains some distance away.

45 *Id.*

46 Ken Roth, *War in Iraq: Not a Humanitarian Intervention, in* HUMAN RIGHTS WATCH WORLD REPORT, 2004: HUMAN RIGHTS AND ARMED CONFLICT 13, 22 (2004), *available at* http://www.hrw.org/wr2k4/download/wr2k4.pdf.

47 Lee Feinstein & Anne-Marie Slaughter, *A Duty to Protect*, 83 FOREIGN AFF. 136, 137 (2004).

48 THE WHITE HOUSE, THE NATIONAL SECURITY STRATEGY OF THE UNITED STATES OF AMERICA 18 (2006), *available at* http://www.whitehouse.gov/nsc (follow "National Security Strategy of the United States of America 2006" hyperlink; then follow "Full PDF Document" hyperlink) (last visited Nov. 25, 2006).

49 Feinstein & Slaughter, *supra* note 47, at 139 (addressing Saddam Hussein's Iraq).

50 *See* INT'L CRISIS GROUP, *supra* note 1.

51 Philip Stephens, *No Retreat From the Global Community*, FIN. TIMES (London), Mar. 18, 2006, at 19.

52 INT'L COMM'N ON INTERVENTION AND STATE SOVEREIGNTY, *supra* note 16, ¶ 3.14.

53 Gareth Evans, President, Int'l Crisis Group, Keynote Address at Channels of Influence in a Crisis Situation Seminar in Helsinki, Finland: Conflict Prevention and Development Cooperation (May 9, 2006), *available at* http://www.crisisgroup.org/home/index.cfm (follow "President" hyperlink; then follow "Speeches" hyperlink; then follow "Conflict Prevention and Development Cooperation" hyperlink).

13

The Misuse of Power, Not Bad Representation
*Why It Is Beside the Point that No One Elected Oxfam**

Jennifer C. Rubenstein

> *"Who elected Oxfam?"*
> —The Economist[1]

On July 21, 2010, the Dodd-Frank Wall Street Reform and Consumer Protection Act, better known as the Dodd-Frank bill, was signed into law by President Obama. Section 1502 of the bill, the Conflict Minerals Provision, requires companies to show that the minerals used in their products did not originate in the Democratic Republic of Congo, or if they did originate in the DRC, that they did not contribute to the conflict there.[2] Support for Section 1502 was spearheaded by ENOUGH, a US-based international non-governmental organization (INGO), and Global Witness, a UK-based INGO. Together with the International Crisis Group's John Prendergast, these two organizations wrote Section 1502.[3] They also helped to shape the lineup of speakers at the Security and Exchange Commission's October 2011 "public roundtable" about rules for implementing the bill.[4]

Even before Dodd-Frank was passed, however, many US- and DRC-based academics and activists argued that Section 1502 would have disastrous consequences. They predicted that mining companies in the DRC, anticipating the difficulty and cost of abiding by the new rules, would shift their operations elsewhere, leaving tens of thousands of Congolese miners jobless, and making them, their families, and communities even more destitute than they had been previously.[5] These academics and activists also argued that regulating the minerals trade would not accomplish the legislation's stated objective of reducing conflict in the DRC, because the minerals trade played only a very small role in driving the conflict there.[6] These predicted outcomes seem to have largely come to pass.[7]

Consider another example of advocacy by an INGO. In March 2011, Oxfam and three Ghanaian non-governmental organizations (NGOs) together released a report that they had jointly commissioned, called "Achieving a Shared Goal: Free Universal Health Care in Ghana." The report asserted that "[t]he current health system in Ghana is unfair and inefficient," that Ghana's National Health Insurance Authority (NHIA) had overstated by 44% the proportion of Ghanaians covered by Ghana's National Health Insurance Scheme (NHIS), and that the scheme should be dismantled and replaced with free-at-point-of-service health care for all, funded primarily by tax revenues.[8] The report also argued that contrary to claims made by the United Nations Development Programme and the World Health Organization, other countries should not adopt Ghana's NHIS as a model.[9]

The "Shared Goal" report generated a "major controversy," both within Ghana and in international development circles.[10] The NHIA slammed the report, arguing that it was a sloppily researched effort by Oxfam to "tarnish a home grown African initiative."[11] But the NHIA did eventually respond to the report's criticisms by altering its methodology for calculating the number of people effectively covered by Ghana's NHIS, leading to a much lower estimate.[12] At the international level, the World Bank issued its own report about Ghana's health care system, partly in response to the "Shared Goal" report. In this report, the World Bank, like the NHIA, repeatedly referred to the "Shared Goal" report as "the Oxfam report," and to its arguments as "Oxfam's critique," largely ignoring the Ghanaian NGOs that co-commissioned the report.[13] How should we think about the advocacy by ENOUGH, Global Witness, and Oxfam in these cases?

Over the past few decades, there has been a dramatic increase in advocacy by INGOs working on issues related to inter-group violence, humanitarian disasters, poverty, and injustice.[14] This increase in INGO advocacy has not gone unnoticed by democratic theorists. Many of these theorists have interpreted INGO advocacy as a paradigmatic example of "non-electoral representation." Viewed through this interpretive lens: a) ENOUGH and Global Witness are non-elected representatives of Congolese miners and Oxfam is a non-elected representative of poor Ghanaians; and b) their advocacy efforts should be evaluated based on how well they meet normative criteria of good (democratic) representation, such as authorization, accountability, deliberativeness, and responsiveness to their "constituents'" preferences and interests.

Yet, in sharp contrast to how democratic theorists characterize INGO advocacy, most INGO advocates themselves vehemently *deny* being representatives. They instead claim to be "partners" of the poor and marginalized groups they seek to assist, and of the domestic NGOs, community-based organizations (CBOs), and domestic governments with which they work. For example, Oxfam describes itself as working "in partnership" with the three Ghanaian NGOs with which it co-commissioned the "Shared Goal" report: ISODEC, Essential Services Platform of Ghana, and the Alliance for Reproductive Health Rights.[15]

What explains this divergence between how democratic theorists conceptualize INGO advocacy and how many INGO advocates describe themselves? Are democratic theorists guilty of wearing representation-colored glasses—that is, of seeing representation wherever they look, even if it is not really there? Or are INGOs' claims to be partners rather than representatives merely a ploy to avoid being held to the demanding normative standard of "good representative"? In this article I show that both of these allegations are partially correct: humanitarian INGO advocacy often includes, but is rarely limited to, representation. Democratic theorists therefore overstate their case when they describe INGOs as (non-elected) representatives or as primarily makers of "representative claims."[16] Likewise, INGOs overstate their case when they deny engaging in representation at all. However, while representation and partnership are both prominent and seemingly promising descriptions, they are also poor starting places for conceptualizing INGO advocacy—or so I shall argue.

I assume that, to be legitimate, INGO advocacy must be consistent with norms of democracy, equality, and justice.[17] Because these terms are so vague, this assumption is not very controversial—but nor does it tell us much. The more controversial—and relevant—question is: how should these norms be interpreted and specified for the context of INGO advocacy? We often think of good representation as promoting or instantiating democratic norms, and good partnership as promoting or instantiating equality.[18] But the normative criteria associated with representation and partnership—i.e., familiar ideas about what it means to be a good representative and a good partner—do not provide adequate guidance for understanding what is required for INGO advocacy to be democratic and egalitarian. Nor do these criteria offer much guidance on what makes INGO advocacy just.

This article therefore asks: what conceptualization of INGO advocacy[19] would most help INGOs and their interlocutors to a) understand the most important and distinctive political ethical predicaments that INGO advocates regularly face; and b) navigate those predicaments in ways that are consistent with democratic, egalitarian, and justice-based norms? I argue that while INGO advocates do sometimes engage in representation or act as partners, for the purposes of normative evaluation we should conceptualize INGO advocacy not as representation or partnership, but rather as *having and exercising quasi-governmental power.* Correspondingly, the main normative standard to which INGO advocates should be held is that they *avoid misusing their power.*

This argument has implications not only for the political ethics of INGO advocacy, but also for democratic theory more generally. It reveals tensions between representation and democracy that are very different from those identified by direct, participatory, and strong democrats. It offers a counterweight to the recent "representative turn" in democratic theory, by asking not only whether we *can* read particular activities as representation, but also whether we *should* do so: what is revealed and elided by the representation lens?[20] Finally, the argument presented here reminds us that how we conceptualize activities and relationships influences what we notice about them, and the normative demands we place on those who engage in them. The choices we make, and fail to make, about how to conceptualize activities and relationships is therefore a political issue.

The next two sections of this article explain the limitations of the representation and partnership lenses, respectively. In Section III, I present my proposed alternative: the power lens. I describe four ways in which INGO advocates tend to misuse their power and propose four corresponding normative principles for avoiding these misuses. Section IV concludes. I illustrate my arguments with reference to the two cases of INGO advocacy described above.[21] Neither is an incontrovertible example of INGO advocacy gone wrong—or right. But Oxfam's advocacy on Ghana's NHIS appears to have been more consistent with democratic, egalitarian, and justice-based norms than ENOUGH and Global Witness's advocacy on Section 1502 of the Dodd-Frank bill. Thus, one burden of this article is to show that the power lens provides more precise and relevant concepts and criteria for explaining this judgment than do the representation and partnership lenses.

I. INGO Advocacy as Non-Electoral Representation

Since the mid-1990s, democratic theorists have become increasingly interested in political representation in general, and "non-electoral" representation in particular. They regularly cite INGO advocacy as a paradigmatic example of non-electoral representation, and describe INGOs as representatives and as makers of representative claims.[22] For example, the Stanford Encyclopedia of Philosophy's entry on "political representation" states that, "[g]iven the role that International Non-Governmental Organizations play in the international arena, the representatives of dispossessed groups are no longer located in the formal political arena of the nation-state."[23] Likewise, Urbinati and Warren write that "advocacy" organizations and "international non-governmental organizations" "claim to represent constituencies within public discourse and within collective decision-making bodies."[24]

The theorists making these arguments are primarily interested in using INGO advocacy to shed light on (non-electoral) representation, not vice versa. But once INGO advocacy is conceptualized as non-electoral representation, the normative question that inevitably arises is: how—if at all—can this advocacy be democratically legitimate? Michael Saward responds to this question by examining "a set of cases of non-elective representative claims" and developing "evaluative criteria against which the democratic acceptability of unelected would-be representatives might be assessed."[25] For Urbinati and Warren, "the challenges for democratic theory are to understand the nature of these [non-elected] representative claims and to assess which of them count as contributions to democracy and in what ways."[26]

These authors' understandings of both the descriptive content of INGO advocacy and the normative questions that it raises therefore seem to be shaped largely by their prior conceptualization of INGO advocacy as representation and/or as the making of representative claims. But, as I mentioned above, advocacy INGOs themselves usually deny being representatives or engaging in representation. In a survey, "less than 10%—of the [I]NGOs examined claimed to be 'speaking for' the South or Southern NGOs ..."[27] Jordan and Van Tuijl note that "many NGOs deny the concept of representation, pointing out that local communities, be they in the North or South, are able to adequately represent themselves."[28] Likewise, a recent search of the websites of several major INGOs yielded virtually no references to the word "represent" or to its cognates.[29]

What is going on here? I will argue that while democratic theorists are correct that INGOs sometimes engage in representation, there are three reasons why INGO advocacy should not be normatively evaluated primarily through a representation lens.

A. Representation as a source of conceptual disagreement

For the allegation that an INGO has represented badly to have any critical force, there must be agreement that the INGO has in fact engaged in representation (or promised to do so, as I discuss below). For instance, the allegation that Global Witness is a bad representative of Congolese miners provides little critical leverage if representing is not what Global Witness is doing. This suggests the need for a clear criterion or criteria for determining when representation is taking place. Even the "representative claim" approach, which emphasizes that representation can take diverse forms, acknowledges that, for judgments of the democratic legitimacy of representation to be relevant, a representative claim must have been made.[30]

We should not expect to find normative criteria for evaluating INGO advocacy that can be applied mechanistically, without judgment or disagreement. But we should search out criteria that direct this disagreement in constructive ways, for example, toward the effects or meaning of the advocacy activity being evaluated, rather than the definition of abstract concepts. Yet, efforts to apply the "good representative" criterion to INGOs are likely to founder on implicit and explicit disagreement about what representation is. Indeed, the literature on representation suggests several possible criteria for determining when representation has occurred, all of which yield different judgments about whether or not many instances of INGO advocacy are cases of representation, and none of which is clearly superior to the others.

One such criterion is *self-identification*. According to this criterion, an actor engages in representation if and only if it claims to be doing so, and is a representative if and only if it claims to be one. Urbinati and Warren's, and Montanaro's discussions of "self-authorizing" representatives allude to this criterion.[31] But while an INGO's claims to engage in representation or be a representative are *sufficient* to justify holding it to a standard of being a good representative, making self-identification a *necessary* condition for representation lets INGOs off the hook too easily.[32] As we have seen, many INGOs deny representing poor and marginalized groups. Accepting such denials at face value, as the self-identification criterion requires, means accepting that any INGO can say anything it wants to about the preferences or interests of any group, without being a bad representative of that group, so long as it denies representing that group.

While self-identification lets INGOs off the hook too easily, a second possible criterion for identifying when representation is occurring—*audience perception*—is too demanding. Rehfeld argues that representation occurs if and only if the audience to whom the putative representation is made thinks it occurred.[33] On this view, if readers of ENOUGH and Global Witness's websites think that these organizations represent Congolese miners, then ENOUGH and Global Witness represent Congolese miners to these readers. (They might not represent the miners *well*, but they do represent them.) The audience perception criterion, therefore, has the opposite shortcoming as the self-identification criterion: it puts no weight at all on the self-description of the putative representative. Using this criterion to identify cases of representation by INGOs, therefore, puts all of the power in the audience's hands, and denies INGOs any role in determining how their activities are conceptualized, and, thus, over the normative standards used to evaluate them.[34]

A third possible criterion for determining when representation is occurring—the *activity* criterion—asks whether the putative representative has made claims about the preferences, interests, or perspectives of some individual or group to a third party.[35] Because it focuses on activities rather than perceptions, this criterion offers a basis for contesting both an INGO's assertion that it is not a representative, and an audience's perception that that INGO is a representative. The main shortcoming of the activity criterion is that, even when an advocacy activity *can* be described as representation, this is often just one of several plausible descriptions of that activity. For example, Oxfam's advocacy about Ghana's health care system could be described as representation. But it could also be described as a set of empirical assertions, participation in public debate, or an effort to "press decision-makers to change policies and practices that reinforce poverty and injustice."[36] Given all of these possible descriptions, how do we know that the representation-description is the one from which we should derive normative standards for evaluating the activity in question? Often, we don't. In such cases, the activity criterion, like the other two criteria discussed above, fails to provide a basis for determining whether a given instance of INGO advocacy ought to be evaluated against a normative standard of "good representation."

B. INGO advocacy includes activities other than representation

A second reason why we should not conceptualize INGO advocacy as representation for the purposes of normative evaluation is that, regardless of what criterion/a we use to identify instances of representation, INGO advocacy includes both representing and other activities. If we evaluate INGO advocates based only on how well they represent, we overlook these other activities. This omission should be of tremendous concern to democratic theorists, who have reason to care about the democratic and anti-democratic potential of *all* aspects of INGO advocacy, not only representation.

Cases of INGO advocacy often involve one or more of three activities that are not (best described as) representation:

1   Assisting other actors, such as domestic governments, NGOs, and social movements, to better represent poor and marginalized groups (e.g., by providing them with information or connecting them with high-level officials). Oxfam describes this as "supporting organizational and institutional capacity strengthening."[37]
2   Pressuring elected officials to better represent their poor and marginalized constituents.[38] For example, the "Shared Goal" report argues that the current Ghanaian government "came to power in Ghana on a promise to deliver a truly universal health insurance scheme" that "still remain[s] unfulfilled."[39] This category of advocacy activities also includes efforts to "improve the workings of the mechanisms and agencies that regulate and frame the behavior of political representatives."[40]

3   Altering the participants in, or the content of, public debate. While representation can do this (e.g., by "calling forth" a constituency), the participants in and content of a debate can also be altered in other ways.[41] For example, Doctors Without Borders' "Starved for Attention" campaign attempted to alter the debate about malnutrition and food aid by arguing that US food aid was not nutritionally balanced.[42] This category of advocacy activity also includes "helping to bring together different actors to work on common problems," "generating and sharing knowledge," "promoting innovation and alternative solutions that may be brought to scale,"[43] and engaging in witnessing or *témoignage*.

To summarize, INGO advocacy includes a wide range of activities, including but not limited to representation, in different and fluid combinations. We therefore need normative criteria for evaluating INGO advocacy that are relevant to as wide a range of INGO advocacy activities as possible, including but not limited to representation (however defined).

C. INGO advocates are sometimes mediocre and second-best representatives

I have argued that we should not conceptualize INGO advocacy as representation because: a) the concept of representation fosters unproductive disagreement about what representation is; and b) whatever criteria are used to identify instances of representation, INGO advocacy includes activities other than representation. But what about situations in which INGO advocates clearly *are* engaged in representation (e.g., cases in which their activities are consistent with all extant criteria for determining when representation is occurring)? One might think that, in such cases, INGOs ought to be normatively evaluated based on how well they represent. I disagree.

Compared to domestic democratic governments, NGOs, CBOs, and social movements, humanitarian INGOs are often, though not always, mediocre representatives in absolute terms and "second-best" representatives in relative terms. This is so for at least three reasons. First, unlike democratic domestic governments and some NGOs, INGOs do not operate under the threat of formal or informal sanction by the people most directly affected by their advocacy. As Michael Edwards writes:

> What if the [I]NGOs who protested so loudly in Seattle turn out to be wrong in their assumptions about the future benefits that flow from different trading strategies—who pays the price? Not the [I]NGOs themselves, but farmers in the Third World who have never heard of Christian Aid or Save the Children, but who will suffer the consequences for generations.[44]

Second, unlike some domestic NGOs and CBOs, INGO advocates that engage in representation often lack a nuanced understanding of the political, social, economic, or religious dimensions of the issues they address.[45] Finally, many INGOs are headquartered in Northern countries and their high-level managers and decision-makers are mostly white people from those countries. When these INGOs represent people living in Southern countries, they can sometimes reproduce, at a symbolic level, and despite the sincere good intentions of the individuals involved, patterns of domination and usurpation by colonial and imperial powers.[46]

Of course, INGO advocates have many strengths as representatives: they often have sources of funding that domestic NGOs lack, and connections, experience, expertise and technical capacities that social movements do not have. They can also be less corrupt than domestic NGOs and governments. However, the three shortcomings just mentioned—lack of accountability to those most affected, limited understanding of the situation "on the ground," and lack of descriptive representation—are, if not constitutive of INGOs, then at least extremely difficult for INGOs to ameliorate. So, even though INGOs are sometimes better representatives than domestic governments, NGOs, or social movements in the short term, the latter actors' features, relationships and capacities mean that they have the potential to be first-best representatives *vis-à-vis* INGOs in the medium to long term.[47]

Because INGO advocates are often mediocre and second-best representatives, what is required for them to act consistently with democratic norms differs from what is required for a better-than-mediocre and first-best representative to act consistently with these norms. While for a first-best representative the best way to be democratic is often to represent as well as possible, for INGOs, being democratic often means *not* representing as well as possible themselves, but rather stepping back, making way for, pressuring, and/or supporting other, potentially superior representatives, such as domestic governments, NGOs, or social movements.[48] Characterizing an INGO as a representative or as engaged in representation is, therefore, problematic because it suggests that that INGO should strive to represent as well as possible.

One might think that INGO advocates should represent as well as possible when they are the best representatives currently available, and step back when they are second-best. But the key point about INGOs is that, because the question of whether they should engage in representation is always contingent on what other (first-best) actors are able and willing to do, they must *always maintain an orientation toward the activity of representing* that is different from the orientation of first-best representatives. While first-best representatives can throw themselves into representing as well as possible, INGOs must constantly ask themselves whether, how, and to what extent they should step back and support or pressure other representatives.[49]

II. INGO Advocacy as Partnership

The previous section described three limitations of the representation lens. Of these, the partnership lens avoids the first two: it does not invite unhelpful conceptual disagreement about the meaning of terms, and it is relevant to a wide range of advocacy activities. But like the representation lens, the partnership lens does not provide an adequate basis for elucidating the political and ethical implications of INGOs being second-best and mediocre representatives—or the political and ethical implications of them being second-best at aspects of INGO advocacy other than representation.[50] This is so in different ways for two distinct conceptions of partnership.

What I will call the "complementarity" conception of partnership reflects the everyday meaning of the word "partner." On this conception, being a good partner means treating one's partner(s) as equal(s), working with them on equal terms, and participating in a division of labor in which partners might perform different roles, but have equal standing. The complementarity conception can be found in Oxfam International's "Partnership Principles":

> Oxfam believes it is only through the collective effort of many actors (civil society, state, private sector and others) that this goal [of reducing poverty and injustice] can be achieved. Each of these actors has a role to play in accordance with its responsibility, legitimacy, its capacities and strengths ... These relationships are not about side-lining ... others; *they seek instead to foster complementarity and to harness the added value each may bring.*[51]

While initially appealing, this conception of partnership is inadequate because it does not acknowledge Oxfam's status as a sometimes second-best actor. To see this, consider a passage from Oxfam Canada's Partnership Policy, which invokes what I will call the "redundancy" conception of partnership:

> Whatever can be done with sufficient quality, effectiveness and efficiency by local organizations must be done by them ... Every effort will be made to live up to the aspiration embodied in OI Program Standard 6 which states that "effective partnering is a fundamental strategy through which *Oxfam seeks to become redundant.*"[52]

Unlike the complementarity conception, the redundancy conception of partnership acknowledges Oxfam's status as a sometimes second-best actor—with regard to not only representation, but also a wide range of other activities ("whatever can be done ... by local organizations must be done by them"). The redundancy conception, therefore, offers a picture of Oxfam's role that differs sharply from the picture offered by the complementarity conception: rather than complement local organizations indefinitely, Oxfam should continually support other actors and reduce its own involvement, until it eventually becomes redundant. The redundancy conception therefore acknowledges the long-term comparative advantage of some other actors over INGO advocates, in terms of accountability, local knowledge, and mirror representation. It also acknowledges that the differing strengths and capacities of INGOs and domestic NGOs are sometimes not happy coincidences to be exploited (e.g., "harnessing the added value each may bring"), but rather effects of injustices that should be overcome.[53]

Yet, while the complementarity conception relies on the ordinary language meaning of "partnership," and so, (despite its other flaws) has a rich set of associations attached to it that can contribute to practical judgment about what good partnership requires in a given case, the redundancy conception redefines partnership so dramatically that, in applying it, we have little more than the definition itself to go on. In blunt terms, the redundancy conception is normatively attractive, but it is not really partnership.

The partnership lens also has an additional shortcoming that the representation lens does not have: partnership pertains primarily to interactions between actors; it says little about the structural inequalities that condition these interactions. Yet, such inequalities are widespread in INGOs' relationships with NGOs, largely because NGOs rely on INGOs for funds. The effects of these inequalities can be mitigated in various ways. However, so long as NGOs depend on INGOs for funds, it is difficult for the relationships between them to be fully consistent with egalitarian norms, even if employees treat each other as equal partners in their everyday interactions.[54]

III. INGO Advocacy as the Exercise of Quasi-Governmental Power

Recall that our aim is to find a way of conceptualizing INGO advocacy that will yield helpful normative criteria for evaluating it—criteria that are keyed to the political and ethical predicaments that INGO advocates regularly face, and that shed light on how they might navigate these predicaments in ways that are consistent with democratic, egalitarian and justice-based norms. The shortcomings of the representation and partnership lenses suggest that such a conceptualization should ideally: 1) not be based on concepts such as representation, that are likely to generate endless unhelpful dispute; 2) apply to a wide range of INGO advocacy activities, including but not only representation (however defined); 3) address the political and ethical implications of INGOs being often second-best and mediocre representatives (and second-best and mediocre at other advocacy activities); and 4) attend to structural inequalities, not only interactions between actors. It should also preferably reflect ordinary usage of terms, such that prior discussion and examples can be brought to bear.

I think we can go a considerable way toward meeting these desiderata by conceptualizing INGO advocacy not as representation or partnership, but rather as *holding and exercising quasi-governmental power*.[55] "Governance" is, of course, a very broad term. By "governmental power" I here mean the power to shape the policies and practices of coercive institutions, either directly or by influencing public opinion. INGOs' governmental power is "quasi" because INGOs shape coercive policies and practices more than entirely non-governmental actors (such as individual Good Samaritans), but less than at least some full-fledged governmental actors (such as well-functioning democratic states).

If we conceive of INGO advocacy as holding and exercising quasi-governmental power, then the normative standard to which INGO advocates should be held is that they avoid excessively accumulating and misusing this power. This "power lens" helps us see that the unintended negative effects of INGO advocacy (such as those associated with Section 1502 of Dodd-Frank) are usually manifestations of ongoing and persistent—but not entirely unchangeable—power inequalities. That is, they are more systemic than random, one-off mishaps, but they are not so deeply entrenched that it is impossible for INGOs to escape or alter them.

In the rest of this section I argue that compared to the representation and partnership lenses, the power lens provides a more nuanced and penetrating account of how INGO advocacy enacts, supports, and undermines democratic, egalitarian, and justice-based norms. I focus on four ways in which INGO advocates tend to misuse their power, and propose four corresponding normative principles for avoiding these misuses, presented in roughly decreasing order of importance.[56]

A. Misuse of power #1: Significantly undermining the basic interests of poor and marginalized people

The most obvious way in which INGO advocates misuse their power is by undermining the interests of poor and marginalized people. Correspondingly, the most obvious specification of the normative requirement that INGOs avoid misusing their power is that they should not undermine the interests of poor and marginalized people. Of course, most policies and practices of coercive institutions—including policies and practices advocated by INGOs—benefit some poor people and undermine the interests of others. As Riddell notes, "in most cases [of advocacy], some poor people will tend to benefit, either relatively or absolutely, from the consequences of changes in the external policy regime, and some will tend to be adversely affected."[57] For this reason, requiring that INGOs avoid advocating for any policy that might make any poor or marginalized person even a little bit worse-off would likely exclude advocacy that is on the whole beneficial. So, by the *basic interests principle*

I will mean that: a) INGO advocates should not *significantly* undermine the *basic* interests of any poor or marginalized individual; and b) the anticipated net benefits of the policies for which INGOs advocate, and their advocacy itself, should outweigh the anticipated net negative effects of the policies for which they advocate and their advocacy itself for poor and marginalized groups.

The basic interests principle has several advantages: unlike the representation lens, it does not invite unhelpful conceptual disagreement, nor does it apply to only a narrow subset of INGOs' advocacy activities.[58] The main shortcoming of the basic interests principle is that it can be difficult to judge whether a particular instance of INGO advocacy has, in fact, significantly undermined the basic interests of poor and marginalized people. For example, the available evidence suggests that ENOUGH and Global Witness's advocacy on Section 1502 of Dodd-Frank violated the basic interests principle. Yet, this assessment is contested; it might well turn out to be incorrect as events unfold and/or as new information becomes available.

One seemingly promising way to get around this problem is to treat due diligence as a proxy for compliance with the basic interests principle. That is, even if it is difficult to tell whether an INGO has actually undermined the basic interests of poor and marginalized people, we can ask whether it took reasonable precautions to avoid doing so. However, determining what counts as due diligence by INGO advocates can also be difficult. For example, Global Witness has posted or linked to several reports about the situation in the DRC on its website, including a report summarizing a survey of the residents of seven mining communities.[59] If Global Witness did violate the basic interests principle, then either its seemingly extensive research did not amount to due diligence, or due diligence is a poor proxy for complying with the basic interests principle in this case.[60]

A final difficulty with the basic interests principle is that INGOs and (some members of) a poor or marginalized group can disagree about what (some members of) that group's interests are. Such disagreements can sometimes be resolved through discussion.[61] When discussion fails, democratic norms suggest that INGOs have not only a moral permission, but also a moral obligation, to shift their efforts and attention to groups with whom they have more of a shared vision (especially when the relevance of democratic norms are themselves the subject of the disagreement).[62]

B. Misuse of power #2: Displacing poor and marginalized groups and their (more) legitimate representatives

Now, suppose that ENOUGH and Global Witness turn out to be correct about Section 1502. We would then have to conclude that the policies that these INGOs supported, in fact, did not significantly undermine the basic interests of poor and marginalized people. But it would not necessarily follow from this that ENOUGH and Global Witness did not misuse their power. This is because, as I noted above, ENOUGH and Global Witness wrote the text of Section 1502 and shaped the lineup of speakers at the SEC hearings about the bill. Regardless of whether the policies that they supported significantly undermined the basic interests of vulnerable people, this constituted a different sort of misuse of power, a misuse on democratic procedural grounds.

The problem that this second type of misuse of power captures is difficult to see using the representation lens. The representation lens tells us that by helping to write Section 1502, and by shaping the lineup of speakers about the bill, ENOUGH and Global Witness represented mining communities poorly. They were not authorized by, nor accountable to these communities, nor did they accurately convey community members' wishes or interests to US officials. But ENOUGH and Global Witness might dispute this allegation, by saying: "We never claimed to represent the Congolese mining communities. We were simply offering our expert opinion on US legislation." For the reasons elucidated in Section I above, this statement is difficult to refute from within the representation framework.

Now consider another way of spelling out the intuition that there is something wrong with ENOUGH and Global Witness's actions. By writing Section 1502 and shaping the lineup of speakers at the SEC roundtable, ENOUGH and Global Witness helped to *displace* other actors—including those who, if given the chance, would likely have done a better job than ENOUGH and Global Witness of representing the Congolese miners who were going to be significantly affected by the bill. In short, the representation lens only enables us to say that ENOUGH and Global Witness failed to fulfill the positive requirements of the role of representative—a role that they claimed not to occupy. In contrast, the power lens enables us to say that ENOUGH and Global Witness failed to fulfill a negative duty: to avoid blocking (more) democratically legitimate representation by others.

This latter argument is not only more difficult to counter with the "but that's not what we (said we) were doing" response; it also offers a more perspicacious description of the problem. The problem is not that ENOUGH and Global Witness's statements and actions amounted to bad representation. Rather, it is that these INGOs—together with legislators and industry representatives— helped to silence *other* voices that could have contested their version of events.[63] Had these other voices been heard, ENOUGH and Global Witnesses' own statements and actions would likely have been less damaging.

This "displacement" of (more) legitimate representatives, or of actors who are better than INGOs at other aspects of advocacy, can have at least three kinds of negative effects. First, it can lead to policies that undermine the basic interests of vulnerable people (i.e., it can collapse into violations of the basic interests principle). This appears to have happened in the case of ENOUGH and Global Witness. As Seay writes:

> Many of the problems with Section 1502 and its unintended consequences were anticipated by Congolese civil society leaders and scholars and could have been avoided had their perspectives been integrated in the advocacy process [of US-based organizations] before strategies were released and advocacy activities had already been determined.[64]

Second, displacement can make it more difficult for actors that are potentially more legitimate representatives than INGOs, such as domestic NGOs based in poor countries, to hone their skills. For example, the Congolese civil society leader Eric Kajemba stated that: "[t]here are NGOs here in the East [of the DRC]—BEST, Pole Institute, there are many organizations working on this. I agree, we have problems, but some are trying to do good work."[65] By helping to displace Congolese NGOs from participating in debates about Section 1502, ENOUGH and Global Witness not only deprived US lawmakers of these NGOs' expertise; they also made it more difficult for these NGOs to gain the experience and connections that might have helped them overcome the "problems" to which Kajemba refers.

Third, displacement can prevent the involvement of actors whose involvement is intrinsically valuable. As Markell argues with reference to what he calls "usurpation," a crucial question is: "whatever it is that's happening, and however it's being controlled, to what extent is it happening *through you*, through your activity?"[66] For example, as I noted above, both Ghana's NHIA and the World Bank consistently referred to the "Shared Goal" report as "the Oxfam report," and to its arguments as "Oxfam's critique." This focus on Oxfam might have reduced the extent to which the things that were "happening" in Ghanaian civil society, such as vigorous debate about Ghana's NHIS, were happening through the Ghanaian NGOs.[67]

Unlike usurpation, which on Markell's account appears to be largely intentional and direct, displacement is often unintentional and indirect.[68] Oxfam did not intentionally push its Ghanaian "partners" aside. Insofar as the Ghanaian NGOs were displaced, this was due to the indirect and joint effects—some intended, some not—of Oxfam, Ghana's NHIA, the World Bank, and other entities. Historical conditions also played a role: the history of British colonialism in Ghana provided a rhetorical opening for the NHIA to attack the "Shared Goal" report as neo-colonial by attributing it to Oxfam.[69] In short, displacement encompasses both activities directly undertaken by a small number of identifiable actors, such as Global Witness and ENOUGH writing Section 1502 of Dodd-Frank and helping to shape the lineup of speakers about the bill, and the indirect and joint effects of many different actors interacting under conditions of inequality, such as the possible displacement of the Ghanaian NGOs from a more prominent role in the debates prompted by the "Shared Goal" report.

Given these negative effects of displacement, I propose a *minimize displacement principle*: INGOs should minimize the extent to which they displace vulnerable groups and their (more) legitimate representatives and advocates, taking into consideration other ethical constraints. This principle requires INGO advocates to address two questions: how much should they undertake an advocacy activity themselves versus how much should they step back; and insofar as they do step back, what form(s) should that stepping back take (e.g., active support of a first-best actor, leaving the scene, or something else)? The minimize displacement principle does not provide specific answers to these questions, but it crystallizes them in a way that the representation and partnership lenses do not. The minimize displacement principle can also be applied to a wide range of advocacy activities (not only representation); it addresses issues of structural inequality, and it attends to the implications of INGOs being mediocre and second-best actors. While admittedly complicated, it does not appear to invite unhelpful disagreement about abstract concepts. Unlike the redundancy conception of partnership, it does not contravene ordinary language and it identifies a harm that INGOs should avoid (i.e., displacement).

C. Misuse of power #3: Cultivating and retaining the capacity for arbitrary interference

What if ENOUGH and Global Witness had been asked by Congressional staffers to help write Section 1502 and shape the lineup of speakers at the hearings about the bill, but declined to do so, citing other commitments? One might think that under these circumstances, ENOUGH and Global Witness would not have misused their power. Indeed, they would not have significantly undermined the basic interests of poor and marginalized persons or displaced anyone. But, by not questioning the legitimacy of the request, they would have retained and reinforced their *capacity to arbitrarily interfere* with vulnerable groups. In so doing, they would have misused their power in a third way, albeit one that is milder and more passive than the two misuses of power just described.

By "capacity to arbitrarily interfere," I mean the capacity (i.e., the power) to take actions that significantly affect others, without being pressured to ensure that those actions track the interests and preferences of those significantly affected ("track" here means "take into account" not "act consistently with").[70] Even if ENOUGH and Global Witness had declined to help write Section 1502, they still would have had the capacity to interfere arbitrarily with the Congolese mining communities and with domestic NGOs based in the DRC. This capacity appears to have had real effects: as Congolese civil society leader Eric Kajemba stated, "we are not very happy with Global Witness or ENOUGH, but we feel they are very influential, and we are ready to work with them. On the other hand, we are *also* afraid of our government and what they are doing."[71] On one plausible reading of this statement, Kajemba is suggesting that the Congolese NGOs were afraid of ENOUGH and Global Witness, presumably because they are "very influential." That is, it was these organizations' *capacities* to act, not only what they actually did, that constrained the Congolese NGOs.

The capacity to arbitrarily interfere is objectionable on egalitarian grounds because, when A has the capacity to interfere arbitrarily with B, B has an incentive to "toady" and "fawn" to A, in order to stay on A's good side.[72] In his well-known elucidation of this idea, Philip Pettit focuses on cases in which the threatened interference is an intentional or quasi-intentional effort to make other people's lives worse.[73] In contrast, when INGOs interfere arbitrarily with poor and marginalized groups or domestic NGOs, they usually do not intend to make anyone's lives worse. But INGOs' capacity to interfere arbitrarily with these groups still gives those groups a reason to "work with" INGOs, in Kajemba's terms. Thus, a third normative principle for evaluating INGO advocacy is that INGOs—and other actors—should *minimize INGOs' capacity to arbitrarily interfere with vulnerable groups and those groups' (more) legitimate representatives*, again taking into consideration other ethical commitments. This principle does not invite conceptual disagreement, can be applied to a wide range of advocacy activities, and addresses structural inequalities.

Can INGOs really be held morally responsible for having the *capacity* to interfere arbitrarily with vulnerable groups and their (more) legitimate representatives, as opposed to actually interfering with them? I think that they can be, insofar as they intentionally or knowingly cultivate and/or retain this capacity. For example, while US politicians and industry leaders bear some responsibility for ENOUGH and Global Witness's capacity to help write Section 1502 of the Dodd-Frank bill and influence the lineup of speakers at the SEC hearings about the bill, it appears that ENOUGH and Global Witness also sought to develop their capacity to do these things. Either way, attending to advocates' capacity for arbitrary interference requires expanding our focus beyond advocates themselves, to also include other actors and the contexts in which advocates operate.

For example, in contrast to ENOUGH and Global Witness, Oxfam does not seem to have had the capacity to interfere arbitrarily with the Ghanaian people or Ghanaian NGOs. This appears to be in large part because Ghana is a stable and inclusive democracy with a vibrant civil society.[74] The "Shared Goal" report was, therefore, actively debated and criticized, not taken as marching orders by Ghanaian NGOs, the Ghanaian people, or the Ghanaian government (quite the contrary!). In other words, there were strong democratic institutional constraints on Oxfam's capacity to influence domestic public policy in Ghana. Whereas the representation lens prompts us to look for accountability mechanisms that do or could constrain Oxfam, the misuse of power lens casts a much wider net. It enables us to see that other actors—including Ghanaian government officials and Ghanaian NGOs—contested, diluted, contextualized, and qualified Oxfam's claims in ways that constrained Oxfam's power and rendered the effects of its advocacy more consistent with democratic norms, even in the absence of formal (or informal) accountability mechanisms. No one elected Oxfam, but Oxfam was constrained in other ways.

D. Misuse of power #4: "Low Balling"

Oxfam has thus far fared well in our analysis: while it might have contributed unintentionally to the displacement of Ghanaian NGOs, it seems not to have violated the basic interests principle. It also had limited capacity to interfere arbitrarily with poor Ghanaians or Ghanaian NGOs. But what should we make of the circumstances surrounding the commissioning and release of the "Shared Goal" report? The agreement between Oxfam and the Ghanaian NGOs was that Oxfam would assist with funding, but that all four organizations would co-author the report together, on equal terms.[75]

The literature on INGO-NGO "partnerships" suggests that in this type of arrangement, the INGO (in this case, Oxfam) has more power. (As the saying goes, "he who pays the piper calls the tune.") While a Ghanaian consultant wrote the report, the partnership literature predicts that Oxfam would have had more say than the Ghanaian NGOs in determining—if not the content of the report—then its scope and the questions it addressed.[76] An official from Oxfam-Ghana stated that this was *not* the case. She argued that "[the report] was handled equally." "Round table discussions were held with various stakeholders in health, trades unions, civil society etc. Ideas were shared, discussed and interrogated at various stages of the research process. As a result, the report was "fairly [*sic*] ghananian."[77] An official from a Ghanaian NGO agreed with the Oxfam official's assessment in some respects, but also noted the difficulty for both the Ghanaian NGOs and Oxfam in retaining their identities as individual organizations while working together. This official thought that the correct model for Oxfam was to "lead from behind."[78]

Without trying to definitively characterize the relationship between Oxfam and the Ghanaian NGOs, I want to investigate the implications of one possibility: that while the Ghanaian NGOs viewed their arrangement with Oxfam as the best available option under the circumstances, they would not have accepted it under better conditions (e.g., had they been able to fully fund the report on their own).

Suppose, then, that the Ghanaian NGOs accepted Oxfam's offer, but that this offer was the most appealing of the Ghanaian NGOs' options in part due to structural and/or historic injustices (such as the history of British colonialism in Ghana). Philosophers call offers such as this "mutually advantageous exploitative" (MAE) offers. An MAE offer is one in which "*A* gets *B* to agree to a mutually advantageous transaction to which *B* would not have agreed under better or perhaps more just background conditions …"[79] Because MAE offers stand at some remove from other forms of exploitation, I will here call them "lowball" offers.[80] Lowball offers present a seeming paradox. On the one hand, these offers are structurally very similar to price gouging, and it is widely accepted that price gouging—e.g., charging $100 for a $15 shovel after a snowstorm—is unethical, because it involves reaping a windfall profit at the expense of someone who is especially vulnerable through no fault of her own. But on the other hand, someone who accepts a lowball offer is presumably better off than she would have been without the offer. Assuming that Oxfam is under no obligation to make the Ghanaian NGOs any offer at all, how could it be unethical for it to make them an offer that, if accepted, would make the Ghanaian NGOs better off than they would have been without the offer?[81]

I think the answer to this question is that, by entering into what philosophers call a "special relationship" with the Ghanaian NGOs (by making them an offer), Oxfam takes on a responsibility to treat the Ghanaian NGOs in a particular way.[82] This is why Oxfam does not have a duty to make an offer to the Ghanaian NGOs, but if it does make them an offer, it should not try to extract the best deal possible if doing so requires taking advantage of historic and ongoing injustices in ways that makes things worse for the Ghanaian NGOs than they could otherwise reasonably be.[83] To do so would be a misuse of power on Oxfam's part. The representation and partnership lenses offer little traction on this issue.

While lowball offers are misuses of power, they are not necessarily unjustified, all things considered. Lowball offers can sometimes be in the best interest of poor and marginalized people—for example when domestic NGOs are corrupt or inefficient, or lack the capacity or motivation to deal with broader issues (such as health care policies in other countries). I therefore propose that INGOs should adopt a principle of *wariness about making lowball offers*.[84] The main strength of this principle is that it addresses issues of structural inequality.

E. The exercise of power lens

The four principles just described together meet the four desiderata discussed above (see Figure 13.1 below). As such, they provide a plausible and attractive specification of what it means for INGO advocates to avoid

		Desiderata			
		Does not invite unhelpful conceptual disagreement	Relevant to a wide range of INGO advocacy activities	Accounts for INGOs being second-best and mediocre representatives	Addresses structural inequality
Principles derived from the power lens	Do not undermine basic interests	X	X		
	Minimize displacement	X	X	X	X
	Minimize capacity for arbitrary interference	X	X		X
	Be wary of lowball offers		X		X

Figure 13.1   Desiderata met by each of the four principles suggested by the power lens

misusing their power, and so to act consistently with democratic, egalitarian and justice-based norms.

Although it is framed as a negative duty, the requirement that INGO advocates avoid misusing their power is still very demanding; complying with the four principles outlined above would require many INGOs to significantly alter their existing practices. But recall that these principles are meant to function as possible specifications of the misuse of power lens; they should not be construed as hard-and-fast rules for normatively evaluating INGO advocacy. This is, first, because these principles are not exhaustive: INGOs almost certainly misuse their power in ways other than those discussed here. There are also other standards relevant to normative evaluation of INGO advocacy that do not involve the misuse of power, most notably whether INGOs are effective at achieving their (justified) objectives.[85]

In addition, while I have presented these principles in what I take to be roughly descending order of importance, this is not a lexical ordering: severe displacement might be more objectionable than a modest violation of the basic interests principle, for example. Likewise, acting consistently with these principles has costs, and the principles say nothing about how these costs should be traded off against compliance with the principles. In particular, INGOs can sometimes face conflicts between not misusing their own power, and preventing misuses or abuses of power by other actors. For example, if Ghana's NHIS really is much less effective than Ghana's NHIA claims, and if other countries really are on the verge of adopting versions of this scheme, then perhaps some displacement of Ghanaian NGOs is a reasonable price to pay to ensure that the truth about Ghana's NHIS emerges. The power lens helps to clarify what is at stake in these trade-offs, even though it does not yield all-things-considered judgments about which trade-offs INGOs should accept.

Finally, while there are, no doubt, situations in which INGOs are justified in misusing their own power in order to prevent gross abuses of power by others, the case of Section 1502 reveals the danger of this highly consequentialist logic. Global Witness and ENOUGH might argue that they slightly misused their own power over Congolese NGOs in order to prevent far greater abuses of the Congolese people by armed groups. But in so doing, Global Witness and ENOUGH helped to silence the activists and scholars who were arguing that reducing the trade in conflict minerals would, in fact, have little effect on the violence in the DRC.

IV. Conclusion

In this article, I have asked what conceptualization of INGO advocacy would most help INGOs and their interlocutors to understand the ethical predicaments that INGO advocates regularly face, and to navigate those predicaments in ways that are consistent with democratic, egalitarian, and justice-based norms. I argued that for INGO advocates, being democratic sometimes does not mean representing as well as possible, and being egalitarian is not merely a matter of acting as an excellent partner. Rather, given the kinds of actors that INGOs are and the contexts in which they operate—given, especially, that they are often second-best and mediocre representatives—consistency with these norms is more precisely and relevantly cashed out in terms of not misusing power. Although there are many intersections among democratic, egalitarian, and justice-based norms, such that it is difficult to talk about them in isolation from each other, the foregoing analysis suggests that for INGO advocates, being just means, at a minimum, not undermining the basic interests of poor and marginalized people and being wary of making lowball offers that exploit historic or ongoing injustices. Being democratic means minimizing the extent to which INGO advocates displace poor and marginalized groups, and those groups' (more) legitimate representatives, from contexts in which coercive policies likely to significantly affect those groups are being shaped. Being democratic, for INGO advocates, also means minimizing the extent to which they cultivate and retain the capacity to interfere arbitrarily with these groups. Finally, being egalitarian for INGOs means minimizing their capacity for arbitrary interference and being wary of making lowball offers.[86]

This, then, is why it is beside the point that no one elected Oxfam: the normative challenges posed by INGO advocacy are far more diverse—but also addressable in a wider variety of ways—than *The Economist*'s rhetorical question "Who Elected Oxfam?" suggests. This question implies that bad representation is the problem and elections, or other forms of accountability, are the solution. But as we have seen, Global Witness and ENOUGH did not only represent badly; they also undermined the basic interests of poor and marginalized people and cultivated and exercised the capacity to interfere arbitrarily with Congolese NGOs. Oxfam (possibly) and Global Witness and ENOUGH (almost certainly) displaced poor and marginalized people and/or their (more) legitimate representatives. Oxfam might have made a lowball offer to Ghanaian NGOs that took advantage of historic injustice. These issues go far beyond bad representation. Yet, possible strategies for addressing them go far beyond elections.

When one has a hammer, everything can look like a nail. Likewise, when one studies representation, everything can look like representation. I have argued that democratic theorists, especially theorists of representation, need to take off our representation-colored glasses and look anew at advocacy through the lens of power, and not only representation. In so doing we will not only see important aspects of INGO advocacy that are not representation; we will also see representation itself in a new light.

Notes

* For comments on the present and/or a previous version of this article, I thank Elizabeth Arkush, Lawrie Balfour, Colin Bird, Suzanne Dovi, Chad Flanders, Harrison Frye, Archon Fung, Pete Furia, Michael Kates, Colin Kielty, George Klosko, Jane Mansbridge, Charles Mathewes, Kirstie McClure, Jennifer Petersen, Allison Pugh, Andrew Rehfeld, Michael Saward, Jalane Schmidt, Melissa Schwartzberg, Molly Scudder, Denise Walsh, Ron Watson, Kit Wellman, Stephen White and audiences at the University of Virginia Political Theory Colloquium, Wellesley College, Washington University of St. Louis, Harvard University, the 2008 American Political Science Association Annual Meeting, the 2008 conference "Beyond Elections: The Democratic Legitimacy of New Forms of Representation" at Princeton University, and the 2012 Association for Political Theory Conference. Two anonymous referees for this journal provided exceptionally helpful feedback. Claire Timperley provided excellent comments and research assistance. All errors and omissions are of course my own. For a more extended discussion of the themes addressed in this article, see Chapter 5 of my book, *Between Samaritans and States: Political Ethics for Humanitarian INGOs*, forthcoming from Oxford University Press. This article is dedicated to Gertrude Kleinberg and to the memory of Iris Marion Young, both advocates committed to fighting misuses of power.
1 "Angry and effective," *The Economist*, September 21, 2000, pp. 85–7.

2 Full text available at: <http://www.sec.gov/about/laws/wallstreetreform-cpa. pdf>, pp. 838–43.

3 "John Prendergast, The Enough Project, and Global Witness are directly responsible for this completely predictable havoc, as are the American legislators and industry personnel who took their testimony as gospel, let them write section 1502 of the legislation, and ignored dissenting voices in the debate over the minerals"; Laura Seay, "The DRC minerals mess," August 4, 2011, <www.texasinafrica.blogspot.com> (accessed February 20, 2013). Because this issue is ongoing and contentious, much of the available information comes from blog posts and other unpublished sources.

4 "[M]embers of Congress like Jim McDermott and their staffs seem to have taken Enough's word at face value, going so far as to let the advocacy organization choose most of the witnesses at hearings on the Dodd-Frank measure, which meant that any dissenting voices—Congolese or American— went mostly unheard"; Laura Seay, "The Dodd-Frank catastrophe," August 8, 2011, <www. texasinafrica.blogspot.com> (accessed February 20, 2013). ENOUGH claims that it "wasn't involved with this event," but acknowledges that "several members of our team attended the hearing"; John Bagwell, "Hijacking the Congo conflict minerals narrative," May 22, 2012, <http://www.raisehopeforcongo.org/blog/ post/hijacking-congo-conflict-minerals-narrative> (accessed February 20, 2013).

5 Congolese civil society organizations estimated that 5–12 million people (miners and their dependents) have been significantly negatively affected by Section 1502; Laura Seay, "What's wrong with Dodd-Frank 1502? Conflict minerals, civilian livelihoods, and the unintended consequences of western advocacy," *Center for Global Development*, Working Paper 284, January 2012. See also: David Aronson, "How Congress devastated Congo," *New York Times*, August 7, 2011; Jason Stearn's response to Aronson, "Thoughts about conflict minerals," August 10, 2011, <http://congosiasa.blogspot.com/2011/08/thoughts-about-conflict-minerals.html> (accessed February 20, 2013); Mvemba Dizolele, "The costs and consequences of Dodd-Frank Section 1502: impacts on America and the Congo," May 10, 2012, <http://dizolele.com/?p=958> (accessed February 20, 2013); and "Conflict minerals in the Congo: let's be frank about Dodd-Frank," August 22, 2011, <http://www.huffingtonpost.com/mvemba-dizolele/conflict-minerals-congo-dodd-frank_b_933078.html> (accessed February 20, 2013).

6 Séverine Autesserre, "Dangerous tales: dominant narratives on the Congo and their unintended consequences," *African Affairs*, 111 (2012), 202–22.

7 See the sources cited above, especially Seay, "What's wrong with Dodd-Frank 1502?" The ENOUGH Project disagrees with this assessment. (Sasha Lezhnev, "What conflict minerals legislation is actually accomplishing in Congo," August 9, 2011, <http:// www.huffingtonpost.com/sasha-lezhnev/what-conflict-minerals-le_b_922566.html> (accessed February 20, 2013)) However, a more recent ENOUGH report on the effects of Dodd-Frank paints an only somewhat positive picture: "From Congress to Congo," August 7, 2012, <http://www.enoughproject.org/files/ConflictMinerals_ CongoFINAL.pdf> (accessed February 20, 2013). While it is impossible to adjudicate definitively among these positions, one reason to give more weight to those critical of Section 1502 is that, as Autesserre ("Dangerous tales") explains, ENOUGH and Global Witness had economic and institutional incentives to accept and perpetuate the idea that conflict minerals are a main driver of the DRC conflict.

8 Alliance for Reproductive Health Rights et al., "Achieving a shared goal: access to free health care in Ghana," 2011, <http://oxf.am/Z2D> (accessed November 06, 2012), pp. 7, 8 and 25. (The NHIA implied a coverage rate of 62%, but the report argued that it "could be as low as 18%.")

9 Alliance for Reproductive Health Rights et al., "Achieving a shared goal," p. 8; George Schieber et al., "Health financing in Ghana at a crossroads," *World Bank* (2012), p. ii.

10 Schieber, "Health financing in Ghana at crossroads," p. 8.

11 National Health Insurance Authority, "NHIA Position on OXFAM/ISODEC report on free universal health care in Ghana," March 17, 2011, <http://www.ghanaweb.com/GhanaHomePage/NewsArchive/artikel.php?ID=205271> (accessed February 20, 2013).

12 Schieber, "Health financing in Ghana at crossroads," p. 8.

13 Ibid., pp. 8, 9, 66, 82, 108, 109.

14 Roger Riddell, *Does Foreign Aid Really Work?* (Oxford: Oxford University Press, 2007), ch. 17. Unless otherwise stated, by "INGO" I mean INGOs working on these issues, in particular those headquartered in wealthy Western countries.

15 See discussion of the "Shared Goal" report on Oxfam's website: <http://www.oxfam.org/en/policy/achieving-shared-goal-ghana-healthcare> (accessed June 6, 2013). There is a large critical literature about "partnership" in the field of international development. See, e.g., Alan Fowler, "Beyond partnership: getting real about NGO relationships in the aid system," *IDS Bulletin*, 31 (2000), 1–13; Rita Abrahamsen, "The power of partnerships in global governance," *Third World Quarterly*, 25 (2004), 1453–67 and the citations therein.

16 Michael Saward, *The Representative Claim* (Oxford: Oxford University Press, 2010).

17 I focus on these three norms because they are often invoked by INGOs themselves, and so can provide the basis for an immanent critique. But even when INGOs do not explicitly adopt them, these norms have some relevance to INGOs. For example, even INGOs that pursue humanitarian aims rather than political justice must act justly rather than unjustly.

18 David Plotke, "Representation is democracy," *Constellations*, 4 (1997), 19–34; Nadia Urbinati, "Representation as advocacy: a study of democratic deliberation," *Political Theory*, 28 (2000), 758–86.

19 By "advocacy" I mean the activities that INGOs themselves describe as "advocacy" or "campaigning." While describing these activities as advocacy is not neutral among possible normative criteria for evaluating them, the term has fewer normative criteria embedded in it than "representation" and "partnership" do.

20 Sofia Näsström, "Where is the representative turn going?" *European Journal of Political Theory*, 10 (2011), 501–10.

21 I don't claim that these cases are typical of INGO advocacy in general. In social scientific terms, my use of them is "hypothesis-generating."

22 Some right- and left-leaning critics of INGOs, legal scholars, and scholar-practitioners also describe INGOs as non-elected representatives. See Paul Wapner, "Introductory essay: paradise lost? NGOs and global accountability," *Chicago Journal of International Law*, 155 (2002), 155–60 and other articles in this issue; Erik

Bluemel, "Overcoming NGO accountability concerns in international governance," *Brooklyn Journal of International Law*, 31 (2005), 139–206; and Warren Nyamugasira, "NGOs and advocacy: how well are the poor represented?" *Development in Practice*, 8 (1998), 297–308.

23 Suzanne Dovi, "Political representation," *Stanford Encyclopedia of Philosophy*, ed. Edward Zalta, <http://plato.stanford.edu/entries/political-representation/>.

24 Nadia Urbinati and Mark Warren, "The concept of representation in contemporary democratic theory," *Annual Review of Political Science*, 11 (2008), 387–412. See also Michael Saward, "Authorisation and authenticity: representation and the unelected," *Journal of Political Philosophy*, 17 (2009), 1–22; Joshua Busby, "Bono made Jesse Helms cry: Jubilee 2000, debt relief, and moral action in international politics," *International Studies Quarterly*, 51 (2007), 247–75; and Laura Montanaro, "The democratic legitimacy of self-appointed representatives," *Journal of Politics*, 74 (2012), 1094–107.

25 Saward, "Authorisation and authenticity." Saward discusses many types of non-elected actors, including INGOs. See also Montanaro, "The democratic legitimacy of self-appointed representatives."

26 Urbinati and Warren, "The concept of representation." See also Terry MacDonald, *Global Stakeholder Democracy* (New York: Oxford University Press, 2008), p. 163.

27 Alan Hudson, "NGOs' transitional advocacy networks: from 'legitimacy' to 'political responsibility'?" *Global Networks*, 1 (2001), 331–52. I doubt that INGOs deny being representatives for legal reasons (e.g., to retain their 501c3 status), because they still make partisan political claims. Also, some INGOs, such as Oxfam America, have separate advocacy arms for precisely this reason.

28 Lisa Jordan and Peter van Tuijl, "Political responsibility in NGO advocacy," *World Development*, 28 (2000), 2051–65.

29 A search for "represent," "representation," and "representative" on the web pages of 15 of the largest humanitarian and development INGOs in August 2012 revealed no instances of INGOs claiming to represent poor and marginalized people. Details of analysis on file with the author.

30 Saward, *The Representative Claim*, ch. 6.

31 Urbinati and Warren, "The concept of representation"; Montanaro, "The democratic legitimacy of self-appointed representatives."

32 This appears to be why Montanaro's definition of "self-authorizing" representatives does not require that actors describe themselves as representing.

33 Andrew Rehfeld, "Towards a general theory of political representation," *Journal of Politics*, 68 (2006), 1–21. What about the perceptions of the people who are (allegedly) being represented? Their belief that they are being (well-) represented is a necessary condition for *democratically legitimate* representation, but it is neither necessary nor sufficient for representation itself (unless they are coterminous with the audience).

34 An INGO's protestation that it does not represent poor and marginalized groups might well lead some audiences to view that INGO as an especially good representative of those groups, precisely because of its humility in claiming not to speak for others.

35 Saward, "Authorisation and authority," esp. p. 305. Montanaro, in "The democratic legitimacy of self-appointed representatives," p. 1096, describes this activity as "aim[ing] to provide political presence for a constituency to an audience."

36 Oxfam International's website at: <http://www.oxfam.org/en/grow/about/what> (accessed August 20, 2012).

37 Oxfam International, "Working together: Oxfam's partnership principles," <http://www.oxfam.org/en/about/what/partnership-principles> (accessed November 6, 2012). See also Jordan and Van Tuijl, "Political responsibility in NGO advocacy."

38 An INGO that pressures elected representatives on behalf of a group can also be described as representing that group. But when an INGO pressures an elected representative to do something for which that representative has already been democratically authorized (e.g., Oxfam holding elected Ghanaian officials to their campaign promises), the criteria for democratic legitimacy suggested by the representation-description are less relevant than they are when an INGO pressures elected representatives to do something for which these representatives have not already been democratically authorized (e.g., Global Witness and ENOUGH pressing US Congresspersons to include Section 1502 in the Dodd-Frank bill).

39 Alliance for Reproductive Health Rights et al., "Achieving a shared goal," p. 8.

40 Enrique Peruzzotti, "Civil society, representation and accountability: restating current debates on the representativeness and accountability of civic association," *NGO Accountability: Politics, Principles and Innovations*, eds. Lisa Jordan and Peter van Tuijl (London: Earthscan, 2007), pp. 43–60, at p. 47. In contrast, Montanaro, "The democratic legitimacy of self-appointed representatives," at p. 1097, cites Oxfam's claim that it "seek[s] to influence the powerful to ensure that poor people can ... have a say in decisions that affect them" as evidence that Oxfam is a self-identified representative.

41 Cf. Montanaro, "The democratic legitimacy of self-appointed representatives"; Saward, *The Representative Claim*.

42 Starved for Attention, "Malnutrition," <http://www.starvedforattention.org/about-malnutrition.php> (accessed October 1, 2012).

43 Oxfam International, "Working together."

44 Michael Edwards, *NGO Rights and Responsibilities: A New Deal for Global Governance* (London: Foreign Policy Centre, 2000). Also, see Clifford Bob, "NGO representation and accountability: a skeptical view," *NGOs, International Security and Global Governance*, Johns Hopkins University, October 9, 2007, <http://ssrn.com/abstract=1023021>. In "Political responsibility in NGO advocacy," Jordan and van Tuijl describe local NGOs in India having the capacity to influence international activists by threatening to cut them off from important information, but such cases are rare.

45 Jordan and van Tuijl, "Political responsibility in NGO advocacy."

46 More generally, insofar as INGOs are poor "descriptive" representatives of poor and marginalized groups, they cannot provide the epistemic, psychological, symbolic, and other benefits that such representation provides; Jane Mansbridge, "Should blacks represent blacks and women represent women? A contingent 'yes'," *Journal of Politics*, 61 (1999), 628–57. See also Linda Alcoff, "The problem

of speaking for others," *Cultural Critique*, 20 (1991–1992), 5–32. This division of advocacy groups between "Northern" and "Southern" is an oversimplification. For example, Justice Africa is based in London, but is "run by, for and with Africans and African communities; guided by the Pan-African slogan: '*Nothing for me without me*'" (italics in original); see <http://www.justiceafrica.org/about-us/> (accessed October 31, 2012). The inequalities here can be material as well as symbolic, as the jobs, prestige, and expertise associated with advocacy flow to advocates from already wealthy countries.

47 Jordan and van Tuijl, in "Political responsibility in NGO advocacy."

48 Suzanne Dovi, "In praise of exclusion," *Journal of Politics*, 71 (2009), 1172–86.

49 Stepping back and supporting first-best actors might seem unnecessary for humanitarian INGOs, such as Doctors Without Borders, that speak out against gross violations of human rights that they witness directly. But it is still appropriate for INGOs that do this sort of work to consult widely and carefully with those affected, regarding the possible effects of speaking out. For an example of what happens when INGOs do not do this, see Claire Magone, Michael Newman and Fabrice Weissman, *Humanitarian Negotiations Revealed: The MSF Experience* (New York: Columbia University Press, 2011), pp. 45–6.

50 The representation lens does not acknowledge this either because it does not acknowledge that there *are* aspects of INGO advocacy other than representation.

51 Oxfam International, "Working together" (my italics). This passage is also in Oxfam Canada, "Partnership policy," February 25, 2011, <http://www.oxfam.ca/who-we-are/partnership-policy> (both accessed November 06, 2012). See also Jordan and van Tuijl's discussion of "cooperative" advocacy in "Political responsibility in NGO advocacy."

52 Oxfam Canada, "Partnership policy" (my italics). All but the last sentence of this passage can also be found in Oxfam International's Partnership Policy. The fact that the last sentence refers to an OI document suggests that OI also recognizes the attractiveness of the redundancy conception.

53 For example, an INGO's inability to decipher an article in a local Indian newspaper and a local Indian NGO's inability to decipher a highly technical World Bank report are in a sense symmetrical, but they are also the result of historic and ongoing inequalities. Cf. Jordan and van Tuijl, "Political responsibility in NGO advocacy."

54 Cf. ibid., describing an advocacy campaign that was successful in part because the NGOs did not receive funding from their INGO partners. But see Tigenoah's assessment of Oxfam in Ghana below.

55 This conceptualization does not deny that INGOs sometimes do, and sometimes should, act as representatives and partners; it only states that, for the purposes of normative evaluation, we should view them under the more general rubric of quasi-governmental power.

56 These principles also indicate that other actors and institutions can be evaluated based on how well they constrain INGOs from misusing their power. Moreover, INGOs can be evaluated based on the degree to which they support external constraints on their own power.

57 Riddell, *Does Foreign Aid Really Work?*, pp. 300–1.

58 While it might generate discussion of the *content* of people's basic interests, it is unlikely to lead to extended debate about of what an "interest" is.

59 Global Witness, "Artisanal mining communities in eastern DRC: seven baseline studies in the Kivus," August 22, 2012, <http://www.globalwitness.org/library/artisanal-mining-communities-eastern-drc-seven-baseline-studies-kivus> (accessed October 1, 2012).

60 Due diligence is also a poor proxy for not undermining basic interests when actors have an incentive to undertake a particular course of action, regardless of the consequences. Seay, "What's wrong with Dodd-Frank 1502?" and Autesserre, "Dangerous tales," argue that this was the case with ENOUGH and Global Witness.

61 Of course, "agreements" achieved under conditions of extreme inequality or duress are highly suspect.

62 While paternalism can sometimes be justified in severe public health emergencies (e.g., when medical experts and the local population disagree about how a disease spreads), it is generally not justified in the context of advocacy. The situation is more complicated when an especially oppressed minority within a group for which an INGO wants to advocate wants the INGO to be involved, but the majority within the group does not.

63 Seay, "What's Wrong with Dodd-Frank 1502?" and Seay, "The Dodd-Frank catastrophe."

64 Seay, "What's wrong with Dodd-Frank 1502?"

65 Interview with Eric Kajemba (translated from French), <http://congosiasa. blogspot.co.nz/2011/08/interview-with-eric-kajemba-on-conflict.html> (accessed September 30, 2012).

66 Patchen Markell, "The insufficiency of non-domination," *Political Theory*, 36 (2008), 9–36.

67 The story here is complicated. Oxfam's participation created more public discussion of the "Shared Goal" report (both within Ghana and internationally) than there would have been if Oxfam hadn't been involved; the Ghanaian NGOs participated in those discussions (Shang-Quartey, personal communication). However, much of the public narrative around the report, especially outside of Ghana, focused on Oxfam's role in it, rather than on the issues of concern to the Ghanaian NGOs. See Amanda Glassman, "Really Oxfam? Really?" March 14, 2011, <http://blogs.cgdev.org/globalhealth/2011/03/really-oxfam-really.php> (accessed February 20, 2013). But see also substantive responses (in comments section) by Apoya and Shang-Quartey. Duncan Green reports that "The [Ghanaian NGO] partners were actually pretty hacked off at this being described as an 'Oxfam report', and rightly so"; Duncan Green, "Really CDC, really?" March 25, 2011, <http://www.oxfamblogs.org/fp2p/?p=4868> (accessed February 20, 2013).

68 Patchen Markell, "The insufficiency of non-domination."

69 The NHIA stated that it "hereby serves notice to Oxfam that its parochial agenda cannot succeed in an era that 'divide and rule' has been banished into the annals of history never to be resurrected again in an independent nation such as Ghana." (NHIA, "NHIA position on OXFAM/ISODEC report on universal health care in Ghana").

70 Philip Pettit, *Republicanism* (Oxford: Oxford University Press, 1997).

71 Interview with Eric Kajemba, <http://congosiasa.blogspot.co.nz/2011/08/interview-with-eric-kajemba-on-conflict.html> (accessed February 20, 2013), my italics.

72 Pettit, *Republicanism*, p. 5.

73 Ibid., pp. 52–4, 272. Pettit seems to think that he must limit his focus to intentional or quasi-intentional interference because non-volitional events such as natural disasters do not respond to toadying or fawning in the way that a slave-owner or abusive husband might. But this excludes the category of unintentional harm by volitional actors. Cf. Sharon Krause, "Beyond non-domination: agency, inequality and the meaning of freedom," *Philosophy and Social Criticism*, 37 (2013), 1–22.

74 The US is also a democracy with a vibrant civil society, but Congolese people and activists were largely excluded from discussions of Section 1502.

75 Shang-Quartey, personal communication and email correspondence, May 14, 2013.

76 See footnote 17 above. This literature also suggests that the power dynamic between INGOs and NGOs might have influenced what NGO officials were willing to say to me.

77 Clara Tigenoah, email correspondence, April 3, 2013.

78 Interviewee, personal communication.

79 Alan Wertheimer, "Exploitation," *Stanford Encyclopedia of Philosophy*, ed. Edward Zalta, <http://plato.stanford.edu/entries/exploitation/>.

80 I thank Suzanne Dovi for suggesting this term.

81 I thank Michael Kates for helpful discussion of this issue.

82 Cf. Karen Stohr, "Kantian beneficence and the problem of obligatory aid," *Journal of Moral Philosophy*, 8 (2011), 45–67.

83 An example of a non-lowball offer in this context would be one that gave the Ghanaian NGOs a say in the report proportional to their expertise or the size of the group they represented, not their capacity to pay.

84 Of course, the best way to reduce lowball offers is to reduce the circumstances of inequality that make them more likely to be offered and accepted.

85 The four principles discussed here are derived from an analysis of only two cases. I hope that other scholars, INGOs, activists and critics—including people on whose behalf INGOs have advocated—will engage with other cases in a similar fashion. This could result in a collectively-authored, empirically-based, morally-nuanced account of the various ways in which INGO advocates tend to misuse their power and the political and ethical implications of them doing so. This account could be helpful for avoiding normatively objectionable INGO advocacy in the future.

86 I suspect that some of these arguments can be extended to types of actors other than INGOs, but I leave this for another occasion.

Index

Political Theory Without Borders, First Edition. Edited by Robert E. Goodin
and James S. Fishkin.
© 2016 John Wiley & Sons, Inc. Published 2016 by John Wiley & Sons, Inc.